Routledge Library Editions

MARX'S CRITIQUE OF POLITICAL ECONOMY

ECONOMICS

HISTORY OF ECONOMIC THOUGHT
In 23 Volumes

I	A Select Bibliography of Modern Economic Theory	*Batson*
II	Early British Economics	*Beer*
III	Nassau Senior	*Bowley*
IV	The Theory of Marginal Value	*Birck*
V	Ricardo and the Theory of Value Distribution and Growth	*Caravale & Tosato*
VI	Productive Labour and Effective Demand	*Coontz*
VII	London Essays in Economics	*Gregory & Dalton*
VIII	Capitalism and the Historians	*Hayek*
IX	The Origins of Scientific Economics	*Letwin*
X	The Individual in Society	*Macfie*
XI	Essays on Hayek	*Machlup*
XII	The Economics of Physiocracy	*Meek*
XIII	Karl Marx	*Mehring*
XIV	Marx's Critique of Political Economy I	*Oakley*
XV	Marx's Critique of Political Economy II	*Oakley*
XVI	J R McCulloch	*O'Brien*
XVII	A Key to Ricardo	*St Clair*
XVIII	Roads to Freedom	*Streissler*
XIX	Economics in the Twentieth Century	*Suranyi-Unger*
XX	Elements of Pure Economics	*Walras*
XXI	The Common Sense of Political Economy I	*Wicksteed*
XXII	The Common Sense of Political Economy II	*Wicksteed*
XXIII	Social Economics	*von Wieser*

MARX'S CRITIQUE OF POLITICAL ECONOMY

Intellectual Sources and Evolution

Volume II: 1861 to 1863

ALLEN OAKLEY

Routledge
Taylor & Francis Group
LONDON AND NEW YORK

First published in 1985

Published 2014 by Routledge

2 Park Square, Milton Park, Abingdon, Oxfordshire OX14 4RN
711 Third Avenue, New York, NY 10017

First issued in paperback 2014

Transferred to Digital Printing 2007

Routledge is an imprint of the Taylor & Francis Group, an informa business

British Library Cataloguing in Publication Data
A CIP catalogue record for this book
is available from the British Library

Marx's Critique of Political Economy II

ISBN 978-0-415-31335-3 (hbk)
ISBN 978-1-138-87861-7 (pbk)

Miniset: History of Economic Thought

Series: Routledge Library Editions – Economics

MARX'S CRITIQUE OF POLITICAL ECONOMY

Intellectual sources and evolution
Volume II: 1861 to 1863

Allen Oakley

Department of Economics
University of Newcastle, Australia

Routledge
Taylor & Francis Group
LONDON AND NEW YORK

First published in 1985
by Routledge

2 Park Square, Milton Park, Abingdon, Oxon, OX14 4RN

270 Madison Ave, New York NY 10016

Set in Sabon, 10 on 12pt
by Columns of Reading

Library of Congress Cataloging in Publication Data

Oakley, Allen.

Marx's critique of political economy.
(International library of economics)
Bibliography: v. 1, p. v. 2, p.
Includes indexes.
Contents: v. 1. 1844 to 1860—v. 2. 1861-1863.
1. Marxian economics. I. Marx, Karl, 1818-1883.
II. Title. III. Series: ILE.
HB97.5.022 1984 335.4'12 83-23111

British Library CIP data also available

ISBN 0-7100-9945-2

Contents

Preface

The first volume of this study of the intellectual sources and evolution of Marx's critique of political economy dealt with the period from 1844 to 1860. During this time, Marx undertook his first studies in political economy. He took what he read to be the abstract representation of the nature of capitalism as it was generally understood. Marx's own observations and reasoning led him to consider political economy to be a 'false consciousness' in this respect. Consequently, he set out to develop an alternative *critical* paradigm that reflected the true nature of the system and adequately explained its observed phenomena. His approach involved an internal critique of political economy and an exposure of the contradictions upon which capitalism was founded. The investigations that Marx pursued and the process of the evolution of this critical paradigm have been considered in the first volume of my study.

In this second volume, the period treated is much shorter. During 1861 to 1863, Marx consolidated and refined the arguments of his evolving critique of political economy in a massive set of manuscripts under the general title 'Critique of Political Economy'. My attention here centres mainly on those manuscripts written over a period of about a year from early in 1862 to early in 1863 to which Marx gave the title 'Theories of Surplus Value'. They represent approximately one-half of the 'Critique' manuscripts written in this period.

This choice of emphasis was motivated by two factors. First, in spite of their ready availability in published form, these manuscripts have been relatively neglected by Marx scholars. At this time, I am aware of no other study which devotes a sustained effort to tracing the evolution of Marx's critique of political economy in this particular context. The primary importance of these manuscripts is that they reveal Marx's endeavours to differentiate and distance his critical paradigm of political economy from the work of his antecedents. This effort also brought with it some significant advances in the analytical sophistication of his critique over the seminal version found in the *Grundrisse* manuscripts. Especially, then, is the situation of Marx's critique in the historical evolution of political economy made more evident by a study of the 'Theories' with the bonus of some additional insight into the preparations for *Capital.*

Secondly, access to the remaining manuscripts is more restricted. The whole set of the manuscripts of this period is held in the archives of the Institute of Marxism-Leninism in Moscow. Those other than the 'Theories' have only recently been published in part. The parts that have appeared comprise drafts of material that was to be used in *Capital*, Volume I as it was published by Marx, or were included in the manuscripts upon which Engels drew when preparing *Capital*, Volume III. In this sense, their contents are, perhaps ironically, 'less neglected' than those of the 'Theories' manuscripts.

Once again I would like to acknowledge the assistance that I have received in the preparation of this study. Geoffrey Harcourt has given me great support and encouragement from the beginning of the project as a doctoral thesis in the University of Adelaide, South Australia. Others who have made helpful comments on my work along the way are Jon Cohen, Ben Fine, Peter Groenewegen, Samuel Hollander, David Laibman, the late Ronald Meek, and Anwar Shaikh. I thank each of these scholars for his assistance, but the responsibility for the interpretations expressed below rests entirely with me.

Special thanks are due to my wife, Renate. She has contributed so much to the completion of the study by undertaking the tasks of editing and typing the manuscript, clarifying points of translation and preparing the index. I am deeply grateful for her efficient and enthusiastic assistance.

Allen Oakley
Newcastle, Australia

Abbreviations

The following abbreviations are used for works frequently cited in the text. More details about the editions of these works are given in the Bibliography.

CCPE	Marx, *A Contribution to the Critique of Political Economy*
CW	Marx and Engels, *Collected Works*
G	Marx, *Grundrisse: Foundations of the Critique of Political Economy*
G(EV)	Marx, *Grundrisse der Kritik der politischen Ökonomie* (Europäische Verlagsanstalt)
K	Marx, *Capital: a Critique of Political Economy* (Progress Edition)
K(PE)	Marx, *Capital: a Critique of Political Economy* (Penguin Edition)
MEGA	Marx and Engels, *Historische-kritische Gesamtausgabe*, Sections I and II
MEW	Marx and Engels, *Werke*
TSV	Marx, *Theories of Surplus Value*, Parts I to III

Notes:

1 The Sections of the Marx-Engels *Gesamtausgabe* referred to in the text comprise more than one volume. A citation such as *MEGA*, I/3, 410 refers to page 410 in Section I, volume 3 of the work.

2 In other multi-volume works, the abbreviated form is followed by a volume number and a page number, e.g. *MEW*, 31, 534 refers to page 534 in volume 31 of the Marx-Engels *Werke*.
3 In the passages quoted from these works, *any emphasis is Marx's unless otherwise stated.*

CHAPTER 1

Introduction

BIBLIOGRAPHICAL MATTERS, 1861–3

When Marx took up his critique of political economy project again around August 1861,[1] his immediate concern was to complete the long-promised 'third chapter' on 'Capital' that was supposed to have been published with *A Contribution to the Critique of Political Economy* (*CCPE*) in 1859.[2] The general objective of the *Contribution* was to publish in the form of presentation the investigations that had been undertaken in the *Grundrisse* manuscripts (*G* and *G*(EV)).[3] However, Marx had evidently had great difficulty with organising and reworking the material that he had accumulated. As a consequence, the *Contribution* as published comprised only two chapters: one dealt with the commodity and its Value[4] and the other with the process of 'simple circulation' which embraced the role of money in circulating capital in its commodity form (see *CCPE*).

Having sent the incomplete manuscript for the *Contribution* off to the publisher early in 1859, Marx faced the task of arranging and redrafting the remaining material for presentation as the 'third chapter'. This was now to be published as a companion volume to the 1859 work. He devised a plan for the chapter that comprised three sections under the heading 'Capital' (G(EV), 969ff.):

I Production Process of Capital
II Circulation Process of Capital
III Capital and Profit

This plan was set down in the spring of 1859, but it was to be more than two years before Marx was seriously to begin re-writing the relevant *Grundrisse* material.[5]

The work that Marx then began was to grow well beyond its apparently intended scope and involved him in further extensive critical *investigations* into political economy. Such was his enthusiasm, though, that by the end of the summer of 1863, he had written a massive manuscript in 23 notebooks, together with eight supplementary notebooks containing excerpts from his wider reading. It is possible to set out much of the contents of the main manuscript, but little is known of the contents of the eight excerpt notebooks designated A to H and written in the spring of 1863 (see editorial note 119 in *TSV*, I, 488). These are extant but no details of them have been published to date.

The main notebooks were numbered by Marx from I to XXIII and carried a continuous pagination running from 1 to 1472 (probably amounting to some 3,000 printed pages). The contents of the main manuscript notebooks are outlined below.

'CRITIQUE OF POLITICAL ECONOMY' MANUSCRIPTS

I to V: (1) Transformation of money into capital.
  (2) Absolute surplus Value.
  (3) Relative surplus Value.
VI to XV: (5) Theories of surplus Value.
XVI to XVIII: Capital and profit.
  Mercantile capital and interest.
  (5) Theories of surplus Value (conclusion).
  Plans for Part I and Part III of what became *Capital.*
XIX to XXIII: [Draft of some remaining material for *Capital*, Part I – no details have been published.]
  Short essays in the historical critique of political economy.

As Marx had begun the manuscripts with the intention of completing the 'third chapter' on 'Capital', the first five notebooks were devoted to a drafting of the first three topics of Section I, 'Production Process of Capital'. Having considered Value and the simple circulation of commodities and money in the *Contribution*, Marx now turned his attention to capital as the basis of the production process under capitalism (these notebooks have been published in *MEGA*, II/3/1, 3ff.).

The drafting of these three sections continued until the end of 1861. At this point, Marx digressed from the 'third-chapter' programme that would have involved moving onto topic (4), which according to the 1859 plan (*G*(EV), 969ff.) was to be 'Original Accumulation'. It seems, though, that Marx had now changed his mind on this fourth section, for he wrote towards the end of notebook V that he would go on to analyse absolute and relative surplus Value 'in their combination'. This section was not drafted at the time, and instead he turned his attention to another topic not previously mentioned, viz. '(5) Theories of Surplus Value'. Having considered the principles of surplus Value in some detail, Marx decided, for some reason, to begin an intensive, and, as it turned out, extensive, critical re-reading of his antecedents on this theme and its associated analyses. The substantive scope of this critique under the rubric of surplus Value attests to the central status which Marx ascribed to the category.

Marx worked on 'Theories' continuously for about a year. In this period, he completed the main part of the critical history, filling notebooks VI to XV. When he began again on the 'third chapter' on 'Capital' in December 1862, his first concern was to draft out the section 'Capital and Profit' (*MEGA*, II/3/5, 1598ff.). In notebooks XVI to XVII, he examined several aspects of the relationship between the essential categories of capital and surplus Value and the phenomenon of profit in both the 'static' and 'dynamic' contexts. He went on in the last part of notebook XVII and in part of notebook XVIII to consider the topics of merchant capital and the theory of interest. Beyond notebook XVIII, little is known of the contents of the remainder of the 'Critique' except for the few essays in critical history that have been included with the 'Theories' material. Engels reported in passing, in the Preface to *Capital*, Volume II, that the last notebooks of the series contained mainly the draft text for the remaining topics of Book I of *Capital* that had not been covered in the *Contribution* or in notebooks I to V (*K*, II, 2). Unfortunately, this part of the 'Critique' has not yet been published.

'Theories of Surplus Value' grew to occupy notebooks VI to XV during 1862. This was not the end of it, either, for Marx continued to work sporadically up until the middle of 1863 with a substantial piece in notebook XVIII and shorter critical essays in parts of notebooks XX to XXIII. The detailed contents of all these notebooks dealing with the critical history of the theory of surplus Value are set out below (*TSV*, I, 37ff.).

'(5) Theories of Surplus Value' notebooks

VI	(a)	Sir James Steuart.
	(b)	The Physiocrats – François Quesnay.
	(c)	Adam Smith.
VII	(c)	Adam Smith (continuation): Theories of productive labour. John Stuart Mill (Digression).
VIII		John Stuart Mill (Digression – continuation).
	(c)	Adam Smith (conclusion): Theories of productive and unproductive labour.
IX	(c)	Adam Smith. Conclusion: Theories of productive and unproductive labour.
	(d)	Jacques Necker.
X	Digression: Quesnay's *Tableau économique*.	
	(e)	Simon Linguet.
	(f)	John Francis Bray.
	(g)	Johann Rodbertus-Jagetzow.
XI	(g)	Rodbertus. New theory of rent (Digression).
		Digression: Note on the history of the discovery of the so-called Ricardian Law of Rent.
	(h)	David Ricardo.
		Ricardo's and Adam Smith's theory of cost-price (refutation).
		Ricardo's theory of rent.
		Tables, with elucidation, of differential rent.
XII	(h)	Ricardo.
		Table, with elucidation, of differential rent.
		Ricardo's theory of rent.
		Adam Smith's theory of rent.
		Ricardo's theory of surplus-value.
		Ricardo's theory of profit.
XIII	(h)	Ricardo.
		Ricardo's theory of profit.
		Ricardo's theory of accumulation. Critique of this (development of crises from the basic form of

		capital).
		Ricardo's Miscellanea.
		Conclusion of Ricardo (John Barton).
	(i)	Thomas Robert Malthus.
XIV	(i)	Malthus.
	(k)	Decline of the Ricardian School (Robert Torrens, James Mill, Guillaume Provost, polemical writings, John McCulloch, Edward Gibbon Wakefield, Patrick James Stirling, [John Stuart Mill – to be transferred from notebooks VII and VIII above]).
	(l)	Adversaries of the economists (Bray – [to be transferred from notebook X above]).
		Anonymous pamphlet: *Source and Remedy of the National Difficulties*.
		Piercy Ravenstone.
XV		Ravenstone (conclusion).
		Thomas Hodgskin.
		Episode: Revenue and its sources.
		Vulgar political economy.
XVIII		Hodgskin (continuation).
		George Ramsay.
		Antoine-Elisée Cherbuliez.
		Richard Jones.
XX		Thomas Hobbes, John Locke, David Hume, Joseph Massie.
XXI		Productivity of capital. Productive and unproductive labour.
XXII		William Petty, Sir Dudley North.
XXIII		Sir Dudley North, Quesnay's *Tableau économique*, anonymous pamphlet [John Gray].

In preparing this massive 'digression' into the critical history of political economy, it is probable that Marx *began* his investigations with the intention of preparing a synopsis of the implicit role that surplus Value had taken in the evolution of political economy. This intention is suggested by the way he had used the critical history in the first two chapters which comprised the *Contribution*. That is, '(5) Theories of Surplus Value' was to be a historical section to supplement and bolster the exposition of the critical theory of the category in sections (2) to (4) of the 'third chapter'. Quite evidently, though, it went well beyond this brief in both length and substance.

In substance, the work led Marx to some critico-theoretical developments that advanced beyond those adumbrated in the *Grundrisse* manuscripts. These developments involved especially the Value-distribution articulation problem in the transition from the capital-in-general analysis to the many-capitals and competition context. Here he especially found a detailed study of the work of Adam Smith and David Ricardo of immense assistance and his critical method was never more effective. By exposing what he believed to be logical and substantive limitations in the analyses of these antecedents, Marx was able to advance the sophistication of his own critical theory of how capitalism functioned. The ultimate rationale for 'Theories' thus became *self-clarification* and *critico-theoretical development*.

The manuscripts as we have them, represent a work of critical *investigation* more than anything else. They certainly were not in their form of *presentation*. As with the *Grundrisse*, much work on the manuscripts would have been required to prepare them for publication. Marx gave no indications as to what this work would have involved and the pervasive and loose talk about 'Theories' *actually being* 'Volume IV' of *Capital* is likely to mislead readers and interpreters of the manuscripts. There is no doubt that Marx intended that his historical critique would be *prepared* for Book IV of his *magnum opus*, but its precise form of presentation can only be guessed at.

READING 'THEORIES OF SURPLUS VALUE'

In the present study, my analysis of Marx's 1861–3 manuscripts is limited to those that comprised 'Theories of Surplus Value' (*TSV*). Several general observations about my reading of these manuscripts are in order before proceeding. The premise upon which these observations are based is that while the work contains the results of some of Marx's most informative investigations, care is needed in order correctly to interpret the situation and role of 'Theories' in Marx's evolving critique of political economy. From his critical discussions of the works of antecedent writers, we can gain some useful insight into what he intended to achieve through the critique of political economy as it ultimately appeared, albeit unfinished, in *Capital*.[6]

Four aspects of 'Theories' require preliminary emphasis to prepare the way for the study that follows. First, Marx's intention in his critical exposé of the work of his antecedents was to *differentiate* and *distance* his own critical theory from what they had written. He found them to have posited a superficial and misleading interpretation of the relations and operations of capitalism, with some having adopted obscurantist and apologetic approaches. Marx wanted to reveal the *contradiction-ridden essences* of the system that had been overlooked or obscured by his antecedents in their limited use of phenomenal categories as the means of analysis.

Secondly, and consequently, it must be recognised that *the work was never meant to be a history of political economy*, even a critical one. Its *scope* in terms of the writers and topics treated was just too narrow and specialised. Marx's particular focus was on his core critico-theoretical category *surplus Value* around which 'Theories' was written, as its title suggests. His reading of political economy was designed to elicit only antecedent analyses that in some unconscious way foreshadowed his development and application of the concept. This was the thrust of the passage with which Marx began in notebook VI of the manuscripts:

> *All economists share the error of examining surplus Value not as such, in its pure form, but in the particular forms of profit and rent.* What theoretical errors must necessarily arise from this will be shown more fully in Chapter III, in the analysis of the greatly changed form which surplus Value assumes as profit. (*TSV*, I, 40, emphasis added.)

There are two pertinent comments to be made about this piece. First, as things turned out, most of the 'theoretical errors' were revealed in the course of writing out the critical history itself. It is evident that its contents grew well beyond what was initially intended for the work. Secondly, the reference to 'Chapter III' is puzzling in that it refers to it as *future* work. As he was already engaged in writing the '*third chapter*' on 'Capital', this reference must have been to *Section III* in which he planned to write about 'Capital and Profit'.[7]

Thirdly, and again consequent upon the first point, the work is only of limited assistance in tracing the *origins* and *process of formation* of Marx's critique of political economy. It must be emphasised that the *Grundrisse* manuscripts already contained the essential core of the critical theory, a part of which had been presented to the public in the *Contribution.* 'Theories' does, however, give some indication of his *sources* in that the critical history involved makes clear how his own analytical paradigm about the nature, relations and operations of the capitalist economy was distinctive. It must be supposed that this endeavour reflected a retrospective assessment of the writings that he had studied and found useful in a positive or negative sense over the years. It is appropriate to emphasise at this point that it is not possible realistically to argue that Marx's critical theory was somehow created in an intellectual vacuum; that is, without any filiated attachments to antecedent political economy. His concept of *critique* included both intellectual preservation and transcendence, a point that should be kept in mind no matter how distinctive the interpreter finds Marx's critical theory and the issues with which it was concerned.[8]

This raises the fourth point of preliminary concern here regarding my reading of the 'Theories' manuscripts, viz. what can be said about the question of the 'accuracy' of Marx's critique of antecedent political economy? As I have already suggested, the importance of the investigations in the critical history that are analysed in this study does not depend upon it being read *as history.* Marx was sometimes a tendentious critic, with his intention being to maximise the effectiveness of what he wrote as propaganda. His objective was to provide a theoretical basis for the revolutionary transcendence of capitalism. For this purpose, the courtesies of intellectual historical accuracy and 'fairness' were not so relevant. However, this observation is not intended to suggest that Marx's critique had *only* contemporary propaganda value. Far from it. It will be my contention that he was often a perceptive and penetrating critic of the analytical shortcomings of the political economists that he read, albeit often within the scope of his own problematic. At times, though, his critique also had a strictly 'internal' dimension in the sense that it exposed the limitations in the logic of the particular arguments posited by the political economists, even when approached on their own terms.

THE PRESENT STUDY

The exposition below is divided into several parts with a view to bringing some coherent pattern of organisation to the critical *notes* that comprise the 'Theories of Surplus Value' manuscripts. In doing so, I implicitly reject the idea that there was necessarily something sacrosanct about the arrangement of the notes as they were set down by Marx.[9] They were, after all, only *investigations*, and as I have already mentioned, we have no way of knowing what arrangement he would have used in any published version. At the same time, I am not suggesting that the format I have used has any merit beyond providing a meaningful frame of reference for the interpretation presented.

Two interdependent, but analytically separable themes are present in 'Theories'. These were mixed together in the notes, but expositional clarity demands that they be treated separately. First, Marx was concerned with the theme of exchange value and distribution as it had been dealt with by the political economists. Several aspects of the theme were especially important in formulating any adequate critical comprehension of the capitalist economy and these provided the reference points for Marx's readings of the political economists reported in 'Theories'.

The existence of non-labour incomes in an economic system that valued its commodities in terms of embodied labour could not be taken for granted. They had to be *explained*, and for this purpose, Marx evoked his category surplus Value. He argued that it originated in the exploitation of workers whose living-labour services were only partly paid for by the capitalists in the Value of labour power. Further, the categories Value and surplus Value embodied in the commodity form, had to be recognised as *essential* reflections of the very nature of capitalist relations of production as well as the roots of the empirical phenomena of exchange value and income distribution.

It followed from this that the *essential* forms were required to be formally articulated to the *phenomenal* forms. This presented no difficulty when the analysis was confined to the aggregate level of 'capital-in-general' or to a multi-sector situation where all methods of production involved the same composition of capital expressed as the ratio between constant and variable capital advances, each measured in Value terms. These latter conditions ensured that immediate embodied-labour Value generated in production would, when realised as exchange values, yield the general Value rate of profits required by the assumption of competitive capital mobility between sectors of production. The problem arose when the different sectors employed technical methods that involved capitals of varying Value compositions. Then the requirement of inter-sector uniformity of the rate of profit could be met only by realising exchange values that were *systematically* different from immediate Values. In these exchange values, the surplus Value component *realised* was generally different from that directly generated in the production of the commodity. By this means, Marx identified exchange values that realised just that amount of surplus Value required to yield the same Value rate of profit in each sector of production. To this category of exchange value he variously ascribed the names 'cost price' or 'average price', although the term ultimately used towards the end of 'Theories' and in later works was 'price of production' (see, e.g., *TSV*, III, 333, 377). Unlike the political economists, then, Marx was able to formalise this category of exchange value and present an analysis which explained its systematic difference from immediate Value, even though it is now clear that his analysis was incomplete.[10]

For this dimension of his critique, Marx adopted a 'static' methodology. That is, his critical analyses focused on a particular *phenomenal* exchange value and distribution vector and pursued its 'hidden' *essential roots* in the transcendental domain of Values and surplus Value. For this 'X-ray snapshot' approach,[11] no concept of historical time or analytical change was needed, and one of Marx's critical premises was that the political economists had not realised this.

Marx's ultimate critico-analytical concern with explicating the 'law of motion' of the capitalist system is the second theme to be found in 'Theories'. The analysis centring on this theme required a 'dynamic' methodology. Marx's objective here was to understand the logic of the various dimensions of historical 'motion' that were consequent upon the premise that individual capitalists would strive to maximise their capacity to generate surplus Value. The means of acquiring this capacity was capital accumulation. Marx found the 'motion' so induced to be crisis prone, reflecting the contradiction-ridden nature of the capitalist system of socio-economic relations. By contrast, with some exceptions, the political economists had perceived economic growth and development as processes that could proceed without inherent or significant social or economic impediments.

In Parts I to III of the study, the first theme is dealt with and the arrangement of the exposition is chronological. The evolution of exchange value and distribution theory is divided into three phases along lines suggested by Marx. In the 'Theories', he was overwhelmingly concerned with British political economists. He wrote only some brief notes on the Physiocrats and Turgot, and some even briefer scattered jottings on Say and Sismondi. The crucial period of the development of *Classical* political economy began with Petty in Britain (and Boisguillebert on the Continent). This was the phase in which the ideas of the 'Monetary' and 'Mercantilist' writers (*G* 103, 327-8; *CCPE*, 158) dominated the general approach to economic thought. Within this approach, Marx identified those facets that were to be of lasting relevance and thus began his pursuit of the evolution of Classical analyses to their zenith in the work of Ricardo (and Sismondi on the Continent) (*CCPE*, 52). Beyond Ricardo, with few and limited exceptions, Marx felt that the analytical potential of the Classicals for a *critical* comprehension of capitalism had not been realised. Political economy was 'vulgarised' to varying extents by a succession of 'Ricardian' disciples and critics alike, each intent on explaining away or 'correcting' Ricardo's analytical limitations while overlooking his more profound insights into the workings of the economy. To some extent, the more 'radical' of Ricardo's interpreters, the so-called 'Ricardian Socialists' had come closer to Marx's critical reading of the *Principles*. Their work, too, was constrained, for various reasons, from realising what potential Ricardo's *magnum opus* held as a critical source.

The first three Parts of this study, then, deal in turn with Marx's critique of the rise and decline of Classical exchange value and distribution theory prior to Ricardo, in Ricardo's *Principles* and beyond Ricardo. In these Parts, I discuss the critique that emerged as Marx traced the theory through the works of a series of political economists. He dealt extensively and intensively with some, the key figures being Adam Smith and Ricardo, while devoting less effort to writers whom he considered to have contributed little of significance to the theme.

Part IV is approached somewhat differently. It deals with Marx's scattered and desultory treatment of the analysis of 'motion' in its various dimensions culminating in the discussion of the crisis. Here the critique is less able to be related meaningfully to his reading of particular political economists. Consequently, in this Part, I have adopted a thematic method of analysis and endeavoured to provide some coherence by bringing together Marx's piecemeal discussions of the various dimensions of 'motion' from throughout the 'Theories' manuscripts. These were all written in the context of criticising some individual political economist, but their substance was often not related directly to the text at hand.

Part I

Exchange value and distribution before Ricardo

CHAPTER 2

Exchange value and distribution analysis before Adam Smith

THE MERCANTILIST AND CLASSICAL FOUNDATIONS

In the *Grundrisse* manuscripts, in *A Contribution to the Critique of Political Economy* and in many places in the 'Theories of Surplus Value' manuscripts, Marx referred briefly to the work of the earliest group of writers on matters of political economy to whom he could give some classification. He identified this group with a perception of the economy that he called 'The Monetary System' (*G*, 103, 327–8). Although the particular writers that comprised the group were never listed by Marx, he did specify the relevant period of their work as the 'sixteenth and seventeenth centuries' (*CCPE*, 157–8). Then, at some unspecified time during the latter century, he identified the emergence of the 'commercial, or manufacture, system' (*G*, 103–4) which he saw as a 'variant' of the 'Monetary System'. He finally called this the 'Mercantile System' (*CCPE*, 158; cf. *G*, 327–8). Again, no writers were specifically identified as Mercantilist, but those who wrote in the period from about the middle of the seventeenth century to the middle of the eighteenth would seem to comprise an appropriate coverage (*G*, 103, ed. n. 19).

The interpretation of Marx's taxonomic thought about the writers of this period prior to the mid-eighteenth century is made more problematical by his definition of Classical political economy as beginning with William Petty in England and Pierre Boisguillebert in France (*CCPE*, 52). As Marx himself recognised, these two writers and their contemporaries wrote very much in the

Mercantilist tradition (*CCPE*, 54–5). Granting this, the point of the definition seems to have been that certain of the core ideas that were to characterise Classical political economy *began to appear* in the writings of this period. From then on, the Classical 'school' traversed a process of intellectual evolution and consolidation through the work of the Physiocrats ('the true fathers of modern political economy' – *TSV*, I, 44; cf. *G*, 328),[1] Anne-Robert-Jacques Turgot, James Steuart ('the first Briton to expound a general system of bourgeois economy' – *CCPE*, 57) and Adam Smith. The evolution culminated and reached its apogee in the work of Jean-Charles-Léonard Simonde de Sismondi and David Ricardo ('who gave to Classical political economy its final shape' – *CCPE*, 61). Thus, it was Marx's view that certain key writers contributed to the ultimate form of Classical political economy *in specific ways*. To this extent, writers before Sismondi and Ricardo, including those of the Mercantile period, expressed *some* ideas around which the Classical paradigm developed over time.

For Marx, the central premise of the Monetary writers was their belief that ultimate wealth comprised exclusively accumulated gold and silver (*G*, 103, 327; *CCPE*, 54, 158). On the basis of this narrow perception, though, he felt that these writers had grasped quite well the way the political-economic system of the day worked. In this vein, Marx noted:

> *It was consistent with the rudimentary stage of bourgeois production* that those misunderstood prophets should have clung to the solid, palpable and glittering form of exchange value, to exchange value in the form of the universal commodity as distinct from all particular commodities. (*CCPE*, 158, emphasis added.)

The Mercantilists had appropriately emphasised the sphere of commodity *circulation* as the dominant operational dimension of the economy, for in this period, the form of the production process did not have the relevance that it would acquire in the late eighteenth century and beyond (*CCPE*, 158–9). The actual owners of the means of production very largely worked with them to produce the products to be traded. Only when they had entered circulation did the commodities become of economic concern and give the opportunity for artful merchants to transform them into the maximum possible amount of the universal form of wealth, gold and silver. As Marx went on to note many times in the 'Theories' notebooks, these writers *necessarily* stressed the generation of 'profit on alienation' as the only source of a surplus given the mode of production that underpinned commerce at this stage (see, e.g., *TSV*, I, 41, 43, 62, 66, 154, 205, 209, 380, 383).[2]

In the later analyses of bourgeois political economy, the *emphasis* shifted away from the *ultimate* accumulation of gold and silver *per se* towards the recognition and pursuit of 'productive' forms of wealth. However, the *motive* for participation by wealth owners in economic activity remained the maximisation of the realised surplus in 'money' form, even if the *origin* of this surplus was increasingly sought in production rather than in circulation (*CCPE*, 158–9). Thus, the Mercantilist writers who provided the first Classical insights into the burgeoning 'modern' capitalist economy were increasingly conscious of the *activity of generating wealth*, both through manufacturing and commerce (*G*, 103–4, 327–8; *TSV*, I, 304).

It was in the last notes written for the 'Theories' manuscripts that Marx gave some more definition to these general ideas of the Mercantilist writers as the founders of Classical political economy (*TSV*, I, 353ff.). The notes comprised several pages of short quotations from the works of Thomas Hobbes, William Petty, John Locke, Dudley North, Joseph Massie and David Hume (although none was *referred to* as Mercantilist), along with some equally short critical observations by Marx. His reading of these works emphasised two main themes, viz. the treatment of the notion of exchange value and the explanation cum justification for the specific, non-labour incomes paid as rent and interest.

The writings of the period revealed a preoccupation with the interest rate on money lent to finance activity in manufacturing and commerce.[3] Especially were these writers concerned with the issues of the legal versus the 'natural' determination of the interest rate and the merits and significance of the progressive decline of the legal rate from 10 per cent to 5 per cent per annum in England between 1625 and 1714.[4] This led them into a continuing debate about the complex of cause and effect relations between interest rates and economic activity.[5] Two schools of thought emerged concerning these issues.[6] The first argued for the continuation of legally controlled interest rates and their progressive reduction as a stimulus to economic activity and wealth accumulation. The second school took the position that declining interest rates should be left to occur as a 'natural' effect of economic progress and that to force the legal rate below the 'natural' rate would lead to hoarding and a reduced availability of loans to facilitate the growth of wealth.

With respect to the notion of exchange value, the latter half of the seventeenth century saw an increasing interest in the link between what appeared as market price and the cost of producing the commodity involved.[7] This interest accompanied the perceived changes in the mode of production and the emerging intellectual concern with the production aspects of political economy. It became apparent to observers that *labour* input was a dominant and decisive element in the determination of the cost of production and, as a consequence, the initial investigations of the links between labour and exchange value were undertaken. These investigations led to two main arguments about the links involved.[8] First, the exchange value of a commodity remained firmly attached to its use value, but now the use value was largely ascribed to the activity of labour. Secondly, the labour input measured as the cost of wages was argued to be the dominant cost of production. In no case in this period could a writer's position on the *importance* of labour in determining exchange value be considered as a labour *theory* in the fully developed Classical sense. However, as Marx was aware when he chose Petty as the first of the Classicals, this group had at least provided the foundations for future theoretical developments.

PETTY

When Marx considered Petty's work in the *Contribution* of 1859, the particular reasons for citing him as the founder of Classical political economy and, indeed, as 'the father of English political economy', were not made explicit (*CCPE*, 52–4). One thing that caught Marx's attention was Petty's '*political arithmetic*, the first form in which political economy is treated as a separate science' (*CCPE*, 53–4). This led Marx to suggest that Petty would claim to be the 'founder of a new science' (*CCPE*, 52n.). Here he was probably referring to Petty's claim, in the Preface to his *Political*

Arithmetick, written in the early 1670s, to some originality and innovation in his attention to quantitative-empirical observations as the most appropriate substance of social and political-economic analysis and argument. In the spirit of 'science', Petty resolved to leave to others, arguments that 'depend upon the mutable Minds, Opinions, Appetites, and Passions of particular Men' (quoted *CCPE*, 52 n).[9] For Marx, too, observations and data had a role to play in his critique of political economy and capitalism. *Capital*, Volume I, as it was published by Marx, was replete with such details, although *in support* of reasoned theoretical argument rather than in any sense instead of it (see, e.g., Chapter 10: 'The Working Day' and Chapter 15: 'Machinery and Large-Scale Industry'; *K*(PE), I, 340ff. and 492ff. respectively). Petty's identification of and emphasis on the need to found political economy on a sound knowledge of its empirical object must have appealed to Marx.

In the *Contribution*, Marx also made reference to Petty's emphasis on the role of labour in the production of use values, the *original* form of wealth, and on the division of labour as a means of increasing the productivity of labour (*CCPE*, 52 and n.). As well as arguing the merits of the division of labour *in production*, Petty also revealed an awareness of the *social* dimension of such a division and its essential role as the *basis* for post-production trading between interdependent specialist producers.[10] It was in this context of socially interdependent producers that the nature and significance of exchange value would ultimately be grasped. Petty did not formulate his views on exchange value in this way. He confined his attention largely to the sphere of simple circulation and 'accepts exchange value as it *appears* in the exchange of commodities' rather than probing its *immediate* origins in the production process (*CCPE*, 54). In accordance with his Monetary preconceptions, Petty located ultimate exchange value in 'the particular kind of concrete labour by which gold and silver is extracted' (*CCPE*, 54). However, as Marx noted, this reflected some insight into the link between the expression of exchange value and one, generalised form of labour, an insight which was to underpin the embodied-labour principle in the future.[11]

Marx's discussions of Petty in the 'Theories of Surplus Value' manuscripts were found mostly in notebook XXII (*TSV*, I, 354ff.), with some earlier pieces in notebooks VII and VIII (*TSV*, I, 179ff.). The main focus of Marx's comments in these pieces was Petty's earliest economic work, *A Treatise of Taxes and Contributions* (1662).[12] He had apparently also consulted some of Petty's other works, although the depth of his reading was not evident in 'Theories', for these were mostly mentioned only in passing. The works were:[13]

> *The Political Anatomy of Ireland* [1672] to which is added *Verbum Sapienti* [1664], (1691).
> *An Essay Concerning the Multiplication of Mankind* (1682).
> *Political Arithmetick* [1676], (1690).
> *Quantulumcunque Concerning Money* [1682], (1695).

From among these works, it was the *Political Arithmetick* that was quoted from at any length, and then only in the earlier notebooks.

On the basis of what Marx wrote in these later investigations in 'Theories', two main ideas appear to have reinforced his high regard for Petty's contributions to the early development of Classical political economy. These ideas were first, the link between labour exercised in production and exchange value, alluded to in the *Contribution*; and secondly, the origin of rent as a surplus associated with the employment of labour and land, along with the notion that the interest on money was integrally related to this rent.

With respect to Petty's treatment of exchange value, Marx quoted a passage from *A Treatise of Taxes* to the effect that an equivalence between the labour time involved in preparing an ounce of silver and relocating it in London and the labour time required to produce a bushel of corn meant that 'one is the natural price of the other' (quoted *TSV*, I, 181 and 356).[14] And, in this same passage Petty added that a decrease in the labour input required to produce the silver would mean that the bushel of corn would have its exchange value expressed in terms of more than one ounce of silver, *ceteris paribus*. Moreover, Marx found in *A Treatise of Taxes* the notion that what mattered for the understanding of exchange value was not the *type* of labour involved in the production process, but *labour time as such*. Thus Marx felt that the following passage foreshadowed the notion of 'abstract labour' and reinforced his view that Petty had grasped that exchange value *expressed* in terms of silver had its roots in labour time:[15]

> And forasmuch as possibly there may be more Art and Hazzard in working about the Silver, then about the Corn, yet all comes to the same pass; for let a hundred men *work ten years* upon Corn, and *the same number of men, the same time*, upon Silver; I say, that the *neat proceed* of the Silver is the *price of the whole neat proceed of the Corn*, and like parts of the one, the price of like parts of the other. (quoted *TSV*, I, 357; cf. 181.)

Petty's thought on exchange value in *A Treatise of Taxes* ultimately included three interdependent but separable conceptual forms of the category (*TSV*, I, 355).[16] The first form was a 'natural' exchange value which 'depends upon the *few or more hands*' (quoted *TSV*, I, 356) required to produce a commodity; the second form was a 'political' exchange value which reflected a distortion of the 'natural' value because of 'Supernumerary Interlopers into any Trade over and above all that are necessary' who raise the unit cost of producing a commodity; and the third form was an 'artificial' exchange value expressed in terms of silver and called 'the true Currant'. For Marx, the 'natural' exchange value was the category which would have continuing significance for Classical political economy.

By way of conclusion, Marx identified 'three ways of determining [exchange] value' that were 'running alongside of each other' in Petty's work (*TSV*, I, 361). There was first: '*The magnitude of [exchange] value*, determined by equal labour time, *labour* being here considered *as the source of value*', although the latter point represented somewhat of an overstatement. Secondly, with respect to the idea that exchange values were expressed through the common mediation of money, Marx generously granted Petty the insight that value took 'the form of social labour'. Thirdly, though, while Petty was supposed to have had these important insights, he did not, in Marx's view, always clearly distinguish labour as the producer of use value from labour as the producer of exchange value; probably, it should be added, for the reason that Petty did not attempt to make this distinction at all.

The premise upon which Marx founded his critique of Petty's

analysis of the non-labour incomes rent and interest, was the theory of surplus Value – or, at least, the principle of a realised exchange-value surplus above the cost of a commodity to its final seller. Marx read Petty as having some idea that the outlay on labour to produce a commodity comprised the exchange value of 'subsistence' needs. In a Mercantilist way, Petty made this point as follows in *A Treatise of Taxes*: 'the law . . . *should allow the Labourer but just wherewithal to live*; for if you allow double, then he works but half so much as he could have done, and otherwise would; *which is a loss to the Publick of the fruit of so much labour*' (quoted *TSV*, I, 356).[17] Marx had found the idea that the worker's capacity to perform labour could be conceived of as a commodity in the earlier work by Hobbes: *Leviathan: on the Matter, Form and Power of a Commonwealth, Ecclesiastical and Civil* (1651). In the context of discussing the various dimensions of man that can be elicited to describe his capacity or 'Power' to 'obtain some future Good', Hobbes wrote that 'The *Value*, or WORTH *of a man*, is as of all other things, his Price; that is to say, so much as would be given *for the use of his Power*' (quoted *TSV*, I, 353).[18] To this idea, Marx added Hobbes's later argument that '*a man's Labour* also, is a *commodity* exchangeable for benefit, as well as any other *thing*' (quoted *TSV*, I, 353).[19] Together, these ideas of Hobbes and Petty provided some historical roots for the Classical analysis of 'labour' purchased as an input to production, or labour power as Marx would more meaningfully call it.

For Marx, some comprehension of the exchange value of 'labour' as an input was vital in identifying the realisation of a surplus when a commodity was sold. He chose to quote a passage from the *Political Arithmetick* to illustrate Petty's 'anticipation of the nature of *surplus Value*' (*TSV*, I, 180) on the basis of a known exchange value of the 'labour' required to produce a bushel of corn.[20] The simple notion argued by Petty was that with a given corn price, fixed by international trade arbitrage, an increase in the 'labour' cost of producing corn due to an increase in the demand for labour with the development of 'trade and manufacture', must result in a decrease in the surplus available for the payment of rent. This passage was backed up with one quoted from *A Treatise of Taxes* in which the surplus principle was even more obviously implied:[21]

> Suppose a man could with his own hands plant a certain scope of land with Corn, that is, could Digg, or Plough, Harrow, Weed, Reap, Carry home, Thresh, and Winnow so much as the Husbandry of this Land requires; and had withal *Seed* wherewith to sowe the same. I say, that when this man *hath subducted his seed out of the proceed of his Harvest*, and also, what himself hath both eaten and given to others in exchange for Clothes, and other Natural necessaries; that the *remainder of the Corn* is the *natural and true Rent of the Land for that year*. (quoted *TSV*, I, 356–7; cf. 181–2.)

Here a 'corn' surplus was ascribed to the *fact* that it cost less corn in terms of seed and sustenance for the farmer than could be produced by the farmer's labour *on the land*.

What Petty did not canvass in his discussions was the *origin* of the surplus corn. For him, the total corn produced and its exchange value was the result of *labour and land* working together. He went on to make this explicit when he wrote that 'all things ought to be *valued by two natural Denominations, which is Land and Labour*; . . . a Ship or garment is worth such a measure of Land, with such another measure of Labour' (quoted *TSV*, I, 360).[22] As far as *expressing* such exchange value was concerned, Petty wanted to preserve the use of the universal measure of silver. When he posed the question: 'how much English money this Corn or Rent is worth?', his answer was to draw the analogy with an equivalent amount of labour to that involved in producing the corn, net of its cost of sustenance, devoted to the procurement of silver (*TSV*, I, 357).[23] Again, this argument did not *explain* the existence of the surplus.

On the basis of the principle of valuation espoused by Petty, it is evident that he considered the generation of rent to be the result of the 'productivity' of land. In an endeavour to give some coherence to this determination of rent in the light of the dominant relation between exchange value and labour, mediated by silver money, Petty devised the idea that the 'natural Par between Land and Labour' should be sought. This would enable the 'contribution' of land to production to be made directly equivalent to a certain volume of labour time and the exchange value of a commodity, including the surplus, could then be fully expressed in terms of labour input (*TSV*, I, 357–9, 362).[24]

Petty went on to link the payment of interest on money to the 'inconvenience' to its owner of forgoing the *control and use* of that money for a period of time.[25] More importantly for Marx, the *amount* of interest to be paid was based upon the existence of rent on land. Petty argued this quite explicitly with respect to the 'natural Standard' of usury: 'As for *Usury*, the least that can be, is the *Rent of so much Land as the Money lent will buy*, where the security is undoubted' (quoted *TSV*, I, 359).[26] Thus Petty posited a 'natural' view of interest and he consequently took a stand against any endeavour to control interest rates by legal *fiat*. He wrote of 'the vanity and fruitlessness of making *Civil Positive Laws* against *the Laws of Nature*' in this context (quoted *TSV*, I, 361).[27]

In Marx's view, the particular significance of Petty's conception of interest was that it provided a bridge between the appearance of the surplus as rent 'attached' to land and its burgeoning form as a return that must bear some relation to the capital advanced to facilitate production. With respect to 'Petty's deep insight into the matter', Marx concluded that 'From the standpoint of the *buyer* of rent (i.e., of land) *rent* thus appears merely *as interest on his capital* used to buy it; and in this form rent has become completely unrecognisable and appears as *interest on capital*' (*TSV*, I, 359). Once again, then, Petty was seen by Marx as having foreshadowed an important subsequent development in the evolution of Classical political economy.

LOCKE AND NORTH

Marx interpreted the contemporaries Locke and North as having developed contrasting views about the determination of the 'natural' rate of interest. He found that Locke had emphasised the supply of and demand for money *per se* as the crucial market factors while North's version went beyond this and was transitional in the sense that it looked forward to the explicit relation of non-labour incomes to the *activity* of production and trade by identifying money as the basis for productive capital or stock formation (*TSV*, I, 364).

From among the many works of John Locke, Marx chose to

quote and comment on some brief passages from only two (*TSV*, I, 356ff.):

> *Some Considerations of the Consequences of the Lowering of Interest and Raising the Value of Money* (1692)
> *Two Treatises of Government*: Book II: *An Essay Concerning the True-Original, Extent, and End, of Civil Government* (1690).[28]

He emphasised the former work as his main source and was concerned with three main themes, viz. interest on money, private property and labour.

Marx began by noting the similarity between Locke's views about the lowering of interest rates and those of Petty (*TSV*, I, 364; cf. 369, 373). In the *Political Arithmetick*, Petty made the point that 'the natural fall of Interest, is the effect of the increase of Money'.[29] It was this theme, *inter alia*, that Locke took up and elaborated when he considered the concern over interest rates during the latter part of the seventeenth century. He emphasised the 'natural' (market) determination of interest rates and was opposed to the legal approach to lowering them,[30] although he recognised several pressures which would influence where the rates *should* settle. First, he recommended some legal upper limit on interest rates in order to prevent the excessive levels that may result from monopoly forces in lending by intermediaries[31] (in this sense of 'compulsory regulation', Marx's assertion that Locke rejected it was incorrect – *TSV*, I, 369). Secondly, though, he recognised the need for interest rates to be at a level that would ensure an adequate availability of money for lending in order to meet the 'needs of trade'.[32] This availability required that the opportunity cost of hoarding be sufficient to prevent it on any significant scale and that the return on money in England be sufficient to prevent the export and/or repatriation of funds.[33] Thirdly, he noted that if the legal rate of interest was forced below the 'natural' rate, the problem of evasion would arise.[34]

For Locke, the 'natural' rate of interest appeared to be determined by the interplay of two factors: first, the supply of loanable funds, which he related to the volume of money in circulation;[35] and secondly, the demand for loans to facilitate commerce and production, a demand that was indicative of the level and growth of economic activity.[36] With respect to 'the natural interest of money', then, its value would be raised: 'When the money of a country is but little, in proportion to the debts of the inhabitants' and 'when money is little in proportion to the trade of a country'.[37]

What especially attracted Marx's attention in Locke's discussions of interest was his concern also to explore the *origin* of and *explanation* for the payment of interest on money (*TSV*, I, 365ff.).[38] In Locke's perception of the '*natural*' world, man's *immediate* right to property arose only through the actions of his *personal labour*. Thus he wrote in *Of Civil Government* that 'every man has a property in his own person: this nobody has any right to but himself. The labour of his body, and the work of his hands, we may say are properly his' (quoted *TSV*, I, 365).[39] Consequently, *nature* tended to limit the possession of property to those things that could be acquired by personal labour *and* made use of directly and immediately. Thus Locke went on: 'The measure of property nature has well set *by the extent of men's labour*, and the conveniences of life' (quoted *TSV*, I, 366).[40] Any property beyond this 'belonged' to others and its accumulation impeded their rights to what nature could provide (*TSV*, I, 365–6).[41] The effect of this principle, though, was not to rule out the accumulation of property *per se*, for 'different degrees of industry were apt to give men possessions in different proportions'.[42] Rather, Locke's point was that any 'surplus' property beyond personal needs must be made available for others to use and not be allowed to 'perish'. This was ensured by the process of exchange with the mediation of money and the consequent accumulation of wealth in the form of this *durable* medium represented no loss to anyone of the services of nature. So man 'might heap as much of these *durable* things as he pleased; the exceeding of the bounds of his just property not lying in the largeness of his possession, but the perishing of any thing uselessly in it' (quoted *TSV*, I, 366–7).[43] With respect to the means of production – only land in Locke's perception – the justification of property rights was expressed as follows:[44]

> it is plain that men have agreed to a disproportionate and unequal possession of the earth; they having, by a tacit and voluntary consent, found out a way how a man may fairly

> possess more land than he himself can use the product of, by receiving, in exchange for the overplus, gold and silver, which may be hoarded up without injury to anyone; these metals not spoiling or decaying in the hands of the possessor.

Here Marx read the origins of private property in the means of production and an early justification for its existence, in spite of the inequality of possession that it entailed.

In his *Some Considerations*, Locke argued that the possession of wealth in the form of money was analogous to the possession of land in the sense that both could be employed to facilitate production and commerce: 'For as the unequal distribution of land, (you having more than you can or will manure, and another less) brings you a tenant for your land; and the same unequal distribution of money . . . brings me a tenant for my money' (quoted *TSV*, I, 367).[45] Analogously also, the lending of money must, then, bring some income and money 'comes to be of the same nature with land, by yielding a certain yearly income, which we call use or interest' (quoted *TSV*, I, 367).[46] Here the analogy seemed to break down, for Locke posed the question of how money could provide an income, noting that 'land produces naturally something new and profitable, and of value to mankind; but money is a barren thing, and produces nothing' (quoted *TSV*, I, 367).[47] The analogy remained robust, though, and Locke went on to argue that '*my money is apt in trade, by the industry of the borrower*, to produce more than six per cent. to the borrower, as well as your land, *by the labour of the tenant*, is apt to produce more fruits than his rent comes to.' Thus, the advancing of money as a loan gave the *owner* access to the 'industry of the borrower' and the right to share in the results of that 'industry', for 'by compact', this money '*transfers that profit, that was the reward of one man's labour, into another man's pocket*' (quoted *TSV*, I, 367).[48]

Two things of importance for Marx emerged in Locke's discussion: first, the idea that an income could be paid through the mediation of 'a *political* invention', the contract, by virtue of the *ownership* of money capital alone; and secondly, the idea that this income was to be paid out of a *surplus* generated by the labour activity of another person (*TSV*, I, 356, 367). With respect to this second point, care is needed in interpreting the *origin* of the surplus. Marx's comment that '*Locke* reduces both [rent of money and rent of land] to [the] exploitation of labour' (*TSV*, I, 369) can be misleading. Under the conditions of production in manufacturing with which Locke would mainly have been familiar, viz. workers working with their own means of production on a small scale, the emergence of a surplus in the circulation process depended upon 'profit on alienation' being received by the merchant seller. There was no general capacity to exploit labour in production as Marx would later understand it and the 'industry' that the owner of money capital tapped was that of the merchant and not the immediate commodity producer.[49] Be this as it may, Marx appropriately concluded that Locke had begun formally to draw attention to incomes appropriated by owners of accumulated property in a form other than land and independently of any feudal traditions. Locke's insights concerning the origin of interest on money represented 'the classical expression of bourgeois society's ideas of right as against feudal society' (*TSV*, I, 367).

In relation to man gaining access to the resources of nature, Locke gave prominence to the role of *labour*. The useful products available to man were directly the result of his own efforts except in rare circumstances where nature yielded something useful without effort (such as air). As Locke observed in *Of Civil Government*: 'it *is labour indeed that put [sic] the difference of value on everything*' and 'which puts the greatest part of the value upon land, without which it would scarcely be worth anything' (quoted, in part, *TSV*, I, 366).[50] However, as Marx realised, Locke was not arguing an embodied-labour view of *exchange* value. Rather he was referring to labour as the source of *use* value. The point remained, though, that this perception of the role of labour was an important founding principle, for as Marx noted, 'the measuring of exchange value by labour is in reality based on the fact that the labourer creates use value' (*TSV*, I, 366). That is, the exchange value of a commodity to be realised in the market was probably envisaged by Locke as the *consequence* of the *use value* additions provided by labour in the production process. It was in this indirect sense that labour 'generated' exchange value at this early stage of Classical political economy.[51]

As far as Marx was concerned, Dudley North's main distinction in his book *Discourses upon Trade; principally directed to the*

Cases of the Interest, Coynage, Clipping, Increase of Money (1691) was the separation of a 'definite concept of *stock* or *capital*, or rather [of] *money* as a mere *form of capital*' from money *per se* as the circulating medium (*TSV*, I, 364). North wrote that gold and silver as money were 'nothing but the Weights and Measures by which Traffick is more conveniently carried on, then could be done without them'. He continued, in recognition of money's store of value function, that it was the 'proper Fund for a *surplusage of Stock to be deposited in*' (quoted *TSV*, I, 369).[52]

The important point, then, was that these roles of money could be distinguished from its conception as a fund that could be set to work as capital in order to facilitate production and trade with the intention that it should yield a net return to the owner. North made it clear that 'from all the Money that lies dead, no benefit is to be expected' (quoted *TSV*, I, 371)[53] and, more graphically, that:[54]

> No Man is richer for having his Estate all in Money, Plate, etc., lying by him, but on the contrary, he is for that reason the poorer. That Man is richest, whose Estate [is] in a *growing condition*, either in Land at Farm, Money at Interest, or Goods in Trade. (quoted *TSV*, I, 370.)

For Marx, this idea, so clearly expressed by North, represented a crucial step in the evolution of Classical political economy. It enabled North to formulate what Marx considered to be 'the first correct conception of interest' (*TSV*, I, 364; cf. 369).

North argued more distinctly than Locke had done that the 'natural' rate of interest was a consequence of the market relation between the supply of and demand for *money capital*. More significantly, he aligned the payment of interest with rent in the sense that just as 'the Landed Man letts his Land', so those who had accumulated money capital and who 'either have not the skill, or care not for the trouble of managing it in Trade' could be considered to have 'lett their *Stock*' (quoted *TSV*, I, 369).[55] The reward in both cases was a form of *rent*, as North saw it, even though that paid in the latter case was called interest. Furthermore, North made the point that relative risk mattered in computing 'rent' and that 'Land ought to yield *less Profit* than Stock' (quoted *TSV*, I, 369)[56] because of the risk that a 'borrower' could abscond with the principal in the latter case but not in the former case.[57]

It was North's view that the rate of interest was an *effect* of the level of economic activity rather than its cause. The supply of and demand for money capital, or stock, on which the rate depended, were reflections of the volume of trade and wealth in a nation. More specifically, the 'price' of money capital was determined in the same way as the market price of a commodity and 'if there be more Lenders than Borrowers, Interest will . . . fall'. As a consequence, North concluded that 'it is not low Interest makes Trade, but *Trade increasing the Stock of the Nation* makes Interest low' (quoted *TSV*, I, 369).[58] His empirical judgment was that the observed fall in English interest rates had been caused by the growth of trade and wealth generating a constant excess supply of money capital.[59]

MASSIE AND HUME

North's endeavour to present interest as a payment due to the owner of money capital consequent upon its use in production and trade was taken up again and further developed in the mid-eighteenth century by Joseph Massie and David Hume. Marx's brief consideration of these two writers (*TSV*, I, 373ff.) included references to Massie's anonymously published work *An Essay on the Governing Causes of the Natural Rate of Interest; wherein the Sentiments of Sir William Petty and Mr. Locke, on that Head, are considered* (1750) and Hume's essay 'Of Interest' (1752).

Both Massie and Hume were concerned to refute the notion that the rate of interest was merely a monetary phenomenon, as had been argued most especially by Locke (*TSV*, I, 373, 375).[60] The central argument posited by these writers, and on which Marx focused was that the *origin* of interest was to be sought more explicitly in the use of stock to make a profit through engaging in production and trade. Hume described the nexus between interest and profit in the following terms:[61]

> It is *needless* . . . to enquire which of these circumstances, to wit, *low interest* or *low profits* [emphasis original], is the *cause*, and which is *the effect*. They both arise from an extensive

> commerce, and mutually forward each other. . . . An extensive commerce, by producing large stocks, diminishes both interest and profits; and is always assisted, in its diminution of the one, by the proportional sinking of the other. (quoted *TSV*, I, 375.)

Moreover, he formed the view that the level of profits and the rate of interest were both a *cause* and an *effect* with respect to economic activity and wealth: 'as low profits arise from *the encrease of commerce and industry*, they serve in their turn to its farther encrease, by rendering the commodities cheaper, encouraging the consumption, and heightening the industry' (quoted *TSV*, I, 375).[62]

Massie's argument was similar and he stated categorically that: 'The *natural Rate of Interest* is governed by the *Profits of Trade* to Particulars' (quoted *TSV*, I, 376).[63] In order to emphasise this view, Marx cited two further pieces of Massie's analysis in which observed interest rate differences were associated with empirical assessments of profits. First, the decline in the dominant rate of interest in England from 8 per cent to 4 per cent over the past one hundred years was ascribed to the fact that in earlier times, traders returned 'double the Profits they now make' (quoted *TSV*, I, 376).[64] Secondly, the different interest rates currently observed in various countries were argued to be due to the fact that 'the Profits of Trade in these several countries differ from the Profits of Trade here, and so much as to produce all those different Rates of Interest' (quoted *TSV*, I, 376).[65] The basis for such differences in profits and interest was, in Massie's view, simply that: 'The Profits of Trade in general, are governed by the Proportion *which the Number of Traders* bears to the *Quantity of Trade*' (quoted *TSV*, I, 376),[66] along with his judgments that this proportion had risen in England during the period cited and was highest in those other countries which had relatively low rates of interest.

Massie found the *justification* for the payment of interest in the recognition that money capital facilitated the *potential* to generate profit. Thus, '*that which Men pay as Interest* for what they borrow . . . [is] *a part of the profits it is capable of producing*' with the qualification that 'The equitableness of taking Interest, depends not upon a Man's making or not making *Profit* by what he borrows, but upon its being capable of producing Profit if rightly employed' (quoted *TSV*, I, 376).[67] This argument posed the corollary question of how the actual division of the immediate profit of trade between the borrower and the lender of money capital was to be explained. Massie felt that this division would be resolved by the emergence of a general consensus, presumably expressed through the market rate of interest. He recognised, though, that there would be exceptional cases where the general *proportional* division would not apply. Such cases would involve traders of great skill and/or those engaged in highly risky ventures '*which Lenders have nothing at all to do with*' (quoted *TSV*, I, 376).[68]

Marx finally summarised his conclusions about the place of Massie and Hume in the early evolution of Classical political economy in the following passage:

> Massie, even more definitely than Hume, presents interest as a mere *part of profit*; both attribute the fall in interest to the accumulation of capitals (Massie [speaks] especially of competition) and the fall of profits resulting from this. Both [say] equally little about the *origin of the profit of trade* itself. (*TSV*, I, 377.)

Thus, as Marx saw it, the challenge for those that followed Massie and Hume was to identify the *source* of profit independently of the 'profit on alienation' that had, not unreasonably, preoccupied the Mercantilist writers.

STEUART

Marx chose James Steuart's book *An Inquiry into the Principles of Political Œconomy: Being an Essay on the Science of Domestic Policy in Free Nations* (1767), with which to begin his initial draft of the 'Theories of Surplus Value' manuscripts (notebook VI, *TSV*, I, 41ff.). The reason for this choice appears to have been that Steuart's contribution represented a systematic culmination of the evolution of British political economy prior to Adam Smith's *Wealth of Nations*. As already noted at the beginning of this chapter, the detailed consideration of the other main pre-Smithian writers came only in the last few notebooks of the series in which 'Theories' appeared. It seems likely, though, that any rearrangement of the material for *presentation* in published form would have required these later pieces to be included prior to the treatment of Steuart. This would have enabled Marx to situate Steuart's work more completely in its intellectual-evolutionary context.

It was in his handling of the issue of the explanation of the profit of stock that Steuart stood out, in Marx's view, as the last of the Mercantilist writers. When situated alongside the works of the Physiocrats and of his approximate contemporary Adam Smith, Steuart's thought looked backwards rather than forwards in the evolution of Classical political economy. In Marx's words:

> Before the Physiocrats, surplus Value – that is, profit in the form of profit – was explained purely from *exchange*, the sale of the commodity above its Value. Sir James Steuart on the whole did not get beyond this restricted view; he must rather be regarded as the man who reproduced it in scientific form. (*TSV*, I, 41.)

Steuart's work was the '*rational* expression of the Monetary and Mercantile systems' (*TSV*, I, 43) in its recognition that the 'profit upon alienation' which appeared in exchange was not the creation of new wealth.

Steuart distinguished 'positive profit' from 'relative profit'. The former manifestation of the economic surplus Marx interpreted to involve a net addition to *use value* by way of the production process. In Steuart's words, the 'positive profit' was the result of 'an *augmentation* of labour, industry, or ingenuity, and has the effect of swelling or augmenting the *public good*' (quoted *TSV*, I, 41).[69] By contrast, 'relative profit' was argued by Steuart to represent 'a vibration of the balance of wealth between parties, but implies *no addition to the general stock*' (quoted *TSV*, I, 41).[70] And any exchange may involve the realisation of a 'compound' of both forms of profit.

Steuart did not fully clarify the relationship between these concepts of 'profit' and exchange value as the means of their realisation. In his discussion of price determination, he distinguished two components that were involved: 'In the *price* of goods, I consider two things as really existing, and *quite different* from one another [. . .]; the *real value* of the commodity, and the *profit upon alienation*' (quoted *TSV*, I, 42).[71] He elaborated on these categories and explained that the 'real value' originated in production as the result of the combined effects of three considerations: first, the volume of labour time, *on average*, required to produce the commodity; secondly, the exchange value of the worker's 'subsistence and necessary expence', in which were included 'his personal wants' *and* 'the instruments belonging to his profession', again *on average*; and thirdly, 'the [exchange] value of the materials' (quoted *TSV*, I, 42).[72] Just how these things were to be combined in order to determine exchange value was not specified by Steuart. Marx interpreted 'real value' to comprise the average labour time for production, 'valued' in terms of 'subsistence and necessary expence' for that period, plus the exchange value of raw materials used up. Steuart's conclusion was somewhat confusing: 'These three articles being known, the price of manufacture is determined. It cannot be lower than the amount of all the three, that is, than the *real value*' (quoted *TSV*, I, 42).[73] Although Marx did not comment here, it is not clear why 'all the three' needed to be added together and if so, how the 'amount' of the first would be valued independently of the latter two elements.

Given Marx's interpretation of the 'real value' determination, he concluded that if all commodities were sold at this value, 'no profit would exist' (*TSV*, I, 42). Steuart probably recognised this, too, because his concept of profit in this context was strictly 'profit upon alienation'. He explained it as emerging *in exchange* as the excess of *realised* exchange over 'real value', with this '*manufacturer's profit*' being 'in proportion to *demand*' and fluctuating 'according to circumstances' (quoted *TSV*, I, 42).[74] As Marx noted, this form of profit could only be what Steuart would soon call 'relative profit' and which represented 'a vibration of the balance of wealth between the parties' and 'implies no addition to the general stock'.[75] In relation to exchange value, Steuart did not clarify the origin or mode of realisation of what he would call 'positive profit'. Subsequent references to profit in the *Principles* concerned the 'vibration' idea rather than this latter form.[76]

There was very little in Steuart's *Principles* which treated the issues of production and distribution that concerned Marx. However, Marx made the best of what there was and noted two particular merits of Steuart's contribution (*TSV*, I, 43). First, he was impressed by the fact that Steuart was under no illusions about the *source* of 'profit upon alienation'. It did not represent a genuine surplus or addition to wealth and only emerged for an individual trader by virtue of the loss incurred by another. It was this argument which led Marx to conclude that Steuart's work was 'the *rational* expression of the Monetary and Mercantile systems' (*TSV*, I, 43). Secondly, and unfortunately with no supporting exegesis, Marx asserted the merit of Steuart's 'service to the theory of capital' in that he showed 'how the process of separation takes place between the conditions of production, as the property of a definite class, and labour power'. More generally, he gave 'a great deal of attention to this *genesis* of capital' in agriculture first as a precondition for its emergence as the basis of large-scale manufacturing industry (*TSV*, I, 43).

THE PHYSIOCRATS AND TURGOT

Marx's treatment of the Physiocrats in 'Theories of Surplus Value' comprised three stages. Immediately after his consideration of Steuart's *Principles*, he discussed their work in quite general terms, largely without any references to individual members of the 'school' or their works (*TSV*, I, 44ff.). In this context, Marx made some comments about the Physiocrats' concept of the burgeoning capitalist mode of production in France, their treatment of capital and their recognition of the surplus as the basis for the payment of rent. Next, Marx undertook an exegetical critique of the work of Anne-Robert-Jacques Turgot, whom he thought of as essentially a Physiocrat. Then, later in the 'Theories' manuscripts (notebooks X and XXIII), Marx provided an interpretation of the analytical centrepiece of Physiocracy, the *Tableau économique* (*TSV*, I, 308ff. and 378ff.). The sources and substance of this interpretation will be considered in the context of discussing Marx's 'law of motion' of capitalism in a later Part of this study.[77]

For the present, Marx began by drawing attention to the merit of the Physiocrats' perception of the emerging capitalist economic system *as an organic whole*. That is, their analyses reflected the essential interdependence of the totality of elements and forms that comprised the abstract representation of the self-reproducing socio-economic system. Thus, in spite of the Physiocrats thinking in terms of a 'natural' basis for such a system: 'It was their great merit that they conceived these forms as physiological forms of society: as forms arising from the natural necessity of production itself, forms that are independent of anyone's will or of politics, etc.' (*TSV*, I, 44). One additional difficulty that pervaded their work, according to Marx, was a failure to separate clearly the *material* dimension of production and circulation from its socio-historical form. In formulating their 'material laws', the Physiocrats' 'error is only that the material law of a definite historical social stage is conceived as an abstract law governing equally all forms of society' (*TSV*, I, 44). However, this limitation did not detract from their insight into the interdependence of production and circulation, mediated by capital, as the basis for understanding the reproduction process (*TSV*, I, 44).[78]

Two aspects of the Physiocrats' theory of production warranted recognition, in Marx's view. First, they had given *capital* a prominent role in the production process: 'The analysis of *capital* within the bourgeois horizon, is essentially the work of the Physiocrats. It is this service that makes them the true fathers of modern political economy' (*TSV*, I, 44).[79] Secondly, they had emphasised that *the* significant phenomenon of capitalist production that had to be explained was the generation of an economic surplus. It was the *raison d'être* of capitalism: 'Thus the Physiocrats saw the production of surplus Value as the essence of capitalist production. It was this phenomenon that they had to explain' (*TSV*, I, 62). In their approach to this problem, moreover, they made a very real analytical advance in arguing that the *origin* of the surplus was to be found in production: 'The Physiocrats transferred the enquiry into the origin of surplus Value from the sphere of circulation into the sphere of direct production, and thereby laid the foundation for the analysis of capitalist production' (*TSV*, I, 45). Circulation was ascribed its correct role in the Physiocrats' analyses, viz. that of the integrated extension of the production process in which the realisation of commodity sales would ensure continuing reproduction.

In spite of these important contributions to the analysis of capitalist production and reproduction, the Physiocrats were unable fully to realise what would later be recognised as the potential of their work. They were severely constrained by the object of their analysis being a form of capitalism in which agricultural production predominated. As Marx put it: 'while feudalism is . . . made bourgeois, bourgeois society is given a feudal semblance' (*TSV*, I, 50; cf. 52). The fundamental Physiocratic thesis which followed from this was that only agricultural production could generate an economic surplus. This surplus was appropriated by landowners as rent, and was argued to be a bounty of nature, a part of the 'Natural Order' which framed economic and social activity for the Physiocrats. 'For them', Marx noted, 'the bourgeois forms of production necessarily appeared as natural forms' (*TSV*, I, 44).

Within this analytical framework, though, Marx did find a perceptive interpretation of the involvement of labour in the generation of the economic surplus. He argued in this context that 'the foundation of modern political economy, whose business is the analysis of capitalist production, is the conception of the *Value of labour power* as something fixed, as given magnitude – as indeed it is in practice in each particular case' (*TSV*, I, 45). The Physiocratic notion was that the wages of labour should be confined to the '*strict necessaire*' in commodity (use-value) terms. The '*strict necessaire*' was, in effect, a *commodity* value of labour power rather than an exchange value form, as Marx recognised. Thus, 'without being in any way clear as to the *nature* of Value, they could conceive the Value of labour power, so far as it was necessary to *their* inquiry, as a definite magnitude' (*TSV*, I, 45, emphasis added).[80] On the basis of this conception, Marx argued, the Physiocrats had formulated an essentially correct principle of the surplus couched in commodity (use-value) terms. 'The agricultural labourer, depending on the minimum of wages, the *strict necessaire*, reproduces more than this *strict necessaire*, and this more is rent, *surplus Value*, which is appropriated by the owners of the fundamental condition of labour – nature' (*TSV*, I, 50–1). In spite of the ascription of the surplus to a '*gift of nature*', the correct concept of *productive* labour was employed in this formulation. For Marx, such labour was that which, in production, generated surplus Value. 'Hence for the Physiocrats agricultural labour is the only *productive labour*, because it is the only labour that *produces a surplus Value*, and rent is the *only form of surplus Value* which they know' (*TSV*, I, 46). Marx saw the particular nature of the production process that the Physiocrats observed, along with their lack of concern to elaborate the exchange value dimension of economic phenomena, as two reasons for this narrow perception of productive power.[81] So it was that:

> In manufacture the workman is not generally seen directly producing either his means of subsistence or the surplus in excess of his means of subsistence. The process is mediated through purchase and sale, through the various acts of circulation, and the analysis of value in general is necessary for for it to be understood.

By contrast, Marx continued:

> In agriculture . . . [the surplus] shows itself directly in the surplus of use values produced over use values consumed by the labourer, and can therefore be grasped without an analysis of value in general, without a clear understanding of the nature of Value. (*TSV*, I, 46; cf. 48–9, 50.)

The Physiocrats did not transfer this principle of the surplus to capitalist production in general. Because only 'Nature' was productive, non-agricultural production was 'sterile' in that it merely processed and transformed use values. The upshot of this was their failure to recognise that it was *capital* which *facilitated* the production of the surplus and that this was independent of the particular sector of production involved. Moreover, they also did not accord *profit* its correct status as the most immediate manifestation of the surplus in *capitalist* production.

> *Profit* on capital in the true sense, of which rent itself is only an offshoot . . . does not exist for the Physiocrats. Profit is seen by them as only a kind of higher wages paid by the landowners, which the capitalists consume as revenue (and which therefore enters into their costs of production in the same way as the minimum wages of the ordinary workmen). (*TSV*, I, 47.)[82]

It was Turgot's work that went beyond this and in which it was recognised that the surplus was associated with capitalist production in general, and that profit was the immediate return on advances.

Marx found in his rather brief critical reading of Turgot's *Reflections on the Formation and the Distribution of Wealth* (1766),[83] an extended version of the Physiocratic analyses in which the burgeoning influence of capital on production and distribution was now made more explicit (*TSV*, I, 54ff.). In the work of Turgot's immediate antecedents, the feudal and bourgeois aspects of the mode of production coexisted side by side. Turgot broke away from this vision and examined the historico-analytical emergence of a capital-dominated mode of production from within its feudal origins. In Marx's interpretation of Turgot, the 'illusion' of this coexistence 'disappears completely, and the Physiocratic system is presented as the new capitalist society prevailing within the framework of feudal society'. And, Marx added: 'This therefore corresponds to bourgeois society in the epoch when the latter breaks its way out of the feudal order' (*TSV*, I, 50; cf. 54).

The *Reflections* comprised 101 numbered passages. In passage XXVI,[84] the idea of capital advanced to facilitate agricutural production emerged after a discussion of pre-capitalist forms. Beyond this, after a series of passages dealing with money and exchange value, Turgot began to analyse the profound changes that the *general* application of capital in production must bring to the form of distribution and to the form of society itself (passages XLIXff.).[85]

A mode of production dependent upon capital brought with it a class of owners of accumulated wealth whose function it was to facilitate manufacturing, agriculture and commerce by organising and financing the material means of production required and who expected and received a financial reward for doing so. The emergence of this class of owners of capital was accompanied by the appearance of a class of propertyless workers whose access to 'subsistence' required that they work for wages paid by the owners (passage LXV).[86] These two classes now existed alongside that of the landowners and the analysis of this extended and modified socio-economic system required, *inter alia*, more careful attention to the determination and role of exchange value and a theory of distribution which included wages and 'profits'. Turgot's achievements with respect to developing this analysis were considerable.[87] Unfortunately, Marx did not fully elaborate them in his critique, although he did draw attention to some of the key analytical advances that Turgot made beyond the work of the Physiocrats proper.[88]

The *Reflections* began with a consideration of the productive activities of the 'Husbandman' who worked his own land. His labour was rewarded with a net product that covered the 'wages of his toil' *and* provided a surplus as well. This capacity to produce a surplus gave the 'Husbandman' a unique economic status which Turgot argued was to be found in the fact that the 'labour of the Husbandman *produces more than* his wants' and generates a 'superfluity *that nature accords him as a pure gift*'. Non-agricultural labour was 'sterile', in the sense that its produce covered only the 'livelihood' of the worker, while the 'Husbandman' was '*the only one whose labour produces over and above the wages of labour*' (quoted *TSV*, I, 55).[89] The significance of this argument for Marx was the emphasis that it placed on the *direct labour* of the 'Husbandman' as the source of the total product, even though the surplus was posited as a 'gift of nature'. The results of the 'Husbandman's' labour were effectively divided into two parts: one to 'pay' his 'wages' and one left over as the surplus (*TSV*, I, 55).

For Marx, it followed that when the direct labour came to be performed by a class of wage labourers, while all of the useful land was owned by another class, the true nature of the surplus was exposed. As Turgot recognised: 'The mere workman who has only his arms and his industry, has nothing unless he suceeds in selling his labour to others.' What is more, these 'others' were prepared to pay the workman 'what is necessary to procure him his subsistance' (quoted *TSV*, I, 56).[90] The simple result of this arrangement was that the landowner could reap much of the rewards of cultivation without providing any labour. Furthermore, Turgot was very clear as to the nature and origin of the return to the landowner. He argued that: '*The proprietor has nothing except through the labour of the cultivator*' (quoted *TSV*, I, 57), which effectively overruled the 'gift of nature' idea.[91] Turgot continued that the proprietor 'has need of the Cultivator because of a necessity which arises from the *physical* order of things, by virtue of which the land produces nothing at all without labour'. By contrast:[92]

> the Cultivator has need of the Proprietor only by virtue of *human conventions* and *the civil laws* which guaranteed to the original Cultivators and their heirs the ownership of the land which they had occupied, even after they ceased to cultivate it. (quoted in part *TSV*, I, 57.)

The two conditions from which the surplus arose, and by means of which it was perpetuated, were, then, the propertyless working class who were paid only their 'subsistence' and the landowners' property rights over the means of production. It was these conditions, when set in the context of a society dominated by the capitalist class as the owners of the means of production, that comprised the two pillars of Marx's theory of exploitation and surplus Value (*TSV*, I, 55–7).

It was in passage XXVI of the *Reflections* that Turgot introduced the mode of cultivation of land which involved the mediation of a third class of participants. The idea of 'tenant farming, or the letting out of Land' was that a wealthy cultivator with farming and entrepreneurial skills became the means by which the landowner could avoid working his own land.[93] The motivation for this capitalist farmer was his belief that he could improve the productivity of land by capital-intensive methods and thereby reap a larger surplus than that available to the landowner employing labour-intensive methods. This would enable the farmer to offer the landowner a fixed rent per year for the contracted period of tenancy while at the same time the latter's degree of effort and risk was reduced substantially.

Turgot went on to explore this capitalist approach to the organisation of production in the passages from number XLIX onwards.[94] He introduced the idea of savers with accumulated money wealth who were prepared to advance such wealth in order to facilitate economic activity of various kinds. For Turgot, 'these accumulated values are what is called *a capital*' and he discussed five alternative 'employments of capitals': the purchase of a landed estate, advances for manufacturing and industrial enterprises, advances for agricultural enterprises, advances for commercial enterprises, and lending at interest.[95]

In the cases of industrial and agricultural production that most interested Marx, Turgot considered two further aspects of the conversion of the mode of production to one dominated by capital. First, Turgot noted the consequences for socio-economic class structures in a situation where now 'a large part of society had *only their arms to maintain them*' and must be employed as wage labourers in order to subsist (quoted *TSV*,I, 58).[96] The social manifestation of this situation was that the 'Class of cultivators' and the 'industrial stipendary Class' were 'divided into two orders of men, that of the Entrepreneurs or Capitalists who make all the advances, and that of the ordinary Workmen on wages' (*TSV*, I, 59).[97] Here Turgot revealed a fundamental insight into the class nature of capitalism much as Marx himself perceived it.

Secondly, Turgot reflected upon the need for profit as a return on capital advanced in these production ventures. His summary of the bases of such profit in the following piece covered a broad range of considerations that he thought to be relevant. The capitalist could expect that the sale of his commodity[98]

> returns to him not only all his advances, but also a profit sufficient to compensate him for what his money would have been worth to him had he employed it in the acquisition of an estate, and, in addition, for the wages due for his work, his trouble, his risks, and his ability itself; for there is no doubt that if the profit were the same he would have preferred to live without any exertion on the revenue of an estate which he could have acquired with the same capital. (quoted in part *TSV*, I, 59.)

The *source* of this profit was not explicitly argued by Turgot at this point and it is interesting to note that in the case of agriculture, the above considerations combined to represent only 'a *return of the costs of cultivation*' rather than 'a *revenue*' on the grounds that they were the minimum necessary conditions for production to take place at all.[99] The only *surplus* referred to was that revenue accruing beyond these 'costs' and paid to the landowner as rent. Turgot's Physiocratic heritage remained quite evident here and its presence was reinforced later in the *Reflections* when he insisted that 'there neither exists nor can exist any revenue other than the net product of the land' and added that 'it is evident that the capitals come from the land just as much as the revenue does' (*TSV*, I, 59).[100] It was to be Adam Smith whom Marx found to be the first Classical political economist to have broken free of the legacies of Monetary–Mercantilist and Physiocratic thought in the analysis of exchange value and distribution.

CHAPTER 3

Adam Smith's *Wealth of Nations*

INTRODUCTION

By the time Marx came to formulate his interpretation and critique of Adam Smith's *An Inquiry into the Nature and Causes of the Wealth of Nations* in 'Theories of Surplus Value', he was already well acquainted with its content. He read the book as early as 1844 and had used its analyses as the main basis for his critical discussion of capitalism, as it was portrayed by political economy, in the *Paris Manuscripts* (CW, 3, 235ff.). There were also numerous references to it in the *Grundrisse* manuscripts and in the *Contribution*. In 'Theories', the essential core of the work was subjected to a critique in depth and it was the second most detailed part of Marx's critical history of political economy, after that dealing with Ricardo's *Principles*.[1] Marx's critique was directed at both the *methodology* and *substance* of Adam Smith's work. The critique of Smith occupied much of notebooks VI to IX and was taken up again in notebooks XI and XII. The former part contained Marx's analysis of Smith's exchange value theory and a lengthy analysis of various theories of productive and unproductive labour which centred around Smith's views on the subject. Smith's theory of 'cost price' was dealt with in notebook XI and his theory of rent in notebook XII.

With respect to the methodology evident in the *Wealth of Nations*, Marx's assessment was based upon standards of what the 'science' of political economy should endeavour to achieve. Adam Smith had stated his objectives at the beginning of the book in the section entitled 'Introduction and Plan of the Work'. He intended to account for certain observed phenomena of the burgeoning industrial capitalist society. In particular his two, more theoretical, Books on which Marx's critique centred, dealt with the following topics:

> The causes of . . . improvement, in the productive powers of labour, and the order, according to which its produce is naturally distributed among the different ranks and conditions of men in the society, make the subject of the First Book of this Inquiry.
>
> . . .
>
> The Second Book . . . treats of the nature of capital stock, of the manner of which it is gradually accumulated, and of the different quantities in labour which it puts into motion, according to the different ways in which it is employed. (*WN*, 2–3.)[2]

By Marx's methodological criteria, Smith had not adequately explicated the nature and origin of the capitalist phenomena of production, distribution and accumulation referred to and implied in these summary headings.

The basic reason for Smith's analytical limitations was that he had been unable to clarify the precise dimensions of his method.

> Smith himself moves with great naivete in perpetual contradiction. On the one hand he traces the intrinsic connection existing between economic categories or the obscure structure of the bourgeois economic system. On the other, he simultaneously sets forth the connection as it appears in the phenomena of competition and thus as it presents itself to the unscientific observer just as to him who is actually involved and interested in the process of bourgeois production. One of these conceptions fathoms the inner connection, the physiology, so to speak, of the bourgeois system, whereas the other takes the external phenomena of life, as they seem and appear and merely describes, catalogues, recounts and arranges them under formal definitions. With Smith both these methods of approach not

> only merrily run alongside one another, but also intermingle and constantly contradict one another. (*TSV*, II, 165.)

Marx referred here to an unconscious duality in Smith's thought. At one level, Smith was concerned to ensure that the categories which *describe* the observed phenomena of capitalism are established and arranged to present a coherent representation of the nature of the system. For Marx, this type of empiricist description could explain or account for very little. Rather, it set out the *objects* of explanation itself. The topography or anatomy of capitalism did not explain how it became the way it is or how it functions.

Marx credited Smith with the simultaneous endeavour to elicit genuine explanations for what he described. At times, Smith probed the phenomena in pursuit of a logical account of their appearance. The analogy here was with the physiology of the system, the objective of which was to comprehend the phenomena by analysing functions and operations. Unfortunately, Smith did not seem to recognise this methodological duality and he continuously conflated phenomenal description with essential explanation in a mixture that led him into analytical contradictions.

Smith's methodological confusions were most evident in his puzzles over the theory of exchange value. He himself recognised a potential difficulty in this aspect of his work when he entreated his readers for their concentrated attention to his discussion of value 'in order to understand what may, perhaps, after the fullest explication which I am capable of giving of it, appear still in some degree obscure.' And 'some obscurity may still appear to remain upon a subject in its own nature extremely abstracted' (*WN*, 33). On Smith's handling of the theory, Marx observed that at one level in the *Wealth of Nations* he revealed a potential fully to grasp the essences involved: 'the value of the commodity is examined, and in some passages correctly determined – so correctly determined that he traces out in general form the origin of surplus Value and of its specific forms, hence deriving wages and profits from this Value.' Beyond this, though, Smith turned this approach on its head and Marx added immediately: 'then he takes the opposite course, and seeks on the contrary to deduce the Value of commodities (from which he has deduced wages and profits) by adding together the natural prices of wages, profit and rent' (*TSV*, I, 97). For Marx, it was quite wrongheaded to give the *phenomenal forms* of distribution a logical priority in the *explanation* of exchange value. Later in 'Theories' this point was reiterated: 'The meaning of this change of approach is that first he [Smith] grasps the problem in its *inner relationship*, and then in the *reverse form, as it appears in competition*. These two concepts of his run counter to one another in his work, naively, without his being aware of the contradiction' (*TSV*, II, 106).

Thus, Marx found Smith to have confused the analytic with the synthetic dimensions of formulating and presenting an explanation of the exchange value phenomenon and its articulation with distribution. In particular, Smith had failed to realise that logico-analytical procedures applied to the dissection of phenomenal forms produced the *means* of explanation but not the explanation itself. The latter required a process of logical synthesis: that is, the application of reason to generate an argument which totally accounts for the phenomenon that is the object of explanation. In the discussion above, this object was the *form of appearance* of exchange value.

Smith's methodological limitations, then, led him into his well-known advocation of the labour-commanded *measure* of exchange value and his retreat from providing any *explanation* of the *capitalist* exchange value form at all. The duality apparent in his treatment of exchange value was taken up by subsequent writers and this gave Smith a somewhat peculiar status in the development of political economy as the originator of two different lines of thought.

> Adam Smith's contradictions are of significance because they contain problems which it is true he does not solve, but which he reveals by contradicting himself. His correct instinct in this connection is best shown by the fact that his successors take opposing stands based on one aspect of his teaching or the other. (*TSV*, I, 151.)

One of these strands led to the phenomenal interpretation of exchange value which links it to observable market events, while the other led to the concerted endeavour to preserve the direct links between exchange value and its embodied-labour essence originating in production.[3]

In spite of the methodological inconsistency evident in the *Wealth of Nations*, Marx admired the scope and scale of Smith's project. Smith had described, and to some extent analysed, for the first time the emerging system of *industrial* capitalism. Marx had recognised this as early as 1844 and a considerable respect for the seminal work of Smith pervades his critique in 'Theories'.

EXCHANGE VALUE AND THE IMPLIED PRINCIPLE OF SURPLUS VALUE

The main problem that Marx experienced in formulating his detailed critical investigations of Adam Smith's analysis of exchange value and its relationship to the structure of distribution was its lack of a coherent and consistent argument. In his exegesis, Marx endeavoured to make the best he could out of Smith's largely seminal contributions to these central aspects of an understanding capitalism. As Marx saw it, the objective of this part of Smith's analysis was to provide a systematic account of the observed pattern of capitalist distribution as it is mediated by the generation and realisation of the exchange value of commodities. In this particular analytical sense, Smith pursued an objective similar to Marx's own, albeit without the critical orientation. Unfortunately, and not unexpectedly given its position in the history of political economy, Smith's work did not fully account for these capitalist phenomena. Marx's critique exposed the limitations of the analysis and, in so doing, he reinforced the status of his own, more complete critical insights into the system.

It is to be noted that Marx had a particular view of what an exposition of the political economy of capitalism should achieve. He expected it to account for the phenomena that the system exhibited in a *logically consistent* way. This test had nothing to say about the ultimate purpose towards which a particular work was directed. If it purported to say anything about the capitalist system, it had to be based on a logically sound core of analysis that could explain at least the most important features of the system.

For Marx, the absolutely essential foundation of any exposition of the nature of capitalism was the embodied-labour theory of Value. This theory followed from what he perceived to be the essential nature of the capitalist relations of production. The theory *necessarily entailed* certain important consequences for the way in which capitalist phenomena were to be accounted for. The logic of capitalism was definitive for Marx and his critical test of the validity of explanations of its phenomena was their consistency with the labour theory of Value. Whatever a writer set out to do in his work on political economy, if it *began* with the labour theory it was bound to follow it to its logically entailed conclusions.

Such, then, was the standard that Marx set in his critical assessment of Adam Smith's analyses. Marx had established in his *Grundrisse* investigations what he considered to be at least the rudiments of the essential critico-logical core of capitalism as an economic system. This analysis was reinforced through the partial development and presentation of the ideas in the *Contribution* of 1859. His critique of Smith's analysis of exchange value and distribution thus involved checking its *logic* against that of his own account of the same phenomena. *As a whole*, Smith's achievement in these analyses had many limitations. In places, though, his insights were profound and had already been of crucial importance in the evolution of Marx's own critical position.

As Adam Smith saw it, the argument that embodied-labour content provides a basis for *explaining* exchange value could not be sustained once this value of the commodity did not accrue wholly to the worker (*WN*, 53–4). In *capitalist* production, the profit which accrues to the capitalist has to form part of exchange value along with the wage cost of labour. It is apparent from this that such value can only be *expressed* by summing the values shared amongst those involved in the production of the commodity.

Marx agreed with the labour-production approach to exchange value determination in its *orientation* but not in its details. He concurred with Smith that the exchange value of 'labour', that wage which provides for subsistence and reproduction, is a fundamental component of exchange value theory. But, along with Ricardo, Marx did not see any need for a shift of value theory between the pre-capitalist and capitalist economies.

Exchange value generation is not a function of the form of distribution of that value. Marx's thought on this was made clear in two passages: 'The relation between the labour time contained in commodities A and B is in no way affected by how the labour time contained in A and B is appropriated by various persons' (*TSV*, I, 74); and

> the distribution or appropriation of Value is certainly not the source of the Value that is appropriated. If this appropriation did not take place, and the workman received the whole product of his labour as his wage, the Value of the commodities produced would be just the same as before, although it would not be shared with the landowner and the capitalist. (*TSV*, I, 94.)

Clearly for Marx, the current and past labour embodied in a commodity during production was the only *source* of its Value. He found it quite misleading to infer, as Smith did (*WN*, 59ff.), that exchange value somehow has its *source* in the revenue flows of wages, profit and rent.

The root of Smith's problem with exchange value theory, as Marx saw it, was his failure to formulate a correct concept of the exchange value of 'labour'. Smith had not comprehended that the capital-labour 'exchange' in which the capitalist purchased labour services was not appropriately classified as an *exchange* at all. The capitalist purchased a *capacity* to labour for which he paid a social 'subsistence' equivalent in Value terms. Without the category labour power, Smith was unable correctly to analyse the capital–labour relationship. Commodities could exchange at their embodied-labour Values in an economy which included the receipt of non-labour income. Smith's analysis had foundered, Marx argued, upon the distinction between the 'quantity of labour' and the 'Value of labour'. The *Value* of labour embodied in a commodity had to be differentiated from the quantity of labour embodied (*TSV*, I, 73).

In a direct production economy, the exchange value of labour to the worker *was* the exchange value of the commodity he produced. Exchange may ensue on this basis with materialised labour and living labour having a quantitative identity. In this situation, Marx argued: 'a definite quantity of living-labour time would always command a quantity of commodities which represents an equal amount of materialised labour time' (*TSV*, I, 72). Once the means of production to be used by labour were owned by one or more classes who employed that labour as a separate class, then the situation was different: 'A definite quantity of living labour does not command the same quantity of materialised labour, or a definite quantity of labour materialised in a commodity commands a greater quantity of living labour than is contained in the commodity itself' (*TSV*, I, 72). According to Smith, under these circumstances, the embodied-labour theory of exchange value was invalidated. However, his subsequent discussion involved a most unsatisfactory analysis of the relationship between exchange value and distribution.

In the *Wealth of Nations*, Book 1, Chapter VI, Smith attempted to find a *causal explanation* for exchange value generated in capitalist production. His attention centred upon the *composition* of exchange value implied by the 'natural' distribution of the value produced. Marx quoted the following passage from the *Wealth of Nations* in demonstrating Smith's appreciation of the basic rationale of capitalist production:

> As soon as *stock has accumulated in the hands of particular persons*, some of them will naturally employ it in setting to work industrious people, whom they will supply with materials and subsistence, *in order to make a profit by the sale of their work, or by what their labour adds to the value of the materials.* (WN, 54; quoted *TSV*, I, 78.)

Marx noted that in this passage, profit emerged through value added by labour prior to exchange. This idea was reiterated in a further passage which he quoted from the *Wealth of Nations*:

> The *value which the workmen add to the materials*, therefore, resolves itself . . . *into two parts, of which the one pays their wages, the other the profits of their employer upon the whole stock of materials and wages which he advanced.* (WN, 54; quoted *TSV*, I, 79.)

What this amounted to was that Smith saw profit (and rent) as *deductions* from the total exchange value added by the efforts of labour in production. In the particular case of private property in land, '*rent makes the first deduction from the produce of labour which is employed upon land*'; and '*profit makes a second deduction from the . . . labour which is employed upon land*'. To these pieces, Smith added the generalisation that: 'The produce of almost all other labour is liable *to the like deduction of profit*' (*WN*, 73; quoted *TSV*, I, 84). For Marx, then, it was quite evident that Smith recognised that all exchange value *originates* in production and is *realised* in the sale of commodities. Moreover, the exchange value is the product of *labour alone* and any revenue accruing to the other factors of production, capital and land, represents *deductions* from the product of labour. That Smith recognised these deductions as a *surplus* of exchange value was made clear also when he wrote of 'the *surplus, from which are drawn both the profit of the farmer and the rent of the landlord*'; and 'the *surplus* which remains after replacing the seed and *maintaining all that labour*' (*WN*, 164 and 165; quoted *TSV*, II, 355). From these pieces, it is hardly surprising that Marx found in Smith's work an awareness of the principle of surplus Value as the origin and explanation of non-labour incomes.

If he had followed through in these arguments, Smith would not have found it necessary to suggest that in a *capitalist* economy, the embodied-labour principle of exchange value could not be applied and still account for profit and rent payments. The labour-commanded principle could provide a *measure* of exchange value but it could not explain its determination. Marx ascribed Smith's failure fully to recognise the analytical potential of his ideas to the conflation of surplus Value with its phenomenal forms.

> Thus Adam Smith conceives *surplus Value* – that is, surplus labour, the excess of labour performed and realised in the commodity *over and above* the paid labour, the labour which has received its equivalent in wages – as the *general category*, of which profit in the strict sense and rent of land are merely branches. Nevertheless, he does not distinguish surplus Value as such as a category on its own, distinct from the specific forms it assumes in profit and rent. (*TSV*, I, 82.)

Most importantly, it could not follow logically from Smith's arguments that capital and land are *independent sources* of profit and rent respectively as he suggested (*WN*, 59). And, the labour-commanded perception of exchange value could not *account for* its appearance in capitalist markets (*TSV*, I, 92ff.). It was appropriate for Smith to see exchange value (or natural price) as being *resolved* into its wage and profit (and rent) components, but 'it would be wrong to say that the Value of the commodity arises from adding together or combining the price of the wages and the price of the profit which are regulated independently of the Value of the commodity' (*TSV*, I, 96).

In the context of discussing the theory of rent in the *Wealth of Nations*, Marx returned briefly to his critique of Smith's difficulties with formulating a consistent account of exchange value determination (*TSV*, II, 345–6). Marx reiterated his view that Smith had, at times, conflated the processes of exchange value formation and distribution and had not maintained the mediating role of the surplus that he had quite clearly recognised.

A passage at the end of Book I, Chapter VI of the *Wealth of Nations* served to demonstrate Smith's failure to give due prominence to the form of the analytical articulation between exchange value and distribution. In this passage (*WN*, 61; quoted *TSV*, II, 345), Smith began by expressing the point that 'in a civilised country there are but few commodities of which the *exchangeable value* arises *from labour only*'. Marx read this as a clear assertion of *causality* that denied the embodied-labour theory of Value. The exchange values of the majority of commodities must '*arise*' from elsewhere if they are not to be attributed to labour. According to Smith, the *origin* of this *additional* exchange value was accounted for as '*rent* and *profit* contributing largely to that of the far greater part of them'. Again Marx found here an assertion of causality in the term '*contributing*' ascribed to *pre-existing* forms of distribution, surely an inconsistency given Smith's explicit awareness elsewhere that these forms were but parts of a surplus contributed by labour.

The passage concluded with an expression of the labour-commanded view of exchange value in which Smith compounded his inconsistency by referring to the total exchange value of the commodities produced in a country as the '*annual produce of its labour*'. This total exchange value was envisaged to be 'sufficient *to purchase* or *command a much greater quantity of labour than what was employed in raising, preparing and bringing that produce to market.*'

Marx's response to this passage was to reword it according to the logic of Smith's own discussion elsewhere. Smith was quite correct to point out that under developed capitalism, exchange value is rarely *resolved* into a payment for labour only. The exchange value of a commodity is generally *resolved* into profit and rent components as well. But, this says nothing about the *origin* of the exchange value or *why* it is so resolved. The crucial twist came in Marx's revision of the last part of Smith's piece to read: 'the annual produce of its labour will always be sufficient to purchase or command a much greater *quantity of labour* than what had to be *paid* (and therefore employed) in raising, preparing and bringing that produce to market' (*TSV*, II, 346). Here the origin of the extra labour commanded was re-emphasised as being the exercise of *unpaid* living labour activity. For some reason, at this point Smith did not evoke his own recognition of the existence of a surplus generated by labour, and from which profit and rent are drawn. This omission left his overall analysis with a confusing ambivalence about the vital exchange value–distribution nexus.

PRODUCTIVE AND UNPRODUCTIVE LABOUR

In dealing with the critical history of the theory of surplus Value, Marx was concerned to include some discussion of the distinction between productive and unproductive labour. For Marx, this dichotomy was a vital one. Productive labour employment is the origin of surplus Value and the very basis for the continued existence of capital (*TSV*, I, 153). The operation of the capitalist mode of production requires that living labour be employed by means of capital advances to purchase labour power. Thus: 'Only labour *which is directly transformed into capital is productive*'; and Marx added that productive labour is 'labour which produces surplus Value or serves capital as agency for the creation of surplus Value, and hence *for manifesting itself as capital*, as self expanding Value' (*TSV*, I, 393, latter emphasis added). Productive labour 'transforms the objective conditions of labour into capital and their owner into a capitalist', and it 'produces it own product as capital' (*TSV*, I, 396).

Marx noted that both Mercantilist and Physiocratic writers had, in effect, made this distinction. In some of their works it was argued that labour was productive if its commodity output exceeded the 'cost' of producing the output. For the Mercantilists, this meant that in foreign trade, money returned from the export of the commodities produced should exceed the money cost of production. For the Physiocrats, the notion applied to labour in agriculture where the commodity (use value) production exceeded the commodity input. Marx thus found that even though the Physiocrats had not argued the concept of surplus Value correctly, they had viewed productive labour as that which produced the surplus. This was, in principle, correct (*TSV*, I, 153–4).

It was Adam Smith who generalised the concept of productive labour in the capitalist production and accumulation context.[4] Marx found in the *Wealth of Nations* two conceptions of productive labour. One of these was the essentially 'correct' conception, in the light of Marx's own, that labour is productive if it generates an output *Value* which exceeds the input *Values*, i.e. labour that generates *surplus Value*. In this definition, Smith followed the basic principle which had been suggested by earlier writers and was consistent with his implied notion of surplus Value.

> This conception of productive labour follows naturally from Adam Smith's view of the origin of surplus Value, that is, of the nature of capital. In so far as he holds to this conception he is following a course that was taken by the Physiocrats and even by the Mercantilists; he only frees it from misconceptions, and in this way brings out its inner kernel. (*TSV*, I, 153.)

The 'inner kernel' was that productive labour is at the root of surplus Value generation. This befitted the context of Smith's discussion for the central theme of the *Wealth of Nations* was capitalist growth and development and the means of maximising it.

A significant point about the concept of productive labour involved here was neglected by Smith in that he did not emphasise that its 'productivity' originates in the particular form of the capital–labour relation under capitalism. That is, he did not situate the productive labour category in its context as logically entailed by the very nature of capitalism.

Marx argued this theme late in the 'Theories' manuscript (notebook XXI). There he reiterated the notion that the 'exchange' between capital and labour comprised two dimensions. First, the capitalist purchases labour power in exchange for the wage and obtains *control* over the workers' capacity to perform living labour. Secondly, the capitalist extracts surplus Value by exploitation, for it is a condition of the employment of the worker that he provides living labour beyond that socially necessary to produce the commodity wage Value (*TSV*, I, 397–8). It is in this form of the capital–labour relation, then, that the productivity of labour *as viewed by the capitalist* is to be found. As Marx put it: 'when we speak of *productive labour*, we speak of *socially determined* labour, labour which implies a quite specific relation between the buyer and the seller of labour' (*TSV*, I, 396). The capitalist mode of production is viable because access to productive labour can be arranged through the capital–labour relation.

> Productive labour is only a concise term for the whole relationship and the form and manner in which labour power figures in the capitalist production process. The distinction from *other* kinds of labour is however of the greatest importance, since this distinction expresses precisely the specific form of the labour on which the whole capitalist mode of production and capital itself is based. (*TSV*, I, 396).

This appropriate definition of productive labour was not used consistently by Smith as Marx had argued (*TSV*, I, 155–6, 160ff.). The second conception to which Smith resorted involved labour that produced *Value* embodied in a *commodity*. In this approach, two separate conceptions of productive labour can be identified. One of these relates purely to the production process out of which *Value* emerges irrespective of any surplus Value content, while the other relates to the view that production of non-material services cannot be considered productive. Marx's interpretation did not bring out this subtlety explicitly, but both aspects were present in his critique of Smith.

For Marx, the origin of Adam Smith's confusing use of the productive-labour concept in relation to both the production of surplus Value and Value was to be found in the Physiocratic notion that non-agricultural industries were 'sterile' in the sense that they produced commodities with Value but generated no surplus Value. Smith was aware that all industries should be viewed as generating the surplus, but in Marx's view he still allowed himself to revert to the fallacious alternative in his conception of productive labour (*TSV*, I, 162–3).

The latter of the two variations of the commodity-based conception of productive labour was related in Marx's argument to Smith's definition of the *commodity*. Marx quoted the following piece from the *Wealth of Nations* in order to illustrate the point: 'the labour of the manufacturer *fixes and realises itself in some particular subject or vendible commodity, which lasts for some time at least after that labour is past* . . . [while the] labour of the material servant, on the contrary, *does not* [*so*] *fix or realise itself* . . .' (*WN*, 351–2; quoted *TSV*, I, 161). The particular view of the commodity espoused here was inappropriate in Marx's interpretation. A product becomes a commodity not on the basis of its *material* existence but rather because, in the capitalist context, it is produced as a vehicle of surplus Value to be realised in exchange. As Marx put it:

> The materialisation, etc., of labour is however not to be taken in such a Scottish sense as Adam Smith conceives it. When we speak of the commodity as a materialisation of labour – in the sense of its exchange value – this itself is only an imaginary, that is to say, a purely social mode of existence of the commodity which has nothing to do with its corporeal reality; it is conceived as a definite quantity of social labour or of money. (*TSV*, I, 171.)

Thus Smith went on to list as unproductive those forms of labour which produced services only. In this he gave no recognition to the 'vendible commodity' as possibly a service produced as a consequence of capital advanced by a capitalist with the objective of accruing surplus Value.

Some services are paid for out of *revenue* when they are destined for immediate consumption (*TSV*, I, 164ff.). And, it does not matter if the consumption of these services is mediated by a material product, they still remain unproductive in the capitalist sense. Marx used the example of a jobbing tailor who called at his home to make a pair of trousers (*TSV*, I, 402–3). The exchange value of the services of the tailor was included in the price paid for the trousers. The point made by Marx was that 'The mere *direct* exchange of money for labour . . . does not transform money into capital or labour into productive labour' (*TSV*, I, 403). However, the same form of service labour may be *productive* where the tailor is employed by a capitalist to make trousers for sale. The trousers themselves are no longer the immediately important thing, for the service rendered to the capitalist by the tailor is that the tailor 'works six hours for nothing', and 'that this takes place in the form of making trousers only *conceals* the real relationship' (*TSV*, I, 403). Similarly, directly consumable service labour might be employed by the capitalist where he can arrange for the labour to generate and to realise surplus Value. It was Marx's conclusion that

> The same labour can be productive when I buy it as a capitalist, as a producer, in order to create more Value, and unproductive when I buy it as a consumer, a spender of revenue, in order to consume its use value, no matter whether this use value perishes with the activity of the labour power itself or materialises and fixes itself in an object. (*TSV*, I, 165; cf. 166–7.)

EXCHANGE VALUE, NATURAL PRICE AND DISTRIBUTION

While Marx found an implied principle of surplus Value generation in the *Wealth of Nations*, Adam Smith's explicit analysis referred only to the phenomenal forms of this category. Smith's analysis was locked into the manipulation of 'undeniable empirical phenomena' (*TSV*, I, 89) and he failed to see the significance of surplus Value as the *essence* of these forms. In his attempts to link the 'natural' rates of return to the factors of production directly to the appearance of exchange value or natural price, he was left without any account of how such returns originated. Smith was, though, but a victim of the *deceptive appearances* of capitalist operations and his analysis did not reach beyond them in this case.

It was Marx's view that Smith's treatment of *capital* in the exchange value–distribution articulation was inadequate. In particular, Smith neglected its role as the determinant of the form of the *social* relations of production. This was a significant omission, for: 'Capital is productive of Value only as a *relation*, in so far as it is a coercive force on wage labour, compelling it to perform surplus labour . . .' (*TSV*, I, 93). Smith's notion of surplus Value was not linked to exploitation as a consequence of this omission. For him, *profit did not have to be explained*; it was an empirical fact that just had to be fitted into his account of the appearance of exchange value.

The sort of fallacy which Smith's argument involved was illustrated in a passage of the *Wealth of Nations* in which he was concerned to establish that profit was not basd upon payment for the 'labour of inspection and direction' (*WN*, 54–5; cited *TSV*, I, 91–2). Marx found in Smith's arithmetic an analytical weakness rooted in the acceptance of the empirical identification of surplus Value with profit. The example given by Smith included two factories. The production details for each are set out in Table 3.1 (in Marx's terms). The reasoning implied by this example was that by increasing raw material (constant capital) inputs tenfold the profit return was raised from 100 to 730. How this increase was to be explained Smith did not say. He applied the *given* rate of profit to all capital employed to illustrate his point that profit had increased manyfold without any addition to the labour of superintendence. He did not notice that this additional profit was 'generated' *without any additional labour of any kind.* Twenty men were employed in both cases even though a much greater throughput of production was involved in Factory 2. It was Marx's view that this result could not be explained by Smith's approach. Moreover, the method employed by Smith became orthodox in subsequent political economy. Thus, Marx concluded:

> The seven times greater profit in the one manufactory as compared with the other – or in general the law of profit, that it is in proportion to the magnitude of the capital advanced – thus *prima facie* contradicts the law of surplus Value or of profit (since Adam Smith treats the two as identical) that it consists purely of the unpaid surplus labour of the workmen. Adam

> Smith puts this down with quite naive thoughtlessness, without the faintest suspicion of the contradiction it presents. All his disciples – since none of them considers surplus Value in general, as distinct from its determinate forms – followed him faithfully in this. With Ricardo . . . it merely comes out even more strikingly. (*TSV*, I, 92.)

Table 3.1

	Factory 1	*Factory 2*
Rate of profit	10 per cent	10 per cent
Variable capital	300	300
Constant capital	700	7,000
Total capital	1,000	7,300
Total profit	100	730

In discussing Marx's critique of Adam Smith's analysis of the exchange value–distribution connection, it is appropriate to recall that for Marx, *four* concepts were linked to the idea of exchange value, with the last three *expressed* both in labour and money terms. These four concepts were *Value*, the directly generated embodiment of abstract labour entailed by the *logic* of capitalist production relations; the immediate manifestation of Value as an embodied-labour *exchange value*; the modified form of this exchange value derived to include a uniform (Value) rate of profits on the many capitals involved in production and variously called the 'cost of production', 'average price' and 'price of production'; and, the actually realised *market price*, a modification of the 'average price' which results from the influence of supply and demand inequality.

Early in 'Theories of Surplus Value', Marx noted, 'The market price of the commodity . . . stands either above or below its Value. Indeed, as I shall show later, even the average price of commodities is *always different* from their Value' (*TSV*, I, 95). He went on to establish the point referred to here (*TSV*, II, 64ff.) before his critique of Smith's analysis of 'cost price' (*TSV*, II, 216ff.) and rent (*TSV*, II, 342ff.). This Value–distribution articulation analysis (the familiar 'transformation problem'), which resulted in the formal emergence of the category 'price of production' that had been missing from the *Grundrisse* investigations, is considered in the next chapter of this study.

For the present, Marx's critique of Smith centred upon Smith's direct identification of exchange value with 'natural price' (the equivalent of an 'average price' in the above sense), a reflection of his abandonment of the embodied-labour theory of value formation. In Marx's view, Smith had not comprehended the true nature of capitalist Value and its ramifications for the exchange value – distribution articulation (*TSV*, I, 95). Once again the difficulty experienced by Smith could be ascribed to his empiricist vision of the capitalist system, as Marx explained in the following passage. For Smith:

> the value of the *commodity* is identical with its *cost price* and the latter with the *natural price* of the commodity. The rate of profit, as of wages, is *presupposed*. They are indeed given for the *formation* of the cost price. They are *antecedent* to the cost price. To the individual capitalist therefore they also appear as given. The hows, whys and wherefores do not concern him. Adam Smith here adopts the standpoint of the individual capitalist. . . And since Smith transports himself right into the midst of competition, he immediately reasons and argues with the peculiar logic of the capitalist caught up in this sphere. (*TSV*, II, 218–19.)

Thus Smith's analysis was concerned only with the apparent, phenomenal world of competition in his dealings with price formation. This allowed him only to formulate two price categories, 'natural' and market price, with the latter fluctuating around the former.

For Marx, the issue was more complex. The challenge that he took up, and was eventually able *partially* to meet, was fully to articulate the immediate Value of capitalist production with its ultimate manifestation as a realised market price by way of an analysis that was consistent with a uniform general rate of profits on the various capitals involved in production. Adam Smith did not even perceive the issue as having so many analytical dimensions because his 'natural price' was formed from a *given* uniform rate of profits (leaving aside rent for the present).

It was clear to Marx that Adam Smith had recognised the link between exchange value and distribution and, in so doing, also recognised that exchange value is the essential mediation between production and distribution in the capitalist system. In *some* of his discussion, Smith had argued exchange value to be analytically prior to distribution. The embodied-labour value of the commodity was what gave quantitative content to the distribution process. In this aspect of Smith's discussion, Marx had been able to identify the principle of surplus Value. But Smith went beyond this and reversed the link between exchange value and distribution. For the major part of Smith's analysis, it was distribution which was prior to value determination, and this left him with a most unsatisfactory circular argument which he could not resolve. The formulation of exchange value or 'natural price' by adding up the observed distributional quantities which were generated in producton *left the distribution itself unexplained.*

> Having *compounded* the Value of the commodity from the separate and independently determined *Values of wages, profit* and *rent*, Adam Smith now asks himself how these primary values are determined. *And here he starts out from the phenomena as they appear in competition.* (*TSV*, II, 218, last emphasis added.)

Chapters VIII, IX and XI of Book I of the *Wealth of Nations*, it seemed, were to be devoted to explaining the determination of the 'natural' rates of wages, profit and rent. Marx found Smith's approach less than satisfactory in general and in its details.

In his critique of these chapters of the *Wealth of Nations*, Marx found little analysis of any substance (*TSV*, II, 222ff.). Smith's reasoning on the 'natural' wage was circular in that the subsistence commodity wage had to be valued using the very exchange values which were in part compounded from the 'natural' wage itself. Marx concluded that indeed 'the chapter [on wages] contains nothing relevant to the question except the definition of the *minimum wage*, alias the Value of labour power' (*TSV*, II, 223). Smith's discussion of the 'natural' rate of profits also failed to get to the point. His analysis centred upon fluctuations in the rate of interest, and whatever these inferred about the rate of profits, based upon a supply and demand mechanism. In no way did this analysis contribute to an *explanation* of the 'natural' rate of profits: 'he does not tell us at all what it is or how it is determined although we are supposed to determine the "natural price" of the commodity by means of this "natural rate of profit" ' (*TSV*, II, 229).

Marx's critique of Adam Smith's analysis of rent was more substantial, reflecting the multi-dimensional nature of Smith's argument on this subject (*TSV*, II, 342ff.).[5] Marx's reading emphasised his concern with the idea that a 'natural' rate of rent could be found to form a component of exchange value in its 'natural' price form. He touched briefly on some other, less definitive dimensions of Smith's analysis, but these discussions are not pursued here.

In reading Smith's discussion of rent, it became apparent to Marx that Smith did not argue the 'natural' rent category as a definitive quantitative measure, although he seemed to retain the *concept* of it in the sense that he sought a consistent principle to account for its origin.

In its most elementary conception, rent was envisaged by Smith as paid out of the surplus generated by labour. As Marx read it, the following passage from the *Wealth of Nations* reflected a 'Physiocratic' vision of agricultural production and distribution:

> But [why?] land, in almost any situation, *produces a greater quantity of food* than what is sufficient *to maintain all the labour* necessary for bringing it to market, in the most liberal way in which that labour is ever maintained. The *surplus* too is always more than sufficient *to replace the stock which employed that labour, together with its profits*. Something, therefore, always remains for a rent to the landlord. (*WN*, 164; quoted *TSV*, II, 354.)

Smith had earlier made it quite explicit that rent is extracted from the surplus by virtue of the private property rights of the landowner:

> As soon as land becomes private property, the landlord demands a share of almost all the produce which the labourer can either raise, or collect from it. *His rent makes the first deduction from the produce of the labour which is employed on*

> *the land.* (*WN*, 73; quoted *TSV*, I, 84: cf. *WN*, 56; quoted *TSV*, I, 82.)

Now while such property rights are necessary for the appropriation of rent, they are not a sufficient condition in that the surplus realised must be adequate to pay rent after returning the normal profit on the farmer's capital advances. The process of exploitation by the capitalist farmer may not, in itself, explain the quantitative capacity to pay rent. As Smith argued, some 'extra' surplus may need to be realised through the market price of the commodities being sufficiently high (*TSV*, II, 354).

Before considering this latter point further, Marx referred to Smith's idea that rent is effectively a 'monopoly' based income. He read of this at several points in the *Wealth of Nations*, but most explicitly in the dictum that: 'The rent of land [. . .] considered as the price paid for the use of the land, is naturally a monopoly price' (*WN*, 162; quoted *TSV*, II, 343). Thus Marx argued that: 'It is in fact a price which is only enforced through the monopoly of landed property'; and regarded 'as a mere effluence of *landed property*, rent is *monopoly price* . . . since it is only the intervention of landed property which enables the product to be sold for more than the cost price' (*TSV*, II, 343). Such a 'monopoly' comprises the right to appropriate part of the *realised* surplus rather than to set its quantity through any capacity to control the exchange value of a commodity. This use of the term monopoly contrasted with Smith's more general discussion of the market orientated use of it to infer control over price by means of deliberately restricting supply (*WN*, 69). The link between the two settings of the term is that an 'extra' surplus is realised in each situation. But, while the capitalist can appropriate it where no land is involved in production, the landowner usurps that right where land is an input to production. All that Smith said in the present context was that the rent would be the maximum that the farmer could afford to pay after being allowed the 'natural' profit return on his capital advances. This was his common standard upon which the *principle* of a 'natural' rent was based. The *excess* of the surplus above the 'natural' profit was referred to explicitly by Smith as 'the *natural rent* of land' (*WN*, 161; quoted *TSV*, II, 342).

This argument left the *value* of the 'natural' rent undetermined as a residual payment until the value of the surplus is actually realised. It was evident to Marx that this outcome was argued by Smith through the state of supply relative to demand, because the market for agricultural production (dominated by corn) fluctuates accordingly. It followed that because the 'natural' rent had no predetermined value, the formation of the exchange value of agricultural commodities (and some other commodities linked directly to natural sources, such as minerals) could not be approached in the same way as for the commodities produced by industry. The wage and profit components were argued by Smith to be predetermined 'natural' components of 'natural' price formation. While they represented *causes* of changes in the 'natural' prices, and hence in market prices, rent was rather a *result* of fluctuations in *market* prices. Thus it was that Smith argued that rent '*enters INTO THE COMPOSITION of the price of commodities in a DIFFERENT WAY FROM WAGES AND PROFITS*' (*WN*, 163; quoted *TSV*, II, 352, Marx's emphasis).

In his critique of Smith's analysis, Marx objected to the apparent shift in the view taken of exchange value formation between Book I, Chapters VI and VII of the *Wealth of Nations*, dealing with the components of exchange value and then the particular forms of 'natural' price and market price, and Chapter XI on rent.

> Although he does not turn back, even for one moment, to glance at Chapters V, VI and VII, he admits to himself (not as a contradiction, but as a new discovery which he has suddenly hit upon), that with the sufficient price, he has overthrown his whole doctrine of natural price. (*TSV*, II, 352.)

Marx based this strong assertion on his reading of Smith's explicit argument in these earlier chapters that the 'natural' prices of *all* products were to be viewed as being formed in the same way from the addition of the 'natural' returns to the factors concurring in their production. Where land was a factor, the 'natural' price included a *particular value* of 'natural' rent. Marx quoted several pieces from the *Wealth of Nations* to substantiate his reading (*TSV*, II, 348–9). For instance:

> When the price of any commodity is neither more nor less than

> what is sufficient to pay the *RENT OF THE LAND, the wages of the labour*, and *the profits of the stock* employed in raising, preparing and bringing it to market, according to their *natural* rates, the commodity is then sold for what may be called *its natural price*. (*WN*, 62.)

Most importantly, this notion of the 'natural' price implied that it exists logically prior to any market induced effects on *realised* exchange value. Rent as its 'natural' rate cannot be a residual here. In these chapters on exchange value formation, land had a factor status akin to that of capital, including the suggestion that it could pursue its preconceived 'natural' rent by mobility between lines of production. Once again, Marx quoted several pieces from the *Wealth of Nations* to this effect (*TSV*, II, 349).

Marx found a different argument in Chapter XI on rent, an argument which he read as inconsistent with Smith's earlier expressed ideas on the formation and analytical status of the 'natural' price (*TSV*, II, 350ff.). According to Marx's reading, Smith supplemented his 'natural' price concept with two additional exchange value forms called 'ordinary' price and 'sufficient' price. It was now the 'sufficient' price that exists logically prior to the realisation of the exchange value of a commodity under particular market conditions. But, this price does not include any rent. It is a purely *production*-based price linked to the *activity* of the capitalist farmer and covers the return of his capital advances plus profit at the 'natural' rate (*TSV*, II, 361). The 'ordinary' price then appears to be a common expected market price for the commodity which Smith argued as follows: 'Such parts *only* of the produce of land *can commonly be brought to market*, of which the *ordinary price* is sufficient *to replace the stock which must be employed in bringing them thither, together with its ordinary profits*' (*WN*, 162; quoted *TSV*, II, 350). Any commodity with an 'ordinary' price greater than its 'sufficient' price will provide a rent residual for the landowner to appropriate. This is dependent upon the most usual state of the market being in excess demand and, for such commodities, a rent will always be available. For other commodities, the market conditions are less predictable and these may or may not deliver a rent depending upon periodic circumstances (*WN*, 163; quoted *TSV*, II, 351).

For Marx, then, it was the 'sufficient' price that was analogous to his price of production category which included a uniform general rate of profits on all capitals. This price is the '*sine qua non* of the existence of the commodity' under the capitalist mode of production (*TSV*, II, 351).

Marx found in Smith's principle of the 'sufficient' price a more or less correct statement of the role that capital plays in the determination of price. The analysis was confined to appearances, but the correct notion of capital advanced for production being returned with a profit through price formation and realisation was present. Smith did not pursue this line of reasoning consistently, though, and in places he experienced difficulty in explaining just how capital could be fitted into price. The issue for Smith was to reconcile price as a sum of revenues with the existence of capital as an input whose exchange value had to appear in the price as well. His dilemma in this was summarised by Marx in the following passage.

> One can see . . . why Adam Smith – despite his considerable scruples on this point – resolves the entire value of the commodity into rent, profit and wages and omits constant capital, although of course he admits its existence for each 'individual' capitalist. For otherwise he would have to say: The value of a commodity consists of wages, profit, rent and that part of the value of the commodity which does not consist of wages, profit, rent. It would therefore be necessary to determine value independently of wages, profit and rent. (*TSV*, II, 219.)[6]

A ruse used by Smith to overcome the difficulty was to endeavour to resolve non-wage capital into its revenue components. These were traced back through a sequence of capital inputs setting up what was, in effect, a series of dated revenues to add to the immediate revenues in price formation (*TSV*, I, 98). As Marx saw it, 'it is of no avail for Adam Smith to send us from pillar to post' (*TSV*, I, 99) in this way.

To demonstrate that Smith was unable to escape the dilemma, Marx quoted two passages from Book II, Chapter II of the *Wealth of Nations*. In the first, Smith reiterated his view that commodity exchange value is resolvable into three revenue components:

> *The whole price or exchangeable value* of that annual produce

> [in aggregate], must resolve itself into the same three parts, and be parcelled out among the different inhabitants of the country, either as the wages of their labour, the profits of their stock, or the rent of their land. (*WN*, 302; quoted *TSV*, I, 100.)

Then, immediately following this point, Smith proceeded to argue for the exclusion of capital replacement from gross revenue to give a *net revenue.* Marx built some of his critique around the following passage.

> The gross revenue of all the inhabitants of a great country, comprehends the whole annual produce of their land and labour; the neat revenue, what remains free to them after deducting the expence of maintaining; first, their fixed; and, secondly, their circulating capital; or what, without encroaching upon their capital, they can place in their stock reserved for immediate consumption, or spend upon their subsistence, conveniences, and amusements. Their real wealth too is in proportion, not to their gross, but to their neat revenue. (*WN*, 303; quoted *TSV*, I, 101.)

In this analysis, then, Smith could not sustain the idea that exchange value is compounded only from revenues. From arguing that distribution is effectively prior to price formation he had to revert to his earlier position that revenue could only be paid out of price, recognising now that capital has to be replaced as well.

Another aspect of Smith's analysis also revealed his confusion over the exchange value–price–distribution issue, Marx argued. The object of Smith's analysis was the competitive capitalist economy. Competition ensures that, allowing for some specific differentials, the 'natural' rates of return to all three factors of production are effectively the same in all sectors of production. Smith was aware that this distribution pattern is sustained by factor mobility and flexible *market* prices which signal non-'natural' rates of return in particular sectors of production. Thus he wrote that the market price may be sustained above the 'natural' price for a considerable time, but below it for only a limited time. He continued:

> Whatever part of it was paid below the *natural* rate, the persons

> whose interest it affected would immediately feel the loss, and would immediately *withdraw either so much land, or so much labour, or so much stock, from being employed about it*, that the quantity brought to market would soon be no more than sufficient to supply the effectual demand. Its *market price*, therefore, would soon rise to the *natural price*. This at least would be the case where there was perfect liberty. (*WN*, 70; quoted *TSV*, II, 221–2.)

Marx objected to this argument on two grounds: first, Smith's own analysis did not consistently follow the concept of the 'natural' price inferred here; and secondly, that the understanding of the price and distribution determination process displayed by Smith was incomplete because he failed to penetrate the appearances involved and expose the essence of the process.

As Marx saw it, the driving, primary force behind production is *capital* and the interests of capitalists. Capital mobility is important and competition establishes a uniform general rate of profits. Labour is paid its Value as labour power and has no incentive to be mobile. Marx was not concerned to fit land into any *fundamental* critical analysis of the capitalist economy, for he argued that the *essential* nature of the system could be grasped without reference to land. And, as the above discussion has suggested, Marx found that Smith got into considerable difficulty in maintaining his concept of 'natural' rent as a *price-determining* element. In spite of his earlier argument, Smith had resolved to leave it as a *market determined* residual. In his 'sufficient' price concept, though, he had grasped the appropriate form of a central price towards which competitive market prices would gravitate if supply and demand imbalances could be corrected by the initiative of *capital* mobility (*TSV*, II, 353).

By focusing on appearances, Smith had not fully accounted for the existence of this central price form as necessary to ensure the continuous and constant supply of a particular commodity to meet a given demand (*ceteris paribus*). He correctly perceived that competitively flexible market prices would level out to such a central price, in spite of his difficulties with the 'natural' price concept. His *description* here corresponded to the actual events occurring in the operations of the capitalist markets. What this empiricist view of the competitive process could not explain was the *actual level of the price* towards which a market price would settle. In this respect, Marx found Smith's price theory to be signally incomplete. Smith lacked the methodological and analytical sophistication required to pursue the 'sufficient' price's essential logical roots in the embodied-labour origin of exchange value. This procedure was, in Marx's view, crucial in order fully to account for the appearances.

As I will demonstrate in the next two chapters of this study, Marx found that Ricardo had made some advances towards formulating such an analysis. Marx noted that Smith's perception of the *apparent* 'natural' price formation process was the basis for

> an essential difference between Smith's and Ricardo's conceptions of the levelling out to the *natural price*. Smith's [conception] is based on his false assumption, that the three elements independently determine the value of the commodity, while Ricardo's is based on the correct assumption that it is the *average rate of profit* (at a given level of wages), which alone determines cost prices. (*TSV*, II, 222.)

Later, he reiterated this view:

> Thus the *sufficient price* is in fact the *price of production* or *cost price* as abstracted by Ricardo from Adam Smith and as it indeed presents itself from the standpoint of capitalist production, in other words the price which, apart from the outlay of the capitalist, pays the ordinary profit; [it is] the average price brought about by the competition of capitalists in the different employments of capital. (*TSV*, II, 351.)

However, given Smith's, albeit belated, recognition of the 'sufficient' price idea, Marx somewhat overstated the *conceptual* advance made by Ricardo on this particular point. What Ricardo did do was to rid the analysis of the ambivalence apparent in Smith's work with respect to the appropriate central price concept.

Part II

David Ricardo and the apogee of Classical political economy

CHAPTER 4

Ricardo's *Principles*: exchange value and profit

INTRODUCTION TO MARX'S CRITIQUE OF RICARDO

Marx's critique of Ricardo's *On the Principles of Political Economy and Taxation* (3rd edition, 1821)[1] is an especially controversial subject about which much has been written in the history of political economy. Several different positions on the *degree* and *nature* of the critical-intellectual filiation between Marx and Ricardo are evident in the literature. Some writers have been most concerned to dissociate Ricardo from Marx's revelations about the conflict- and crisis-ridden nature of capitalism.[2] Others have been concerned to dissociate *Marx* from Ricardo's bourgeois political economy by arguing that his critique represents a distinct rupture in the evolutionary progress of the history of political economy. In the work of this group, Marx becomes an 'a-Ricardian' whose critique of political economy and capitalism is independent of any intellectual filiations with Ricardo or anybody else.[3]

At the other extreme, some historians of political economy have claimed that Marx's Ricardian heritage is beyond doubt.[4] For this group, Ricardo and Marx are situated in a direct line of Classical evolution in political economy that runs at least from the Physiocrats and Adam Smith in the eighteenth century to the work of Piero Sraffa (and in 'dynamics' especially, to Michal Kalecki, Wassily Leontief and Adolph Lowe) in more recent years.[5] It will be one of my objectives in the present study to provide the detailed textual-exegetical evidence required for a proper assessment of Marx's situation in this Classical-Ricardian heritage.

In the case of at least one historian of political economy, though, Alfred Marshall's claim to lineage with Ricardo has been restaked and even extended to involve an implicit link with the general equilibrium world attributed to Léon Walras. And the Ricardo–Marx filiation has been preserved by a simultaneous endeavour to situate Marx in this world, too.[6] This view has met with much opposition despite the erudition of its presentation.[7]

With respect to the nature and status of Marx's critique of the *Principles*, few *detailed* studies have been undertaken. The main two that have been published take a strongly critical stance against Marx's position.[8] It will be one of my objectives, also, to attempt a more empathetic and relativistic interpretation of the critique than those available at present. It is my view that Marx's critique of the *Principles* can be *comprehended* only by recognising two dimensions of its situation: first, within the confines of the analytical preconceptions and standards of the era; and secondly, within the evolving methodology, premises and substance of Marx's total critique of capitalism. Given this delimiting situation, my objective is to explicate the actual bases on which Marx drew his critical conclusions about Ricardo's work.

In any endeavour to account for the specifics of Marx's critique of the *Principles*, several factors are of preliminary importance. First, Marx approached the critique with the central tenets of his own critical theory well developed through his *Grundrisse* investigations and through the presentation of Value theory and the simple circulation analysis in the *Contribution*. In addition, the critical discussions of Ricardo in 'Theories of Surplus Value' were immediately preceded by Marx's first formal exposition of the Value-distribution *articulation* analysis.[9] The conceptual clarifications which this involved served him well in the critique.

Secondly, it cannot be emphasised too strongly that the crucial and essential foundation of Marx's critique of political economy was the embodied-labour theory of Value. For Marx, this theory reflected the absolutely indispensable essence of the relations and operations of the capitalist mode of production and its integrated processes of exchange and distribution. Any theoretical exposition of capitalism that did not begin from the first principles of Value formation must miss the essential nature of the system. More importantly, any theoretical exposition that *began* with the embodied-labour principle of exchange value and then did not fully elaborate its entailed logic did not realise its full explanatory potential.

Thirdly, and apropos the previous point, whatever may be thought of the embodied-labour theory of exchange value today, and whatever may have been revealed about its inherent analytical difficulties,[10] our comprehension of *Marx* is not helped by omniscient and absolutist criticisms of his critique that pay little regard to the situation, status and stage of analytical development of the theory in the early and mid-nineteenth century. It formed the premise from which all *orthodox* and *recognised* political economists of the period worked. Marx would have seen no reason to question it. What he did was to *adapt* it in such a way that its critico-explanatory powers were enhanced remarkably. However, to expect him to have had the prescience needed in order to anticipate the subtle logico-analytical problems that the theory has been revealed to entail in modern debates is unreasonable. It is against the analytical standards and the limited, socially 'sterile' perception of the significance of the labour theory *in his own time* that Marx's critical theory should be assessed.

The final point of preliminary importance in the understanding of Marx's critique of Ricardo is that his reading of Ricardo's works was limited in its scope. His focus was virtually exclusively on the *Principles* as Ricardo's *magnum opus* and he paid little attention to any earlier works. In 'Theories', he referred in passing to *An Essay on the Influence of a Low Price of Corn on the Profits of Stock etc.* of 1815 (*TSV*, II, 123, 125) and *On Protection to Agriculture*, 4th ed., 1822 (*TSV*, II, 125; III, 55), but neither work was the object of any critical analysis.[11] Nor was Marx concerned with earlier editions of the *Principles* and their differences from the third edition, which he took to be the definitive statement of Ricardo's political economy.[12] It is also important to note that modern-day standards of Ricardo scholarship have been set through access to Ricardo's voluminous correspondence. This has proved to be a very rich source of analytical clarification. Marx did not have access to this source and his critique was constrained to some extent as a consequence. Moreover, Marx was not aware of two other writings of Ricardo which bore directly upon the themes with which he was concerned. One was the 'Notes on Malthus', written during 1820, in which Ricardo expressed his views about Malthus's analyses which contradicted his own in many ways. The source of these 'Notes' was Malthus's *Principles of Political Economy*, 1820. The other piece which Marx could not consider was Ricardo's 1823 essay 'Absolute Value and Exchangeable Value'. Both of these writings would have provided Marx with additional insights into Ricardo's thought on political economy.

Marx was a trenchant but sympathetic critic of Ricardo. He considered the *Principles* to be the apogee of the development of bourgeois political economy and his reading of Ricardo's work led him to cite several significant aspects which gave it this status.

For Ricardo, the progress of human society could be assessed by its capacity to produce flows of commodity wealth. In this sense, capitalism had been an historically unrivalled success and Marx considered it quite appropriate that Ricardo had concentrated upon this dimension of the system (*TSV*, II, 117–18, 125; III, 52). Ricardo had learnt from Adam Smith that this capacity could expand through capital accumulation and that, in principle at least, such expansion could be achieved in a socially harmonious way. It seemed to Marx that Ricardo's analysis of the dynamics of distribution cast some doubts upon this potential for harmony. And, in his own critique of political economy, Marx's central thesis was that the immanent nature of capitalism negated this potential completely.

What appealed to Marx most particularly in Ricardo's work was his preparedness to expose the contradictions and conflicts of the capitalist system. It was no surprise to Marx that Ricardo seemed to espouse the interests of the members of the bourgeoisie given their central role in the production of commodity wealth, the key to increasing social welfare (*TSV*, II, 118, 166). Similarly, Ricardo's perception of the proletariat as 'machinery or beasts of burden or commodities' Marx found to be a 'scientific' judgement in the context of his analyses rather than one based on any class prejudice (*TSV*, II, 119).

So it was, then, that in spite of the limitations of Ricardo's perceptions imposed by his lack of an explicit sense of history and his consequent absolutist attitude towards capitalism (*TSV*, II, 153, 238; III, 52, 55, 402, 500), Marx found great merit in Ricardo's 'scientific honesty' and 'ruthlessness' (*TSV*, II, 118) when it came to explicating the roles of social classes in wealth creation. Indeed, for Ricardo, no class was above sacrifice if analysis revealed that a dominant pursuit of its interests impeded social progress in this sense. Thus: 'Ricardo championed bourgeois production insofar as it [signified] the most unrestricted development of the social productive forces, unconcerned for the fate of those who participate in production, be they capitalists or workers' (*TSV*, III, 52), and 'Where the bourgeoisie comes into conflict with this, he is just as *ruthless* towards it as he is at other times towards the proletariat and the [landowning] aristocracy' (*TSV*, II, 118).

In two rare references to Ricardo's works other than the *Principles*, Marx quoted passages which supported this reading of Ricardo's attitude (quoted *TSV*, II, 125). In the second edition of *An Essay on the Influence of a Low Price of Corn on the Profits of Stock etc.* of 1815, Ricardo wrote that 'I shall greatly regret that *considerations for any particular class*, are allowed to check the progress of the wealth and population of the country.[13] He confirmed this view some years later in *On Protection to Agriculture*, 4th edn., 1822, when he showed a similar disregard for the short-term interests of the capitalist class in the following passage:[14]

> That *some capital would be lost* cannot be disputed, but is *the possession or preservation of capital* the end, or the means? The means, undoubtedly. What we want is an *abundance of commodities* [wealth in general], and if it could be proved that by *the sacrifice of a part of our capital we should augment the annual produce* of those objects which contribute to our enjoyment and happiness, we ought not [. . .] to repine *at the loss of a part of our capital.*

Marx claimed also that Ricardo's impartiality was further demonstrated in the *Principles* when he added Chapter XXXI, 'On Machinery', to the third edition and publicly recanted on his previously expressed view that technological change would not adversely affect the employment prospects of workers (*TSV*, II, 555).

When Marx drew together his critical investigations in 'Theories of Surplus Value' (*TSV*, III, 453ff.), he distinguished between the 'Classical' political economists[15] and those whose work he considered to be 'vulgar'. In his view, the bases for which will be discussed in chapter 6 below, the latter had failed to develop Ricardo's unbiased insights into capitalism and had effectively obscured the conflicts and contradictions that had begun to be exposed in the *Principles* (*TSV*, III, 501). Ricardo was at the forefront of the Classicals' endeavour 'to grasp the inner connection in contrast to the multiplicity of outward forms' (*TSV*, III, 500). That is, he sought, probably unconsciously, analytically to penetrate appearances and apply reason without immediate reference to empirical forms. Unfortunately, these 'inner connections' were often short-circuited in his explanations in that the complex of logico-analytical linkages involved were not worked out adequately. For Marx, this was the general point at which his own 'criticism and understanding must begin' (*TSV*, III, 500). Moreover, in spite of the Classicals' lack of any historical dimension in their analyses, their merit was that they had at least begun to get the analysis of contemporary capitalism into a coherent form. Marx concluded that such analysis 'is the necessary prerequisite of genetical presentation, and of the understanding of the real, formative process in its different phases' (*TSV*, III, 500). Thus it was that he made clear his dependence on the contributions to the political economy of capitalism by the Classicals, and by Ricardo especially, in the formulation of his critique of political economy.

As is well known, Marx had great faith in abstract reasoning as the basis of critical understanding. This was made clear in his methodological 'Introduction' to the *Grundrisse* (*G*, 100ff.). He later reflected on this method explicitly in his Preface to the first edition of *Capital*, Book I when he wrote that 'in the analysis of economic forms neither microscopes nor chemical reagents are of assistance. The power of abstraction must replace both' (*K*(PE), I, 90). And, in the Preface to the second edition of this Book of *Capital*, he concurred with the view of the Russian Nikolai Sieber, expressed in Sieber's 1871 book *David Ricardo's Theory of Value and of Capital*, that the pure theory in *Capital*, far from being metaphysical, was based on 'the deductive method of the whole English school, a school whose failings and virtues are common to the best theoretical economists' (quoted *K*(PE), I, 100). Marx evidently had no qualms about this methodological link with Ricardo, although the metaphysical (*qua* non-empirical) status of many of Marx's own categories could hardly be denied.

What had impressed Marx was the adoption of this abstract approach by Ricardo, especially in the core theoretical chapters of the *Principles*. Marx read the *Principles* as an endeavour progressively to establish the laws which regulate capitalist income distribution under conditions of growth. Ricardo saw this as 'the principal problem in political economy' (*Principles*, 5) and his method involved the formulation of logico-deductive conclusions from the premise of the embodied-labour theory of exchange value.

On the basis of this theory, one of Ricardo's concerns was to show how far 'the relations of production and commerce' under capitalism were consistent with it and the extent to which they contradicted it. This led him to reveal 'how matters stand with the contradiction between the apparent and the actual movement of the system' and to make some progress in understanding the links between the *phenomena* of the system and the 'basis on which the inner coherence, the actual physiology of bourgeois society, rests or the basis which forms its starting-point' (*TSV*, II, 166).

In Marx's terms, there existed two levels at which analysis could be pursued. He referred first to the abstract analysis of the '*inner relationships*' of capitalism and drew the analogy of the study of the hidden functioning of the body through physiology, which provides an 'understanding of its internal organic coherence and life process' (*TSV*, II, 166). The second level of analysis was the descriptive exposition of the '*reverse form, as it appears in competition*', a possible analogy for which would be the study of anatomy (*TSV*, II, 106, 165, 166; cf. *CCPE*, 20). Ricardo had brought political economy to the point where the analytical potential of the former level could have been realised and Marx was full of praise for this achievement. He noted the 'theoretical satisfaction' afforded by Ricardo's 'originality, unity of fundamental approach, simplicity, concentration, depth, novelty and comprehensiveness' and concluded that Ricardo had provided 'with concise brevity a critique of the old, diffuse and meandering political economy'. The result was the presentation of 'the whole bourgeois system of economy as subject to one fundamental law' and the extraction of 'the quintessence out of the divergency and diversity of the various phenomena' (*TSV*, II, 169).

Despite his respect for Ricardo's seminal efforts in the use of abstraction, Marx considered that Ricardo had not realised the full potential of his method. In his abstract analyses, Ricardo had resorted to the logically premature inclusion of empirical phenomena and the appearances of competition. That is, Ricardo had not followed through the intricate logical detail entailed by the assumption of the embodied-labour premise of exchange value. Thus, 'when he analyses the *value* of the commodity, he at once allows himself to be influenced by consideration of all kinds of concrete conditions'. Moreover, Ricardo must be reproached for regarding 'the phenomenal form as *immediate and direct* proof or exposition of the general laws' and 'for failing to *interpret* it' (*TSV*, II, 106; cf. 165).

The most evident indication of the limitations of Ricardo's application of the abstract method was, for Marx, the structural organisation of the argument in the *Principles*. Having isolated the embodied-labour basis for exchange value at the beginning of Chapter I of the work, Ricardo was anxious to confront the theory with empirical phenomena in order to 'test' its degree of consistency with them, or to discover the extent to which some 'modification' of the theory was required in order to ensure such consistency (*TSV*, II, 164). That is, Ricardo's primary concern was *to confirm rather than to explain the appearances of capitalism* on which he chose to focus his attention. As a consequence, he did not make the best use of the *explanatory* power of his method and *some key economic phenomena were added to his analyses but left as unexplained assumptions*. Especially was this the case with the *general rate of profits*, which was a crucial empirical tendency of competitive capitalism for both Ricardo and Marx (see, e.g., *TSV*, II, 174, 190). The *presumption* and *use* of such an empirical phenomenon in the 'bottom line' of abstraction in Ricardo's analysis was quite unacceptable to Marx. The power of abstraction could do much better, as he would show.

In general terms, it was Marx's view that the *Principles* exhibited a 'faulty architectonics' (*TSV*, II, 166, 167) as a result of Ricardo's limited use of the abstract method. In particular, Marx referred here to the first six chapters of the work, beyond which the remaining twenty-six chapters comprised only 'applications, elucidations and addenda which, by their very nature are jumbled together and make no claim to being systematically arranged' (*TSV*, II, 167; cf. 169).

The point of Marx's general critique of the six, fundamental theoretical chapters[16] was that while their coverage gave the scope for Ricardo to have developed his explanatory thesis in a logically progressive pattern, he rushed ahead of himself in such a way that 'the entire Ricardian contribution is contained in the first two chapters' on exchange value and rent (*TSV*, II, 169).

> Thus one can see that in this first chapter not only are *commodities* assumed to exist – and when considering Value as such, nothing further is required – but also wages, capital, profit, the general rate of profits and even . . . the various forms of capital as they arise from the process of circulation, and also the difference between 'natural and market price'. (*TSV*, II, 168.)[17]

With the second chapter covering rent (together with its supplementary Chapter III), the three chapters dealing respectively with natural and market price, wages and profits were left with little substantive contribution to make, beyond filling in a few definitional and theoretical gaps. The essential dimensions of these categories had been taken for granted in the first two chapters (*TSV*, II, 168–9) and put to static and dynamic 'tests' of consistency with the embodied-labour theory of exchange value. The consequence of these Chapter I 'tests' was that Ricardo confronted logico-analytical inconsistencies that he could not, or at least did not, resolve *formally*, an issue which will be considered in detail below (see pp. 88ff.).

THE INTRODUCTORY 'DIGRESSION' ON THE VALUE-DISTRIBUTION ARTICULATION ISSUE

Marx's critique of Ricardo in 'Theories of Surplus Value' effectively began with a section entitled 'Herr Rodbertus: New Theory of Rent: (Digression)' (*TSV*, II, 15ff.). Rodbertus's work with which Marx was concerned dated from 1851,[18] so, in terms of any chronological evolution of political economy, to treat it prior to Ricardo's *Principles* was a digression. However, the placement of this section had an important critico-logical rationale and its substantive content represented a significant stage in the evolution of Marx's critique of political economy. In particular, it included a concise statement of his position on the Value-distribution articulation issue in mid-1862 when the piece was drafted and the initial developments in his critique of Ricardo's theory of differential rent.

Some explanation of the circumstances of the 'Digression' is in order first. Two stages were involved.[19] First, there was a letter from Ferdinand Lassalle on 9 June 1862 in which Marx was requested to return the Rodbertus book, which he had on loan, by the beginning of October that year. This gave the *impetus* for the section to be written when it was. Secondly, and more significantly, Rodbertus was also a critic of Ricardo and had attempted to formulate a theory of *absolute* rent on the basis of the embodied-labour theory of exchange value as a critical response to Ricardo's efforts with *differential* rent. Marx, too, took up the omission by Ricardo of any treatment of absolute rent and saw this as indicative of his deficient handling of the Value-distribution articulation issue. In effect, Rodbertus was an intellectual 'competitor' who might be seen as having pre-empted part of Marx's projected critical work. It was important, then, that Rodbertus's contribution be subjected to critical scrutiny before Marx formalised his own critique.

In the present Section, I am concerned to examine one of the two substantive critical developments that Marx undertook in the context of his critique of Rodbertus. In his formalisation of the Value-distribution articulation analysis and the development of what was to become known as the price-of-production category, Marx overcame the most essential limitations of his 1857–8 *Grundrisse* work on this issue.[20] This formalisation also represented a crucial step in the preparation for the critique of Ricardo's *Principles*.

Marx's development of the absolute rent concept and the initial stages of his critique of Ricardo's differential rent theory, also set in the context of the Rodbertus 'Digression', will be considered in chapter 5 below. I have delayed the treatment of this part of Marx's critique until after the Value-distribution analysis has been considered in its essentials relating to the capital-labour antithesis. In this, I am following Marx's own assessment of the relative critico-analytical insignificance of land and its revenue. He expressed the view that the essence of the capitalist mode of production was to be found in the capital-labour relation and that it was appropriate to 'bring in the landowner who draws rent [only] at a later stage, as a special excrescence'. For Marx: 'The circumstances under which the capitalist has in turn to share a part of the . . . surplus Value which he has captured, with a third, non-working person, are only of secondary importance' (*TSV*, II, 152).

Marx dealt initially with the logical formation of a uniform rate of profit (or general rate of profits) in a multi-sector model of capitalist production and distribution characterised by variations in the Value composition of capital between sectors (*TSV*, II, 25ff.). The essential basis of this uniform rate of profit was competition between capitals and their free mobility between sectors. What was required was to deduce a vector of realised exchange values that would return such a uniform rate on each individual sector capital. As Marx recognised in a critique of Rodbertus on this point, the realisation of the uniform rate could not be linked *directly* to immediate embodied-labour exchange values. This concept of exchange value thus could not act as the competitive 'centre of gravity' for the commodity market (*TSV*, II, 27).

In his discussion of this issue, Marx *assumed* a uniform rate of generating surplus Value from variable capital employed. This assumption included as its bases a particular embodied-labour exchange value of the uniform commodity wage and a given level of labour productivity in wage commodity industries, along with a fixed length of the working day (*TSV*, II, 27; cf. 21–2, 66). But, he emphasised, a knowledge of this rate was not sufficient to indicate the rate of generating surplus Value relative to *total* capital advanced. Sector capitals have different compositional characteristics which affect their capacity to produce surplus Value in a given period. Marx noted three such characteristics (*TSV*, II, 28): first, the relationship between their technical or 'organic' components expressed in the category organic composition of capital as the ratio of the Value of the means of production in use to the Value of the labour power commanded; secondly, their period of circulation determined by the mix of fixed as against circulating capital employed; and thirdly, the period of production determined by the nature of the physical production process involved. In order to simplify the logic, though, Marx assumed uniformity for the second two characteristics and concentrated on differences stemming from the first.

Now given that surplus Value is only generated by variable capital, and given a uniform rate of surplus Value (although as Marx later recognised (*TSV*, II, 208 n.), this latter assumption is not necessary, as a given vector of sector rates of surplus Value will do, albeit with a little added complexity), it is self-evident that the Value rate of profit on total capital is affected by its organic composition. The issue that Marx faced, then, was to devise an abstract analysis that would reflect the forces of competition acting to ensure that each capital, irrespective of its organic composition, returned the same rate of profit. What he needed was a *modified* embodied-labour exchange value that would compensate for the compositional variations in the sector capitals.

Here Marx introduced the *metaphorical idea*[21] of the individual capitalists being 'shareholders' in the aggregate capital and therefore in the aggregate surplus Value that it generated per period (*TSV*, II, 29–30). The 'shares' of the surplus Value were argued to be in proportion to the relative shares of total capital held by each capitalist. The 'redistribution' of surplus Value required occurred as a consequence of *realised* exchange values that differ from immediate exchange values in the appropriate way. These *average prices*, as Marx called them at this stage, reflected a competitive situation in which each capital received the same rate of profit, assumed here to be the only relevant signal for capitalists. Any deviation from average price would, through capital mobility, change the supply and demand relations in the sectors and generate market pressures to change exchange values in such a way as to remove the resulting excesses (*TSV*, II, 26–7).

Care is needed in interpreting the implications of Marx's metaphorical 'process' analysis. It must be emphasised that the analysis, as far as it involves the 'transformation' of Values into average prices, should be considered in a 'static' sense. That is, the emergence and existence of the average price vector reflects *no observable process of change or adjustment vis-à-vis* the vector of Values (in spite of suggestions to the contrary in some of Marx's discussions – see, e.g., *TSV*, II, 29, 209). The appropriate analogy is that of an X-ray photograph which reveals the underlying structures 'supporting' a physical appearance.[22] In this case, the appearance is highly abstract in that average prices would operate as the basis for empirical prices only under the special circumstances of perfect equality of supply and demand patterns. Any market induced divergence from average prices will be corrected by competitive adjustments such that there is always a *tendency* for these prices to be sustained. None the less, Marx's important point was that they are essentially founded upon a vector of immediate embodied-labour Values determined in the production processes of each sector.

For the capitalist and his apologetic political economists, this competitive result of a uniform rate of profit independently of any particular capital composition belied the idea that profit only came from labour. As Marx put it: 'This *illusion* confirms for the capitalist – to whom everything in competition *appears* in reverse – and not only for him, but for some of his most devoted pharisees and scribes, that capital is a source of income *independent* of labour' (*TSV*, II, 69). The point of Marx's analysis was to dispel this illusion through an *abstract-logical* extension of the implications of the essential principle of embodied labour Value to a model reflecting the empirical conditions of capitalist production.

Marx was soon able to extend and formalise the principles of the Value-distribution articulation issue sketched out above (*TSV*, II, 66ff.). This represented his first attempt to 'solve' the so-called 'transformation problem'. His analysis involved some oversights and limitations and the degree of significance to be attached to these, indeed to the 'problem' itself, varies among interpreters of Marx.[23] The only points worth making here in this respect are first, that as a seminal effort to solve an extremely difficult analytical puzzle, and relative to other contemporary failures even to *perceive* the problem correctly, Marx's analysis represented a conceptual achievement of a high order. And secondly, an unfortunate fact to be faced by critics and the faithful alike, is that the analysis of the 'problem' to be found in the manuscripts for *Capital*, Book III is not much more sophisticated in its *substance* than that from 1862 set out below (cf. *K*(PE), III, Chapter 9, 254ff.).

In the 'Digression', Marx devised the five-sector model summarised in Table 4.1 (adapted from *TSV*, II, 67–8). Each sector has a capital input of 1,000 units of immediate, embodied-labour Value (*expressed* in constant Value monetary units), but there are wide variations in the organic compositions of these capital. These range from 2/3 in sector III to 4 in sector I. The average organic composition of 3/2 coincides with that in sector II. Marx found the appropriate average rate of profit by aggregating the immediate ratios of surplus Values to capitals advanced in the sectors and averaging them. Alternatively, he aggregated the surplus Values generated and expressed this as a ratio to the aggregate capital advanced. The result was a uniform Value rate of profit of 20 per cent, given the assumed uniform rate of surplus Value of 50 per cent. Note again that this latter assumption is in no way necessary and the solution for the rate of profit can be obtained quite easily with any vector of rates of surplus Value.

Each sector's capital 'shares in' the aggregate surplus Value in proportion to its Value. This means that the commodity 'prices', i.e. embodied-labour exchange Values expressed in money terms, *realised* for each sector's production must be such as to return the appropriate surplus Value share. Some of these average prices will be above immediate Values, as in sectors I and IV where the organic compositions of capital are greater than average; and some average prices will be below immediate Values, as in sectors

Table 4.1

Sector	*Constant Capital*		*Variable Capital*	*Surplus Value*	*Rate of S.V. (%)*
	Mach.	*Raw Mat.*			
I	100	700	200	100	50
II	500	100	400	200	50
III	50	350	600	300	50
IV	700	nil	300	150	50
V	nil	500	500	250	50
Totals	1350	1650	2000	1000	

III and V where the organic compositions are less than average. In one case, that of sector II, by coincidence, the organic composition is average and average price and immediate Value are the same. These results depend upon *realised* sector profits being respectively greater than, less than and equal to the immediately generated sector surplus Values.

At this stage, both of the invariance conditions that are implied in the analysis were taken for granted by Marx. He made no comment on the fact that the total surplus Value equals the total profit and the total immediate exchange value equals the total average price, probably because the 'redistribution' of surplus Value metaphor made these self-evident results. And later, when he explicitly mentioned the conditions, it was *en passant* with little evident importance being attached to them (*TSV*, II, 190).[24]

One aspect of the Value-distribution articulation analysis that has puzzled interpreters since the publication of Book III of *Capital* is that Marx failed explicitly to note that the *input* side of his tables involved immediate embodied-labour Values while the *output* side emerged with average prices (all expressed in money units). The point has often been made by supporters and

Profit	*Immed. Rate of Profit (%)*	*Immed. Value*	*Average Price (Modified Value)*	*Modified Profit*	*Uniform Rate of Profit (%)*
100	10	1100	1200	200	20
200	20	1200	1200	200	20
300	30	1300	1200	200	20
150	15	1150	1200	200	20
250	25	1250	1200	200	20
1000		6000	6000	1000	

dissenters alike that Marx's tables are inconsistent in that the inputs originating in capitalist production should already be in average prices. Consequently, the use of immediate Values on the input side appears to be quite inappropriate.[25] Now it cannot legitimately be argued that Marx was unaware of this point. When he concerned himself explicitly with input–output issues, he noted that inputs had to be produced and were thus outputs that had passed through the circulation process at exchange values that were consistent with the requirements of distribution (see, e.g., *TSV*, II, 61, 62, 63; III, 167).

What, then, are we to make of Marx's apparent oversight in this aspect of his articulation analysis? Opinions vary widely, but what is often not done is to try to provide some rationale for what Marx did rather than simply writing it off *on our own terms* as an elementary blunder. It is evident that the important pedagogic impact that he probably intended to make on his ultimate readers was that indeed a vector of labour Values could be systematically transformed into a vector of average prices. For Marx, it was crucial to *begin* with Values on the input side. Some scholars have taken his treatment seriously and undertaken to find its rationale. And, there are reasons to believe that *for Marx's purposes*, given the situation of the issue in his critique, the analysis was correctly worked out. These arguments depend on a careful interpretation of the methodology and the meaning of the categories that he used. Such care has too frequently not been taken in the rush to defeat or defend Marx. The important conclusion to be drawn from the work of these scholars is that while the average-price valuation of inputs is ultimately an appropriate 'correction' to the analysis presented by Marx, this analysis had a legitimate place in the critique as he saw fit to argue it.[26]

THE LIMITATIONS OF RICARDO'S VALUE-DISTRIBUTION ARTICULATION ANALYSIS

In appreciating Marx's critique of Ricardo's treatment of the Value-distribution articulation problem, some differences between the two writers are relevant. These concern their perceived problematic and some aspects of their methodology.

Ricardo's central concern in the *Principles* was the presentation of an explanation for what would happen to distribution and to the rate of growth itself as the growth of capital stock and population proceeded. In the Preface, he referred to his intention to consider the situation of the tripartite class distribution of income in the 'different stages of society', the latter being his way of referring to the growth of capitalism rather than to any general historical phases. For Ricardo, as I have already noted, 'To determine the laws which regulate this distribution, is the principal problem in political economy'. He went on to add that while contemporary and past improvements had been made to political economy in general, these efforts 'afford very little satisfactory information respecting the natural course of rent, profit and wages' (*Principles*, 5).

At the epistemological level, Ricardo's background was in the Anglo-Saxon empiricist tradition. The appearance of the world as immediately perceived by the senses provided the medium for any analysis. *Reason was used only to give coherence to these appearances*. With respect to political economy, this meant working within a framework of empirical categories immediately reflecting the phenomena of capitalism in the abstract. Ricardo simply would have perceived no cause to pursue any explanation for the *existence* of such categories because of their immediate and obvious empirical relevance.

Two things about Ricardo's political economy follow from the above discussion. First, he was not explicitly concerned with what we would call the 'static' equilibrium analysis of price and quantity vectors. His focus was immediately upon *change*, as becomes apparent quite early in Chapter I of the *Principles*. The *static logic* of the embodied-labour theory of exchange value did not concern him. Rather, his interest was in the theory as the basis for establishing a valuation process that was independent of *changes* in distribution.[27] This would enable the actual effects of a change in wages on non-wage incomes to be analysed in isolation from changes in the national product to be distributed.

Secondly, Ricardo was not influenced by metaphysical modes of reasoning using *non-empirical* categories as the basis of explanation. Such use of essential categories and applied transcendentalism just would not have occurred to him.

The contrast with Marx's essentialism is evident. He was concerned to expose what he considered to be the *hidden essence* of capitalist phenomena such as exchange value and profit. In so doing, he sought the reasoned explanation of the *existence* of these phenomena by making specific the conceptual *differences* between essences and their phenomenal forms. Moreover, Marx had no compunction about resorting to categories that had no immediate empirical manifestation according to the set of categories used in political economy. To him, it was clear that the social and economic forms and events of capitalism could not be accounted for by the mere manipulation of empirical categories. Such an approach effectively assumed much of what it was to explain and served only to describe and to confirm the immutability of the capitalist system. It could provide no basis for a critical comprehension that would give impetus to revolutionary change.

It is against this background of contrasting approaches and concerns that Marx's critique of the *Principles*, especially its theoretical core, should be assessed. What Marx sought in the work could not have been there to find and this accounts for some of his critical disappointment with it. Then, depending upon how intellectually paranoid we are about Marx's critique, it can be interpreted either as misguided, insensitive and mostly unfounded, or as an ingenious adaptation of existing knowledge to a quite distinct revolutionary problematic in which the critical content was but a means to an end. I prefer the latter interpretation.

The initial substantive appeal for Marx in his re-reading of the *Principles* must have been Ricardo's unequivocal adherence to the embodied-labour principle of exchange value determination.[28] This adherence was so obvious to him that he did not work through any critical exposition of Ricardo's thought on this matter *per se*. Ricardo's *analytical* dependence upon it was taken as given by Marx. And, on that understanding, he went on critically to explicate the limitations evident in Ricardo's development of the embodied-labour premise and its logical articulation to the phenomena of capitalist distribution.

On the subject of exchange value itself, Marx only made the point that for Ricardo it was less of a socio-philosophical category than a pragmatic one. Marx thought much more about the *nature* of Value and its exchange value *form* as reflections of the essence of the capitalist mode of production and distribution (*TSV*, II, 164, 172). At one point in the *Principles*, though, Marx found that Ricardo had some insight into the essential *meaning* of exchange value. In Chapter XX, 'Value and Riches, Their Distinctive Properties', Ricardo disagreed with Say's view that exchange value is a purely relative and subjective phenomenon linked to perceptions of use value and expressed in quantitative terms *through* exchange activity. Here he quoted a piece from Destutt de Tracy in support of his view that labour forms the 'common measure' which gives *existence* to exchange value (*Principles*, 284–5; *TSV*, III, 181). Marx read this as indicative of Ricardo's recognition of the existence of exchange value of commodities as the *representation* of social labour as a human activity independently of any particular use-value form.

Earlier in his critique, Marx was not so confident that Ricardo understood the essence of exchange value in this sense. Especially did he argue that Ricardo confused the issue by resorting to the term 'relative value' (*TSV*, II, 170ff.). In accordance with the *superficial appearance* of exchange value, the term was appropriate, reflecting what Adam Smith had referred to as 'the power of purchasing other goods' (*WN*, 32; cf. *Principles*, 11). And, of course, Marx recognised this relativity of exchange value between the different use-value forms as a legitimate dimension of Value theory (see *CCPE*, Chapter 1). What Ricardo did, though, was to continue the confusing use of 'relative value' when he had a clear concept of 'absolute value' whose primary analytical significance he seemed to underestimate. As Marx pointed out, a change in 'absolute value' is only a *necessary* condition for a change in 'relative value'. It is not *sufficient* because equal proportional changes in embodied-labour content leave 'relative values' unaltered. What Ricardo had failed to keep to the fore, was the idea that between commodities, 'their relativity consists by no means solely of the ratio in which they exchange for one another, but of the ratio of all of them to . . . [the] social labour which is their substance' (*TSV*, II, 172). But, we should recall that Marx was concerned with explaining *existence* while Ricardo focused on *change*, given existence, and as a consequence, his emphasis on 'relative value' suited his purpose (e.g., *Principles*, 21, 28–9, 34–5, 47).

Marx found Ricardo to be determined to preserve the embodied-labour principle of exchange value as fundamental to the analysis of capitalism. Chapter I of the *Principles* was a testament to this in the particular and explicit sense that as more complex characteristics of the system were added, it was their *analytical consistency* with embodied-labour exchange value that was under logical 'test'. Ricardo felt that Adam Smith had failed adequately to consider this potential of the basic principle of exchange value that he had so clearly recognised (*Principles*, 12ff.). In Marx's view, though, Ricardo had not fully understood the Value-distribution articulation problems that Adam Smith had encountered and thus had compounded rather than clarified the issues.

The stage was set for Marx's critique of Ricardo's treatment of these issues in the following summary passage:[29]

> In competition, the *cost-price* and not the *Value* appears as the regulator of *market-price* – so to speak, as the *immanent price*, the Value of the commodity. But in competition this cost-price appears to be represented by the given average rate of wages, profit and rent. Hence Adam Smith tries to establish these separately and independently of the *Value* of the commodity – rather as elements of the natural price. Ricardo, whose main concern has been the refutation of this Smithian aberration, accepts the result that *necessarily* follows from it – namely *the identity of Values and cost-prices* – although with Ricardo this result is logically *impossible*. (*TSV*, II, 235; cf. 132.)

Here Ricardo stood accused of a serious theoretical oversight. While he had argued correctly for the retention of embodied labour as the essential determinant of exchange value, even under increasingly complex conditions of production, he did not *formally* develop the logical implications of this essence for the comprehension of observed price formation and distribution processes. Furthermore, it was Marx's central critical argument that Ricardo had not pursued fully the *entailed logic* of his own key premise.

The specific problem that Marx had in mind here, as we have seen it worked out in the 'Digression' on Rodbertus (see pp. 81ff. above), was the devising of a formal articulation between immediate embodied-labour exchange values and realised cost prices that would generate a uniform rate of profit on all sector capitals, independently of their technological *cum* Value compositions. There can be no doubt that, in his own way, Ricardo was *aware* of this puzzle, even though he did not formulate its solution (*TSV*, II, 132). However, the important thing for Marx was to reinforce the status of his own analysis through critique. His approach was to arraign Ricardo's analyses against his own 'solution' and to underscore the former's limitations. At this point, it must be emphasised that the limitations so espoused by Marx did not justify his often repeated conclusion that Ricardo 'identified' embodied-labour exchange value with cost price in the sense that there existed no difference between the two categories at the conceptual level (e.g., *TSV* II, 27, 129, 132, 154, 161ff. *passim*). What can be said of Ricardo here is that he opted for assumptions and analytical simplifications which served his particular methods and objectives. And the result of his approach was effectively to ensure that he could avoid having to make the distinction in any formal analytical sense.

The questions of the relations between embodied-labour exchange value and the form of capitalist distribution emerged in Ricardo's analysis in a particular way. Quite early in the *Principles*, he confronted the problem of the *logical* viability of this principle of exchange value in the context of what happens to relative prices when there is a change in the wage component of distribution. Abstracting from any impediments to competition and capital mobility, and from excesses of supply and demand in commodity markets, Ricardo posited a uniform rate of profit as a axiom of his model. On this basis, he reasoned that if the exchange value of the initially given commodity wage (the 'real' wage) increased, then the 'relative values' of commodities would change in such a way as to realise a new, and lower, uniform rate of profit. Commodities produced by fixed capital-intensive processes would have a lower exchange value while those produced by labour-intensive process would have a higher value (*Principles*, 38, 43; *TSV*, II, 174–5). Ricardo described this discovery as involving a 'considerable modification' to the embodied-labour theory of exchange value and cited the outcome as reflecting 'another cause' of variations in exchange value (*Principles*, 30).

Marx's critique of this analysis centred on four interdependent points of difference from his own enquiry, each of which he considered to be the result of the 'faulty architectonics' of the theoretical core of the *Principles* (*TSV*, II, 166–7). First, by virtue of his empiricist bias, Ricardo did not go beyond *positing* the existence of a general rate of profits, although he was conscious of the need to explain how it is *maintained* by competition once it is established. That is, he *imposed* the uniform rate of profit on his model rather than providing an internal formal explanation for how its existence can be consistent with the embodied-labour premise for exchange value and distribution (*TSV*, II, 174, 190). Thus the *precise analytical form* of the 'considerable modification' to the determination of exchange value associated with variations in capital composition and the formation of the general rate of profits was not worked out either as a 'static' problem of conceptual differences or as a 'dynamic' problem of change. Secondly, then, the exact conceptual distinction between exchange value and cost price was not made clear by Ricardo. Indeed, in places, he *appeared* to assert that what *Marx* thought of as two very different concepts were identical. As we have seen, Marx made much of this appearance. Thirdly, *for Marx*, Ricardo's immediate focus on the effects of income redistribution on 'relative values' was a 'subsidiary question' (*TSV*, II, 180) and could not legitimately be considered prior to the independent formalisation of the cost price category. Marx argued that the dynamic analysis undertaken by Ricardo, at least potentially, required this category, for it is *cost prices* that alter with changes in distribution and not embodied-labour exchange values. The exceptions to this are, of course, the trivial cases of a one-sector model or a model characterised by more than one sector with uniform capital compositions, where realised embodied-labour exchange values return a general rate of profits directly. Fourthly, Ricardo's particular approach led him to the argument that the 'modifications' to embodied-labour exchange values brought about by the existence of different capital compositions and a general rate of profits are *quantitatively* insignificant. For his purposes, then, embodied labour remained a 'near-enough' basis for determining exchange values to apply through time as growth in aggregate production occurred (*Principles*, 36; *TSV*, II, 193–4). Ironically, after having made this point, the whole issue disappeared in the rest of the *Principles* beyond Chapter I because Ricardo used a model in which commodities with exchange values determined immediately by embodied labour were appropriate.[30]

What are we to make of these critical points? The first point is crucial in that it represented the *origin* of the remainder of the difficulties that Marx noted. By virtue of his choosing to impose the general rate of profits on his analysis, Ricardo was left with no apparent need to *explain* it as a logical extension of the embodied-labour exchange value premise from which he worked.[31] As regards the second point, Marx's argument that Ricardo thought of immediate exchange value and cost price as identical *concepts* is not to be taken too literally. What Marx wanted to emphasise was that Ricardo had been 'forced' into *appearing* to adhere to such an identity between the categories because he had not been able formally to explain the articulation between them. And, it must be said that at times in the *Principles* such *appearances* were quite blatant. At one point Ricardo noted that 'Mr. Malthus appears to think that it is part of my doctrine, that *the cost* and *value* of a thing should be the same; – *it is*, if he means by cost, "*cost of production*" *including profits*' (*Principles*, 47 n.; quoted *TSV*, II, 199). This cryptic statement can reasonably be read as explaining that under conditions of capitalist production, the *operationally relevant* exchange value form is cost price.[32] Thus, it was not that Ricardo was conflating the two *concepts* because, in spite of his lack of any formalisation of the distinction between them, he was able to express it implicitly. The clearest example of such expression came in the following passage (*Principles*, 34):

> Here then are capitalists employing precisely the same quantity of labour annually on the production of their commodities, and yet the goods they produce differ in value on account of the different quantities of fixed capital, or accumulated labour, employed by each respectively. (quoted *TSV*, II, 181; cf. *Principles*, 37, quoted *TSV*, II, 188.)

Ricardo persisted with his confusing use of the generalised term 'value' instead of referring with more precision to cost price, but his conclusion clearly indicated that *even at the level of 'static' or difference analysis*, he had conceptualised a modified form of embodied-labour exchange value which allowed for differences in capital compositions. It was the case, though, that the arithmetical example to which Ricardo referred centred on a *given* general rate of profits (*Principles*, 33ff., quoted *TSV*, II, 180–1). Even allowing for this inverted approach to the issue, Marx's own conclusion about the arithmetical example is revealing:

> One absolutely cannot conceive what Ricardo intended to elucidate in this example, apart from the fact that the cost prices of commodities – insofar as they are determined by the value of the outlay embodied in the commodities plus the same annual rate of profit – *differ* from the Values of the commodities and this difference arises because the commodities are sold at prices that will yield the *same rate of profit* on the capital advanced; in short, that this difference between *cost prices* and *Values* is identical with a *general rate of profit*. (*TSV*, II, 182; cf. 184.)

Clearly, Marx was aware that Ricardo had *not* confused exchange value and cost price to the degree inferred by some of Marx's balder critical comments. Indeed, later in his manuscript, he referred to Ricardo's treatment of the categories in the following terms: 'But his great contribution remains: Ricardo has a notion that there is a difference between Value and cost price . . .' (*TSV*, III, 71).[33]

Ricardo's lack of any *formalised* distinction between embodied-labour exchange value and cost price was also the focus of Marx's third critical point. Because of this lacuna, Ricardo often did not separate the 'static' *derivation* of the cost price form from *changes* in cost prices due to changes in distribution. The following passage from the *Principles* illustrates the point (*Principles*, 42–3):

> It will be seen . . . that in the early stages of society, before much machinery or durable capital is used, the commodities produced by *equal capitals* will be nearly of *equal value*, and will rise or fall only relatively to each other on account of more or less labour being required for their production; but after the introduction of these expensive and durable instruments, the *commodities produced by the employment of equal capitals will be of very unequal value*, and although they will still be liable to rise or fall relatively to each other, as more or less labour becomes necessary to their production, they will be subject to another, though minor variation, also, from the rise or fall of wages and profits. Since goods which sell for 5000*l* may be the produce of a capital equal in amount to that from which are

> produced other goods which sell for 10,000*l*, the *profits on their manufacture will be the same*; but those *profits would be unequal, if the prices of the goods* did not vary with a rise or fall in *the rate of profit*. (quoted *TSV*, II, 197–8.)

Here, Ricardo's capacity to convey a very important point is marred by the conflation of 'static' and 'dynamic' analytical elements. The introduction of fixed capital in varying ratios to wage capital generates a conceptually different price vector from that which applied when only labour was used in production. It is the *existence* of cost prices that ensures the realisation of a uniform rate of profit, and Ricardo was aware of this in this passage. Then, if a uniform profit rate is to be *preserved* when distribution *changes*, the cost prices will have to vary in the appropriate way. The critical point made by Marx was simply that the formal development of the cost price concept and a demonstration of precisely how its realisation generates a uniform rate of profit is a logically prior issue to the manipulation of cost prices as part of a growth and distribution analysis. As Marx put it, 'the mere existence of a *general rate of profits* necessitates *cost prices* that differ from *Values*' and 'even if *wages* are assumed to *remain constant*, the difference exists and therefore is *quite independent* of the rise or fall in wages' (*TSV*, II, 176). Thus, he concluded after examining Ricardo's various arithmetical examples in Chapter I of the *Principles* (*TSV*, II, 180ff.) that:

> Ricardo *does not dwell on the conclusion which follows from his own illustrations*, namely, that – *quite apart* from the rise or fall of wages – on the assumption of constant wages, the cost price of commodities must differ from their Values, if cost prices are determined by the same percentage of profit. But he passes on . . . to the influence which the rise or fall of wages exerts on *cost prices* to which the Values have already been levelled out. (*TSV*, II, 191.)

Indeed, Ricardo should have noted explicitly that 'cost prices remain unintelligible without Values determined by labour time' (*TSV*, II, 194).

It was in the context of his immediate concern with dynamic matters that Ricardo devised his demonstration that the quantitative influence of capital compositions on 'relative value' changes as distribution changes is insignificant. Embodied-labour exchange values were an acceptable approximation *for Ricardo's purposes.* Marx gave little recognition to this in arguing his fourth point of criticism (although see the hint of recognition at *TSV*, II, 193–4). That he did not appreciate the *purpose* of exchange value theory in Ricardo's work is evident from Marx's brief aside on the 'invariable standard of value' puzzle that plagued Ricardo for much of his life. Marx asserted that Section VI of Chapter I of the *Principles* dealt merely with the measurement of exchange value and 'contains nothing important' (*TSV*, II, 202). The *role* that the 'invariable standard' was to play, and its profound significance for the sort of growth-distribution problem with which Ricardo was concerned, was not discussed by Marx.[34] He undertook to return to this 'unsatisfactory' problem in 'a subsequent revision of the theory of money' (*TSV*, II, 202), but there is no evidence that he ever did so.

In Chapter IV of the *Principles*, 'On Natural and Market Price', Ricardo's central concern was with the more or less 'static' analysis of *realised* price vectors under competitive conditions. Here he was much clearer in his references to the cost price *concept*, now termed 'natural price', as the 'centre of gravity' of exchange values. As Marx noted (*TSV*, II, 211), though, at the beginning of this chapter, Ricardo again left room for potential confusion by his imprecise use of the terms 'value' and 'natural' price' in relation to the 'comparative quantity of labour which is necessary to their production' (*Principles*, 88). However, Marx was soon able to establish that in this context, Ricardo had given a clear definition of the natural price concept (*TSV*, II, 211–12). He quoted two passages from the chapter to this effect. In one, Ricardo had noted that if all commodities sold at their natural price, then the general rate of profits would be realised on all capitals (*Principles*, 90). Ricardo's correct conceptualisation of the natural price was even clearer in the second piece (*Principles*, 91):

> It is then the desire, which every capitalist has, of diverting his funds from a less to a more profitable employment, that prevents the *market price* of commodities from continuing for any length of time either much above, or much below their *natural price*. It is this competition which so adjusts the *exchangeable value* of

> commodities, that after paying the wages for the labour necessary to their production, and all other expenses required to put the capital employed in its original state of efficiency, the *remaining value or overplus* will in *each trade* be in proportion to the value of the capital employed. (quoted *TSV*, II, 212.)

Here Marx added the comment: 'This is exactly the case', for Ricardo had stated precisely the *principle* behind Marx's own formal establishment of the existence of cost prices in the Rodbertus 'Digression' (see pp. 81ff. above).

In his critique of this chapter, Marx focused on Ricardo's analyses of the various aspects of competition relevant to *market price* determination. Marx identified three logical dimensions of the market-price formation process (*TSV*, II, 206ff.): first, the competitive establishment of the uniform rate of profit through the existence and realisation of cost prices; secondly, the competitive process driving market prices, set by short-run supply and demand criteria, towards cost prices; and thirdly, the establishment of a uniform *intra-sector* price for each particular commodity, independently of distribution criteria but related directly to a particular technique of production.

Now we have already seen that Ricardo did not pursue the formalisation of cost price formation even though he was well aware of the conceptual bases and principles involved. With respect to the other two dimensions, Ricardo had recognised both of them and Marx quoted passages from the *Principles* to this effect.

The third dimension emerged as an integral part of Ricardo's theory of differential rent in Chapter II. He argued that the least productive capital was that applied to marginal, no-rent land and it determined the ruling exchange value for all 'corn'. This principle applied to *all* production (*Principles*, 73; *TSV*, II, 203). What Marx noted, but apparently did not occur to Ricardo, was that this uniform realised exchange value caused the immediate rates of profit on *intra-sector* capitals, embodying different technologies, to be non-uniform. The same problem applied to Marx's idea that the ruling exchange value was determined by some quantitatively dominant technique (*TSV*, II, 204–5). What neither of them considered was how such a situation could be sustained in non-agricultural production under competitive conditions with capital mobility. In fact, Marx soon ruled it out when he noted that only in agriculture could 'excess profits' become fixed as rent appropriated by landowners (*TSV*, II, 241; see chapter 5 below).

Regarding the second dimension of competitive effects, that process which ensured that cost prices acted as the 'centre of gravity' for market prices, Ricardo's analysis emphasised correctly that short-run supply and/or demand excesses would generate self-correcting divergences from the general rate of profits by virtue of capital mobility based on rate of profit signals (*Principles*, 88ff.; cf. Chapter XXX; *TSV* II, 207–8). Ricardo went on to note that this process would be facilitated by the existence of 'floating capital' in the form of credit, a phenomenon that Marx considered to be 'both the result and the condition of capitalist production' (*TSV*, II, 211).

The way in which Ricardo handled the category *capital* in his analysis of exchange value also drew criticism from Marx, with his critique centring upon the operational division of capital rather than upon its conception. Clearly, Ricardo's view of capital was *material*, rather than *social*, as Marx would have it. But what was significant here was that Ricardo used the fixed capital-circulating capital dichotomy to analyse capital in what was essentially a *production* problem. This dichotomy was more appropriately associated with circulation problems (*TSV*, II, 174). And, indeed, Ricardo was praised by Marx for recognising this (*TSV*, II, 176).

Ricardo took several approaches to the analysis of capital compositions in the exchange value determination problem, each based upon the above dichotomy. Marx summarised these thus:

1 A difference in the proportion of fixed to circulating capital.
2 A difference in the period of turnover of *circulating* capital as a result of a break in the labour process while the production process continues.
3 A difference in the *durability* of fixed capital.
4 A difference in the relative period during which a commodity is altogether subjected to the labour process (without any break in the labour process or without any difference between production period and labour period) before it can enter the actual circulation process. (*TSV*, II, 178.)

For Ricardo, the significant point was that irrespective of composition, whatever the basis of its variation, each equal capital had to return the same rate of profit. However, Marx found that in spite of this appreciation of the complex mechanics of capital's involvement in production, when Ricardo undertook his formal (arithmetical) analyses (see *TSV*, II, 180ff.) they did not include any effective application of the details outlined (*TSV*, II, 189). Rather, Ricardo emphasised capital advanced to pay wages, what Marx called variable capital, to the virtual exclusion of fixed capital (*TSV*, II, 182). Moreover, what Ricardo referred to as circulating capital turned out to be effectively variable capital by virtue of the exclusion of raw materials from it. This was probably indicative of Ricardo's recognition of the need to isolate capital that employs labour in any analysis founded on the principle of embodied-labour exchange value. Marx gave much more attention to these issues when he considered Ricardo's treatment of non-labour incomes and I shall turn to a discussion of them in the next chapter.

CHAPTER 5

Ricardo's *Principles*: rent and surplus Value

ABSOLUTE RENT AND THE CRITIQUE OF DIFFERENTIAL RENT

In this chapter, I consider Marx's critique of Ricardo's analysis of non-labour incomes. The centrepiece of Marx's critique of all political economy was its general failure to isolate the category of surplus Value as logically prior to its appearance in the phenomenal forms of rent, profit and interest (*TSV*, I, 40). Political economists, including Ricardo, had not *explained the origin* of non-labour incomes before these phenomena were subjected to analysis.

Marx approached the critique of Ricardo's analysis of non-labour income generation in two stages. First, he considered Ricardo's formulation of the theory of rent, a theory which had a significant role in the *Principles* (see the Preface, *Principles*, 5). Marx's critical investigations of this topic were extensive, but were scattered over several parts of the 'Theories of Surplus Value' manuscript and lacked overall organisation. The notes on rent included an initial outline of Ricardo's theory in the context of the critical 'Digression' on Rodbertus (*TSV*, II, 15ff. *passim*), a 'Digression' on the historical development of rent theory (*TSV*, II, 114ff.) and a critique of Ricardo's theory of differential rent, including a mass of supporting arithmetical calculations (*TSV*, II, 236ff.). Throughout these investigations, the one recurring theme was the critical evolution of Marx's theory of absolute rent as the essence of the *existence* of rent. This development was supplemented by Marx's exposure of the limitations of Ricardo's differential rent analysis, both as a principle and in the examples used in the *Principles* to support it. In this process, Marx worked through alternative and extended cases which gave results that were opposed to those implied by Ricardo. In spite of his disclaimer that he did 'not intend to give a detailed exposition of rent until dealing with landed property *ex professo*', and that 'here the purpose is only to set forth the general law of rent as an illustration of my theory of Value and cost price' (*TSV*, II, 269), Marx's analysis went somewhat beyond this brief.[1]

In the second stage of his critique of the analysis of non-labour incomes in the *Principles*, Marx argued that in considering 'profit', Ricardo had *formally* analysed its generation in relation only to capital advanced to employ labour. He gave little attention to fixed capital and raw materials as integral parts of the explanation of this category and this effectively meant that his analysis related to *surplus Value* rather than to *profit* directly (*TSV*, II, 373ff.). Ricardo's analysis was set in a production context dominated by agriculture and he did not abstract sufficiently to consider production *per se* in which the juxtaposition of wage and non-wage incomes, irrespective of the *form* of the latter, could be examined. In this stage of the critique, then, Marx considered Ricardo's treatment of profit as an extension of the *implied* principle of surplus Value (*TSV*, II, 426ff.). Marx's argument here was also that in order actually to consider *profit*, a more complex analysis than that provided by Ricardo was necessary. Especially had Ricardo failed adequately to *explain* the general rate of profits even though he had *used* the category by *imposing* it on his analysis with a *given* rate. These two stages of Marx's critique are considered in turn in this section and the next.

For Marx, it was crucial that *all* facets of the distribution process be shown to be logically consistent with the embodied-labour theory of Value and the theory of surplus Value. Moreover, they must involve the realisation of a general Value rate of profits and the explicit dominance of cost prices in the determination of realised exchange values. The formal recognition of these conditions emerged initially in 'Theories of Surplus Value' in the context of the 'Digression' on Rodbertus's treatment of rent (*TSV*, II, 15ff. – note that Marx's critique of Rodbertus went well beyond the issue of rent: see *TSV*, II, 60–6, 71–94).

Rodbertus had posited a principle of *absolute* rent generation which Marx took up and critically developed. Under this principle, the *capacity* to pay rent in agriculture depended upon establishing that somehow capital invested in such production realised an *immediate* Value rate of profit that exceeded the ruling general rate, the latter rate being that required to maintain an 'equilibrium' allocation of capitals between sectors of production. The principle then entailed two further requirements. Some mechanism had to exist whereby landowners could be shown permanently and legitimately to appropriate the 'excess profit' when the total produced exchange value belonged at the point of realisation to the *capitalist*. This would then ensure that the ultimately realised rate of profit in agriculture remained equal to the general rate and forestall any inflow of new capital into production. In addition, capital should not have access to 'free' land of equal quality to that already in production and on which there is no obligation to pay rent.[2]

How did Marx elaborate upon these principles? He began by noting that Rodbertus's approach to explaining the *capacity* to pay rent was 'absurd'. It depended upon agricultural capitalists perceiving their self-grown raw material inputs as 'costless' or, at least, failing to recognise the *implicit* exchange value of such inputs that do not pass through any market realisation. This lowered their perceived relative capital input and enabled them to return an 'excessive' immediate rate of profit (*TSV*, II, 21ff., 45ff.). Without this miscalculation by farm capitalists, Rodbertus was unable to explain rent at all (*TSV*, II, 92).

Marx recognised that he had to find some other characteristic of agricultural production that distinguished it from industrial production and explained the agricultural capitalists' capacity to pay rent from surplus Value. He argued, as an opening gambit, that agricultural wages, the Value of labour power, might be lower than those paid by industry, allowing the former sector to generate a higher rate of surplus Value (*TSV*, II, 17). This idea was quickly abandoned in favour of the historico-empirical observation that the level of technological development in agriculture had fallen behind that in industry. That is, agriculture remained more labour intensive. As a result, Marx argued, without any analytical support at this stage, that this meant a lower organic composition of capital in agriculture than in industry (*TSV*, II, 18–21). This condition became central to all of his subsequent analysis of absolute rent in 'Theories' (see, e.g., *TSV*, II, 93, 94, 105, 244, 298, 315–16, 331, 376, 394; III, 300–1).[3]

In his analysis of the formation of a uniform Value rate of profit across sectors of production through the realisation of average prices (see chapter 4, pp. 81ff. above), Marx had noted that sectors with lower than average organic compositions of capital returned *immediate* rates of profit that exceeded the general rate. This immediate rate could be realised if the commodity concerned sold at its embodied-labour Value (all *expressed* directly in constant money units – *TSV*, II, 264; cf. *Principles*, 46, 110 n.). It was clear to Marx that agriculture comprised such a sector and its *capacity* to pay rent was self-evident (*TSV*, II, 30ff., 92–3), although he recognised that this capacity might disappear in time due to technological change (*TSV*, II, 93).

Having established the quantitative capacity to pay rent, Marx then confronted the need to explain the fact that such rent is *actually paid* as a permanent qualitative feature of agriculture. That is, to answer the question: why is the 'excessive' rate of profit in agriculture not competed away in the usual sense through agricultural commodities realising average prices instead of embodied-labour exchange values? (*TSV*, II, 37).

Marx found the answer to this question in the monopolisation of land suitable for agricultural production. He summarised his point as follows:

> It is quite simply the *private ownership* of land, mines, water, etc. by certain people, which enables them to snatch, intercept and seize the *excess surplus Value over and above* [average] *profit* . . . contained in the commodities of these particular spheres of production . . . and so to prevent it from entering into the general process by which the general rate of profits is formed. (*TSV*, II, 37; cf. 94.)

The matter was not quite so simple, as Marx realised, for the necessary condition of monopoly over land had to be supplemented by the assumption that no 'free' land is available on which no rent has to be paid and which is of such fertility that capital could return and appropriate (temporarily) 'excess' profits above the general rate (*TSV*, II, 38, 96).

The actual *payment* of absolute rent to the landowner had both a socio-political and an economic rationale. It was socio-political in the sense that:

> Just as it is the *monopoly* of capital alone that enables the capitalist to squeeze surplus labour out of the worker, so the monopoly of land ownership enables the landed proprietor to squeeze that part of surplus labour from the capitalist, which would form a constant *excess profit*. (*TSV*, II, 94.)

Thus the agricultural capitalist is 'exploited' by another class that owns a particular means of production without which his own property cannot bring any return.

As Marx saw it, this 'outsider', the landowner, is able to break into the aggregate surplus Value generated by all capitals and expropriate part that would otherwise be 'shared' out by virtue of the unique economic status of his means of production. The point that Marx recognised was simply that land cannot be reproduced and that therefore, the monopoly position of landowners that he assumed cannot be avoided by capitalists who use land in production (*TSV*, II, 40–2). Moreover, the landowner could exercise his option of withdrawing his land from production. That this was a possibility was evidenced, Marx argued, by 'the large amount of fertile land that is uncultivated in the most developed countries of Europe' along with the amount of land used for quite unproductive purposes (*TSV*, II, 306).

Marx introduced his critique of Ricardo's theory of rent early in the 'Digression' on Rodbertus (*TSV*, II, 18ff.) and developed it gradually and intermittently through several notebooks of the 'Theories of Surplus Value' manuscript.

As is well known, Ricardo's theory involved a particular way of conceptualising and explaining *differential* rent. While Marx accepted the possibility of such a rent form existing, he had two central misgivings about Ricardo's handling of it. First, for Marx, the establishment of the quantitative determinants of the differential rent form independently of any explicit concern with the role of landed property rights could not explain rent adequately. Differential rent not only needed to be integrated with the generation of absolute rent, but also both were to be explained as consequences of the existence of a class of landowners. Thus, the principle of absolute rent 'explains the *existence of rent*, whereas Ricardo only explains the *existence of differential rents* and actually does not credit the *ownership of land* with any *economic* effect' (*TSV*, II, 94). Secondly, Marx worked on the theory of differential rent and found that Ricardo's analysis was too restrictive in its assumed conditions. Such rent differentials could be shown to be generated under more general conditions of relative land fertilities and their order of entering production with a variety of patterns of increasing demand.

For Marx, these difficulties with Ricardo's analysis of rent arose from a 'twofold historical error' comprising a failure to recognise any difference between the labour productivity in agriculture and industry due to the former's relative lack of technological development, and the assumption that the extension of agricultural production necessarily involved margins of decreasingly fertile, no-rent land (*TSV*, II, 244). Marx presented no evidence for his rejection of these 'stylised facts' of economic development in Britain, but it was fundamental to much of his critique of Ricardo on rent.

Another source of Ricardo's failure to recognise the existence of absolute rent was the limited nature of his exchange value–distribution articulation analysis, including his lack of any rigorous formulation of the cost price concept (*TSV*, II, 129ff., 242ff., 318ff.). As we have seen, the recognition of absolute rent depends upon a clear analysis of the generation of a uniform rate of profit along with Marx's assumption about the relatively low organic composition of capital in agriculture. In this context, too, Marx overstated Ricardo's position by invoking again the assertion that he *identified* exchange value and cost price as well as now asserting that he *denied* the existence of absolute rent (*TSV*, II, 129, 130, 243, 244). It was rather the case that Ricardo's objectives and approach, and his different view of the 'facts', just did not allow for the logical possibility of absolute rent. Marx did grant, though, that one of the key contributions made by Ricardo to the analysis of rent was that he endeavoured to link it directly to the embodied-labour theory of exchange value (*TSV*, II, 34, 245). What is more, at one point quite late in the *Principles*, Ricardo implicitly recognised the possibility of absolute rent alongside differential rent even though he had not developed the former idea explicitly. The relevant passage quoted by Marx was the following (*Principles*, 330):

> But, suppose *that there were no land which did not afford a rent; then, the amount of rent on the worst land would be in proportion to the excess of the value of the produce above the expenditure of capital and the ordinary profits of stock*: the same principle would govern the rent of land of somewhat better quality, or more favourably situated, and, therefore, the rent of this land would exceed the rent of that inferior to it, by the superior advantages which it possessed; the same might be said of that of the third quality, and so on to the very best. It is not, then, as certain, that it is *the relative fertility of the land*, which determines the portion of the produce, which shall be paid for the rent of land . . . (*TSV*, II, 336.)

The excess of exchange value above cost price here was argued to provide a source of rent over and above that due to differential fertility. This rent appeared on *marginal* land to which the differential principle could not apply (*TSV*, II, 337).

Marx began his detailed critical analysis of Ricardo's theory of rent with a brief historical excursus as background (*TSV*, II, 114ff.). He found that the principle of differential rent, the principle he called the 'Ricardian Law of Rent', was devised by the Scotsman James Anderson during the 1770s as an incidental by-product of that writer's concern to promote stable agricultural development. Anderson had related the emergence of rent to that excess 'profit' which was associated with wheat production on land of varying fertilities at varying costs (including some general standard of profit) in a situation of uniform market price (*TSV*, II, 146–7). Where the cost of production coincided with the market price, as Anderson thought to be probable on the least fertile land, no rent could be appropriated. Anderson had noted that the fertility of land was not merely a function of nature and that the *pattern* of differential rents could be altered over time by artificial improvements in fertility.

Leaving Adam Smith's treatment of rent aside for later treatment, Marx made the point that Anderson had not been concerned to develop the theory of rent as an explicit topic with theoretical significance *per se*. This development, Marx argued, was left to Sir Edward West and Thomas Malthus whose pamphlets dealing with the subject appeared in 1815. In Anderson's era, wheat prices were not the cause of great concern. The empirical evidence tabulated by Marx (*TSV*, II, 133ff.) revealed that these prices had declined for most of the seventeenth century and during the first half of the eighteenth century. An upward trend began about the middle of the eighteenth century but did not become a problem until the period 1800–20. Then the price of wheat rose very rapidly and debate over the 'Corn Laws' took on a new vigour. In this context, the problem of explaining, and perhaps justifying rents was viewed as an important one by West and Malthus.

As Marx read these pamphlets, West was the more original in his presentation of the rent principle (*TSV*, II, 115). Malthus was viewed by Marx not only as a plagiarist of Anderson in this matter, indeed as a '*plagiarist* by profession' (*TSV*, II, 115), but also as an arch apologist for and defender of the landowners (see also *TSV*, III, 13ff. *passim*). Marx expressed, with considerable vituperation, his finding that Malthus had distorted Anderson's thesis where necessary in order to bring it into accord with his own theoretical and political predilections (*TSV*, II, 115ff.).

Ricardo, also in an environment of very high wheat prices and active 'Corn Law' debate, followed on in this tradition of developing rent theory as a significant responsibility of political economy (*TSV*, II, 236). In the Preface of the *Principles*, Ricardo gave West and Malthus credit for presenting the 'true doctrine of rent' and noted that 'without a knowledge of which, it is impossible to understand the effect of the progress of wealth on profits and wages' (*Principles*, 5).

For Marx, one significant feature of this development of the theory of rent was that its frame of reference was *capitalist production* (*TSV*, II, 236ff.). He argued that, unlike continental European experience, capitalism in agricultural production was well advanced in England by the time that Ricardo formulated his analyses. Unfettered by such deeply ingrained land holding traditions as those evident on the Continent, the English could link land usage to the profit motive more readily. This, Marx argued, had been aided by the enclosure movement which made agriculture a more defined process of production. In all, he observed that:

> nowhere in the world has capitalist production, since Henry VII, dealt so ruthlessly, with the *traditional* relations of agriculture, adapting and subordinating the conditions to its own requirements. In this respect England is the most revolutionary country in the world. Wherever the conditions handed down from history were at variance with, or did not correspond to, the requirements of capitalist production on the land, they were ruthlessly swept away . . . (*TSV*, II, 237.)

Moreover, the colonisation movement, based as it was, to some extent, upon capitalist premises, led to an increased consciousness of the role of capital in agricultural development (*TSV*, II, 239).

It was quite appropriate, then, for Ricardo to begin from the presupposition that agricultural production was capitalist. He proceeded on the assumption that capital was mobile as between sectors of production, including agriculture, and that agriculture would not experience any shortage of capital under conditions of economic growth (*TSV*, II, 239).

As Marx understood it (*TSV*, II, 32–3), the key assumption in Ricardo's theory of differential rent was the existence of a no-rent margin of land (extensive *or* intensive – see *TSV*, II, 95, 332) on which invested capital received only the ruling general rate of profits. Resort to this marginal land was induced by growing demand for 'corn'. For in spite of its lower productivity, and with no rent to pay, capital on such land could be assured of a 'normal' rate of return due to an ability to charge a higher price for 'corn' which reflected its higher *cost price*. The *capacity* to pay rent then emerged at this higher realised market exchange value because the *cost prices* of corn produced on intra-marginal land, including the 'normal' rate of return on capital, were now lower by some degree than the new ruling marginal cost price. This was assured by Ricardo's assumption of the progressively decreasing fertilities of land used to produce 'corn' and by the argument that a uniform market price would be charged for 'corn' based on the cost price on marginal land.[4]

Marx made three main criticisms of Ricardo's analysis of rent. First, it is only the *capacity* to pay rent that arises from excess profit on capital on intra-marginal land. This excess profit does not establish the *existence* of rent, for 'The Ricardian law would prevail just the same, even if *landed property* were *non*-existent' (*TSV*, II, 103). It is the socio-political institution of private property alone which gives landowners the *potential* to claim *rent* from capitalists. Then, it is the fact that access to relatively fertile land is controlled by them that enables this potential to be realised (*TSV*, II, 42–4). Marx objected to Ricardo's inference that rent had something to do with 'nature' and the inherent 'powers' of the soil, arguing instead that rent is paid to *those who control access* to the physical 'powers' of nature in general (*TSV*, II, 245ff.). Only in this sense is rent paid for the *use* of natural resources.

Secondly, Marx criticised Ricardo for not realising that the principle upon which he based his differential rent analysis applied to all classes of production. Positive differential generation of surplus Value is a feature of any production sector in which one market price dominates and where this market price reflects the cost price determined by any productivity level other than the most efficient. In the case where the lowest cost price rules, the differentials will all be negative, while for Marx both positive and negative differentials would emerge because of his assumption of a dominant 'average' productivity (*TSV*, II, 240–1). What Marx made explicit was that:

> Manufacture and agriculture only differ from one another here in that in the one, the excess profits fall into the pocket of the capitalist himself, whereas in the other they are pocketed by the landowner, and furthermore, that in the former they are *fluid*, they are not lasting, are made by this capitalist or that, and always disappear again, while in the latter they *become fixed* because of their enduring (at least for a long period) natural basis in the *variations in the land*. (*TSV*, II, 241.)

Thus, in manufacturing, the competition between capitals would, in a short time, remove any 'excess' profits due to technological differentials in production implemented by particular capitalists. While this sort of differential would always be present, it is '*fluid*' in the sense of moving between capitalists as their relative position in the technology matrix changes. This is not so in agriculture. Differential rent cannot be competed away, but it might disappear due to 'artificial' improvements in fertility.

Thirdly, and most significantly, Marx argued that Ricardo's

comprehension and analysis of the rent issue was too narrow in its scope and restrictive in its assumptions. Ricardo's analysis was devoted to establishing the consequences of a continuation of the 'Corn Laws' that restricted the import of corn, ostensibly in order to ensure that land-rents were not eroded. The effect on which Ricardo focused was that a reliance on domestic production to feed a growing population would result, indeed had resulted, in higher nominal wages (even allowing that the real commodity wage did not rise). This *logical* prognosis was based very firmly on the assumption of declining productivity on marginal land, but also fitted the facts of rising wheat prices at the time (as Marx well knew: *TSV*, II, 135, 143–4).

As Marx showed, this perspective on rent did not capture adequately the *possible* outcomes of an increase in the demand for domestically produced 'corn'. Marx's laborious 'tables of differential rent' outlined cases quite different from Ricardo's by liberalising the assumptions made (*TSV*, II, 251ff.). The results demonstrated that Ricardo's analysis was not only limited by his omission of the absolute rent concept.

It is worth noting that in these 'tables', Marx began to focus on the analysis of *change* and he would soon take up the critical development of his 'law of motion' of capitalism more generally (*TSV*, II, 275ff., 321ff., 438ff.). But for the present, the results of change were confined to some very particular effects in agriculture based upon a development of the 'static' conditions formalised earlier in this section.

The thrust of Marx's critique here was that the assumption of progressive resort to *decreasingly* fertile land in order to meet an increasing demand for 'corn' was a sufficient but not necessary condition for the generation of differential rent. Under conditions of an increase in demand just met by the additional marginal land brought into production (*TSV*, II, 241), he argued that differential rent could emerge even if land was increasingly fertile (*TSV*, II, 272ff.). By positing three grades of land designated in *ascending* order of productivity as I–II–III, it did not matter in which order they were brought into use. If an increase in demand involves progression from III and II to I, which was Ricardo's case, then the total demand would be provided for at a market price determined by the cost price on I, with the differential rent emerging on II and increasing on III. In the reverse case, where expanding demand is met by transition from I to II to III, the highest cost price would still dominate market price. That is, with the cost price on I dominant, as II and III were brought into use, each would bring forth a differential rent. Should it be that the extension to III resulted in the removal of I from production even with the increased demand, then the cost price on II dominates and differential rent on III would emerge.

In amplification of this point, Marx analysed a series of comparative static situations in his arithmetic 'tables' (*TSV*, II, 254ff., 262ff., 289ff.). These analyses revealed that a variety of results with respect to the market price of 'corn' could emerge depending upon assumptions made about the relative expansion of supply and demand. Ricardo's argument that 'corn' would necessarily rise in price with economic growth Marx showed to be but *one* possibility.[5]

RICARDO'S IMPLIED PRINCIPLE OF SURPLUS VALUE IN HIS THEORY OF PROFIT

Before beginning the substantive part of this section, two points are of preliminary relevance to prepare the reader for what is to come. First, in the following discussion, only more or less 'static' analytical issues relating to differences in concepts and levels of analysis are considered. Both Ricardo and Marx were concerned, *inter alia*, with the effects of capital accumulation on profits and this is an important theme in Marx's critique. It is not possible entirely to remove the 'dynamic' elements relating to change rather than difference, but the reader should be aware that such issues will receive detailed attention in Part IV below. In this sense, the present section establishes some principles of Marx's critique that will be developed more fully subsequently.

Secondly, in analysing the theory of capital and profit, both Ricardo and Marx confronted complex technical issues which they were unable to solve or of which they remained ignorant. These issues are still controversial today and without universally accepted solutions.[6] It is worth noting, too, in the present context that even today, after more than 150 years of interpretation and debate, what Ricardo 'meant' on these (and other) issues remains in dispute.[7] The simple preliminary point to be made here is that the reader acquainted with these debates and controversies should, more than ever in this section, keep in mind the intellectual-historical situation of Marx's work and be prepared for the relative technical limitations of his critical developments.

For Marx, the most essential participants in the capitalist system, from a critico-analytical viewpoint at least, were the capitalist and the wage labourer. It was their relationship which manifested the most important characteristics of the system, especially with respect to the nature of the distribution process and the role of capital (*TSV*, II, 152). The *essence* of the system was captured by the embodied-labour theory of Value and its reflection in the theory of surplus Value and the category labour power.[8] The fundamental point of Marx's critique of Ricardo on capital and profit was that he had not clearly *isolated* and *explicated* these categories. It was not that Ricardo's conceptual framework did not include similar *ideas* about the nature of capital, the origin of profit and the valuation of 'labour', for implicitly these were part of his analytical apparatus. At the same time, though, more than semantics was involved in Marx's critical discussion. His point was again, as it had been in the critique of exchange value theory, that while Ricardo's analyses made use of such essential concepts and principles, their full analytical potential was not realised. For Marx, the semantic structure of his own analysis added a degree of explication and clarity not evident in the *Principles*. Ricardo's (not unexpected, we should add) immediate concern was to confront and handle *empirical phenomena*. Marx ultimately wanted to do this too, but he felt that a more abstract and detailed formal critico-analytical basis was needed prior to doing so. Ricardo did not canvass this view.

A key point in this respect was Ricardo's analysis of the surplus as the source of profit (and other non-labour incomes). Marx was in no doubt that Ricardo had based his theory of profit on the surplus concept. For example, Ricardo wrote that profit originated as 'the *remaining value on overplus*' from commodities 'after paying the wages for the labour necessary to their production, and all other expenses required to put the capital employed in its original state of efficiency' (*Principles*, 91; quoted *TSV*, II, 212). Marx read this as arguing that commodity Value essentially included a surplus. To a large extent, though, he found that Ricardo emphasised only variable (wage) capital advances when discussing the residual surplus as it appeared immediately in the *profit* form. And, because, in addition, Ricardo expressed the surplus in embodied–labour terms (mediated by money of a constant value), the surplus was *technically* a surplus *Value* in Marx's sense (*TSV*, II, 427). As Marx put it:

> In his observations on profit and wages, Ricardo . . . abstracts from the constant part of capital, which is not laid out in wages. He treats the matter as though the entire capital were laid out directly in wages. *To this extent*, therefore, he considers *surplus Value* and *not profit*, hence it is possible to speak of his theory of surplus Value. (*TSV*, II, 373.)

Having granted this, though, he hastened to add that Ricardo worked on his analyses as if the principles involved pertained *directly* to profit. The role of surplus Value as an analytical mediation was not made explicit: Ricardo 'seeks to present the laws of profit directly, without the intermediate links, as laws of surplus Value' (*TSV*, II, 374), although it must be granted that this endeavour was an unconscious one for Ricardo.

In providing an explanation for non-labour incomes as part of the embodied-labour theory of Value, the essential point is to account for the difference between the Value of 'labour' and the Value *generated* by this 'labour'; for unless there is a difference, there can be no surplus. Marx argued that Ricardo had not made this *clear* because he had not posited the conceptual issues involved in the appropriate way.

Marx began his consideration of this difficulty with a simple example posed as follows:

> It is clear that the proportional quantity of labour contained in two commodities A and B, is absolutely unaffected by whether the workers who produce A and B receive much or little of the product of their labour. The Value of A and B is determined by the *quantity of labour* which their production costs, and not by the *costs of labour* to the owners of A and B. (*TSV*, II, 395.)

The commodities A and B represent a certain volume of *materialised* labour and are valued accordingly. But the puzzle is, why is the Value of the *living* labour that produced A and B below that of its materialised form? (cf. *TSV*, II, 403–4). Clearly: 'Quantity of [embodied] labour and Value of labour are two different things' (*TSV*, II, 395). This puzzle is accentuated by the argument that in order to facilitate the production process, *past materialised* labour in the form of constant capital is purchased at its full embodied-labour Value while *living* labour *appears* to be purchased at a Value less than its capacity to supply materialised labour in the immediate future (*TSV*, II, 399). In Marx's view this issue could be resolved only by distinguishing very precisely between the form of labour as a *commodity* and the form of living labour as it is exercised in the production process (*TSV*, II, 397–8, 405–6). The embodied-labour principle of Value applied directly to the former, but while it *involved* the latter, it did not *apply* to it in the usual sense.

It was at this point that Marx invoked the category first formulated in the *Grundrisse* to express labour in its *commodity* form, viz. *labour power* (*TSV*, II, 399). Ricardo had approached this problem of valuing 'labour' as a commodity in a way with which Marx concurred as far as it went. The category '*real wage*' represented the 'natural price' of 'labour' through the mediation of the embodied-labour exchange value (perhaps cost price) of the socio-historically modified basket of 'subsistence' wage commodities (*TSV*, II, 404). Ricardo defined this 'natural price' as that which 'is necessary to enable the landowners, one with another, to subsist and to perpetuate their race, without either increase or diminution' (*Principles*, 93). To this piece, Marx added the qualification that Ricardo should have allowed for 'that rate of increase, required by the average progress of production' (TSV, II, 400), an aspect of the issue that Ricardo had treated by resorting to short-run market effects on the real wage, countered by an ensuing population response to increased worker prosperity *as if* it occurred in the short run, too (*Principles*, 93–4). In fact, Marx argued that Ricardo had here effectively resorted to the forces of supply and demand in order to give quantitative meaning to his 'natural price' of 'labour' (*TSV*, II, 400). Marx referred here to Ricardo's assertion that: 'Like all other contracts, wages should be left to the fair and free competition of the market' (*Principles*, 105).

Marx approached the valuation of labour power in a different way, a way that reflected his concern to expose the socio-political conflict inherent in the relationship between capital and labour. It was *exploitation* that Marx wanted to emphasise as the source of surplus Value. While he had been generous in his praise for Ricardo's 'scientific honesty' in facing up to the conflict elements of capitalism (see chapter 4, pp. 73ff. above), this view of the origin of the surplus was not present in the *Principles*, as Marx implicitly recognised.[9] The difference from Ricardo that he did make explicit in this respect related to the *concept* of capital. For Marx, capital represented 'a *definite social relationship*' (*TSV*, II, 400) under which the Value of the workers' only negotiable asset, labour power, is determined solely by what the capitalists tacitly agree to pay in order to maintain the living labour capacity of workers, allowing for socio-historical extensions, or are forced to pay by short-run market conditions. Such a socio-political situation, embracing the laws of private property, means that the workers have no option (beyond starvation or the 'poor house') but to accept the going commodity wage. Marx equated the 'productivity of capital' with 'the *compulsion to perform surplus labour*' (*TSV*, II, 405; cf. I, 394). The existence of surplus Value, then, is not an accident of the physical or technological characteristics of production, but rather the conscious *raison d'être* of *capitalist* production, the perpetuation of which is ensured by the 'rules of the game' overseen by the capitalists themselves (*TSV*, II, 406). In this context, the Value of labour power could not be considered simply as only an outcome of the whims of the market. Its quantitative axis is delimited by the capitalists' pursuit of maximum surplus Value.[10]

Ricardo had expressed the idea that wages, the aggregate exchange value of 'labour', could be considered as a *share* in the total periodic production of exchange value. He referred to this idea at many points throughout the *Principles* and Marx culled out a series of quotations to this effect (*TSV*, II, 420–1). For example, Ricardo wrote, in the context of describing a redistribution of income away from wages, 'that of any given *annual value a less portion would be paid to the labouring class*, and a larger portion to those *whose funds employed this class*' (*Principles*, 420; cf. 35). Implicit in this view of distribution of the *net* product, expressed in embodied-labour terms, between capital and labour was the metaphor of the division of the working day into necessary and surplus labour (*TSV*, II, 404–5, 418–19; cf. III, 33).

Marx said of Ricardo in this respect that:

> by not *directly* showing that one *part* of the labourer's *working day* is assigned to the reproduction of the Value of his own labour power, he introduces a difficulty and obscures a clear understanding of the relationship [between capital and labour] . . . The *origin of surplus Value* does not become clear . . . (*TSV*, II, 405.)

Moreover, Ricardo had not noticed that changes in surplus Value generation could arise not only from a change in the Value of the 'real wage' (what Marx called *relative* surplus Value), but also from a change in the length of the working day (what Marx called *absolute* surplus Value). Marx read Ricardo as having posited a *fixed* working day which did not allow the latter change to emerge (*TSV*, II, 404ff.).

It was Marx's view that in analysing the role of capital in the generation of the surplus in its profit form, Ricardo had neglected *formally* to consider the involvement of fixed capital.[11] Now it is quite evident to any reader of the *Principles* that Ricardo was not unaware that fixed capital had a role to play as much of his discussion included explicit references to this category in both its particular micro-forms and in its more generalised form (see, e.g., *Principles*, 5, 22–3, 30ff., 38ff., 80, 95, 273, 386ff.). What was missing beyond the tentative steps in this direction taken in Chapter I (see chapter 4, pp. 88ff. above), was an *analytical* explication of the role of fixed capital *in general*, aggregated at least to the sector level. For Marx, basing his critique on the concept of constant capital, Ricardo's neglect of raw materials was also a serious omission (*TSV*, II, 182, 189).

In places, Ricardo did touch upon the general analytical problem of fixed capital. His way of handling the situation was to make fixed capital 'disappear' by including in wage capital sufficient advances to cover the immediate labour needed fully to restore the exchange value 'used up' during the period of operation of the particular machine involved. Marx did not notice this ploy even though he quoted one of Ricardo's references to it as the 'expenses required to put the capital employed in its original state of efficiency' (*Principles*, 91, quoted *TSV*, II, 212; cf.

Principles, 39, where Marx would have read the point made even more explicitly).[12]

Perhaps the clearest example which illustrates the tenor of Marx's criticism here relates to Ricardo's assertion that: 'The labour of a million men in manufactures, will always produce the *same value*, but will not always produce the same riches' (*Principles*, 273; quoted *TSV*, II, 414). Marx responded that this would only be the case where *all* capital advanced is variable capital, even assuming a given working day.

> He is . . . only right in the *one* case, where the total capital equals the variable capital; a presupposition which pervades all his . . . observations regarding the capital of society as a whole, but in capitalist production this precondition does not exist in a single branch of industry, much less in the production of society as a whole. (*TSV*, II, 414.)

Once constant capital used up in production is introduced, the immediate Value produced by a given volume of labour could vary upwards from the Value determined in the presence of variable capital only. The constant capital transfers its Value, wholly or in part, to the aggregate of produced Value (*TSV*, II, 414–15). However, if Ricardo meant to include in the 'labour of a million men' that labour which 'corrects' the 'depreciation' of fixed capital (and perhaps replaces raw materials), then the particular criticism by Marx did not apply.

Be this as it may, Ricardo's analytical manoeuvre left the problem of constant capital unsolved as Marx saw it. For Marx, the distinction between constant capital and variable capital represented an essential analytical reflection of his socio-political view of capital. Only by advancing variable capital and thereby exploiting labour could the capitalists appropriate surplus Value. Constant capital was sterile in this sense (*TSV*, I, 395). Ricardo's 'depreciation replacement' approach to fixed capital obscured this point and to some extent reflected a, possibly unconscious, resort to the 'vulgar' view that *all* capital 'generates' profit and therefore its particular *form* is of no analytical importance. As Marx saw it, this was a consequence of Ricardo's failure to keep clearly separate the categories surplus Value and profit and their different origins, and his *imposition* of a general rate of profits in lieu of its analytical derivation (*TSV*, II, 427).

Marx emphasised that 'the laws of surplus Value – or rather of the rate of surplus Value – (assuming the working day as given) do not so directly and simply coincide with, nor are they applicable to, the laws of profit, as Ricardo supposes' (*TSV*, II, 426; cf. 376, 379ff., 410). In particular, Marx argued that the rate of profit on a particular Value of capital employed depends on several factors other than the rate of surplus Value (*TSV*, II, 426–7). The rate of surplus Value itself is expressed by the ratio of surplus labour to necessary labour. This ratio is determined by the commodity basket assumed to be purchased by workers, valued according to the dominant rate of productivity in the relevant industries. This combination of factors gives the Value of labour power and hence the necessary labour component of the ratio. The surplus labour then depends upon the length of the working day. Marx's expression for the Value rate of profit was: $r = e.v/(c+v) = e/(1+g)$; where: e = rate of surplus Value; c = Value of constant capital advanced and used up; v = Value of variable capital; $g = c/v$ = organic composition of capital (cf. *TSV*, II, 22). Most importantly, then, anything which alters the value of the organic composition of capital, without an exactly compensating effect on the rate of surplus Value, will change the rate of profit. This alternative could involve a change in technology which changes the physical composition of capital employed or simply a change in the relative Values of wage commodities and direct inputs to production (*TSV*, II, 380–1). Ricardo had not formulated the rate of profit function in this way. And, it was an important part of Marx's critique of Ricardo's handling of the role of capital that he had not formulated the organic composition of capital *as it related to production* (e.g. *Principles*, 31). Ricardo's perception of the composition related, at least nominally, to a dichotomy between circulating and fixed capital more appropriate to the analysis of circulation and thus supplementary to the issue of identifying the essential determinants of the rates of surplus Value and profit (*TSV*, II, 373). As if instinctively, though, when it came to *analysing* capital in this context, *Ricardo effectively used Marx's dichotomy* (*Principles*, 30, 32, 43, 45–6, 87). Surplus Value was related directly to wages capital and never to raw materials, leaving fixed capital as the constant component in Marx's sense.[13]

Two other factors not considered by Ricardo affected the rate of profits independently of the rate of surplus Value. First, the former is measured after the payment of any rent has been deducted. Secondly, as between sectors of production, for a given rate of surplus Value, the *periodic* rate of profit is also affected by the turnover characteristics of the capital involved along with the periods of production and circulation.

Despite Ricardo's general lack of precision when discussing the nature and origin of profit, Marx recognised that some passages in the *Principles* did reflect an appreciation that the rate of profit is to be distinguished from the more immediate concept that Marx called the rate of surplus Value (*TSV*, II, 374, 427ff.). In the passages quoted by Marx, Ricardo's formulation of the rate of profit relates the surplus to *all* capital advanced to facilitate production, including items of fixed capital. Marx's conclusion that Ricardo thus 'throws overboard his whole theory of profit' and 'his identification of profit with surplus Value' (*TSV*, II, 430–1) was an overstatement of the situation. It was, though, quite evident that Ricardo had not thought through, as carefully as had Marx, the role of non-wage capital in the determination of the rate of profit.

It was in this context that Marx made a brief reference to the tricky problem of the effect on the general rate of profits of a change in the Value of so-called 'luxury' commodities not consumed by workers. Such a change left the Value of labour power the same and Ricardo concluded that therefore profits would be unaffected (*Principles*, 118):

> But suppose the price of silks, velvets, furniture, and any other commodities, not required by the labourer, to rise in consequence of more labour being *expended on them, would not that affect profits*? Certainly not: for *nothing can affect profits but a rise in wages*; silks and velvets are not consumed by the labourer and therefore cannot raise wages. (quoted *TSV*, II, 430–1.)

Marx understood here that Ricardo referred to the *rate* of profit, as suggested at the beginning of the chapter 'On Profits' (*Principles*, 110) and he objected to the conclusion on the basis of his formal analysis of the average price–general rate of profits formation 'process' (see chapter 4, pp. 81ff. above). Once again, it was evident to Marx that Ricardo had not recognised clearly enough the conceptual distinction between the rate of surplus Value and the rate of profit. In the case of the *former*, Ricardo's argument here was quite correct. But, the links to the determination of the general rate of profits were more complex than he made allowance for. The simple fact, as Marx saw it, was that *all* sectors of manufacturing industry are involved in the 'redistribution' of immediate surplus Value in order to ensure the return of a uniform rate of profit in each. The common-sense logic of the analysis then led him to conclude that an alteration in the immediate Value of any commodity would upset the 'equilibrium' average price vector and the resulting inter-sector redistribution of the new aggregate surplus Value would result in a new general rate of profits (*TSV*, II, 423, 431; cf. III, 349–50). Whatever the limitations of Marx's Value-distribution articulation analysis, his conclusion here followed directly and logically from it.

Marx went on more fully to analyse the dynamic aspects of the 'laws' of surplus Value and profit when he took up his critique of Ricardo's work on capital accumulation and its distributional and other effects. I shall consider this dimension of the critique in Part IV below.

APPENDIX TO CHAPTER 5

Absolute and differential rent

In this appendix, the *technical* dimensions of Marx's analysis of absolute and differential rent are developed formally. It must be emphasised that for Marx, understanding rent required more than a technical quantitative exposition. Rent was a category of *property income* that resulted from particular relations of production of capitalism. In no sense should the following 'socially sterilised' presentation be taken to suggest otherwise.

The physical structure of production comprises two sectors; agriculture (a) and manufacturing industry (m). At first, in order to formalise absolute rent, the organic composition of capital in agriculture (g_a) is argued to be less than that in manufacturing (g_m) and the two parcels of land that comprise the agricultural sector are assumed to be of uniform fertility. This latter assumption rules out any differential rent for the present.

The following symbols are used to represent Value quantities converted into constant money units:

- w = embodied-labour exchange value
- c = constant capital advanced *and* used up in one production period
- v = variable capital
- $\bar{e}$ = uniform rate of surplus Value
- r = rate of profit
- $\bar{r}$ = general rate of profits
- p = cost price realising $\bar{r}$
- mp = market price
- AR = absolute rent per unit of commodity output
- DR = differential rent per unit of commodity output

In agriculture:

$$w_a = c_a + v_a + \bar{e}.v_a$$

Agriculture is assumed to be isolated from the determination of the general rate of profits which emerges in manufacturing by the 'sharing out' of total surplus Value. The relevant expression is:

$$\bar{r} = r_m = \frac{\bar{e}}{1 + g_m}$$

And with $g_m > g_a$, the immediate rate of profit in agriculture, r_a, exceeds r_m and determines the *capacity* to pay rent.
Thus:

$$p_a = c_a + v_a + \bar{r}\ (c_a + v_a) < w_a$$

and

$$AR = (w_a - p_a) > 0$$

An analogous approach can be used formally to explicate

Ricardo's analysis of differential rent. In this case, the uniform organic compositions of capital, $g_a = g_m$, assures that no absolute rent will be generated. Agriculture now includes two land qualities each providing, say, one-half of the required 'corn' output. The land of the poorer quality dominates in the determination of the market price of 'corn' such that:

$$w_{a2} = mp_a = c_{a2} + v_{a2} + \bar{e}.v_{a2}$$

Because land of the better quality requires less capital in order to produce a unit of 'corn', then:

$$(c_{a1} + v_{a1}) < (c_{a2} + v_{a2})$$

and:

$$w_{a1} < w_{a2}$$

The *capacity* to pay differential rent is thus given by:

$$DR = (w_{a2} - w_{a1}) = (mp_a - w_{a1}) > 0$$

Marx also argued that differential rent had to be considered as a supplementary addition to the more essential absolute rent (*TSV*, II, 293–4). His argument may be formalised by bringing together the two previous pieces of analysis. The crucial point to notice is that for Marx, the rate of profit which agricultural capitalists perceive as 'normal' is that generated in manufacturing. This assumption is implied by the very nature of his absolute rent analysis. The cost price of 'corn' must be such as to bring the rate of profit realised in agriculture into line with that in manufacturing, for the latter is determined logically prior to the former by the establishment of a vector of cost prices for manufactured commodities.

The situation on the poorer marginal land is:

$$w_{a2} = c_{a2} + v_{a2} + r_a\,(c_{a2} + v_{a2})$$
$$p_{a2} = c_{a2} + v_{a2} + \bar{r}\,(c_{a2} + v_{a2})$$

and because the *immediate* rate of profit in agriculuture, r_a, exceeds the general rate, $\bar{r}$:

$$AR_2 = (w_{a2} - p_{a2}) > 0$$

with $DR_2 = 0$ because $mp_a = w_{a2}$.
On the intra-marginal land:

$$w_{a1} = c_{a1} + v_{a1} + r_a (c_{a1} + v_{a1})$$
$$p_{a1} = c_{a1} + v_{a1} + \bar{r} (c_{a1} + v_{a1})$$

resulting in:

$$AR_1 = (w_{a1} - p_{a1}) > 0$$
$$DR_1 = (mp_a - w_{a1}) > 0$$

The total capacity to pay rent now included that arising because of the lower organic composition of capital in agriculture along with that due to the different fertilities of the land parcels used to meet the demand for 'corn'.

The 'Tables of differential rent'

Marx based his 'tables' on several assumptions. On each quality of land (or mine in the early stages of the analysis), £100 of capital of a uniform composition is applied. The general rate of profits is given as 10 per cent and the *immediate* rate of profit in agriculture is 20 per cent. According to the relative physical productivity of each parcel of land, the unit exchange value of 'corn', what Marx called the 'individual value' (IV), is given by $\frac{120}{T_i}$, where T_i is the physical output of 'corn' from a particular parcel of land (i = I, . . . IV). Similarly, the unit cost price of 'corn' (CP) is given by $\frac{120}{T_i}$. In this context, the market exchange value (MV) was argued by Marx to take various values depending upon the state of demand relative to supply introduced by the changes hypothesised. For each of the situations analysed, the unit rents were calculated as (*TSV*, II, 293–4):

$$DR_i = MV - IV_i$$
$$AR_i = IV_i - CP_i$$

(where these functions are analogous to those devised above, pp. 122–5, as DR = $(mp_{a2} - w_a)$ and AR = $(w_a - p_a)$ respectively).

The arithmetical 'tables' began with a reference situation labelled A in which three mines, numbered I, II and III, of *ascending* productivity are producing to satisfy exactly the level of demand for their product. In this case, the unit MV of £2 is determined by the IV of the product of the least productive mine, number I. With the CP less than IV on I, AR is generated by each mine while DR emerges on II and III only.

The changes introduced in tables B to E then involved extensions of production to the *more* productive mine or land parcel number IV. The particular outcome in each case depended upon what happened to demand relative to the supply effects of bringing IV into production. In each case, though, Marx showed that MV progressively *declined*, a result made inevitable by the ascending productivity cases examined. At the same time, in each case the total rent rose, although in itself this was not very useful information in the absence of any analysis of the overall distributional results, including what happened to relative shares.

Part III

Exchange value and distribution after Ricardo

CHAPTER 6

Reactions to Ricardo's theory: the 'mainstream' critics

INTRODUCTION

Marx's critique of Adam Smith and Ricardo, to which I have devoted most of my attention so far in this study, occupied much of the first eight notebooks of the 'Theories of Surplus Value' manuscript, viz. those numbered VI to XIII. In the last of these notebooks, Marx included an investigation of Ricardo's theory of capital accumulation. This piece of the critique and the general theme of the 'law of motion' of capitalism in antecedent political economy is considered in Part IV. Meanwhile, in the present Part, my focus is on the last two main notebooks of the 'Theories' manuscript, those numbered XIV and XV (*TSV*, III). Here Marx turned his critical attention to a variety of political economists who wrote about exchange value and distribution in the period of the waning dominance of Ricardo's intellectual heritage. In the space of about 450 printed pages, he considered the work of some eighteen writers to varying extents ranging from one page on Wakefield to 55 pages on Malthus.

These brief pieces are characterised by their generally sketchy nature and narrowness of scope. Many of the writers considered had quite substantial written outputs, to most of which Marx would have had access and thus would presumably have read. Yet he contented himself with often superficial critical glosses on selected passages from selected works of the authors concerned.

Part of the reason for this brevity and superficiality was that Marx considered many of the writers concerned to be unworthy heirs of Ricardo's supreme, albeit ambiguous, analytical legacy to political economy. Although he had varying degrees of respect for their contributions, none had been able fully to recognise or realise the *potential* of Ricardo's analyses for the development of a critical comprehension of the essential nature of the capitalist system. This interpretation applied to both Ricardo's critics and those who considered themselves to be his disciples. More than this, it is evident that Marx felt that several of the writers had abrogated their intellectual responsibilities in favour of an apologetic obscurantism in which the interests of one social class or another were allowed to dominate the outcome of the analyses. As we shall see, Marx considered this to be a 'vulgarisation' of Ricardo's heritage and some of his critical remarks against such writers were highly vituperative as a consequence.

All of this resulted in Marx writing a series of brief critical sketches, often of a contentious nature. His critique here was of a different standard from that evident in much of what I have considered so far. The treatment of Adam Smith's *Wealth of Nations* and Ricardo's *Principles* was detailed and exegetical. It has been possible to identify the bases of most of the critical arguments, even where they reflected some misinterpretation on Marx's part. In the present situation, though, the critique often comprised assertions based on highly selective and limited textual evidence. It is not possible, therefore, to assess the veracity of these assertions from the evidence provided by Marx and, *as an intellectual historian*, here he would often rate very low.

Be this as it may, I do not intend to pursue Marx on this particular aspect of his work. I have already emphasised that it serves little purpose to read the 'Theories of Surplus Value' manuscript as an history of political economy *per se*. Its significance is to be found in what the critical discussions reveal about the nature of political economy and in what they add to our understanding of the *evolution and sources* of Marx's critique of political economy, with its objective of exposing the conflict- and crisis-ridden nature of capitalism. The part of the critique that is to be considered in this chapter varies in its contribution to our understanding in this sense and some of it is summarised here more for the sake of expositional completeness than anything else. On the positive side, it will be found that the critique gave Marx a vehicle for a reiteration of some of his key critical ideas and in this sense, it may have helped him to clarify his thoughts. Only a few new critical dimensions were added, though, to what he had firmly established already as the main thrusts of his critique of political economy. This assessment needs to be qualified with respect to those aspects of the critique in these notebooks that related to the evolution of Marx's analysis of the 'law of motion' of capitalism. In Part IV, I shall argue that in this respect the other writers of Ricardo's time and after retained a somewhat greater critical significance for Marx because he was less confident about this part of his critique and did not consider Ricardo's contributions to be so *potentially* definitive.

The brevity and narrowness of Marx's critique in the present context can also be ascribed in part to the particular concerns of his theme. He was interested only in how other writers had handled the analysis of exchange value and the surplus as the origin of profit, along with some immediately related categories, such as labour and capital. These were esoteric concerns that omitted much of the broader sweeps of the political economy of the period. However, such fundamental analytical issues were still prominent in the literature. The more important point to emphasise, then, is that as Marx read things, it had all been said before, and even generally with more acuity, by Ricardo and Adam Smith. Especialy did this apply to those whom I will call the 'mainstream' post-Ricardians as distinct from the 'radicals' and other lesser known writers to whom Marx gave some critical attention. For Marx, the post-Ricardians provided him with little *opportunity* to write much that was new because of their essential adherence to the exchange value and distribution doctrine formulated earlier by one or the other of the two pillars of Classical political economy, Smith and Ricardo. As Marx had written to Engels so perceptively about political economy more than a decade before: 'Basically, this science has made no further progress since A. Smith and D. Ricardo, however much has been done in individual and often very subtle researches' (letter of 2 April 1851, *MEW*, 27, 228). This attitude had its very clear reflection in notebooks XIV and XV of the 'Theories' manuscript.

For the purpose of exposition, it is convenient to group the writers with whom Marx dealt at this stage of his critique under four headings. There is some substantive justification for this also, because in the case of each group, his attitude and emphasis varied.

The first group comprises those whom Marx considered to be predominantly critics of one aspect or other of Ricardo's treatment of exchange value and distribution. It includes Thomas Malthus, Samuel Bailey and Robert Torrens. To the second group, it is appropriate to attach the label 'pseudo-disciples' in that while their immediate objective was to propagate and popularise the doctrine of Ricardo, Marx found that they had largely represented it in such a way that both its limitations and analytical potential were obscured. Especially had the two key writers in this group, James Mill and John Ramsay McCulloch, failed to recognise and pursue the potential of Ricardo's *Principles* and thus to forestall the rising tide of criticism of some of his main ideas. Thomas de Quincey was also given some brief attention by Marx and can be placed in this group.[1] John Stuart Mill, though, is a special case here because although Marx placed him directly in the line-up of this group of Ricardo's 'pseudo-disciples', this placement was based on the critique of only one small, early piece from Mill's mass of writings. Marx chose to overlook most of Mill's independent development of Ricardo's ideas.

All of the writers in these two groups were considered by Marx to have, to varying degrees, 'vulgarised' Ricardo's analyses. In one way or another, they had all contributed to the 'Disintegration of the Ricardian School', as Marx referred to the sequence of intellectual events after Ricardo's death (*TSV*, III, 69). In particular, Marx's concern was that they had neglected and/or obscured the potential *critical* insights into the nature of capitalism that he had found in the *Principles*. In some cases, he ascribed their approach to political apologia for the capitalist system. But, in general, he seemed to be of the opinion that these writers simply lacked sufficient concern over the human-social evils of the system to induce them to seek any explanations for such evils in the relations of production and distribution.

To the third group of writers to whom Marx referred I have given the title 'radical critics' of capitalism. Marx's own heading here was 'Opposition to the Economists (Based on the Ricardian Theory)' (*TSV*, III, 238). These 'radicals' took up Ricardo's analyses for the purpose of giving some formalisation to the exposure of the miserable conditions under which nineteenth-century workers existed. They were critics of capitalism devoted to the reformist cause of improving the workers' conditions. In this group, Marx featured the work of Piercy Ravenstone, Thomas Hodgskin, John Bray and the anonymous author of a pamphlet written in this tradition.

There was finally a fourth group of writers with no particular common element beyond their individual appeal to Marx for having made some identifiable contribution to the development of those dimensions of political economy that he thought important. George Ramsay, Antoine-Elisée Cherbuliez and Richard Jones had each provided some subtle extension of Ricardo's ideas which set him apart from the other post-Ricardians.

Two writers of the period stand out as having been neglected by Marx, viz. the Frenchman Jean-Baptiste Say and the Swiss political economist Jean-Charles-Léonard Simonde de Sismondi. Each was considered in 'Theories of Surplus Value' only in passing and mostly in the context of discussing some other writers.

The neglect of Say is less surprising than that of Sismondi. Marx had a very low opinion of Say, interpreting his work as a superficial, albeit systematic, summary of the very worst aspects of Smith's *Wealth of Nations* (*TSV*, I, 103; II, 165). Although Marx indicated his intention ultimately to deal with Say's work more completely (*TSV*, II, 494; III, 122), this appears never to have been undertaken. In his extant passing references to Say, he was variously described as 'insipid', 'inane', 'tedious' and 'this humbug'; and his work dismissed as 'dull superficiality', 'trash' and 'childish babble'. That Marx devoted so little critical effort to such work was, then, to be expected, whatever may be thought of Say's views today.

As far as Sismondi was concerned, the situation of the neglect is quite different and rather difficult to explain. There were several passing references to Sismondi in 'Theories of Surplus Value' (*TSV*, I, 177, 282, 415; II, 118, 378, 534; III, e.g., 56, 84, 259, 424) and these indicated that Marx had a critical respect for his work. Again it was Marx's expressed intention to undertake a complete critique of this work in the future (*TSV*, III, 53) and, again, this never eventuated as far as is known. Most of the references to Sismondi in the present context remained as integral parts of the discussion of other writers. Malthus was accused of direct plagiarism from Sismondi's *Nouveaux Principes d'économie politique* (*TSV*, III, 53). Cherbuliez's work was also interpreted by Marx to be 'Sismondian', but this was considered more acceptable than was the case with Malthus (*TSV*, III, 362, 382, 396–8). In addition, though, Marx did give some hints of the substantive contributions made by Sismondi. He was aware of the *social* implications of capital and recognised the contradiction that, while labour was argued to be the *source* of Value, most of what was produced accrued to the capitalist giving the *appearance* that it originated with capital (*TSV*, III, 259, 424). Sismondi also interpreted crises to be the consequence of immanent contradictions in capitalism, especially that production was motivated by exchange value without due consideration of effective demand based upon use value (*TSV*, III, 56, 84). It really is to be regretted that Marx did not ever provide a detailed critique of Sismondi's significant contributions to political economy.[2] However, in what was essentially an endeavour to differentiate and distance his work from existing contributions to the political economy of capitalism, Marx possibly felt that there existed sufficient superficial similarities between some of Sismondi's ideas and his own for Sismondi's work to be best left aside as a 'parallel' development. There is just not enough extant evidence to go much beyond such speculation.

The sections that follow in this chapter and the next three consider in turn each of the four summary groups of writers alluded to above.

'MAINSTREAM' REACTIONS TO RICARDO

As I have already indicated, the writers whose work was the object of Marx's critique in the first two groups to be considered in this chapter and the next were all part of what he saw as the 'Disintegration of the Ricardian School'. This was the case, he argued, whether they *intended* to be destructive as critics or constructive as disciples. The fact that Malthus was treated separately from the others in the manuscript does not appear to me to preclude him from a role in the disintegration process as Marx saw it.

Before proceeding to my discussions of the particular writers criticised by Marx, there are some points of a general nature to be made which will help situate his scattered remarks in their proper critical perspective.

Marx's general thesis was that the ambiguity and the unintended open-endedness of Ricardo's core analyses in the *Principles* gave both his critics and 'pseudo-disciples' the scope for their disparate interpretations. The critics attacked what they felt to be the definitional ambiguities and logical flaws in the work and some engaged in public and private controversy with Ricardo through books, pamphlets, journals and letters. The 'pseudo-disciples' sought to prepare and propagate a more definitive and logically consistent version of the exchange value and distribution analyses that Ricardo had worked out. In Marx's view they were unsuccessful in this endeavour and the way was left open for the critics to complete their transcendence of Ricardo's contributions.

The critique of these post-Ricardian writers allowed Marx to work through again some of his central critical ideas. The historical context was more than ever here just a medium for illustrating the power of his own critique by arraigning against it the analytically impoverished endeavours by other writers to preserve, transcend or discredit the main thrust of Ricardo's *Principles*. Marx found the *Principles* to contain many nascent critical insights into capitalism that these writers had largely not even recognised, let alone understood or developed. In addition to these sins of omission, though, their works also involved the sin of commission which Marx referred to as the 'vulgarisation' of Classical political economy.

It is difficult to be clear about how many writers were actually considered to be 'vulgar' by Marx. The period from about 1820 to 1830 seems to have been important in this respect, for he argued that it saw the transition from a situation in which Ricardo's *Principles* dominated political economy to one in which a variety of competing writers jostled with each other in the struggle to be recognised.[3] Marx noted that the period saw 'theoretical tilting for and against the Ricardian theory' (*TSV*, III, 109) and 'a fine old row between the Malthusians and the Ricardians' (*TSV*, III, 22). Later, in the Postface to the second edition of *Capital*, Book I, Marx amplified the circumstances of this transition period (*K*(PE), I, 96ff.). There he alluded to the increasing awareness of the class conflict inherent in the capitalist system as this system became more dominant and clearly identifiable. In Marx's view, the beginning of the end for scientific *bourgeois* political economy came with Ricardo's tentative revelations about 'the antagonism of class interests, of wages and profits, of profits and rent'. Ricardo took this inherent antagonism to be 'a social law of nature'. The consequence of this was that *in its present non-dialectical form*, political economy could proceed no further with any meaningful critical analysis of the system it implicitly assumed to be immutable. Moreover, the very nature of 'mainstream' investigations in political economy were deemed by Marx to have changed. With Ricardo especially, 'what is new and significant develops vigorously amid the "manure" of contradictions out of the contradictory phenomena. The underlying contradictions themselves testify to the richness of the living foundation from which the theory itself developed' (*TSV*, III, 84). That is, while Ricardo's abstract-deductive analyses did not preclude the exposure of the logical contradictions inherent in capitalism, his 'pseudo-disciples' (and, it might be argued, his 'mainstream' critics as well) operated on *ideas* in such a way that their analyses were once removed and insulated from the reality with which they purported to be concerned. For this group, their

> raw material is no longer reality, but the new theoretical form in which the master had sublimated it. It is in part the *theoretical disagreement of opponents of the new theory* and in part the *often paradoxical relationship of this theory to reality* which drives . . . [them] to seek to *refute* . . . [their] opponents and *explain away* reality. (*TSV*, III, 84.)

On top of this abrogation of the need to face up to the reality of capitalism, Marx found *superimposed* the distortions of an *apologetic* approach (*TSV*, III, 453, 485, 496, 501, 503). Thus, he later concluded that in this post-Ricardo period:

> It was thenceforth no longer a question [of] whether this or that theorem was true, but whether it was useful to capital or harmful . . . In the place of disinterested inquirers there stepped hired prize-fighters; in place of genuine scientific research, the bad conscience and evil intent of apologetics. (*K*(PE), I, 97.)

Marx worked on the premise that beyond the 1820s, more

particularly, beyond the 1821 publication of the third edition of Ricardo's *Principles* in Britain and beyond the 1827 publication of the second edition of Sismondi's *Nouveaux Principes d'économie politique* in France, the evolution of what he identified as Classical political economy came to an end (*CCPE*, 52, 61).[4] On this basis, it is possible to infer that all subsequent political economists were to be considered as 'vulgar'. It seems to me that such an extreme interpretation is unwarranted, but the fact remains that Marx never explained the situation adequately. At the *end* of the main part of the 'Theories of Surplus Value' manuscript, he made the point that the 'vulgar political economists' were 'by no means to be confused with the economic investigators we have been criticising' (*TSV*, III, 453). This assertion contradicted previous references to the 'vulgarity' of Malthus (*TSV*, III, 20–1), James Mill (*TSV*, III, 85) and McCulloch (*TSV*, III, 168, 172, 182, 183, 185). It is also worth noting that Marx even referred to 'vulgar' *elements* in the work of Smith and Ricardo (*TSV*, II, 347, 427; III, 502). Thus, rather than applying the term 'vulgar' as an absolute classification, it is more useful to specify the particular aspects of a writer's analyses which would be referred to by Marx as 'vulgarisation'. The *word* was not important, but the characteristics that it implied were because they provided the bases for the particular critical themes that Marx pursued in the writings of the 'post-Ricardians'.[5]

Two related characteristics of an analysis marked it as 'vulgar' in Marx's view. First, where the analysis comprised only the manipulation of categories reflecting the superficial appearances of empirical phenomena to the exclusion of any deeper analytical penetration. For Marx, 'science' was required to provide genuine *explanations* for the *existence* of such phenomena by grasping their essence. Vulgar political economy remained enthralled by appearances and could not get beyond them: 'the vulgar economists . . . only flounder around within the apparent framework of those relations [of bourgeois production], ceaselessly ruminate on the materials long since provided by scientific political economy, and seek their plausible explanations of the crudest phenomena for the domestic purposes of the bourgeoisie' (*K*(PE), I, 174–5n.; cf. *TSV*, III, 485). This superficial endeavour left 'science' without any real point: 'vulgar economy feels particularly at home in the estranged outward appearances of economic relations. . . . But all science would be superfluous if the outward appearance and the essence of things directly coincided' (*K*, III, 817). Moreover, Marx saw the vulgarisation of Classical political economy as a reaction to its revelations about the contradictory nature of the capitalist system:

> the more economic theory is perfected, that is, the deeper it penetrates its subject matter and the more it develops as a contradictory system, the more it is confronted by its own, increasingly independent, vulgar element, enriched with material which it dresses up in its own way until finally it finds its most apt expression in academically syncretic and unprincipled eclectic compilations. (*TSV*, III, 501.)

At this point, it is appropriate to introduce the second, more specific indication of vulgarisation to which Marx referred. This related to how a writer approached the analysis of the category Value and its situation in the distribution process. Here the immanent social conflicts of capitalism were most in evidence and the vulgar endeavour to cover them up most blatant. In the terms of the more general characteristic of vulgarisation discussed above, Marx made the distinction between the appearance and essence of non-labour income: 'Surplus Value and the rate of surplus Value are . . . the invisible and unknown essence that wants investigating, while rate of profit and . . . the appearance of surplus Value in the form of profit are revealed on the surface of the phenomenon [of bourgeois society]' (*K*, III, 43). Value and surplus Value as manifestations of capitalist social relations were not expressed by the vulgar political economists. Instead, they were mesmerised by a vision of distribution to which Marx gave a status analogous to the 'holy trinity': capital, land and labour received their respective 'wages' for 'services' rendered to production in the forms of profit (interest), rent and wages. Value came to depend simply on the addition of these payments and political economy presented the world as it appeared to the capitalist (*TSV*, III, 503; cf. 453, 485 and II, 347). The effect of focusing on this appearance of the distribution process was to render it *socially sterile*. The social relations involved were obscured by being translated into relations between 'things'. That is, between say, a 'thing' called capital and a 'thing' called profit.

Thus: 'the participants in capitalist production live in a bewitched world and their own relationships appear to them as properties of things, as properties of the material elements of production' (*TSV*, III, 514). And it was this appearance on which the 'vulgar' analyst depended for his a-historical, a-social presentation of the process as one reflecting the essentially harmonious nature of capitalism. As Marx put it, this vision 'renders a substantial service to apologetics', for in its presentation the 'configurations of capitalist production do not confront one another as alienated forms, but as heterogeneous and independent forms, merely different from one another but *not antagonistic*' (*TSV*, III, 503; cf. 453 and II, 266–7). And: 'Accordingly, vulgar political economy deliberately becomes increasingly *apologetic* and makes strenuous attempts to talk out of existence the ideas which contain . . . contradictions' (*TSV*, III, 501).

For Marx, the vulgar obfuscation of the true nature of capitalist distribution amounted to a 'fetishisation' of the social relations involved (*TSV*, III, 453, 462). The most obvious form of the distribution phenomena in which this 'fetish' was evident he found in interest-bearing finance capital and he discussed it at some length (*TSV*, III, 453ff.). This phenomenon provided the 'vulgar' political economist with the most extreme demonstration of the independent 'productivity' of capital, for here was the 'purest' and 'most sterile' situation in which capital could, at 'arm's length', appropriate a return: 'Interest-bearing capital is the consummate *automatic fetish*, the self-expanding Value, the money-making money, and in this form it no longer bears any trace of its origin' (*TSV*, III, 455; cf. 462, 466, 467). Such capital stands aside from the production process itself and 'establishes' in the mind of the vulgar analyst that the 'service' of *owning* capital is the key to its return (*TSV*, III, 460–2).

In the 'trinitarian' view of distribution, Marx also found the articulation between embodied-labour exchange value and the distribution categories to be obscured. Inevitably, this approach to distribution led to the circularity of the 'adding-up' distortion of capitalist exchange value determination and left both exchange value and distribution with no effective explanation (*TSV*, III, 510–11, 515).

On the basis of these aspects of the vulgarisation of Classical political economy, it is possible to provide a more explicit profile of the themes with which Marx was concerned in the present stage of his critique of political economy. His highly selective reading of the post-Ricardo literature emphasised these themes and some coherence is made evident in the pieces of the critique by relating them to their thematic context.

The general theme of the manuscript remained 'theories of surplus Value'. In all cases, Marx's primary question was how each writer treated the concept of the surplus as the source of non-labour incomes (*TSV*, I, 40). This led him to several other entailed critico-analytical issues, some of which provided the reference points for his critique of each particular writer (cf. *TSV*, III, 237). First, had the writer appropriately conceived of Value as an absolute category reflecting the essence of the capitalist relations of commodity production and exchange? Secondly, had the writer been able to identify the source of surplus Value in the pseudo-exchange between capital and labour in a way that preserved the consistency of this source with the embodied-labour 'law of Value'? That is, had he clearly distinguished between the Value of labour power and the Value provided by the exercise of living labour? Thirdly, had the writer argued the logical distinction beween the phenomena of profit, interest and rent and their essence in surplus Value? Fourthly, had the writer preserved the logical priority of the technology of the production process in the determination of exchange value, emphasising cost price as prior to and necessary for the existence of supply and demand modified market price? Finally, had the writer demonstrated analytically the logical consistency between the 'law of Value' and the existence of cost prices that, when realised, would generate a uniform general rate of profits on all capitals?

Not unexpectedly, Marx's critical investigations led him through a series of negative answers to these questions and I turn now to a consideration of the textual evidence upon which these were based for particular writers. Ricardo's 'mainstream' critics, Malthus, Torrens, and Bailey are treated in the present chapter and his 'pseudo-disciples', James Mill, McCullouch, and de Quincey, along with John Stuart Mill as a special case, are the subjects of the next chapter.

MALTHUS

Marx exhibited a high degree of animosity towards Malthus. In notebook XI of the 'Theories of Surplus Value' manuscript, he briefly considered Malthus as a political economist in the context of discussing the development of the theory of differential rent (*TSV*, II, 115ff.). By comparison with Ricardo especially, two main things worried Marx about Malthus and his work and evoked the vituperative tirade found in the notebook cited above. In a later notebook, that numbered XIV, Marx's critique was more temperate and had more substantive content (*TSV*, III, 13ff.).

Marx's first point of concern for the present was that Malthus lacked originality to the extent of engaging in extensive plagiarism. According to Marx's reading, he plagiarised Joseph Townsend on population theory and James Anderson on rent theory and based his *Principles of Political Economy* virtually entirely on a plagiaristic summary of Sismondi's *Nouveaux Principes d'économie politique* (*TSV*, II, 115, 119, 120; III, 53, 61–2). Malthus was cited as a '*plagiarist* by profession' and as having engaged in a 'shameless and mechanical plagiarism' (*TSV*, II, 115, 117, 120). Marx never explained the grounds for these allegations and they warrant no further attention here.

The second concern that Marx had with Malthus's work was what he took to be its tendentious and intellectually dishonest nature. Here Malthus was contrasted directly with the '*scientific honesty*', even intellectual '*ruthlessness*', of Ricardo (*TSV*, II, 118–19). It is often argued that Malthus was a political reactionary[6] and Marx found this reflected quite obviously in his political economy. Malthus had a negative attitude towards the human potentials of commercial and industrial development, favouring instead a revival and preservation of a predominantly agrarian society with the accompanying political dominance of the landed aristocracy.[7] Marx found him to be 'a shameless sycophant of the ruling classes' (*TSV*, II, 120), who

> defends the interests of the industrial bourgeoisie only in so far as these are identical with the interests of landed property, of the aristocracy, i.e. *against* the mass of the people, the proletariat. But where these interests diverge and are antagonistic to each other, he sides with the aristocracy against the

bourgeoisie. (*TSV*, II, 115; cf. 118.)

Malthus's promotion of the particular interests of the landowners in the guise of 'scientific' analysis offended Marx's perception of 'science' as pursuing truth, 'warts and all'. It was not a matter of 'science' being 'correct' from any particular viewpoint, but rather that it should impartially follow out and expose the tenets of its own *logic*. Marx objected to the apologetics induced by attempts to give *minority interests* an intellectually respectable status.[8] Thus he wrote that 'when a man seeks to *accommodate* science to a viewpoint that is derived not from science itself (however erroneous it may be) but from *outside, from alien external interests*, then I call him "base" ' (*TSV*, II, 119). The irony here was that despite this 'baseness' Malthus was, in one important sense, more 'honest' than most of the other apologetic vulgarisers of the Ricardian legacy: 'Malthus's . . . merit lies in his pointed emphasis on the disharmonies, which . . . were all emphasised, amplified and publicised by him with complacent sacerdotal cynicism' (*TSV*, II, 120–1; cf. III, 57). However, Marx found that these disharmonies served a conservative rather than any radical purpose for Malthus (*TSV*, II, 117).

The veracity of this reading of Malthus, and the associated inferences about Marx's perception of 'science' and status as a 'scientist', could be debated. On the relevance of Malthus's partiality in political economy, though, all that needs to be added here is that while Marx's abhorrence of the man must have given him a negative attitude towards Malthus's analyses, these were not in any way 'tested' on such a subjective criterion. The substantive critique to which I turn below related to Malthus's position on the particular *analytical* issues that were of immediate critical concern to Marx.

It is appropriate to divide Marx's critique of Malthus into two components in the light of the emphasis in this present chapter on the analytical issues of Value and distribution. Malthus is well known as an advocate of the 'general-glut' potential of capitalism, contrary to the widely espoused tenets of 'Say's Law' in the nineteenth century. Marx took up this issue in his critique (*TSV*, III, 40ff.), but I will leave it for consideration as part of the 'law of motion' analysis in Part IV.

Marx made some reference to most of Malthus's works in the

formulation of his critique, but he emphasised those written during the 1820s, viz.:

The measure of Value stated and illustrated with an Application of it to the Alterations in the Value of the English Currency since 1790. (1823)
Definitions in Political Economy, preceded by an Inquiry into the Rules which ought to guide Political Economists in the Definition and Use of their Terms; with Remarks on the Deviation from these Rules in their Writings. (1827)
– also: new edition, with a preface, notes and supplementary remarks by John Cazenove. (1853)
Principles of Political Economy considered with a View to their practical Application [1820], 2nd ed. (1836)

Any reading of Marx's critique of these works must be tempered by the fact that while he recognised them as reactions to Ricardo's *Principles* and the various dimensions of 'Ricardian' political economy that evolved from that work, Marx had access neither to the extensive Ricardo–Malthus correspondence nor to the 'Notes' which Ricardo wrote on Malthus's *Principles*.[9] Modern appreciation of Malthus's place in the history of political economy has depended very much on these sources.

As we have seen, Malthus objected to the tenor of Ricardo's *Principles* with its inherent acceptance of and faith in the rising dominance of commercial and industrial capitalism. As an intellectual source, Malthus preferred the more open-ended exposition of Adam Smith's *Wealth of Nations* in which the influence of these burgeoning forms of capitalism was less obvious and less formally entrenched. Marx recognised this, but he apparently remained unaware of the circumstances which prompted Malthus's reaction against Ricardo, initially in his *Principles* of 1820. The situation was that Malthus saw the publication and subsequently favourable reception of Ricardo's *Principles* as a threat to the so far unchallenged position of the *Wealth of Nations* as the key to political economy.[10] Marx's assertion that Malthus's reaction was 'largely inspired by envy at the success of Ricardo's book' (*TSV*, III, 14), underestimates the intellectual affinity between Malthus and Adam Smith, the subject of much of Ricardo's critical analysis. Indeed, Malthus's predilections for the values and institutions of an agrarian society led him to espouse, somewhat anachronistically in the context of Britain's booming industry and commerce, Physiocratic ideas about productivity and wealth.[11] For him, Ricardo's *Principles* represented a formal expression of much that he rejected.

It was Marx's view that Malthus's retreat to the *Wealth of Nations* represented an error of judgment, for Malthus chose to develop the 'weak side of Adam Smith' in his endeavour to construct a 'counter theory to Ricardo's theory; which is based on Adam Smith's stronger sides' (*TSV*, III, 53). However, it was Ricardo's own analytical limitations which left the way open for this reactionary revival of Smith's ideas. Marx argued that had Ricardo been more precise and consistent in his use of categories and developed the logic of his premises more formally and fully, then Malthus's critical task would have been more difficult (*TSV*, III, 14, 29).

One of the key points of Malthus's critique was the failure by Ricardo to demonstrate formally the consistency of the embodied-labour principle of exchange value determination with the formulation of capitalist cost prices. By positing the appearance of cost prices as unresolved contradictions of the embodied-labour premise, Ricardo's theory could not be clearly seen as analytically superior to the labour-commanded concept of exchange value which Malthus revived in conjunction with his switch to an emphasis on the primacy of market prices. Despite his continued awareness of the cost price concept in this context,[12] Malthus had no *explanation* for the determination of it beyond the circularity of the 'adding up' of factor costs (*TSV*, III, 32). Ricardo's analysis held the unrealised key to what Marx considered to be the correct derivation and role of the cost price category as he had previously demonstrated (see chapter 4, pp. 81ff. and pp. 88ff. above).

For Marx, though, the labour-commanded expression of exchange value was not without its significance. It led him to suggest that Malthus might have grasped the nature of capitalist income more adequately had he perceived this same significance (*TSV*, III, 14ff.). One of the facts of an essential analysis of capitalism as far as Marx was concerned was the '*unequal* exchange between capital and wage labour' (*TSV*, III, 14). What this amounted to was that the commodity labour power commanded less materialised labour than the commodity produced by the living labour extracted from it. The labour power is paid for by the money equivalent of the embodied-labour exchange value of the real commodity wage. When the worker makes a purchase, he 'receives as much materialised labour in commodities as he gives in money' (*TSV*, III, 19). But, the point that Marx emphasised was that this transaction involved the worker using money for which he had paid 'in kind' as living labour more than it was worth in embodied-labour terms. 'Thus the worker is the only one who pays for all commodities above their Value even when he buys at their Value, because he buys money, the universal equivalent, at above its Value for labour' (*TSV*, III, 19). Should the capitalist sell his commodity to his own workers, then it is quite apparent that the profit that he realises comes from his receiving an embodied-labour exchange value, in money form, which exceeds what he effectively 'paid' his workers for it through their engagement in the production process in the first place.

The problem that Marx thought Malthus should have faced up to in determining exchange value including profit was the same as that recognised by Ricardo: viz. how to reconcile the embodied-labour principle with the surplus that results from the pseudo-exchange between capital and labour when it *seems* that 'labour' is fully paid for in exchange value terms. This is the problem of formulating the distinction between the embodied-labour *exchange value* of 'labour' and the *quantity* of living labour extracted in production (*TSV*, III, 25). Malthus's untenable 'solution' was to adhere to the 'adding-up' idea by arguing that all purchasers were like the capitalist's own workers in that he charged them more than the monetary equivalent of the exchange value that he had laid out on past and present labour in order to produce the commodity involved. In this argument, Malthus reverted to the 'vulgar' notion of 'profit on alienation' by 'deriving profit from the fact that the seller sells his commodity not only *above* the amount it costs *him* (and the capitalist does this), but [also] above what *it costs*' (*TSV*, III, 20; cf. 20–1). The 'unpaid labour' source of surplus Value was apparently not recognised by Malthus, even though a more perceptive treatment of the labour-commanded expression of exchange value may have led him to it (*TSV*, III, 26).[13]

As Marx read things, Malthus had no formal theory of how the general rate of profits that he applied was *determined* and had no idea of its analytical links with the process of exchange value formation *in production*. In order to demonstrate this, Marx chose an arithmetical example from Malthus's *Principles* where these particular issues were dealt with and subjected it to critical scrutiny (*TSV*, III, 36ff.).[14]

Before considering Marx's critique, though, it is appropriate to amplify a little the point of Malthus's example. This was not made clear by Marx. For Malthus, profit comprised the excess of realised exchange value over the 'cost' of advances required to make the commodity. It was the case, furthermore, that the realised exchange value was primarily determined by market forces. Supply conditions were *always* modified by *effective* demand conditions in the determination of exchange value and Malthus saw no point in abstracting from the latter as Ricardo had done.[15] It was this approach which gave some rationale to Malthus's vulgar treatment of 'profit on alienation' in the example that Marx investigated, although he concluded that the whole thing amounted only to a tautology anyway and for that reason had little significance.

What Malthus wanted to establish was that his view of how profits emerged was effectively consistent with Ricardo's position on the inverse relationship between wages and profits, a position which he accepted with qualification.[16] Malthus stated his hypothesis as follows:[17]

> The varying rate of profits . . . in the production of every commodity depends on the excess of its value when sold above the known value of the advances, determined in all cases by the state of supply and demand.
>
> . . .
>
> And it will be found, that this proposition is essentially the same as the proposition which states, that profits depend upon the proportion of the value of the whole produce, which goes to pay the wages of the labour employed to obtain it.

The arithmetic proceeded in two stages. First, the advances comprised wage payments only. In this situation, the ratio proposed by Malthus was that of wages advanced to exchange value, where the denominator included wages plus profits (in effect surplus Value in Marx's view by virtue of being related only to variable capital). Using Marx's symbols (not used by Marx here), Malthus's proposition was:

$$r = f\left[\frac{v}{v+s}\right]$$

where: r = Value rate of profits,
v = wage capital,
s = surplus Value appearing as profits.

That r = s/v follows directly here and represents the most obvious expression of Ricardo's inverse relation.

The example was made more complicated when non-wage capital was introduced, but Malthus held that r could still be related to the ratio of wage advances to exchange value by isolating the fraction of the latter equal to the fraction of wage capital in total capital. The proposition became:

$$r = f\left[\frac{v}{\frac{v}{c+v}(c+v+s)}\right]$$

where: c = non-wage advances (used up in the period of production).

This may be re-expressed as:

$$r = f\left[\frac{1}{1+\frac{s}{c+v}}\right]$$

which makes r dependent upon s/v, once c/v is known, thus keeping Malthus's proposition in line with the inverse ratio between profit and wages.

Marx was not very much impressed by Malthus's arithmetic. In its tautological way, it did reveal some 'inkling that surplus Value must be calculated on the part of the capital expended on wages'. However, it 'proves absolutely nothing about a definite, *special* distinguishing relationship of . . . profit to the part of capital expended on wages' (*TSV*, III, 38, 39). And, it really could not be otherwise 'in view of . . . [Malthus's] conception of value' (*TSV*, III, 36) which did not give primacy to the cost of production in isolation from demand modifications.

Moreover, Malthus had not fully appreciated the analytical significance of 'one of Ricardo's greatest contributions', viz. the category 'relative wages', the wages *share* in net exchange value, which amounted to 'another way of expressing the real theory of surplus Value' (*TSV*, III, 33; see above, chapter 5, pp. 113ff.). According to Marx, it reflected the division between the proportion of the working day in which 'the worker works for himself (producing or reproducing his wage)' and 'that part of his time that belongs to the capitalist' (*TSV*, III, 33). Marx ascribed Malthus's rejection of this development to its importance 'in regard to the social relationship between the two classes' and concluded that 'Malthus smells a rat and is therefore constrained to protest' (*TSV*, III, 33–4).[18]

From Marx's point of view, then, Malthus's version of the political economy of capitalism contained little of substantive relevance in comprehending the essential nature of the system. He had retreated to an anachronistic argument about the origin of profit which gave no recognition to the surplus as attributable to the capitalist relations of production between capital and labour. The analysis of distribution that he pursued provided no *explanation* for its phenomenal categories and, beyond the circular 'adding-up' idea, gave no indication of how these phenomena were articulated to the *production* of exchange value. The few potential insights that Marx identified in Malthus's work were left undeveloped.

TORRENS

Marx's central concern in his critique of Robert Torrens's *An Essay on the Production of Wealth* (1821) was the analytical fate of the embodied-labour theory of exchange value in the comparison between pre-capitalist and capitalist society. The essential puzzle was how to formulate exchange value such that it includes profit at a uniform general rate on all capitals. As Marx had shown, it was possible to retain the embodied-labour principle when the mode of production involved capital owned by a separate class by devising the cost price category. Ricardo had recognised this, but had analysed the relations involved without much precision leaving many of his readers unconvinced about the viability of the principle in the capitalist context.

Robert Torrens was one such reader who, not recognising the logical potential of Ricardo's core analyses in the *Principles*, set out to establish an appropriate exchange value principle of his own and to link it to the phenomena of capitalist distribution.[19] Unlike Malthus's endeavours, Torrens's exposition was not polemical (contrary perhaps to Marx's suggestion, *TSV*, III, 71), and his *Essay* contains few references to other writers beyond the Preface. He set the tone of his contribution as follows: 'As presented by Mr. Ricardo, Political Economy possess [*sic*] a regularity and simplicity beyond what exists in nature; as exhibited by Mr. Malthus, it is a chaos of original but unconnected elements'.[20] Rather than being polemical, Torrens's work was intended to be ecumenical and eclectic.[21] He wanted to begin again with Adam Smith's *Wealth of Nations* and draw on what he considered to be the most appropriate methodological and substantive elements of his contemporaries. In Marx's critique, though, the limitations of Torrens's efforts with respect to exchange value and distribution became quite evident.

Torrens's reading of the *Wealth of Nations* noted that Smith had applied the embodied-labour principle to pre-capitalist production while arguing that it could not be applied when a capitalist class must be paid an income. For Marx, of course, it was absolutely essential that capitalist *commodity* production and the resulting income distribution be shown to be consistent with the 'law of Value', and its applicability or otherwise to pre-capitalist forms of production did not matter here (*TSV*, III, 74). In his eclecticism, Torrens began by focusing appropriately on what is meant by the term 'the labour expended on production' in a capitalist economy. Embodied-labour remained the foundation of exchange value for Torrens, but it ended up as a tautology in his vision of '*accumulated* labour expended on production' as the centrepiece of his analysis (*TSV*, III, 73).[22] Marx commented that, in adopting this category, 'Torrens lands himself in a fine mess' and in 'a fine vicious circle' from which he could not extract himself (*TSV*, III, 75). Here Marx added James Mill's comment to the same effect regarding the circularity implied by such a category in his *Elements of Political Economy* (*TSV*, III, 76).[23]

Marx identified the problem with Torrens's 'capital' theory of exchange value as precisely that which Torrens had thought he had overcome, viz. the articulation of exchange value to distribution.[24] Exchange value became simply a compound of accumulated labour advanced as capital plus profit at the 'customary rate'. And because the 'customary rate' was uniformly applied, exchange value was effectively determined by 'embodied capital'. Of course, this left Torrens with no explanation of how this 'customary rate' was determined. Thus: 'a "*customary rate of profit*" *is presupposed* without explaining how it comes about'; but, what was worse, without 'even the feeling that this ought to be explained' (*TSV*, III, 72).

Torrens's analyses had the merit of making the existence of different capital compositions explicit, especially the fact that the same exchange value of capital advanced may set in motion very different quantities of living labour (*TSV*, III, 72–3). It was for this reason that he rejected the embodied-labour principle as able to explain exchange value, for it applied only 'accidentally' where capitals happened to involve the employment of the same living labour.[25] Torrens's idea was to have equal capitals comprising the exchange value of fixed capital used up, the exchange value of raw materials and the exchange value of the commodity wage bill as always generating the same exchange value in production. So far, then, Torrens was founding his exchange value on constant plus variable capital. What he did not recognise was that such equal capitals, because of their varying compositions, had to be seen as producing different exchange values at the point of production and prior to any concern with the phenomena of distribution.

Although Marx did not mention it, Torrens was also keen to locate the *source* of profit *in production*. He argued in terms of capital 'creating' profit as a 'surplus' above its 'costs'. Indeed his definition of the 'cost of production' or 'natural price' was exactly in line with what Marx referred to as the cost of the commodity *to the capitalist* in terms of his outlays (*TSV*, III, 79–80, 83).[26] But, beyond this, he did not realise that the cost of the commodity to the capitalist did not reflect its 'cost' in terms of accumulated and *living* labour together. Marx's argument was that 'the living labour expended upon the commodity and the living labour paid [for] by the capitalist are two different things' (*TSV*, III, 81) and it followed that 'what the production of a commodity *costs* the capitalist and what the production of the commodity itself costs, are [also] two entirely different things' (*TSV*, III, 80).

Thus it was that Torrens's correct *concept* of a central cost price category comprising capital plus profit at the 'customary rate' was left simply as the consequence of market competition. *Long-run market-determined* price conformed to the cost price concept by virtue of capital mobility and supply and demand based competition.[27] Torrens had no *explanation* for the existence of the 'surplus' above 'costs' and he had no *explanation* for the actual value of the general rate of profits. That is, he had not formally linked the idea of cost price with the production process itself as Ricardo had sensed *could* be done by referring to the 'modifications' to embodied-labour exchange value and as Marx had established analytically (*TSV*, III, 79–81). Marx emphasised that

> cost prices are not only determined by the Values of the commodities and confirm the law of Value instead of contradicting it, but, moreover . . . the very existence of costs of production and cost prices can be comprehended only on the basis of Value and its laws, and becomes a meaningless absurdity without that premise. (*TSV*, III, 82–3.)

The detailed applied arithmetical examples, for which Torrens held such high explanatory hopes,[28] proved nothing. They only described and confirmed the *phenomenal appearances* of the competitive market processes of capitalism (*TSV*, III, 71–3, 77–9).[29] As Marx observed, somewhat harshly in this case, Torrens's whole endeavour with the analysis of exchange value and distribution represented: 'Absolutely nothing but the crude, thoughtless, verbal expression of the phenomenon which has to be explained' (*TSV*, III, 73).

Two further points are of some continuing interest in Marx's critique of Torrens. First, he noted Torrens's introduction of the idea that in a production process using durable capital which was only partly depreciated during the production period, the aggregate of exchange value 'produced' could be considered as including the exchange value of the depreciated fixed capital. Torrens referred to this as the 'residue of capital'.[30] Marx saw no particular analytical significance in this idea and did not pursue it at all (*TSV*, III, 72).[31]

Secondly, in one of Torrens's examples, he worked briefly in *commodity* terms and measured inputs and outputs in corn units (*TSV*, III, 77–9).[32] This was very quickly translated into money terms, but Marx seized on the opportunity to make an important point, albeit overstated in the present context. His point was that the extra 20 quarters of corn that the farmer found himself with after having advanced 100 quarters as 'capital' could not be considered as *profit* in its use-value form. Without the mediation of *Value*, that is, without recognising that the *physical* surplus *manifested* as corn is realised as profit only under capitalist conditions of labour exploitation, the example had nothing to do with explaining *profit* as such. *For Marx*, an analysis which did not keep the embodied-labour origin of Value to the fore as its essential premise could not provide an adequate critical grasp of the nature of the capitalist mode of production.

One aspect of Torrens's discussion not taken up by Marx was his assertion that exchange value was a strictly *relative* concept.[33] Torrens argued that exchange value had a *subjective* basis and ultimately reflected perceptions of utility returns from value in use. It therefore could not be expressed in any objective or absolute terms even though Torrens's extensive analyses of the production origins of exchange value would suggest otherwise. The overriding factor in the determination of exchange value remained for him, in both the short and the long run, market *demand* in conjunction with supply conditions. However, this misconception of exchange value *vis-à-vis* Marx's strict adherence to the absolute, objective determination of long-run cost price did not intrude too much in Torrens's work. This was not the case with Marx's next antagonist, Samuel Bailey, whose work became the *locus classicus* of the exclusively relative conception of exchange value. Bailey's arguments on this point required careful critical scrutiny and refutation.

BAILEY

Marx's critique of Samuel Bailey's *A Critical Dissertation on the Nature, Measure and Causes of Value* (1825) gave him the opportunity to reiterate his thoughts on the essential nature of Value (*TSV*, III, 124ff.). In Bailey's work, the key idea posited was that exchange value had no meaning in *absolute* terms and that its only valid form of existence was in the quantitative relativity between two commodities *in exchange*. This same theme appeared in an earlier polemical pamphlet entitled *Observations on Certain Verbal Disputes in Political Economy Particularly Relating to Value and to Demand and Supply* (1821), which Marx had read (*TSV*, III, 111, 125ff.). The author of this pamphlet remains unknown, but Marx noted the similarity between the arguments expressed therein and those of Bailey.[34] Indeed, Marx went further and accused Bailey of plagiarism, again, as in the case of the similar assertions about Malthus, with little supporting evidence (*TSV*, III, 146, 162, 166). The *Observations* pamphlet was the starting point for Marx's critical discussion of the relative exchange value concept, but it was Bailey's book that he considered more significant and which became the centrepiece of the critique. Bailey also wrote the pamphlet *A Letter to a Political Economist Occasioned by an Article in the 'Westminster Review' on the Subject of Value* (1826) in reply to an anonymous critical review of his book that appeared in the journal.[35] Marx referred to this piece in passing, but did not examine its arguments (*TSV*, III, 125).

The *Critical Dissertation* was an explicit attack on what Bailey considered to be the weaknesses of Ricardo's exposition of the theory of exchange value in the *Principles*.[36] Bailey's complaint was that the exposition was confused and imprecise in its use of words and concepts and, more importantly, fundamentally flawed because of its devotion to the pursuit of an absolute concept and measure of exchange value.[37] Marx considered Bailey's attack ill founded and used the critique of the *Critical Dissertation* to re-emphasise that the absolute essence of Value was the necessary reflection of the nature of the capitalist relations of production. Ricardo was defended by Marx to some extent in this discussion, but this was, as always, tempered by a recognition of the limitations of the development of the embodied-labour premise of exchange value in the *Principles*.

Marx had set out his views on the nature of exchange value in the first chapter of *A Contribution to the Critique of Political Economy* (1859).[38] This explication provided his frame of reference for the critique of Bailey. Marx argued that the commodity was the elementary physical result of the capitalist production process. It is a use value produced only for exchange and becomes the vehicle for the expression and realisation of the exchange value generated in production. The commodity thus represents a unity of exchange value and use value, with the latter being the necessary condition for the former. Exchange value is, though, distinct from its embodiment in a particular commodity and manifests the social relations involved in the capitalist production process. That is, the commodity is the physical expression of a specific form of social labour organised under the auspices of capital. For this reason, Marx emphasised the absolute nature of exchange value as logically prior to and independent of its expression in commodity form.

Antecedent discussions of exchange value had not made this conceptual status of the category clear and Bailey had entered the lists explicitly to obscure it. The difficulty faced by the political economists was to get beyond the appearance that exchange values merely reflected the physical transfer of the ownership of commodities, usually with the mediation of money as the '*external* measure' of the relativities involved. Marx's position was that this left exchange value without any roots in the *production* process and failed to explain how physically different commodities were made comparable as quantities for the purposes of establishing their exchange ratios. This latter explanation could be provided by the mediation of the embodied (materialised, congealed, objectified) abstract labour technically necessary to *produce* the commodity. For Marx, this gave exchange value its 'substance' and provided its '*immanent* measure', without both of which value in exchange could express nothing.

It was with these premises fixed firmly in his mind that Marx approached his reading of Bailey's exposition of the view that exchange value was strictly a relative concept. Marx briefly reiterated some of these premises immediately prior to his critique of Bailey, more or less in the context of some critical remarks on the *Observations* pamphlet, although the pamphlet itself was only incidental to the points that he made (*TSV*, III, 125ff.). In particular, he re-emphasised that the meaning of exchange value went beyond its appearance as a quantitative ratio in the physical exchange process. Ricardo had not delved deeply enough into the *concept* of exchange value to make it clear that the value *manifested* in exchange is logically distinguishable from the prior existence of the commodity as a *Value* consequent upon its *production* (*TSV*, III, 125, 131). Thus, Marx set the tenor of his critique of Bailey as follows: 'the rate at which commodities exchange for one another as use values, although it is an *expression* of their Value, their *realised* Value, it is not their Value itself, since the same proportion of Value can be represented by quite different quantities of use values' (*TSV*, III, 127); and he added: 'The rate at which two commodities exchange does not determine their Value, but their Value determines the rate at which they exchange' (*TSV*, III, 132). Thus, Value is a property of a commodity that exists prior to exchange. Moreover, a valid discussion of Value had to abstract from the use-value form and get beyond the '*fetishism*' of the appearances of exchange 'in the first instance'. Especially, Marx argued, it needed to be recognised that:

> As Values, commodities are *social* magnitudes, that is to say, something absolutely different from their 'properties' as 'things'. As Values, they constitute only relations of men in their productive activity. . . . Exchange of products as commodities is a method of exchanging labour, [it demonstrates] the dependence of the labour of each upon the labour of the others [and corresponds to] a certain mode of social labour or social production. (*TSV*, III, 129.)

As a consequence, the substance of Value or its '*immanent* measure' was appropriately abstract social labour (*TSV*, III, 130, 132).

By contrast, Bailey firmly espoused the notion that exchange value had no meaning beyond that which is perceived as the relative quantities of commodities that will exchange for each other at any point in time. These relative quantities embraced the *nature, expression and measure* of exchange value for Bailey.[39]

The immediate origin of the quantitative relation involved in any exchange was argued to be the relative subjective appeal that the commodities had as use values to the purchasers concerned.[40] There existed no 'intrinsic or absolute quality' of the commodity to which exchange value could be ascribed independently of the commodity's effect on the human 'mind'. The appropriate perception of exchange value thus resolved itself to be but 'a relation in which . . . [commodities] stand to each other'.[41]

The one merit that Marx found in the *Critical Dissertation* was that it potentially brought into focus the correct interpretation of money as the *external measure* of a pre-existing exchange value (*TSV*, III, 125, 133, 137–8). This served to highlight the *immanent* measure of exchange value in Marx's analysis and it became central to his critique of Bailey.[42]

Bailey's idea that exchange value should only be perceived as a *relative quantitative phenomenon* left him without any explanation as to how totally dissimilar physical objects were brought into a consistent and objective congruence and thus made comparable prior to being exchanged (*TSV*, III, 139, 160ff.). Marx regarded Bailey as a fetishist who saw no reason to abstract from appearances in order to grasp the nature and meaning of exchange value. Bailey saw exchange value solely as 'a *relation of objects to one another*' (*TSV*, III, 147).

> This is how matters *appear directly*. And Bailey clings to this. The most superficial form of exchange value, that is the *quantitative relationship* in which commodities exchange with one another, *constitutes*, according to Bailey, their value. *The advance from the surface to the core of the problem is not permitted.* (*TSV*, III, 139; last emphasis added.)

Marx quoted the following passage from the *Critical Dissertation* in order to illustrate the point:[43]

> If the *value* of an object *is its power of purchasing*, there must be something to purchase. Value denotes *consequently* nothing positive or intrinsic, but merely the *relation* in which two objects stand to each other as *exchangeable commodities*. (quoted *TSV*, III, 140.)

And he added the following comment: 'His [Bailey's] entire wisdom is, in fact, contained in this passage'. From this 'wisdom', Marx devised the following tautological summary of Bailey's piece 'accurately expressed':

> *If* the value of an object is the relation in which it exchanges with other objects, value denotes, *consequently* (viz. in consequence of the 'if'), nothing but the relation in which two objects stand to each other as exchangeable objects. (*TSV*, III, 141; cf. 142.)

That is, the argument posited by Bailey had no meaningful substance (*TSV*, III, 140–3).

In his endeavour to give some more concrete meaning to his relative exchange value idea, Bailey used an analogy with distance and its units of expression.[44] Marx was not impressed by this analogy and inverted it to emphasise his own perception of Value (*TSV*, III, 143, 161). Bailey's argument was that exchange value, like distance, had no meaning when attached to one object in isolation. As Marx saw it, the analogy should not stop there. In order for distance to be a meaningful expression, the two objects to which it refers must be *situated in relatable space* and their *positions* compared. 'What is the distance between the syllable A and a table?' was the nonsense question posed by Marx to emphasise his point. Their situation or position became the common 'substance' *possessed* by the objects and *expressed* in the measure of distance. Marx repeated this same type of analogy as an afterthought on Bailey later on in notebook XV of the 'Theories' manuscript (appended as a footnote, *TSV*, III, 143–4). Here Marx referred to two plane figures, a triangle and a parallelogram. Their different physical appearances could be transcended in their comparison by recognising their common 'substance' as the measure of area (cf. *TSV*, III, 160–1).

Furthermore, Marx was not impressed by Bailey's argument that the common *causal* essence of exchange value was to be found in the factors affecting the perceived utility of commodities (*TSV*, III, 144). He quoted Bailey's summary piece about the influence of the 'mind' on exchange value determination: 'Whatever circumstances . . . act with assignable influence, whether mediately or immediately, on the *mind* in the interchange of commodities, may be considered as causes of value' (quoted *TSV*, III, 163).[45] Marx thought that this argument failed to contribute to the comprehension of exchange value: 'Instead of explaining what he himself understands by "value" (or "cause of value") Bailey tells us that it is something which buyers and sellers imagine in the act of exchange' (*TSV*, III, 163). Marx had no time for such a contentless approach to the explanation of the existence of exchange value.

In discussing the causal origins of exchange value, though, Bailey did find himself discussing the primary role of production costs (*TSV*, III, 163ff.).[46] He recognised clearly that the production decision will be taken only in the expectation that realised exchange value will exceed costs. Then, abstracting from the modifying effects of monopoly power,[47] Bailey argued: 'The cost would regulate the point at which the competition of the producers would fix each article, or their ordinary prices'. More than this, though, consistency demanded that he add 'and a knowledge of these prices would *operate on his mind* in the exchanges which he made'.[48] Bailey provided little explanation as to the precise meaning of this argument and hastened on to consider the determination of production costs themselves.[49] As Marx noted, Bailey saw merit in Torrens's version of this determination under capitalist conditions of production[50] and rejected the idea that the embodied-labour principle could be retained under such conditions.[51] Marx's response to this was to repeat his argument that capital advanced related to only part of the requirements in explaining how 'ordinary prices' are determined. Without articulation to the embodied-labour root of exchange value, given the uniform rate of profit axiom, the *existence* of the 'ordinary price' category could not be accounted for except by simply assuming that it does. Marx had established that an appropriately formulated analysis could do much better.[52]

Bailey's treatment of money as a third, mediating commodity in the exchange relation also came in for critical scrutiny by Marx. It was here that Bailey recognised the need for a 'common denomination' in order to give *expression* to exchange value (*TSV*, III, 160).[53] Different commodity forms face each other in the exchange relation. As we have seen, this phenomenon posed for Marx the puzzle of how such a relation could be expressed. Thus, commodities 'insofar as they are Values, [are] only different or equal in quantity, but they are always quantities of the same quality. *The difficulty is to find this quality*' (*TSV*, III, 160, emphasis added). Bailey handled this puzzle only at the phenomenal level and then by assuming the existence of the money medium: 'Since Mr. Bailey . . . demonstrates that money as an external measure of [exchange] value – and expression of [exchange] value – has fulfilled its purpose, even though it has a *variable* value, he thinks he has done away with the question of the concept of [exchange] value' (*TSV*, III, 145). In all this, the logical priorities were confused in that 'it is not the determination of the product as Value which leads to the establishment of money and which expresses itself in *money*, but it is the existence of money which leads to the fiction of the concept of [exchange] value' (*TSV*, III, 145). For Marx, then, the point to be emphasised was that money 'is already a *representation* of Value and presupposes it' (*TSV*, III, 161). The 'external measure' of exchange value was no substitute for the '*immanent* measure', but Bailey would have denied the existence of the latter, anyway, for he had no appreciation of the need to identify any cause of the existence of exchange value that went beyond its phenomenal appearance (*TSV*, III, 145–6, 155–6).

CHAPTER 7

Reactions to Ricardo's theory: the 'pseudo-disciples'

INTRODUCTION

In reading the works of those whom he interpreted to be the followers of Ricardo, viz. James Mill, John McCulloch and Thomas de Quincey,[1] Marx found little that could be considered to represent clarification or development of the analyses in the *Principles*. Marx's view was that the *Principles* had the potential to be reworked into a much more consistent and coherent analysis of the nature of capitalism. This potential had not been adequately pursued, certainly not by this group of so-called disciples. On the contrary, Marx made some harsh comments about their endeavours to clarify and popularise the essentials of Ricardo's contribution. In this sense, though, de Quincey was an exception, for Marx devoted little attention to his work and expressed no particular views about its intellectual status beyond acknowledging its strong links with Ricardo's *Principles*.[2]

It was to James Mill and McCulloch that Marx devoted most critical attention, albeit within the ambit of his own critico-theoretical framework. As far as Marx was concerned, these two writers had done little to close off the openings for the destructive Ricardo-critique underway at the time, in spite of their good intentions. Their superficial and largely oversimplified evangelism on behalf of Ricardo failed to correct the logical deficiencies of the complex theoretical core of the *Principles*. The confusing and incomplete message of Ricardo's legacy was soon to be all but obliterated by a wide range of dissenters.[3]

Marx found James Mill's work to have stayed closer to that of the master, Ricardo, than was the case with McCulloch. In Mill, Marx identified an 'inveterate' and 'zealous' Ricardian (*TSV*, III, 91, 95) who was 'the first to present Ricardo's theory in systematic form, even though he did it only in rather abstract outlines. What he tries to achieve is formal, logical consistency' (*TSV*, III, 84). In so doing, though, the 'real contradictions' of capitalism were turned into 'only apparent ones' and Mill tried to 'disprove the theoretical contradictions' of the *Principles* that were all too evident to himself and to others (*TSV*, III, 85). The irony was that Marx concluded that Mill's analytical endeavours became part of the burgeoning downfall of the 'Ricardian' message, for 'he entangles himself in contradictions and with his attempt to solve these he demonstrates the beginning *disintegration of the theory* which he dogmatically espouses' (*TSV*, III, 84–5).

Marx was much harsher on McCulloch and revealed little respect for his work at all. McCulloch was 'the vulgariser of Ricardian political economy and simultaneously the most pitiful embodiment of its decline' who 'did more to undermine the whole foundation of Ricardian theory than all the attacks of its opponents' (*TSV*, III, 168, 88; cf. 172, 182, 183, 185). Indeed, he did not 'understand the essential kernel of Ricardo's teaching' and led the 'total decline of the Ricardian system into twaddle – a decline which prides itself on being its most consistent exposition' (*TSV*, III, 171). Marx felt also that McCulloch had consciously used Ricardo's work in a distorted way in order to serve the Whigs' political cause (*TSV*, III, 172). And, to cap it all, he made numerous assertions that McCulloch had plagiarised the work of various writers (*TSV*, III, 172, 178, 182, 183, 185, 186, 187).

Overall, then, Marx found that the potentials of the powerful analytical insights in Ricardo's *Principles* had been inherited and taken up by two writers who left them unrealised in their misguided propagandist efforts. It was they 'who, in order to reason the contradictory phenomena out of existence seek to bring them into direct conformity with the general law [of Value] by gabble, by scholastic and absurd definitions and distinctions, with the result . . . that the foundation itself vanishes' (*TSV*, III, 29). And, Marx added, 'Mill begins this process' of decline into scholastic obscurantism, while 'In the case of an *unscrupulous blockhead* like *McCulloch*, this manner assumes a swaggering shamelessness' (*TSV*, III, 87).

In concluding these introductory notes on Ricardo's 'pseudo-disciples' as they were perceived by Marx, it must be added that the extremely damning assessments just outlined were not very effectively backed up by textual evidence. They should be read as suggestive of Marx's *attitude* towards these writers rather than as being indicative of the substantive objectives of his critique. Marx did not ever set out *simply* to discredit the work of his antecedents. His critique remained firmly directed at some particular aspects of the theory of Value and distribution as it was handled by the writers concerned. In this case, the vituperative overburden can probably be ascribed to Marx's extreme intellectual disappointment with the abandonment and loss of the potential of Ricardo's *Principles*.

JAMES MILL

James Mill's *Elements of Political Economy* went through three editions between 1821 and 1826. The second and third editions involved some significant extensions and clarifications of the analyses in their predecessors. These included work on the section on exchange value in the second edition of 1824 and on the section on profit in the third edition of 1826.[4] Marx consulted both the first and second editions, the first in the form of its French translation, but made no reference to the third edition. It is interesting also to recall that the *Elements* was one of the earliest works of political economy that Marx read during his studies of 1844, so his acquaintance with it was a long-established one.[5]

It is perhaps not unreasonable to suggest that Marx expected too much from his reading of the *Elements* as a 'successor' to Ricardo's *Principles*. We are now more sensitive than Marx had chosen to be to the fact that the book was intended only as an elementary textbook on political economy. Today's assessments of its status in the history of political economy are more appropriately tempered as a consequence. Mill made this 'school-book' status of his work explicit in the Preface to the first edition of the *Elements*,[6] and yet it seems to have been read as a *treatise* by Marx. It should really have been no surprise that the work avoided the contradictory and more complex aspects of Ricardo's *Principles*

Marx's critique of the *Elements* revealed a mixed attitude towards Mill. He was variously accused of 'vulgarisation', of 'sophism' and 'scholasticism', of 'absurdity' and of 'tautological circumlocutions' (*TSV*, III, 85, 87, 92, 97). At other points, it is possible to sense a certain respect from Marx for the way Mill had struggled with Ricardo's ideas and kept some of the essentials of capitalism before the reader (*TSV*, III, 85, 85–6, 88, 93, 97–8). It was still the case, though, that the general tenets of Marx's critique applied to Mill just as they had done to Ricardo. Mill's object was the phenomenal appearance of capitalism as an immutable economic and social system. His method was a-historical and non-dialectical. He sought no explanations which reached beyond describing the phenomenal and his categories were strictly empirical.

More specifically, three main aspects of Mill's *Elements* were of concern to Marx in his critique. Two related to the treatment of Value and distribution and are included in the present discussion: first, Mill's failure clearly to identify the origin of surplus Value as the source of profit; and secondly, his unsuccessful endeavour to provide an analysis of the capital–labour relation which explained its nature consistently with the embodied-labour principle of exchange value. Marx also touched very briefly on Mill's arguments about the relation of the agricultural rate of profits to the general rate. The third main aspect of the critique involved Mill's analysis of the circulation and realisation of commodities as exchange values (*TV*, III, 100ff.), and this will be taken up in Part IV below.

With respect to Mill's lack of an explanation of profit that was consistent with and validly articulated to his essential recognition of the embodied-labour premise of exchange value,[7] Marx focused on his handling of the relation of '*time as such*' to profit generation. Mill posed the problem as follows:[8]

> time does nothing. How then can it create value? Time is a mere abstract term. It is a word, a sound. And it is the very same logical absurdity, to talk of an abstract unit measuring value, and of time creating it. (quoted *TSV*, III, 86.)

In effect Mill puzzled over the effect on profit of the total circulation time of capital which reflected the use of more roundabout processes of production. The *time* involved, for no apparent reason was observed to add to the exchange value of a commodity produced by such a process. Couching the problem in terms of the maturation period required to get wine ready for the market, Mill 'solved' the puzzle by imputing additional 'labour' to the time dimension of the process.[9] To Marx, such a sophism was quite unacceptable. It forced the empirical observation into the preconceived mould of theory by means of a distortion rather than presenting an explanation of it that was logically consistent with the tenets of the theory. As Marx rather pointedly put it: '*Mill "lied" his way – so to speak – out of the difficulty by saying that one can consider the time in which the wine* ... is in the cellar as a period when it is soaking up labour' (*TSV*, III, 177). Thus:

> Here the contradiction between the general law [of Value] and further developments in the concrete circumstances, is to be resolved not by the discovery of the connecting links but by directly subordinating and immediately adapting the concrete to the abstract. (*TSV*, III, 87.)

The 'connecting links' were quite obvious to Marx. In the example cited by Mill, it was not *Value* at all that was at issue. In valuing the wine, what was necessary was that the realised exchange value should return the general rate of profits on the capital employed for whatever period was involved in the maturation. The fact that this was constant capital only in the form of maturing wine stock and that no variable capital was involved was irrelevant. The process of competition would ensure that the *cost price* of the wine would be appropriate to return the general rate of profits on wine capital whatever the time profile of the production process itself (*TSV*, III, 86–7). Without an appreciation of the nature of the articulation between embodied-labour exchange value and cost price, and between immediate surplus Value generation and the general rate of profits, Mill could not have hoped to grasp this solution to the 'time' problem.

For Marx, the problem of formulating the relation between capital and labour in such a way as to explain the origin of surplus Value consistently with the embodied-labour principle of Value was a crucial one. Any analysis which took the principle as its premise had to devise a way of distinguishing between the Value of 'labour' and the Value delivered by 'labour' in production. The existence of a surplus Value depended on the latter exceeding the former.

Marx did not pursue Mill's analysis of exchange value determination as such, probably because he found it to be similar to that of Ricardo. In the *Elements* it is evident that Mill was conscious of the need to formulate a cost price category, the realisation of which would yield a uniform rate of profit on all capitals, as the basis for market price, even though this latter price would frequently reflect the modifying effects of supply and demand imbalance.[10] Most important here, though, was the fact that Mill looked beyond the cost price category to its roots in embodied-labour exchange value. Thus he wrote: 'It . . . appears by the clearest evidence, that quantity of labour in the last resort, determines the proportion in which commodities exchange for one another.'[11] But, as with Ricardo, these roots were left without any formal articulation to cost price and the uniform rate of profit, even though Mill wanted to preserve the link between exchange value and embodied labour.

In arguing the form of the capital–labour relation, Mill found it difficult to adhere to the embodied-labour premise in the valuation of 'labour'. His argument on this issue was presented in the following piece:[12]

> Instead, however, of waiting till the commodity is produced, and [. . .] the value of it is realised, it has been found to suit *much better* the convenience of the labourers to receive their share *in advance*. The shape under which it has been found most convenient for all parties that they should receive it, is that of wages. When the share of the commodity which belongs to the labourer has been all received in the shape of wages, the commodity itself belongs to the capitalist, he having, in reality, bought the share of the labourer and paid for it in advance. (quoted *TSV*, III, 88–9.)

Marx took the refutation of this apparently innocuous statement very seriously and devoted considerable critical effort to probing its misleading inferences (*TSV*, III, 88ff.).

First of all, Marx objected to the harmonious tenor of the argument in which the capital–labour relation was portrayed as a simple matter of 'convenience' to the parties involved. The effect of Mill's piece was socially to sterilise the relation by having 'labour' as such disappear. Social conflict was obscured by what appeared to be an exchange based transfer to commodities between two 'owners' (*TSV*, III, 89–90, 93–4). Such an *equal exchange* between capital and labour could not provide any insight into the *origin* of surplus Value.

Marx devised an arithmetical example in order to explain the difficulties which Mill left unresolved by posing the capital–labour relation in this way (*TSV*, III, 90ff.).[13] A worker is engaged to produce linen. In a particular period, the portion of the total output ascribed to him is six yards of the material. That is, the output per worker is six yards. In accordance with Mill's argument, '2 yards are assumed to be equal to the Value of the labour which he [the worker] has added'. These two yards are 'sold' to the capitalist. If the money exchange value of linen is one shilling per yard then the problem posed is what the worker is to receive for 'his' two yards. Since these two yards embody the *Value added* by the worker to the constant capital with which he worked, their Value must comprise both his own commodity wage Value and the surplus Value. Then, if the *worker* receives two shillings for 'his' two yards, the surplus Value would be zero. Or rather, the surplus Value that *must* exist as a result of this capitalist endeavour is left without any explanation that links it directly to the embodied-labour principle and the capital–labour relation *per se*. The only thing possible is that the worker receives less than two shillings for 'his' linen in an *unequal exchange*. But this implied that 'linen, and any other commodity, is sold at its Value when the capitalist sells it, but *below* its Value when the worker sells it' and posed the questions: 'Why then should . . . [the worker] not receive the full Value of the 2 yards, like any other seller of 2 yards of linen . . . ?' and 'Why is the quantity of materialised labour received by the worker as wages not equal to the quantity of immediate labour which he gives in exchange for his wages?' (*TSV*, III, 89, 90). It was evident to Marx that Mill's argument was inconsistent with his espousal of embodied labour as the ultimate determinant of the exchange value of commodities, including 'labour' as a capitalist 'purchase'.

Further difficulties in Mill's handling of the capital–labour relation were evident to Marx in the following passage:[14]

> [. . .] *what determines* the share of the labourer, or the proportion in which the commodity, or commodity's worth, is divided between him and the capitalist [?] Whatever the share of the labourer, such is the rate of wages . . . It is very evident, that the share of the two parties is the subject of a *bargain* between them [. . .] All bargains, when left in freedom, are determined by competition, and the terms alter according to the *state of supply and demand*. (quoted *TSV*, III, 93 and 95.)

Here Mill was in effect referring to the determination of what Marx posited as the 'worker's' two yards of linen in the above example. That is, 'we now ask which is his "share" of the product, that is, *which* is *his* product?' But, if a surplus is to exist, '*his* product and his *product* are two quite different things', and 'His product is thus a mere phrase, since the quantity of Value which he receives from the capitalist is not determined by his own production.' Marx's conclusion was: 'Mill has thus merely removed the difficulty one step' (*TSV*, III, 94) and left the question as to how 'labour' is to be valued unresolved.

Mill's statement superficially comprised some appropriate elements for a solution, but no valid explanation of the capital–labour relation as the source of surplus Value emerged (*TSV*, III, 94ff.). The idea of a 'bargain' necessarily implied some confrontation between capital and labour, a point which Marx noted (*TSV*, III, 96–7). For Mill, though, the confrontation was contained by the socially 'neutral' expedient of supply and demand. This could not *explain* the actual level of the commodity wage. In Marx's vision of the capital–labour relation, logical priority had to be ascribed to the determination of the commodity wage as embodying the Value of labour power. The wage was the result of the capital–labour 'bargain' in which the conflict was eventually contained by the working out of power relativities between the classes (*TSV*, III, 94). The effect of supply and demand imbalance in the 'labour' market was merely to *modify* the necessarily pre-existing resolution of the socio-political process. And, when Mill himself analysed the 'dynamics' of the 'labour' market, the reality of the capital–labour conflict and its containment under the influence of competition remained obscured no longer. The fiction of the equal 'commodity' exchange disappeared to be replaced by a vision of a struggle between the power of the capitalist and the necessary fatalism of the workers. But, without the *concept* of labour power, the working out of the competitive struggle had no quantitative reference point and Mill's analysis of *change* could only begin from an arbitrarily presupposed labour 'share' (*TSV*, III, 96–7).[15]

With respect to the determination of the uniform general rate of profits, Mill argued quite explicitly that it depended on the rate of profit on marginally applied capital in agriculture: 'All other profits . . . must sink to the level of agricultural profits' (quoted *TSV*, III, 99).[16] As we have seen, Marx's interpretation of the relationship between agricultural and manufacturing rates of profit was quite different. It was explained as an integral part of his analysis of *absolute rent* in which the key point was made that the manufacturing sector cost prices returned rate of profits which provided the basis for cost prices in agriculture. Agricultural commodities then sold at their immediate embodied-labour Values and the excess over cost price was expropriated by landowners as rent.[17] Marx simply reiterated here that there was no room for a dominant agricultural rate of profit in this vision of production and pricing (*TSV*, III, 99–100). In short, Mill's argument followed Ricardo's on this point and suffered from the same limitations.

McCULLOCH

It is not possible to be sure just how much of McCulloch's considerable contribution to political economy Marx had read.[18] The critique made direct references to only three pieces, viz. the *first* edition of *The Principles of Political Economy with a Sketch of the Rise and Progress of the Science* (1825), one article from the *Edinburgh Review* (March 1824), and the *first* edition of the 'Notes and Dissertations' appended to McCulloch's 1828 edition of Adam Smith's *Wealth of Nations*. The explicit references to the first two pieces were very brief, although in places Marx referred in general terms to the contents of the *Principles* and compared it with the 'Notes', so it is probable that he had at least read parts of that work. For the purposes of the critique, he relied almost exclusively on the 'Notes' as being adequately indicative of McCulloch's ideas on exchange value and its relation to distribution for his purposes.[19]

In considering McCulloch's handling of the analysis of exchange value and distribution in the light of the potential of Ricardo's contribution, Marx drew attention to three, interdependent issues. First, there was what McCulloch argued to be the *source* of profits; secondly, his endeavour to analyse the capital–labour relations consistently with the embodied-labour origin of exchange value; and thirdly, his views on the formation of a general rate of profits on capital (*TSV*, III, 176). Marx based his critique on the reasonable assumption that McCulloch believed embodied-labour to be the *ultimate* source of a commodity having exchange value, given that it was useful. The existence of capital and its profit was then 'added on', as it were, by appropriate reasoning. In Marx's interpretation of the logic involved, this should have led McCulloch to pursue further the implied principle of surplus Value evident in Ricardo's work. He had failed to do this and, as a consequence, had to resort to some quite peculiar sophistry in order to handle the vital analytical issues raised here.

The problem of 'explaining' the source of profit was 'solved' in the simplest manner by McCulloch. In his 'Notes', the existence of profit was argued to be a *motivational requirement* of capitalist production. From this it followed that profit must exist and therefore, as immediate embodied-labour exchange value could not include such a profit, commodities had to be sold above their exchange value so determined. The argument from the 'Notes' quoted by Marx (*TSV*, III, 173) made these assertions quite clear. McCulloch wrote that a commodity 'will never . . . exchange for, or buy exactly the same quantity of labour that producted it' and added to this the following footnote by way of clarification:[20]

> *In point of fact*, it will always exchange for more; *and it is this excess that constitutes profits*. No capitalist could have *any motive* to exchange the produce of a given quantity of labour already performed for the produce of the same *quantity of labour to be performed*. This would be *to lend* without receiving any interest on the loan. (quoted *TSV*, III, 173.)

There was no logically sound *explanation* for profit here. The exchange of equivalent exchange values realised a profit '*upon alienation* . . . explained not by the fact that it corresponds to the law of Value, but by declaring that buyers and sellers have no "motive" for buying and selling in accordance with the law of Value' (*TSV*, III, 174). For McCulloch, the embodied-labour principle of exchange value could not, *per se*, account for profit.[21]

In considering further McCulloch's argument here, Marx went on to refer to the distinction between different exchange value concepts that appeared in a passage in the 'Notes' (quoted *TSV*, III, 173; cf. 169, 175–6).[22] 'Real value' related to the component of exchange value that existed as a consequence of *production*, while 'relative value' expressed this exchange value through other commodities *and 'labour'* with the same 'real value'. In this distincton, Marx noted once again the inappropriate treatment of the relation between capital and labour as just another exchange. Such treatment left the political economists, including McCulloch, with the need to 'add on' some further exchange value at the point of exchange in order to have a profit appear. The simple logic of the matter, as Marx saw it, was that commodities as capital commanded more living labour time than labour embodied in the exchange value of 'labour' itself. That is, a part of the living labour was not paid for in this 'pseudo-exchange'. McCulloch's logic did not recognise this and he was left with the puzzle of how profit could be *explained* rather than merely *justified*.

The third, related issue of exchange value and distribution analysis that Marx extracted from McCulloch's 'Notes' was that of establishing the existence of a uniformly applicable general rate of profits in the presence of capitals of varying compositions. Or, as Marx saw it: 'This is indeed the unrecognised problem of how Values are converted into cost prices' (*TSV*, III, 176). McCulloch should have been at least astute enough to realise that just 'adding on' such a profit rate was no solution to how the rate emerged from the valuation process. For, as Marx recalled: 'The difficulties arising in this context were discovered by Ricardo himself (although not in their general form) and set forth by him as *exceptions* to the law of Value' (*TSV*, III, 177). It was Marx's reading of the record that McCulloch had taken up this 'exceptions' problem and endeavoured to 'solve' it on the basis of the 'insipid evasion' used by James Mill, viz. by resorting to the absurd idea that embodied labour actually 'worked' to create exchange value during the efflux of time *per se* (*TSV*, III, 177–8). Thus: 'McCulloch gets round the difficulty by calling the use value of commodities – exchange value, and the operations in which they are involved as use values, the services they render as use values in production – *labour*' (*TSV*, III, 179). The astounding piece quoted by Marx from the 'Notes' ran: '*labour* may be *properly* defined to be any sort of action or operation, whether performed by man, the lower animals, machinery, or natural agents, that tends to bring about any desirable result' (*TSV*, III, 179).[23] And, after he had '*happily transformed commodities into workers*', McCulloch followed this with the inevitable idea that the 'services' performed by these 'workers' must be paid for in the form of the '*wages of accumulated labour* – alias *profit*' (*TSV*, III, 180). So it was, then, that he established 'proof that equal profit on equal capitals, whether they set large or small amounts of labour in motion, follows directly from the determination of Value by *labour time*' (*TSV*, III, 180; cf. 184–5).[24]

At this point, Marx felt that it was important to remember that Ricardo had explicitly rejected this Mill–McCulloch approach when it was floated by Say as involving the payment of profit for the 'productive services of capital' (*TSV*, III, 180–1). Ricardo was quite clear on this: '*machines* and natural agents might very greatly add to the riches of a country', but they do 'not . . . add any thing to the value of those riches' (quoted *TSV*, III, 181).[25] For Ricardo, and Adam Smith before him, labour was always and remained a 'socially determined *human activity*'; and, Marx added: 'It is precisely through the consistency with which he treats the [exchange] value of commodities as merely "representing" socially determined labour, that Ricardo differs from the other economists' (*TSV*, III, 181). Here the misguided endeavours of McCulloch were in distinct contrast with probably the most fundamental analytical premise of Ricardo's *Principles* (*TSV*, III, 181–2).

McCulloch complicated matters further for himself by making the point that only the 'labour' of those 'non-labour' forces of production that could be *monopolised* could add to exchange value (*TSV*, III, 182).[26] What he failed to recognise here was that *all such forces*, monopolised or not, were 'natural' in their *operation* and all were *free* to the production process. So, 'what is done by cotton, wool, iron or machinery' is done 'gratuitously';

and: 'The machine costs money, but the operation of the machine is not paid for. No use value of any kind of commodity costs anything after its exchange value has been paid' (*TSV*, III, 182). These forces, then, cannot *add to* exchange value. They merely act to transmit *pro rata* some *pre-existing* embodied labour to the newly produced commodity as their originating physical mechanism is 'used up'. In this argument, Marx was again in accord with Ricardo's views (quoted *TSV*, III, 183).[27] The point that Marx wanted to emphasise was that the idea of monopolisation *as it was expressed by McCulloch* was irrelevant in any discussion of profit. Monopolisation of the means of production did allow the capitalists to exploit labour, but this was a socio-political phenomenon which had nothing to do with the operation of the forces of production themselves. Neither profit itself nor its uniform general rate could be *explained* simply by ascribing productive powers to the operation of 'monopolised' forces or instruments of production.

DE QUINCEY

Marx took de Quincey's 'Ricardian' *bona fides* for granted[28] and did not pursue his work beyond a couple of brief comments (*TSV*, III, 123–4). He considered the *Dialogues of Three Templars on Political Economy: Chiefly in Relation to the Principles of Mr. Ricardo*, originally published serially in the March, April and May 1824 editions of the *London Magazine*,[29] to be de Quincey's main contribution to the progress of political economy. Marx added: 'A later work by the same author: *The Logic of Political Economy*, Edinburgh, 1844, is weaker' (*TSV*, III, 124).[30]

On reading the *Dialogues*, Marx probably found it to be, as far as its argument went, so close to Ricardo's own discussion that it warranted no separate detailed critique.[31] As far as Marx was concerned, that de Quincey had understood *the* central issue of political economy was evident in his premise that 'all [. . .] difficulties' of the science 'will be found reducible . . . [to] this: *What is the ground of exchangeable value*?' (quoted *TSV*, III, 123).[32] In endeavouring to answer this question, he had begun appropriately with the embodied-labour principle and recognised some of its difficulties. Marx's assessment was, though, that de

Quincey had not effectively transcended these Value puzzles:

> In this work, the inadequacies of the Ricardian view are often pointedly set forth, although the dialectical depth is more affected than real. The real difficulties, which arise not out of the determination of Value, but from Ricardo's inadequate elaboration of his ideas on this basis, and from his arbitrary attempt to make concrete relations directly fit the simple relation of Value, are in no way resolved or even grasped. (*TSV*, III, 123–4.)

Marx cited only one particular substantive point from the *Dialogues* as warranting explicit mention. This was de Quincey's argument that the existence of *Value* as such, what he called 'real value', should not be confused with its *expression* as exchange value in relative terms. Marx quoted some extracts from 'Dialogue the Fourth: On the Use and Abuse of Two Celebrated Distinctions in the Theory of Value' (*TSV*, III, 124)[33] in which the Templars were engaged in a discussion about the 'real' and 'nominal' forms of exchange value. In de Quincey's view, this issue was of great significance in political economy while at the same time being of great difficulty and a source of some confusion.[34] The thrust of the argument was that expressions of 'relative' exchange value could not capture the essence of exchange value itself. For this, some *absolute* basis was needed and this could only be found in the embodied labour consequent upon a commodity's production.[35] With this unfinished prelude, Marx fully agreed.

JOHN STUART MILL

The critical notes on John Stuart Mill were found in notebooks VII and VIII of the 'Theories of Surplus Value' manuscript. This location is significant, in that it indicates that the piece was written prior to the critique of Ricardo's *Principles* in notebooks XI to XIII. Consequently, it suggests that Marx's work on Mill was somewhat premature. Ideally, the critique should have been based on a thorough understanding of Ricardo's thought from which Mill worked, an understanding that Marx could not have possessed until after his subsequent major critique of the

Principles. What was evident, though, was that Marx intended to include the piece on Mill in the section 'Disintegration of the Ricardian School' along with the work on the writers so far considered in the present chapter. Mill was cited under this heading in the contents list on the cover of notebook XIV (*TSV*, I, 38) and the critique appears with the material from this notebook in the published version of the 'Theories' manuscript (*TSV*, III, 190ff.; cf. *TSV*, I, 481 ed.n. 63).

One feature of the critique of Mill that can possibly be ascribed to its premature writing is its extremely limited scope relative to Mill's huge intellectual output. Mill wrote much that dealt with the Value and distribution issues upon which Marx focused his critical attention. This applied especially to Mill's *magnum opus*, *Principles of Political Economy with Some of their Applications to Social Philosophy* (1848). And yet Marx rejected any reading of this major contribution to the evolution of political economy. In what amounted to an extreme underestimation of the importance of Mill's work, Marx chose to focus exclusively on *part* of one brief essay, 'On Profits and Interest', from the series *Essays on Some Unsettled Questions of Political Economy* published in 1844. This particular essay was written in 1829, very early in Mill's career, and he had occasion to express his own dissatisfaction with it.[36] Such was Marx's judgment here that he considered that this essay contained 'all that is original in Mr. John Stuart Mill's writings about political economy' (*TSV*, III, 190). Just how he would have treated Mill had he rewritten the critique after dealing with Ricardo in detail and after finally preparing the manuscript for publication, is impossible to say. The many brief pieces on Mill in *Capital* do not suggest that Marx would have broadened the basis of his assessment by very much, although in this later work, the *Principles of Political Economy* received some attention (e.g. *K*(PE), I, 652–4, 760, 998).[37]

There were several respects in which the ideas of Mill appeared to be similar to those of Marx. Some of these were dealt with in the 'Theories' manuscript, although not in any detail and probably not with the appropriate degree of generosity of interpretation. The situation was similar where the same ideas came up in *Capital*.

Marx and Mill shared similar views about the role of the '*productivity*' of capital and labour in the production and distribution processes. Even in the early essay referred to above, Mill wrote very pointedly that '*Capital*, strictly speaking, has no *productive power*. The only productive power is that of labour; assisted no doubt, by tools, and acting upon materials' (quoted *TSV*, III, 236).[38] Moreover, he was careful in separating the *operational functions* of the forces of production from their *mobilisation* by capital: 'Wages have no productive power; they are the price of a productive power.' Mill went on to confirm that 'capital which is expended in the wages of labour, is only the means by which the capitalist procures to himself . . . the use of that labour *in which the power of production really resides*.' Thus Mill concluded: 'We need not . . . altogether proscribe the expression, "productive power of capital"; but we should carefully note, that it can only mean the quantity of *real productive power* which the capitalist, by means of his capital, can command' (quoted, in part, *TSV*, III, 236).[39] Marx recognised this similarity in passing and went as far as giving Mill credit for having seen capital as 'a production relation' on the basis of his having argued that its apparent productive power came from putting in motion the '*real productive power*' of labour (*TSV*, III, 236). Both writers agreed that capital as means of production had a role to play in increasing the physical productivity of labour time, but that it could not *add to* the embodied-labour exchange value already contained in those means and the raw materials with which they and the labour worked jointly in production (*TSV*, III, 190ff.).[40] Unfortunately, Marx did not pay due regard to these similar thoughts in his critique of Mill.

Also in this early essay, Mill was not very clear about the *source* of profit. He situated profit correctly as 'the surplus which remains to the capitalist after replacing his capital' and he well realised that this assertion, in and of itself, did not constitute an *explanation* of profit. The addition of the idea that capital was somehow 'productive' did nothing to help, either.[41] In the following piece, there was some hint of the origin of profit, but the idea was not pursued by Mill at this early stage: 'In short, if we compare the *price paid* for labour and tools with what that labour and those tools will *produce*, from this ratio we may calculate the rate of profit'.[42] Given the reference to the rate of profit *ratio* here, the term 'produce' must have meant production of exchange value. What did not seem clear to Mill as yet was the distinction between 'labour' and 'tools' in this context. A generous reading, though, would have linked this piece to the notion that *only labour* was productive of exchange value and reveal an adumbration that the surplus could have come only from *labour*. Marx's insistence that Mill could only conceive of 'profit on alienation' was quite inappropriate here (*TSV*, III, 192, 200, 201). And, quite inconsistently, he wrote later in the 'Theories' manuscript of Mill's expression of 'the principle that profit is equal to surplus Value, surplus labour' (*TSV*, III, 506). Marx must have referred here to the *Principles of Political Economy* where Mill was much more explicit about the source of profit when he wrote that: 'The cause of profit is that labour produces more than is required for its support . . . We thus see that profit arises, not from the incident of exchange, but from the productive power of labour'.[43] The clear *principle* of surplus Value enunciated here was never referred to by Marx *as such*, even though he quoted this passage in full in *Capital*, Volume I (*K*, I, 483).

Having noted all this, it is still important to keep in mind that Mill did not formulate a *theory* of surplus Value that could be said to *explain* profit in the socio-political sense that was so crucial for Marx. Perhaps this different approach to the same perceived principle of the origin of profit can be explained by the fact that the two writers had different 'visions' of the capitalist system and different purposes in their respective investigations of it.

Mill was a critic of the *form* and some of the *results* of capitalism. He found it to be a socio-economic order that was correct in principle, but which with some adjustment, could improve the equity of its delivery of benefits to the bulk of the population.[44] In the light of these views, Mill's concept of profit based upon a labour surplus was not designed to highlight any *exploitation* of labour by capital. He went no further than to argue that distribution was a social discretionary phenomenon and thus amenable to change.

Marx viewed capitalism and its distribution process quite differently. For him, distribution was an objective consequence of capitalist production and he took exception to Mill's attitude.

> How absurd it is . . . for John Stuart Mill and others to conceive bourgeois forms of production as absolute, but the bourgeois

> forms of distribution as historically relative, hence transistory . . . The form of production is simply the form of distribution seen from a different point of view. The specific features – and therefore also the specific limitation – which set bounds to bourgeois distribution, enter into bourgeois production itself, as a determining factor, which overlaps and dominates production. (*TSV*, III, 84.)

The origin of profit in surplus labour represented an integration of production and distribution based on exploitation of labour by capital in which social discretion could have little role. Capitalism was beset by immanent contradictions of this kind and was, consequently, doomed by its own hand. It was Marx's *raison d'être* in political economy to reveal these contradictions and the inevitable role they would play in the demise of capitalism. In this context, the significance of the principle of surplus labour was much more profound than that envisaged by Mill.

Moreover, Mill watered down the principle enunciated above by bringing in the notion of profit as a reward for 'abstinence', an idea adumbrated by Nassau Senior in *An Outline of the Science of Political Economy* (1836). In 'Theories of Surplus Value', Marx gave little attention to the work of Senior. Only at one point did he mention the idea of 'abstinence' in passing and made no particular comment on its status. At another point in the manuscript, though, he effectively ruled out any relevance of the idea as it related to capital accumulated by saving out of profits because the profit had been expropriated through exploitation of labour in the first place (*TSV*, III, 421). Marx referred again to 'abstinence' in *Capital*, Volume I where he noted that: 'John Stuart Mill . . . copies both Ricardo's theory of profit, and annexes to it Senior's "remuneration of abstinence". He is . . . at home with absurd and flat contradictions' (*K*(PE), I, 744n.). In assessing this inference, it must be recalled that for Mill, the surplus principle of profit had nothing to do with exploitation as Marx understood it. For Marx, the 'abstinence' idea *was* a contradiction to the surplus principle in that it had been posited to *explain*, as well as justify, profit. However, Mill rose above this 'vulgar' viewpoint to some extent in that he applied the 'abstinence' idea to the argument that only by saving could capital accumulate, and only out of profit could saving occur, and that the motive for accumulation was the expectation of profit. It followed, then, that profit was a necessary condition for 'abstinence' in these two senses. A more careful reading of Mill by Marx may have caused him to temper his remark on the use of 'abstinence'.

Most of the critique of Mill comprised a lengthy and somewhat laborious analysis of an arithmetical example used in the essay 'On Profits and Interest'. Mill's example was designed to establish the validity of Ricardo's argument that wages and the rate of profit were inversely related.[45] The idea behind the example was quite straightforward and really did not warrant the extensive critical reworking that Marx undertook (*TSV*, III, 195ff.). As it turned out, the only lasting significance of the critique was that it gave him an opportunity again to work through the factors that affected the determination of the rate of profit as distinct from the rate of surplus Value.

The essence of Mill's example may be summarised as follows.[46] It comprised two stages. In the first stage, during a particular period, sixty men paid one-quarter of corn each as wages and working with tools and seed valued at 60 quarters of corn produce 180 quarters of corn. The tools and the corn with which the workers worked in the current period had been produced in the preceding period by forty men paid one-quarter of corn each and assumed to be working with no inputs other than their own labour.

In the second stage, the current period's production of corn is now assumed to involve only labour. This change is made possible by the invention of 'some contrivance'. The production of 180 quarters now requires more immediate labour and this is assumed to comprise the sixty men previously employed plus forty more no longer required to produce tools and seed. Each worker is again paid one quarter of corn so the real cost of labour remains at 100 quarters in the second stage as it was in the first stage. The difference in the second stage is that there is no 'profit' to be paid on the input of tools and seed, an amount of 20 quarters. Thus, by virtue of the change in the overall production process that involved dispensing with tools and seed as means of production, the 'cost' of producing the 180 quarters of corn has fallen from 120 to 100 quarters.

The effect of this change is perceived in the rate of profit on total 'corn' capital advanced in each stage.

$$\text{stage 1. rate of profit} = \frac{180 - (60 + 60)}{120} = 50 \text{ per cent}$$

$$\text{stage 2. rate of profit} = \frac{180 - 100}{100} = 80 \text{ per cent}$$

The rate of profit has *risen* as between the two analytical stages even though the wage 'cost' of the labour input has not changed.

For Mill, the significance of this example was that it implied that the inverse relation between wages and the rate of profit posited by Ricardo had broken down. However, he hastened to add that this difficulty was only apparent, for: 'It is remarkable how very slight a modification will suffice to render Mr. Ricardo's doctrine completely true'.[47] The 'modification' referred to was to recognise that the '*cost of production*' of the wages of labour had actually fallen in the second stage relative to the first. In the first stage, the cost of producing 180 quarters of corn was 120 quarters, including profit on the production of seed and tools. Then, in the second stage, the cost of producing the same output was only 100 quarters. The cost of production of each unit of corn, and thus of the wages of a worker, had fallen by one-sixth. By contrast, had this fall not taken place, the advances to pay the 100 workers in stage 2 would have been 120 quarters and the rate of profit would have remained at 50 per cent. Mill concluded that his arithmetic had confirmed the relation devised by Ricardo: 'It is, therefore, strictly true, that the rate of profits varies inversely as the cost of production of wages. Profits cannot rise, unless the cost of production of wages falls exactly as much; nor fall unless it rises'.[48]

What Marx did not give Mill credit for in his critique of this example was Mill's implicit recognition of the crucial difference that the addition of constant capital (the tools and seed) made to the determination of the rate of profit involved in producing a particular output of commodities. Marx appropriately objected to Mill's way of arguing the point through the 'removal' of the profit on the constant capital from the inputs to production (*TSV*, III, 191, 194). But the situation remained, *in effect*, that Mill's rate of profit expression was correctly s/(c+v) in stage 1 and s/v in stage 2 (where s = surplus Value, c = constant capital advanced and used up, and v = variable capital), even though he did not identify the latter rate as the separate category rate of surplus Value and did not explain where the surplus Value came from at this stage.

Now it was Marx's argument that in spite of what Mill's example apparently showed, the Ricardian inverse relation could only *strictly* apply between the wage rate and the *rate of surplus Value* (*TSV*, III, 191–2, 228). Marx disputed Mill's conclusion that the *only* thing that could affect the rate of profit was the cost of production of wages and, in a complex sequence of arithmetical analyses, endeavoured to refute the conclusion in two ways. First, he argued that Mill's particular analysis was incorrect in finding that the cost of production of wages had fallen by a small proportion between the two stages of the example. Rather, Marx found that it had *risen* by a similar proportion (*TSV*, III, 202ff.). However, this dispute about whether the wage cost had fallen or risen turned out to be relatively insignificant compared to the second element in Marx's refutation. It will not be considered here for that reason, especially in the light of its extreme prolixity. In the second part of the refutation, Marx moved away from the explicit context of Mill's example, but the important issues raised in this generalised analysis of the *logic* of the determination of the rate of profit (*TSV*, III, 228ff.) can be shown to be decisive in his rejection of the inverse relation as it was presented in Mill's example.

The logic of the Value rate of profit was expressed by Marx in the formula:

$$r = \frac{s}{c+v} = \frac{s/v}{1+c/v}$$

It is possible to situate Mill's analysis in the context of this logical framework as follows. In the first stage of the example, the 180 quarters are produced with a rate of surplus Value, s/v, of 100 per cent and a rate of profit of 50 per cent. At this stage, the organic composition of capital, c/v, is unity. By comparison, the second stage has a higher rate of profit of 80 per cent which is equal to the now lower rate of surplus Value. However, the organic composition of capital has decreased from unity to zero. So, even though the fall in the rate of surplus Value puts downward pressure on the rate of profit, two factors are at work in the example to give a net increase in the latter rate. First, the decrease in the organic composition of capital has a positive effect on the rate of profit. Secondly, in stage 2, more labour is employed in the production process and this helps to compensate for the decline in the *rate* of generating surplus Value.

More generally, the rate of profit in Marx's analysis depended very clearly on the Value of labour power as the determinant of the Value of variable capital required to employ a given number of workers for a particular production period. But, the determination of the rate was more complex than this and involved factors that could change independently of 'wages' (*TSV*, III, 191–2, 228). The organic composition of capital had its roots in technological considerations as well and the rate of surplus Value was additionally affected by the length of the working day. Moreover, in more complicated examples, the periodic nature of the production process as a whole had to be considered and the rate of profit actually realised would depend on rates of capital turnover within the periods of production and circulation combined.

In the end, then, Mill's example was shown by Marx to have fallen well short of establishing the unique inverse relation between the wage rate and the rate of profit that Ricardo had espoused. It was the case, though, that in the bulk of Marx's critique, he was preoccupied by the less important point of whether Mill's arithmetic should have revealed a small fall or a small rise in the wage cost instead of pursuing the logical difficulties inherent in the inverse relation itself.

CHAPTER 8

Reactions to Ricardo's theory: the 'radical critics' of capitalism

INTRODUCTION

The 'radical' opponents of capitalism (as it was developing in Britain in the first half of the nineteenth century) with whom Marx dealt in the 'Theories of Surplus Value' manuscript (*TSV*, III, 238ff.) were those whose critical stance he thought to be founded on the premise of embodied labour as the *essential* source of exchange value and the surplus. The link with Ricardo's political economy in particular, apparently expressed by Marx in terms of the 'opposition evoked by the Ricardian theory' (*TSV*, III, 258) should not be exaggerated. The 'radicals' were *opposed* to political economy's treatment of labour under capitalism, including that in Ricardo's *Principles*, and were 'Ricardian' only in the very limited sense of pursuing the logic of the embodied-labour premise.[1] It will be recalled that Marx found *Ricardo* to have struggled hardest to retain this premise in spite of the apparent analytical contradictions to which it gave rise (see chapter 4, pp. 88ff. above). In interpreting *Marx's* critique of the 'radicals' under the heading 'Based on the Ricardian Theory', and in the light of his introductory remarks that in the works considered, the 'opposition . . . takes as its starting point the premises of the economists' and that 'they all derive from the Ricardian form' (*TSV*, III, 238), it is not appropriate to look beyond this essential premise. A reading of the critique makes it quite clear that Marx was not concerned with the doctrinal matters of what 'Ricardian' meant and to what extent the 'radicals' considered themselves to be 'Ricardian' or anti-'Ricardian'.[2]

Furthermore, Marx emphasised that it was *not* the 'socialist' dimensions of these writers' works, if such dimensions existed at all, which led to their being considered. He expressly ruled out writing about works in which 'socialist' themes dominated in the present context. The 'communism' of Owen and the 'socialism' of Fourier and St Simon were not part of his 'plan' at this stage (*TSV*, III, 238).[3]

In the present critique, Marx selected for brief attention *some* of the ideas of the anonymous author of a 'radical' pamphlet, and of Piercy Ravenstone, Thomas Hodgskin and John Francis Bray.[4] Their writings appeared during the period 1821 to 1839, which saw the repeal of the combination laws in 1824–5, the enactment of the Reform Bill and the formation of the Grand National Consolidated Trades Union in 1834, and the subsequent rise of the Chartist Movement. In all, it was a period of social unrest. The interests of land and capital struggled to *retain* their socio-economic and political status while the interests of labour struggled to *advance* theirs. Marx found in each writer's work a central concern for exposing the theoretical foundations of the realities of the situation and role of labour under capitalism (*TSV*, III, 258–60). In this, the 'radicals' reacted against the apologetic obscurantism and contradictions of political economy. The political economists had recognised the unique, or at least dominant, position of labour activity in the generation of exchange value and the accumulation of wealth. To a large extent, in one way or another, the political economists were seen by the 'radicals' as espousing embodied labour as the *essential source* of exchange value. At the same time, though, these economists accepted without question the 'natural' right of capitalists to control the activity of labour and determine its income position by means of the *socio-legal fiat* of private property. The massive maldistribution of income and wealth must have been obvious to *all* observers, but political economy retained and defended the fiction that somehow it was all 'necessary' and that the position of the capitalists was 'justified' in the interests of all people. The 'radicals' had taken the opportunity of the rising tide of the labour movement to rail against these notions, each implying that some mode and degree of reform was required to bring about an improvement in the social and material well-being of the mass of working people.

The common emphasis of these writers which found *critical* favour with Marx was their stand against the *artificial* 'right' of the owners of capital (and land) to receive an income, or, at least, against the increasing *abuse* of that right by the idle rich. The 'radicals' picked up the fundamental contradiction of the capitalist system as it was reflected in political economy:

> In this contradiction, political economy merely expressed the essence of capitalist production or, if you like, of wage labour, of labour alienated from itself, which stands confronted by the wealth it has created as alien wealth, by its own productive power as the productive power of its product, by its enrichment as its own impoverishment and by its social power as the power of society. (*TSV*, III, 259.)

As Marx saw things, what needed to be conveyed to the workers was that 'Capital is *nothing* but defrauding of the worker. *Labour* is *everything*' (*TSV*, III, 260). However, it was the position of political economy that 'labour' could be treated effectively as just another material-instrumental input to production whose *income* needs were akin to 'maintenance'. What was lost from sight was the social-human dimension of 'labour' *qua* the worker. And, just as significantly, political economy neglected the socio-political nature of '*capital*'. It, too, was perceived as a material-instrumental input, the 'services' of which had to be 'paid for' in the form of an income received by the *owners* of capital. The false 'justification' of this income linked it to the instrumental role of capital, but as Marx argued: 'One can only speak of the *productivity* of capital if one regards it as the embodiment of definite social relations of production' (*TSV*, III, 265). In Marx's view, the political economists resisted the socio-political perception of capital because it would render capital as subject to the whims of social and political change. For them, and for the capitalists they represented, the capital concept had to be seen as immutable and absolute in its link with economic 'productivity' and material welfare. It was this link that the 'radicals' wanted to expose as, in one sense or another and to some degree, misleading.

Marx was not uncritical of these writers in spite of this thrust of their work. He found that their analytical capacity to probe the contradictory essences of the capital–labour relation had been constrained by some degree of adherence to the broad 'spirit' of their period which accepted 'capital' as the appropriate organising principle of production (see Marx's comments: *TSV*, III, 254–7, 260, 261, 265, 274). Their commitment was to *reform* and not to the profound transformation of the situation of workers that only *social and economic revolution* could bring. From among the writers that Marx considered, he found (implicitly at least, see pp. 190ff. below) that Bray was the most radical in his explicit advocation of the *abolition* of private property in the means of production. Bray favoured the perpetuation of the physical productivity of the available means of production under *national* ownership (*TSV*, III, 324). The others were more directly concerned with reforming and managing the '*excesses*' of capitalist exploitation of labour and wealth accumulation. Overall, none of the radicals pursued with any critico-analytical depth the immanent, dialectical 'motion' of capitalism that Marx believed would lead to the total transcendence of the system.

ANONYMOUS, *SOURCE AND REMEDY OF THE NATIONAL DIFFICULTIES*

In considering this brief anonymous pamphlet entitled *The Source and Remedy of the National Difficulties, deduced from Principles of Political Economy, in a Letter to Lord John Russell* (1821), Marx made the preliminary point that could well be applied to all of the 'radical' works:

> The pamphlet is no theoretical treatise. [It is a] protest against the false reasons given by the economists for the distress and the 'national difficulties' of the times. It does not, consequently, make the claim that its conception of surplus Value as *surplus labour* carries with it a general criticism of the entire system of economic categories, nor can this be expected of it. (*TSV*, III, 254.)

Thus Marx gave some indication of the limited scope and expectations of his critique of these works.

The particular merit of the *Source and Remedy* pamphlet to

which Marx drew attention was that its author had been more explicit than either Adam Smith or Ricardo about the source of non-labour incomes. The author argued that once embodied labour was established as the principle of exchange value, then it followed that the explanation of 'interest on capital' was to be found in this principle, too (*TSV*, III, 238–9). The form of this explanation was summarised as follows: 'the interest paid to the capitalists, whether in the nature of rents, interests of money, or profits of trade, is paid out of *the labour of others*' (quoted *TSV*, III, 239). Marx noted that this reflected an appreciation of labour exploitation as the source of the surplus *and* that this surplus existed as a general category, in this case 'interest on capital', logically prior to its specific phenomenal forms of rent, interest proper and profit (*TSV*, III, 239–40, 254). This latter point had been a major omission by Adam Smith and Ricardo, in Marx's opinion.

RAVENSTONE[5]

The main argument of Ravenstone's pamphlet, *Thoughts on the Funding System and its Effects* (1824), as its title suggests, examined the implications of government debt and taxation. At the same time, though, Marx found that Ravenstone had undertaken a critique of wealth accumulation for 'idle' purposes.[6] 'Capital' as such could never be *productive* and, 'To teach that the wealth and power of a nation depend on its *capital* is to make industry ancillary to riches, to make men subservient to property' (quoted *TSV*, III, 258).[7] Ravenstone's view was that true 'wealth' was to be found in setting to work as many workers as possible, thus ensuring the intensive and *productive employment* of all capital. This was best achieved under conditions of small-scale production supported by free trade.[8] As far as Ravenstone was concerned, then, capitalism itself was not the difficulty which disadvantaged the working class, but rather it was the trend away from *laissez-faire* through government intrusion and property accumulations on a scale that encouraged and supported the diversion of capital to 'idle' purposes. Such diversion involved 'excesses' of surplus being used for consumption rather than being used to mobilise more labour in production.[9]

Marx found in Ravenstone's pamphlet a definite awareness of labour as the source of true wealth in the form of exchange value that could be realised through the sale of commodities. But, this source of wealth, magnified by the use of increasingly productive large-scale machinery brought with it the potential avoidance of labour. Thus Ravenstone wrote:[10]

> Property grows from the improvement of the means of production; its sole business is the encouragement of idleness. When each man's labour is barely sufficient for his own subsistence, as there can be no property, there will be no idle men. When one man's labour can maintain five, there will be four idle men for one employed in production . . . (quoted *TSV*, III, 262.)

Implicit in this rather puritanical and reactionary argument, Marx found the notion of relative surplus Value: the increasing capacity of workers to produce beyond their needs depended upon the use of more advanced means of production and this excess production could be appropriated to support the idle (*TSV*, III, 258). Ravenstone identified this phenomenon with the very concept of *capital* itself (*TSV*, III, 262).[11] It must have been this line of argument that appealed to Marx, for the pamphlet contained little that was directed immediately at improving the economic status and welfare of workers. All that Ravenstone seemed to be arguing for was a return to an earlier form of small-scale, *laissez-faire* capitalism and the promotion of *labour* as a key moral virtue. In *this* respect, his ideas were hardly 'radical' in the sense that Marx seemed to have used the term.

HODGSKIN

Marx's main interest in Hodgskin in the 'Theories' critique centred on the treatment of capital in the pamphlet *Labour Defended Against the Claims of Capital, or the Unproductiveness of Capital Proved with Reference to the Present Combinations Amongst Journeymen* (1825) (*TSV*, III, 263ff.). The critique also contained brief references to two of Hodgskin's other books, viz. *Popular Political Economy: Four Lectures Delivered at the*

London Mechanics' Institution (1827), and *The Natural and Artificial Right of Property Contrasted etc.* (1832).[12] Marx quoted a few passages from these latter works (*TSV*, III, 315ff., 319), mostly in support of the ideas about capital with which he was dealing. It is especially important to stress, in the light of some historical debate about Marx's intellectual links with Hodgskin, that the 'Theories' critique was not concerned with the broader content of Hodgskin's contributions to exchange value and distribution analysis, except to the extent that these issues related to the discussion of the concept and role of capital.[13]

The full title of *Labour Defended* set out above is significant because it captures the *intent* and *context* of Hodgskin's pamphlet so explicitly. It was his objective to expose the invalidity of the theory upon which the receipt of income by capital *per se* was founded. He argued that this was especially important in the situation of increasingly organised and effective labour activism as a foil against the defensive response on behalf of the interests of capital. Hodgskin wanted to establish the justice of the pursuit of improved economic welfare by workers, even though it would be at the expense of the profit share of aggregate income, by establishing that capital was independently unproductive. Any income that its owners received was appropriated from the realised exchange value of commodities, the existence of which was due only to the actions of labour. For Hodgskin, the claims of capital rested solely on socio-political tradition.[14]

Marx read Hodgskin as a mere critic of the *operations and effects* of the capitalist system as they involved the working class. The essential principle of Hodgskin's stance he perceived to be that it was exclusively the act of labour that was responsible for the creation of material wealth. The means of production with which labour worked could *produce* nothing independently of that labour. In Hodgskin's terms, there existed an essential *unity* between capital and labour in production: 'PRODUCTIVE CAPITAL and SKILLED LABOUR ARE . . . ONE' and 'capital and a labouring population are precisely synonymous' (quoted *TSV*, III, 267).[15] The sense of this unity was that only to the extent that the use of capital as means of production actually involved the 'masters' as 'a useful class of labourers' could those 'masters' lay claim to any income. Hence, 'there is nothing more than knowledge, skill and labour requisite on which the capitalist can found a claim to any share of the produce'.[16]

Under existing capitalist conditions, the owners of the means of production successfully made much more extensive claims to income than Hodgskin thought justified. He rejected as false the arguments of the political economists that these claims were warranted as a consequence of capital's independent contribution to production.[17] Thus in his *Popular Political Economy* he wrote that 'when it is admitted that labour produces all things, even capital, it *is nonsense to attribute productive power to the instruments that labour makes and uses*' (quoted *TSV*, III, 317).[18] More appropriately, Hodgskin found, the existence of non-labour income could be ascribed to the power of the capitalist to appropriate the exchange value of all commodities produced *by labour* beyond that required to provide 'subsistence' for the workers (and to pay rent).[19] These ideas were presented by Hodgskin independently of any theory of the exchange value of the commodities sold in order to realise income. Marx noted this aspect of Hodgskin's critique in passing (*TSV*, III, 267), but he undertook no further consideration of the relation between exchange value and distribution in Hodgskin's work.

For Marx, the argument supporting the unproductive nature of capital had two interdependent dimensions. First, 'capital' could be said to mobilise and improve the physical productivity of labour only by virtue of its command over means of production. It could not, in itself, *produce* any exchange value. Its pre-existing exchange value was merely transformed into a different use value form by production (*TSV*, III, 264–5, 274–5). Secondly, this apparent involvement in production of 'capital' had nothing to do with the means of production and advances to labour being owned and controlled as *capital*. The physical *forces* of production had to be kept separate from the socio-political *relations* of production. It was only the latter which had any relevance to capital as a category in income distribution as Marx saw it (*TSV*, III, 265), while, as Hodgskin had recognised too, political economists had mostly not been willing to keep this separation to the fore (*TSV*, III, 264, 272, 274–6, 322).

Indeed it was Hodgskin's claim that 'capital' had come to be used deliberately to mystify and obscure the reality that payments to the owners of the means of production were but a social convention backed up by legislated property rights. Thus: 'capital is a sort of *cabalistic word*, like church or state, or any other of those *general terms* which are invented by those who fleece the rest of mankind to conceal the hand that shears them' (quoted *TSV*, III, 268).[20] In spite of his having grasped this so clearly, though, Marx felt that Hodgskin had been unable to give the point its due weight in the critical comprehension of capitalism. What Hodgskin had pointed to was the 'subjective illusion which conceals the deceit and the interests of the exploiting classes'. It was Marx's view that the *appearance* of 'capital' in this sense was not a 'subjective illusion' at all. The origin of 'the way of looking at things' was to be sought in 'the actual relationship [between capital and labour] itself' (*TSV*, III, 296). Appearances were, for Marx, always solidly rooted in essences and it was this articulation that Hodgskin had not grasped and explicated.

BRAY

The apparently unfinished notes on Bray's *Labour's Wrongs and Labour's Remedy: or, the Age of Might and the Age of Right* (1839) were found in notebook X of the 'Theories' manuscript. Evidently they were written well before Marx considered the other 'radical' writers, although he attached a note to the contents table of notebook XIV indicating his intention to shift them into their appropriate context with the other 'adversaries of the economists' (*TSV*, I, 38). In the published version of 'Theories', the notes have been placed after those on Hodgskin which were found in notebook XV (*TSV*, III, 319ff.).

It is of interest to recall that Marx had previously referred extensively to the work of Bray in the *Poverty of Philosophy* published in 1847. At that time he quoted several long passages from *Labour's Wrongs* dealing with exchange value and the origin of profit in relation to capitalist property rights (*CW*, 6, 139ff.).[21] The richness of Bray's insights must have been apparent to him then for it was quite evident that Bray understood the source of profit to be the effectively unequal exchange between capital and labour. The argument that Marx quoted embraced the principle of exploitation with the resulting surplus being appropriated by the capitalists by virtue of their property rights, although at that stage, he did not seem to have appreciated the significance of such insights. Indeed, Marx made virtually no substantive comment at all on the pieces quoted, a fact which must have been designed to convey to the reader his complete agreement with them.

Once again, in the present context, the results of Marx's investigations concerning Bray were set down in the same format. Presumably he again agreed with what he read more or less completely, although in this case the intended form of presentation of the treatment of Bray is unknown. To some extent the passages quoted coincided with those used in the earlier work, but different pieces used indicate that he probably re-read *Labour's Wrongs* and selected additional pieces on the basis of his now much more substantial critical grasp of political economy. In the outline of the ideas posited by Bray presented below, it will be quite evident that Marx would have wanted to add very little in the way of actual criticism.

Bray's analyses quoted by Marx pursued the notion that labour was the essence of human material survival. Where labour was able to be avoided by one person through some socio-political contrivance such as private property rights over the means of production, then, *ipso facto*, the labour of some other person or persons must be extended to compensate. In Bray's view, such a situation, as it existed in a class society, was contrary to the original intentions of social existence (*TSV*, III, 319–21).

Under a regime of capital, the capitalists could avoid working by engaging in legally sanctioned unequal exchange with those who *must* work for their own survival. As Bray put it, 'the workmen have given the capitalists the labour of a whole year, in exchange for the value of only half a year – and from this [. . .] has arisen the inequality of wealth and power which at present exists around us' (quoted *TSV*, III, 320).[22] This view of the capital–labour relation defied the usual image of voluntary and equitable exchange presented by political economy, for it amounted to 'no *exchange* whatever' and amounted to 'a palpable deception, a mere farce' (quoted *TSV*, III, 320).[23]

It must have been evident to Marx that Bray had at least adumbrated the principle of labour exploitation as the source of the wealth of the capitalists. Bray wrote that 'the capitalists and proprietors do no more than give the working man, for his labour of one week, a part of the wealth which they obtained from him the week before! – which just amounts to giving him *nothing* for *something*' (quoted *TSV*, III, 320).[24] And, he went on, 'this wealth has all been derived from the bones and sinews of the working classes during successive ages, and it has been taken from them by the fraudulent and slavery-creating system of unequal exchanges' (quoted *TSV*, III, 321).[25] Bray also recognised that the process of exploitation was facilitated by the capitalists' private property rights over what is produced: 'When the workman has produced a thing, it is his no longer – it belongs to the capitalist – it has been conveyed from the one to the other by the unseen magic of unequal exchanges' (quoted *TSV*, III, 323).[26]

Bray objected to the idea, prevalent in political economy, that labour needs to be dependent upon *capital* (*TSV*, III, 321–2). He argued that this represented a confusion of socio-political relations with the physical dimensions of the production process: 'this mutual dependency between Capital and Labour has nothing to do with the relative position of the capitalist and the working man; nor does it show that the former should be maintained by the latter' (quoted *TSV*, III, 322).[27] Marx supported this with the following comment:

> For the economists, the material element of capital is so integrated with its social form as capital – with its antagonistic character as the product of labour dominating labour – that they cannot write a single sentence without contradicting themselves. (*TSV*, III, 322.)

It followed from this type of argument that the evils of capitalist exploitation and inequity could be removed by the abolition of the private property rights that facilitated them while preserving the material-physical powers of the existing means of production. As Bray saw it: 'The machinery itself is good – is indispensable; it is the application of it – the circumstance of its being possessed by individuals instead of by the nation – that is bad' (quoted *TSV*, III, 324).[28] For Bray, the required socio-political change to bring about distributional justice was clear. Marx may have objected to such reformist moralising in lieu of 'scientific' critical analysis, but he could not deny that Bray had grasped relevant issues as well as any other writer, and probably better.

CHAPTER 9

Some particular post-Ricardians

INTRODUCTION

At the end of notebook XIV of the 'Theories of Surplus Value' manuscript, Marx selected three further political economists of the post-Ricardian era whose work he considered warranted some critical recognition. The three writers that he chose were George Ramsay, Antoine-Elisée Cherbuliez and Richard Jones whose works appeared between 1831 and 1852. They had little in common, although there was some overlap evident in the work of Ramsay and Cherbuliez. In each case, though, some particular aspects of their contributions to political economy caught Marx's attention and lifted them, in his view, above the general 'also-rans' of the period.

Both Ramsay and Cherbuliez had treated capital in a way that corresponded in principle to Marx's dichotomy of constant and variable capital. Each had also followed up some of the arguments that Marx considered to be entailed in such a premise, but neither had pursued the logic of their analyses fully. By contrast, Jones was less directly concerned with the issue of defining the nature and role of capital and it was his rare appreciation of historical processes as they influenced the evolution of the social nature of income distribution that caught Marx's attention.

RAMSAY

Considering the length and detailed nature of the contribution to political economy contained in Ramsay's book *An Essay on the*

Distribution of Wealth (1836), Marx's critique was rather brief and superficial. As always, Marx's focus was on those particular elements of the work which related more or less directly to the analysis of exchange value and distribution. In the present context, he concentrated on Ramsay's treatment of the nature of capital and its role in the production and distribution processes. Marx found that while Ramsay had some pertinent ideas about capital, especially with respect to its division into analytically relevant categories, he had not *applied* them in such a way as to grasp the essential nature of capitalism as a system which depended upon exploitation of labour by capital for its survival.

Marx recognised that Ramsay's treatment of the division of capital into two categories was quite careful and definitive as far as it went. Instead of relating the terms circulating and fixed to capital in accordance with some turnover criteria, as was common in political economy, Ramsay drew the more definitive dichotomy between advances to pay wages and advances to purchase means of production, including raw materials. To these two categories, which corresponded to Marx's variable and constant capital, he continued to apply the terms circulating and fixed capital respectively (*TSV*, III, 326).[1] Marx's view was that the retention of this terminology did not enable Ramsay to emphasise sufficiently that he had broken away from relating the dichotomy to *circulation* criteria in favour of considerations pertinent to the analysis of *production* (*TSV*, III, 327).

Ramsay's rationale for the formulation of this dichotomy was that the role of each category of capital in production was quite different. He perceived circulating capital to be strictly unnecessary for the process of production in the sense that if wages could be paid *after* production and commodity realisation such capital would not be needed.[2] It was the *labour* that was necessary for production and the existence of circulating capital was merely a reflection of the fact that the impoverished state of the workers required that the capitalist must provide their sustenance while they performed labour for him. As Ramsay put it: 'circulating capital is not an *immediate* agent in production, *nor even essential to it at all*, but merely a *convenience rendered necessary by the deplorable poverty of the mass of the people*' (quoted *TSV*, III, 327).[3]

Marx objected to this perception of the dichotomy on the

grounds that it did not capture the essence of the capital–labour relation (*TSV*, III, 327–8). For Marx, the distinction between constant and variable capital was a manifestation of the very nature of the capitalist relations of production. *Capitalism* required that labour be *wage*-labour and that advances to pay wages be considered as *capital*. Ramsay was, in effect, abstracting from one of the fundamental conditions for the existence of the system that he intended to analyse. At the same time, he sterilised the socio-political ramifications of the production relations facilitated by circulating capital.

It was evident to Marx, though, that Ramsay grasped the need for a surplus to emerge through the employment of labour by capital. This was a necessary *outcome asserted* by Ramsay as follows:[4]

> a circulating capital will always maintain more labour than that formerly bestowed upon itself. Because, could it employ no more than had been previously bestowed upon itself, what advantage could arise to the owner from the use of it as such? That it is used, is the clearest proof that some profit is thereby derived, and if there be a profit, the quantity of labour which a circulating capital can command, must be greater than that which produced it. (quoted in part, *TSV*, III, 328.)

As Marx recognised, this *assertion* could not *explain* the existence of the surplus. Ramsay ascribed 'gross profit', his term for realised surplus exchange value, to a commodity exchange value that exceeded the wages of labour plus the replacement cost of fixed capital used up in production.[5] However, while he explicitly ruled out 'profit on alienation' which located the *origin* of profit in exchange,[6] his analysis of exchange value still amounted to an *assumption* that profit existed as a reward for the 'sacrifice' of the capitalist in tying up his capital in the production process for a period of time. Beyond noting that Ramsay considered capital to be an independent source of exchange value in this sense (*TSV*, III, 330–1), Marx did not explicitly consider the extensive discussions of these issues in the *Essay*.[7] Having perceived the surplus idea, at least superficially, Ramsay had not gone on to probe its logic fully enough to realise its analytical potential (*TSV*, III, 329ff.). Thus: 'Ramsay's analysis . . . does not go far enough to draw the correct conclusions from his premises, from the new definition which he has given to capital in the immediate production process' (*TSV*, III, 328).

Included in Ramsay's analyses, Marx found the notion that the establishment of a uniform rate of profits on all capitals required a 'modification' of embodied-labour exchange value. While Ramsay was unable to specify a precise analytical format for this 'modification', Marx noted that he had linked it to a 'redistribution' of the aggregate 'gross profit' (*TSV*, III, 330–2).[8] This 'process' would be induced by competition between capitals.[9] In addition, Ramsay clearly delineated the factors affecting the rate of profits as the productivity of industries producing wage commodities and those producing fixed capital items, together with the real (commodity) wage itself (*TSV*, III, 351).[10] Despite these insights, and the others alluded to above, Marx found that Ramsay was unable to put them all together in a *formal* analysis which articulated the realised uniform rate of profits to the principle of embodied-labour exchange value and to the generation of a surplus.

CHERBULIEZ

In Cherbuliez's book, *Richesse ou pauvreté: Exposition des causes et des effets de la distribution actuelle des richesses sociales* (*Wealth or Poverty: an Essay on the Causes and Effects of the Present Distribution of Social Wealth*) of 1841, Marx also found the dichotomisation of capital between advances to pay wages and advances to purchase means of production (*TSV*, III, 362–4). As was the case with Ramsay, Cherbuliez did not realise the analytical significance of the dichotomy for understanding the essentials of the capital–labour relation and the generation of profit. Cherbuliez did not find in it any clue to the *origin* of a surplus as the basis for profit and his argument that there had to be a difference between produced exchange value and input exchange value *explained* nothing. This merely formed a *vulgar definition* of profit (*TSV*, III, 374). But, at least Cherbuliez had related profit to *production* rather than to exchange.

Cherbuliez's attempt to express profit formation in formal terms did not transcend the tautology of definition as the following sample passage revealed:

> Let P be the aggregate product of a given period of time, C the capital invested, π the profit, r, the *ratio* of profit to capital (rate), c the capital used up, then $P - c = \pi$, $r = \pi/C$, therefore $Cr = \pi$. Therefore $P - c = Cr$; therefore $r = (P - c)/C$. (quoted, *TSV*, III, 374.)

As Marx pointed out, this passage did nothing more than *define* profit and the rate of profit (*TSV*, III, 375).

There was, though, a little more of substance in Cherbuliez's further analysis of the rate of profits as the following passage indicated:

> After the deduction of rent, what remains of the *amount of profit* . . . is divided between the capitalist producers *in proportion to the capital each has invested*, whereas the portion of the product which corresponds to the capital used up and is intended to replace it, is divided in proportion with the capital actually used up. This *dual law of division* comes about *as a result of competition*, which tends to equalise the advantages of the different investments of capital. Finally, this dual law of division determines the respective *values* and *prices* of the different kinds of products. (quoted *TSV*, III, 376.)

Although informally expressed, the links between production, price formation and the determination of the rate of profits argued in this passage were correct in Marx's view. The weakness remained, though, that exchange value and price were conflated and the logical priority of exchange value was not emphasised. The Value–surplus Value domain of analysis was not separated clearly from the price of production-profit domain as Marx thought essential (*TSV*, III, 377).

Cherbuliez also revealed an appreciation of the capital–labour relationship which Marx found essentially correct (*TSV*, III, 377). The workers under capitalism have no option but to sell their 'labour' to the capitalist. From this sale, they receive a subsistence wage and, as a consequence, they also renounce any claim on whatever is produced with their labour. They are 'entitled' to receive only what is given to them by the capitalist. This argument was an integral part of Marx's thought also, but he went further to reveal the deceptive nature of the *apparent* exchange between the capitalist and the worker. Cherbuliez did not elaborate upon how it was possible that a part of the labour input was appropriated by the capitalist without being exchanged for anything. This contradicted the law of exchange upon which capitalism was supposed to be founded. In Marx's view, Cherbuliez sensed only that some inconsistency was involved (*TSV*, III, 377–8).

RICHARD JONES

Marx's discussion of Jones's contribution to political economy made reference to the following works (*TSV*, III, 399ff.):[11]

> *An Essay on the Distribution of Wealth, and on the Sources of Taxation,* 1831;
> *An Introductory Lecture on Political Economy delivered at King's College, London, 27th February, 1833.* To which is added a Syllabus of a Course of Lectures on the Wages of Labour, London 1833; and
> *Textbook of Lectures on the Political Economy of Nations etc.,* 1852.

In each of these pieces, Marx found that it was Jones's broad historical 'vision' of the object of political economy, as well as the analytical substance of his work that warranted critical consideration and comment.

What impressed Marx so much about Jones's political economy was that it situated the discussion of the capitalist mode of production in its historical context. Jones emphasised that capitalism was but one stage in the continuing evolution of human society. This elicited the observation from Marx that Jones's work was 'distinguished by what has been lacking in all English economists since Sir James Steuart, namely, a sense of the *historical* differences in modes of production' (*TSV*, III, 399; cf. 428–30). These differences, as they were perceived by Jones, involved largely the nature of the income distribution process and its relationship to the manifest social structures and relations of each era. In his analyses, he especially referred to the situation of the worker and his labour and to the role of private property in the means of production. Thus it was that Jones appeared to Marx to have been sensitive to the primary significance of and human-social impact of each particular mode of production in the stages of history, a perception which Marx found highly congenial and meaningful.

One aspect of Jones's work to which Marx gave no explicit attention was its methodological foundations. Jones stood out in this post-Ricardian era as a writer who favoured the inductivist approach. His objective was to extricate political economy from what he saw as the intellectual restrictions imposed by the essentially deductive method employed by Ricardo.[12] Jones tried *immediately* to grasp, in more or less formal terms, the *reality* of the socio-economic world through the detailed observation and recording of its relations, institutions and phenomena.[13] His objection to Ricardo's approach was that knowledge of the perceived real world could not be meaningfully 'constructed' by a process of logical argument from simple premises alone. The complexities from which Ricardo abstracted were integral parts of what was to be comprehended and logic could not restore them. However, Jones's approach to knowledge through the 'facts' led to description rather than to analytically sound explanations of phenomena. He implicitly realised this when he was forced to impose theoretical constructs on his observations in order to give his work some substantive and coherent content.[14]

Now Marx's own methodology also involved this integration of the historico-inductive and abstract-deductive approaches.[15] However, he recognised more explicitly that it was only through the latter that the phenomenal world could be presented and comprehended formally. The analytical dissection of history remained as the process by which relevant issues and problems expressed through phenomenal categories could be posed. These then became the objective substance of formal explanations.[16] In the present context, though, Marx noted implicitly only that Jones had endeavoured to formulate a logico-historical method which had some characteristics similar to his own.

In the first, and only completed, part of Jones's *Essay*, the category considered was rent. At the beginning of the work, he gave some indications of the broader purpose and scope of his intended project on income distribution. His concern was that the subject had been isolated from its historical context by political economists, whereas he felt that it could only be adequately presented and comprehended by a process of careful and detailed historical exposition.[17] On this premise, Jones planned to consider in turn the various phenomena of income generation and payment associated with land, labour and capital in such a way that their historical dimensions would receive due emphasis.[18] The *raison d'être* for this endeavour expressed by Jones would not have found much favour with Marx, although he made no comment on it. For Jones, the project was aimed at establishing the essentially harmonious and conflict-free nature of the stages of human progress.[19] This included the contemporary stage, although he perceived the need for the mediation of 'wise laws and honest government'[20] in order to ensure this state of affairs.

It was Jones's view, and one with which Marx would have concurred, that the income distribution process should be understood as an extension of the production process. This had not always been made clear enough by political economists.[21] Jones retained the idea evident in political economy that labour was the most essential source of all exchange value when he asserted that: 'All wealth, whatever be its source, is made available for the purpose of man by human labour'.[22] The principle then posited in order to link distribution to production was that even though this wealth passed through the hands of labour initially, the worker 'is rarely in a condition to retain the whole produce of his exertions' because 'some tie, or some want, makes him to a certain extent dependent upon others'.[23] If this 'tie' was to the land, the worker must face the appropriation of his surplus product by the landowner. When capital succeeded land as the dominating force over labour, the surplus was appropriated by the capitalist. What remained for the worker in each case was referred to by Jones as the wages of labour. Although he made no comment on these insights by Jones, Marx did object to this last point in the context of his critique of the 'Syllabus'. For Marx, the term wages should be preserved for the category of labour income associated with the capitalist mode of production in order to emphasise that the domination over labour in this mode took a form that was different from any earlier form (*TSV*, III, 416).

The discussion of rent in the *Essay* comprised an historical exposé of the forms that the category had taken based on the general principle that 'The power of the earth to yield, even to the rudest labours of mankind, more than is necessary for the subsistence of the cultivator himself, enables him to pay [. . .] a tribute: hence the origin of rent' (quoted *TSV*, III, 399).[24] But it was not on this 'power' alone that *rent* depended. Two additional necessary conditions were noted by Jones: 'the *appropriation of the soil*' and 'the scanty capital of implements, seeds, etc.' of most people that are 'utterly insufficient to secure their maintenance in any other occupation than that of agriculture' such that they are 'chained . . . to the land by an overpowering necessity', land they must 'cultivate . . . on such terms as they can obtain, or starve' (quoted *TSV*, III, 399).[25] Here Jones grasped the two essential conditions for exploitation that were of such importance for Marx's critique of capitalism: viz. the appropriation of the means of production by a class of owners, and the inability of most people to sustain themselves except by working with these means on terms dictated by the owning class. As Jones made explicit in his later *Textbook*, it was this combination of historical factors that gave rise to the initial generation and appropriation of a 'surplus produce' in the form of what he variously called 'primitive', 'peasant' or 'primary' rent (*TSV*, III, 449).[26]

Jones's historical-inductive analysis led him from this 'primitive' rent form to the emergence of a form of rent based on the capitalist mode of production and which he called 'farmer's' or 'secondary' rent.[27] He noted that this form of rent could be traced to the accumulation of capital by some 'artizans and mechanics' who became a class of capitalists (*TSV*, III, 402).[28] Some capital ultimately appeared in farming and transformed the peasant into an agricultural labourer paid by the capitalist farmer. Under these conditions, the new form of rent was paid out of the surplus which was now initially appropriated by the capitalist. It was to Jones's credit, Marx noted, that he 'by no means shares the illusion that capital has been in existence since the beginning of the world' (*TSV*, III, 399).

Most importantly for Marx, Jones also expressed the idea that different forms of landed property and rent payment corresponded to specific forms, relations and conditions of labour (*TSV*, III, 400–1). In particular, the capitalist era brought with it the condition that the agricultural worker must relate to the capitalist farmer through the mediation of what appeared to be an exchange process involving wages and labour services. This mediation replaced the legal 'ties' of slavery and the legal cum traditional 'ties' of feudalism. In Marx's perception, the general emergence of the wage-labour form did not mean the end of '*forced labour*', whatever the appearance of the capital–labour 'exchange' may suggest. Workers still had no sensible option but to take up opportunities for labour offered by the capitalist in agriculture or elsewhere, *whatever the conditions*. Thus, as Marx put it, 'real forced labour' merely '*displays in the most brutal form, most clearly the essential features of wage-labour*' (*TSV*, III, 400).

Jones recognised clearly the role of capital in the establishment of the modern form of landed property and rent. The landowner ceased to be the direct appropriator of the agricultural surplus under capitalist conditions. Moreover, the size of the rent share came to depend upon the division of the surplus between the capitalist and the landowner rather than on the size of the surplus itself (*TSV*, III, 402–3).[29] In order to explain the resolution of the conflict implied by this mode of distribution, Jones had to provide some argument which indicated how the *capacity* of the capitalist to pay rent came about. The actual appropriation of rent by the landowner was then taken for granted.

In order to explain 'farmer's' rent, Jones relied on the principle of *absolute* rent, as Marx had subsequently labelled it. This principle recognised the axiom of the general rate of profits as a *minimum* return on capital in agriculture, with any 'excess' profit providing the capacity for rent. In Jones's words: 'Rent . . . necessarily consists merely of *surplus profits*' over and above what could be obtained on capital 'in any other occupation'.[30] Having stated this initial principle, though, Jones went on to investigate the payment of rent in more detail and he ended up with an analysis which combined the capacity to pay absolute rent with that which emerged *additionally* as a consequence of the different fertilities of land in use (*TSV*, III, 403ff.).[31] This general approach was similar to that adopted by Marx in his critique of Ricardo's theory of differential rent earlier in the 'Theories of Surplus Value' manuscript (*TSV*, II, 236ff.).[32] As Jones explained it, the absolute rent component arose only under conditions where a monopoly price of 'corn' could be obtained such that even if land were of the same fertility, the capital applied in agriculture would realise an immediate rate of profit in excess of the general rate.[33] In Jones's view, this was not the usual case and his analysis of rent was dominated by situations in which the 'surplus profits' appeared on lands of varying fertility as *differential* rent, with the land of least fertility yielding only the minimum acceptable general rate of profits.[34]

In principle, then, Jones's analysis of rent was similar to Ricardo's. However, when it came to considering the 'dynamics' of rent in the process of growth, the similarity ended. Jones objected to the simple 'diminishing returns' approach adopted by Ricardo, an objection with which Marx concurred (*TSV*, III, 405–6, cf. II, 236ff.).[35] Jones's analysis of rent was much more elaborate in this respect and he concentrated explicitly on the role of the growth of capital in agriculture as it influenced the productivity of new and old land in use. The thrust of his argument was that the improvements in agriculture due to new machinery and farming methods could be seen to have dominated any tendency for increasing costs of production associated with reduced fertility of land. As a consequence, the fall in the *share* of rent, which Jones found to have accompanied the absolute increase in the volume of rent, could not be ascribed to decreasing returns on land. Rather, it occurred because of the profit demands of the increasingly dominant and growing stock of capital used in agriculture.[36]

This approach to the 'dynamics' of rent, with its emphasis on the primacy of capital accumulation effects, impressed Marx considerably. He considered the particular case examples used by Jones in some detail, but did not find it necessary to offer any significant criticism of the arguments and conclusions involved (*TSV*, III, 404ff.).[37]

One further point made by Jones concerning capital accumulation also caught Marx's attention in passing. According to Jones, the accumulation process resulted in an increase in the *relative* proportion of 'auxiliary capital' in use, where this form of capital was equivalent to Marx's constant capital, at the expense of capital advanced to pay wages (*TSV*, III, 411–12, 417–18).[38] In his work on the 'law of motion' of capitalism,[39] this was one of Marx's most essential premises, especially with respect to the falling rate of profits dimension of 'motion'. Marx found that

Jones, too, had considered the 'dynamic' fate of the rate of profits in each of his works.[40] The tendency of the rate to fall was *asserted* on the basis of observations rather than *explained* by Jones, and Marx concluded that he had 'as yet not the faintest notion of the real law of [the] declining rate of profit' (*TSV*, III, 409), mainly because he had not thought out fully the *origin* of profit itself (*TSV*, III, 417–18, 439, 446–7).

When he turned his attention to Jones's *Introductory Lecture*, with its attached 'Syllabus', and the *Textbook*,[41] Marx found that these works dealt further with the situation of labour under various historical modes of production. As Marx read it: 'The main point . . . in Jones's work is that the whole economic structure of society revolves around the *form of labour*, in other words, the form in which the worker appropriates his means of subsistence, or that part of his product upon which he lives' (*TSV*, III, 414; cf. 415). Jones's attention centred on what he called the 'labour fund'; that is 'the aggregate amount of revenues consumed by the labourers, whatever be the source of those revenues' (quoted from the 'Syllabus', *TSV*, III, 414). On this basis, the 'labour fund' could take one of three historical forms: (1) the unmediated accumulation of revenue by the worker himself; (2) revenues accumulated by any classes separate from the workers; and (3) revenues accumulated as capital for the express purpose of obtaining profits (*TSV*, III, 415–17, 431).[42] It was especially to Jones's credit that he saw these stages in the development of the 'labour fund' as having changing implications for the nature of the social relations of production (*TSV*, III, 415). In particular, Marx expressed the view that Jones had been aware that 'the essential feature of capital is its socially determined form' (*TSV*, III, 424). Here Marx drew a comparison between the contributions of Ramsay and Jones on this matter (*TSV*, III, 428).[43] For Ramsay, the need for capital advances to pay wages was of no particular significance *per se*. Rather it stemmed from the 'accidental' situation that workers were poor and, having no accumulated resources of their own, it was 'convenient' for them to have their wages paid in advance during the production process. By contrast, Jones made much more of the emergence of capital as a particular form of the labour fund which had significant social ramifications in and of itself.

In general, Jones's emphasis on the social dimensions of wage capital was in accord with Marx's own view that it was the emergence of *wage*-labour that represented one of the most essential distinguishing features of the capitalist mode of production *vis-à-vis* those modes that went before (*TSV*, III, 427, 432). Unfortunately, though, Jones's use of the term capital in its historical setting was not as precise as it might have been, as was indicated by the following piece from the *Textbook*: 'Capital, or accumulated stock, after performing various other functions in the production of wealth, only takes up late that of *advancing* to the labourer his wages' (quoted *TSV*, III, 427).[44] Here the identification of capital with 'accumulated stock' as such was quite inappropriate in Marx's view, for analytical clarity required that the term *capital* in this sense be reserved for the advances to pay *wages* only. This difficulty was similar to, and compounded, that which arose concerning Jones's application of the term 'wages' to all pre-capitalist payments to labour in the 'Syllabus' (*TSV*, III, 416). One of Marx's endeavours was to stress the importance of historical changes in the nature of socio-economic systems. This required careful attention to the categories to be used in comprehending the stages of development involved. Precision in the use of categories would avoid confusion, and, in this sense, Marx's chiding of Jones for his loose use of 'capital' and 'wages' was more than mere pedantry.

Part IV

Political economy and the 'Law of Motion' of capitalism

CHAPTER 10

The dimensions of 'motion' and the process of reproduction

INTRODUCTION TO MARX'S 'LAW OF MOTION' ANALYSIS

So far, in the present volume of this study, attention has centred on those aspects of Marx's critique involving the theory of exchange value and distribution in which historical time had no analytical role. For Marx, this level of critical analysis was not an end in itself. His ultimate concern was to provide a formal critical analysis of the historical 'motion' of the capitalist economic system and the crisis-ridden consequences of such 'motion'. From time to time, throughout the 'Theories of Surplus Value' manuscripts, then, Marx's attention shifted to the 'dynamics' of the capitalist mode of production that was his critical object.

Marx's explicit search for what he would call the 'economic law of motion' of the capitalist economic system (*K*(PE), I, 92) began in the *Grundrisse* manuscripts of 1857–8 and underwent partial development for presentation in *A Contribution to the Critique of Political Economy* of 1859. As I argued in volume I of the present study, when considering these earlier parts of Marx's critique (see chapters 7 and 8 of the volume), the evolution of Marx's ideas about the 'motion' of capitalism is appropriately understood as involving several interdependent, but analytically separable, dimensions of the process. This same approach is pursued in the present context.

For Marx, the 'motion' of the capitalist system was induced most fundamentally by the endeavours of *individual* capitalists to maximise the valorisation[1] of their capital through production and circulation activities. The essential unity of the production and circulation dimensions of the operation of the system was expressed formally by Marx in the reproduction schema. These schemata of simple reproduction, i.e. reproduction on a constant scale, and expanded reproduction became the foundation pieces for the analysis of the other dimensions of 'motion'. Each schema revealed the *potential* of the capitalist economy to reproduce itself under *idealised*, *analytically assumed* conditions. Here Marx established the necessary and sufficient quantitative and qualitative requirements for reproduction and growth to proceed smoothly without impediments and without disruptions. Of course, as he well knew, the schemata could provide only a starting point, for they abstracted from the very immanent contradictions of the system that gave its 'motion' the phenomenal characteristic of constant instability so evident to any honest observer.[2]

Imbedded in the *expanded* reproduction schema was another dimension of 'motion' which Marx singled out for analysis. One of his fundamental assumptions about the *individual* capitalist's behaviour was that each was determined to seek out ways to maximise surplus Value generation *and* ways to increase the capacity for such generation through capital accumulation and technological change. Marx was concerned to investigate the logic of this endeavour and the contradictions that it necessarily involved. These contradictions had *aggregate* consequences for the working class, for the structure and operations of capital and for the destiny of the capitalist economic system itself. Marx's view was that political economy had not pursued and exposed these consequences adequately.

Marx's observations led him to perceive the contemporary mode of production to be highly 'dynamic'. Capitalist decision-makers were predisposed towards emphasising growth and change. However, his reasoning suggested to him that much of this dynamism acted against the *collective* interests of the very participants whose *individual* actions were responsible for it. By contrast, the writings of the political economists often revealed a more sanguine view. They presented a 'vision' that emphasised the potential of capitalism smoothly to absorb, or at least adjust to, capital accumulation and its effects.[3] Marx's intention was to refute such 'false consciousness'.

Capital accumulation was a process that immediately affected the forces and relations of *production*. In analysing this dimension of 'motion', Marx again abstracted from any impediments to or disruptions in the circulation process. The contradictions of capital accumulation, as they involved production, were considered in isolation first. But, Marx always stressed the essential *unity* of production and circulation and, consequently, his analysis of 'motion' included a substantial critique of the latter process. The effect of this was to reach another layer of contradictions that would compound the difficulties that arose from the production process itself.

The *collective* manifestation of the decisions of individual capitalists affecting the forces and relation of production and the process of circulation was summarised by Marx under the rubric of the *crisis*. The crisis represented for him the logical culmination of the immanent contradictions embodied in the constituent dimensions of 'motion'. But, it was a complex category and Marx's treatment of it in the 'Theories' manuscripts was very limited. Many important analytical issues were left unattended, perhaps even unrecognised.

These dimensions of the analysis of 'motion', and the search for its 'law' in order to demonstrate the necessity of continuously recurring and deepening crises, provide the frame of reference for my discussion of Marx's critique of political economy on this theme in the 'Theories' manuscripts. The rest of this chapter is devoted to Marx's development of the reproduction schemata. In the subsequent two chapters, I consider first, the issues of capital accumulation and its consequences, and secondly, the crisis phenomenon in the context of the production–circulation unity espoused by Marx.

This format of my approach is quite different from that adopted in the previous Parts of this volume. Up until now, I have followed out Marx's critique of the work of particular political economists within the narrow confines of his concerns about exchange value and distribution analysis. In the present context, a change to a thematic approach is desirable because Marx's investigations of the dimensions of 'motion' were much less dependent upon textual exegetics. Even where a particular writer's work was in focus, the critical discussion concerned especially one or other of the dimensions and generally consisted largely of distinct developments in Marx's own thought independently of the textual context.

The overall analytical results of Marx's scattered investigations of the phenomenon of 'motion' in the present context left much scope for future development. By no means had he come to grips with all of the dimensions and ramifications implicit in his critique. The formal and 'complete' understanding of and explanation for the complex issue of capitalist crises as the culmination of all the aspects of 'motion' was a long way off for Marx. His results at this stage remained rather impressionistic and mostly descriptive rather than formal-analytical. Be this as it may, his work in the critical history of political economy did give Marx the opportunity further to develop some important ideas that were carried forward into the *Capital* manuscripts.

FOUNDATIONS: THE FORMULATION OF THE REPRODUCTION SCHEMA

Marx's formulation of the notion of reproduction represented a crucial advance in the perception of the sectoral division of the macroeconomy appropriate to understanding its continuing perpetuation and expansion. What he did was to move away from the Physiocratic dichotomy between manufacturing and agriculture that continued to pervade political economy towards a clear exposition of the interdependence between the sector producing means of production and the sector producing commodities purchased by workers.[4] Marx had adumbrated such a division of production in the *Grundrisse* manuscripts when he first approached the analysis of reproduction (*G*, 439ff.).[5] Now, in combination with the analytical framework provided by Quesnay's *Tableau économique*, Marx was to develop this production dichotomy into the schema of reproduction that was to prove such a substantial foundation for the critical analysis of the 'motion' of capitalism.

Curiously, though, as was pointed out earlier in this study (see above, chapter 2, pp. 35ff.) Marx's first contact with the Physiocrats' work in the 'Theories' investigations did not concern the *Tableau économique* or raise the issue of reproduction except in passing (*TSV*, I, 44). The need to return to the analysis of the reproduction problem arose in the context of the critique of Adam Smith's handling of the *gross social product* and *net revenue* categories in the *Wealth of Nations* (*TSV*, I, 106ff.).

The issue raised by Marx concerned the problem of arguing exchange-value generation in a way that was consistent with the replacement of constant capital. He found that Adam Smith had become 'entangled . . . in all kinds of contradictions' as a result of trying to resolve this problem (*TSV*, I, 166). Once exchange value was resolved wholly into the *incomes* of labour and capital (leaving aside land for the sake of argument) there was, as it were, no 'labour' left over to replace the means of production. The puzzle was posed by Marx in the following terms:

> So the whole capital must be resolvable, directly or indirectly, into wages and profit. Or is labour somewhere performed which consists neither of wages nor profit, and merely has the purpose of replacing the Values used up in production which are, however, the conditions of reproduction? But who performs this labour, since all labour performed by the labourer is resolvable into two quantities, one which maintains his own power to produce, and the other which forms the profit of capital? (*TSV*, I, 106.)

In effect, Marx recommenced his analysis of reproduction by considering the *processes* which could be represented as a consistent schema once they had worked themselves out.

Marx was evidently quite uncertain about how best to proceed with his analysis of the issue of constant capital replacement through circulation. He stated *the problem* over and over and his investigations were long and laborious with little definitive result. The essential problem to be resolved was that the total *net revenue* had to be adequate, it seemed, to purchase the *gross social product* in order for reproduction to proceed. As Marx stated at one point:

> It is . . . impossible for the Value of the revenue to cover the Value of the total product. But since, apart from the revenue, *no fund exists from which this product sold by producers to (individual) consumers can be paid for*, it is impossible for the

> Value of the total product, minus the Value of the revenue, ever to be sold, paid for or (individually) consumed. On the other hand it is necessary for every product to be sold and paid for at its price (on the assumption that price is here equal to Value). (*TSV*, I, 123–4, cf. 108, 112, 113, 114, 115, 133, 135, and 149–50.)

The question was, then, how could the constant capital component of gross product be realised when revenues comprised only newly added labour, i.e. wages plus surplus Value?

It is to be noted that at this stage, Marx was not concerned with *additions* to constant capital, expanded reproduction, but only with simple reproduction (*TSV*, I, 107, 114, 135, 230, 252). Indeed, expanded reproduction was initially expressed as an issue to be treated later (*TSV*, I, 252), and Marx mentioned it only in passing when considering capital accumulation (*TSV*, III, 250–1, 380–1).

Marx began his analysis of the present problem by positing linen production for direct, final consumption as a microcosm of production in aggregate. The output Value was assumed to comprise 2/3 constant capital and 1/3 Value added, the latter being the source of wage and surplus Value revenue. In this simple context, the issue was the *purchase* of the 2/3 of the linen produced which represented the constant capital input (*TSV*, I, 112–13). This sale was essential if the linen producer was to be able to replace the looms and yarn used up in production. The production of these inputs was proceeding at the same time as the production of the linen. But, in itself this could not ensure reproduction without a prior explanation of where the funds were to come from to purchase the 2/3 of the linen in question (*TSV*, I, 115).

Now it was at this point that Marx turned his investigation away from what would ultimately be the appropriate line of argument. Instead of immediately recalling from the *Grundrisse* that the interdependence of the means of production and consumption commodities production sectors was sufficient to provide the conditions for simple reproduction, he proceeded to extend the number of sectors with a view to providing an adequate revenue to purchase the whole of the linen produced (*TSV*, I, 115ff.). After considerable arithmetical effort, his conclusion was clear that: 'It has thus not helped us at all to shift through nearly 800 branches of production the difficulty of the 8 yards [2/3] of linen of sphere A . . . representing in its product the Value of the constant capital' (*TSV*, I, 122). All that he had achieved was to re-present the problem in a more complex way (*TSV*, I, 133–4).

The correct principle was soon stated, though, and Marx moved into an investigation of its analytical ramifications:

> the constant capital remains equal to itself and replaces itself out of that part of the Value which represents the constant capital in the total product. The exchange between various commodities, the series of purchases and sales between different spheres of production, brings about a change in form only in the sense that the constant capitals in the various production spheres mutually replace each other in the proportion in which they were originally contained in them. (*TSV*, I, 125, cf. 135.)

The analysis to which Marx now proceeded involved the backward vertical integration structure of linen production. The idea here was appropriate in the sense that the role of the producers of the means of production, represented initially by the yarn- and loom-makers, was now brought into the analysis. But the precise structure of the simple reproduction schema did not emerge at this point and Marx went on to extend the sectors considered into those producing increasingly primary inputs. Ultimately, sectors were reached in which output was the only required material input to production, i.e. constant capital was replaced in kind. An example of this was flax growing where the seeds were part of the output. Marx realised, though, that in this extension of the analysis he was not solving the problem (*TSV*, I, 141) and he continued to mull over this approach with little success (*TSV*, I, 141–50). With the benefit of hindsight, we can see that in all of this Marx was still carrying forward the correct principle. For example, he wrote that

> Between different spheres of production, where the products of each enter into the other as means of production, an exchange in kind takes place too (even though concealed by a series of money transactions) between the constant capital of the one and that of the other. In so far as this is the case, the consumers of

> the final product which enters into consumption have not got to replace this constant capital, since it has already been replaced. (*TSV*, I, 149.)

The principle had been posited in the *Grundrisse*, but Marx was now having great difficulty in utilising it to formalise simple reproduction.

Marx returned to the reproduction issue some pages later in the manuscript and again it can be seen that the principle of mutual interdependence between sectors and within sectors was to be the basis of a formal solution (*TSV*, I, 191). What was now evident was that reproduction involved two forms of exchange. In disposing of consumer commodities, revenue was exchanged for revenue and revenue was exchanged for constant capital in each transaction. In order to close the reproduction loop, it was necessary that constant capital be exchanged for constant capital within the means of production sector (*TSV*, I, 197).

This view was reiterated when, some pages later in the manuscript, Marx again took up his analysis of reproduction (*TSV*, I, 230). He considered first the mutual exchanges within the consumption commodities sector (*TSV*, I, 231–5). What emerged from this was that a requirement for reproduction would be the production of these commodities to match the qualitative and quantitative pattern of demand. The exchanges here were revenue for revenue and revenue for constant capital. Reproduction then also required that the revenue of the means of production sector be exchanged for revenue and constant capital in the consumption commodities sector. Only then could the complete realisation of consumption commodities Value be achieved enabling the producers in this sector to replace their constant capital.

By introducing a two-sector model of the economy, Marx was now able more formally to express the reproduction requirements (*TSV*, I, 237ff.). The two sectors were A, which produced consumption commodities, and B, which produced means of production as commodities. Sector A produced Value which comprised 2/3 constant capital and 1/3 newly added labour (Value added) as revenue. It was thus able to purchase 1/3 of its own output. For simple reproduction, the remaining 2/3 had to be purchased by revenue generated in sector B, such revenue not being able to be expended on its own non-consumable product. In this way, sector A realised the Value of constant capital used up in production. This constant capital could then be replaced by exchange with sector B, with mutual consistency requiring that the Value of this exchange be equal to the Value of newly added labour in sector B's production.

The essential requirement for reproduction which followed from this analysis was that 'the total product [of] A is equal to the total revenue of society' (*TSV*, I, 239; cf. 244). It was still necessary further to consider the exchanges within sector B where the Value of its output which comprised means of production had to be realised. There was no fund of newly-added labour Value within the sector for such exchanges so the situation was not analogous to that in sector A. Marx's solution to this part of the reproduction analysis required that mutual exchanges of capital for capital take place between producers within sector B (*TSV*, I, 248–50).

What was missing from the above struggle by Marx to resolve the reproduction issue satisfactorily was a framework for its coherent presentation. He had earlier in the manuscript mentioned in passing that the Physiocratic *Tableau économique* would have a role to play in formulating a reproduction analysis.

> In addition to this analysis of the material elements of which capital consists within the labour-process, the Physiocrats established the forms which capital assumes in circulation (fixed capital, circulating capital, even though as yet they give them other names), and in general the connection between the process of circulation and the reproduction process of capital. We shall come back to this in the chapter on circulation. (*TSV*, I, 44.)

As it turned out, the analysis of reproduction was not left until Marx dealt with circulation as a separate issue, but rather it emerged within the 'Theories of Surplus Value' manuscript. Marx was very impressed by the *Tableau économique* as an analytical device and he was moved to refer to it as 'an extremely brilliant conception, incontestably the most brilliant for which political economy had up to then been responsible' (*TSV*, I, 344). He devoted considerable effort to an assessment of at least one of the forms of the device and the result of this was a formal and coherent presentation of the potential reproduction conditions for capitalism.

The main part of Marx's assessment of the *Tableau économique* appeared in notebook X of the 'Theories' manuscripts and was drafted around April 1862 (*TSV*, I, 308ff.). The form of his notes suggests that he did not work directly from the works of the Physiocrats, but rather probably from a secondary source instead.[6] However, the original format of the *Tableau* on which the secondary interpretation depended was evidently that of Quesnay's article *Analyse du Tableau économique* published in 1766. The table that Marx recorded (*TSV*, I, 308) and that in the *Analyse* were very similar.[7] He used the same version, probably directly from the reprint of the piece in the Eugène Daire collection,[8] when he made some additional brief notes on the *Tableau* in notebook XXIII around July 1863 (*TSV*, I, 378ff.) and again when he composed his substantial letter to Engels on the matter (6 July 1863, *MEW*, 30, 361ff.). This 'simplest version of the *Tableau économique*' (*TSV*, I, 378) appears to have been considered adequate for Marx's purpose of providing a more rigorous expression of his ideas on reproduction. It is uncertain whether he ever studied the more complex and more obviously 'dynamic' zig-zag versions of the *Tableau* not included in the Daire reprints.[9]

The Physiocrats had considered the problem of capital circulation and its integration with the process of production.[10] For Marx, this was an essentially correct basis for understanding the 'motion' of capitalism. He summarised his assessment of the *Tableau économique* in this context in the following passage:

> it was an attempt to portray the whole production process of capital as a *process of reproduction*, with circulation merely as the form of this reproductive process; and the circulation of money only as a phase in the circulation of capital; at the same time to include in this reproductive process the origin of revenue, the exchange between capital and revenue, the relation between reproductive consumption and final consumption; and to include in the circulation of capital the circulation between consumers and producers (in fact between capital and revenue); and finally to present the circulation between the two great divisions of productive labour – raw material production and

manufacture – as phases of this reproductive process . . . (*TSV*, I, 343–4.)

The *Tableau économique*, then, was perceived by Marx as presenting in concise form the essential interdependencies between sectors of *production* in order to ensure *reproduction*. For the Physiocrats, the appropriate division of production was between agriculture (raw materials) and manufacturing, rather than between means of production and consumption commodity production which Marx considered to be a correct simplification of capitalist production. The principle of interdependence remained correct, however. In extending production to reproduction, the Physiocrats had integrated circulation into the analysis, and this circulation was centred around the role of capital. It was Marx's view that this focus upon capital brought the Physiocrats to prominence as the 'true fathers of modern political economy' (*TSV*, I, 44), although their *raison d'être* was the advocation of the capitalisation of agricultural production on a large scale (*TSV*, I, 64–5). Thus, in analysing the role of capital, they had confined their attention to *agricultural* capital to the neglect of manufacturing capital (*TSV*, I, 379) and had divided capital into its circulation-based dichotomy of fixed and circulating to the neglect of the requirements to analyse production (*TSV*, I, 44).

The Physiocrats' analysis was also a *class analysis*. The sectors of the economy involved in reproduction were designated in class terms as the 'productive class' involved in agricultural production, the 'landowner class' and the 'sterile class' involved in manufacturing. What the Physiocrats had not done was to integrate the *material* side of capital and its role in production with the *social* relations of production (*TSV*, I, 44). The social class structure followed the dictates of the 'Natural Order' and the pattern of distribution and involvement in production presented in the *Tableau* was geared purely to that 'Order'. However, their important achievement for Marx was that they had made the *economic* reproduction process dependent upon the existence of a particular *social class* structure, even though it was not clear that the mode of production itself dictated the class forms.

In his assessment of the *Tableau économique* itself, Marx largely took the form of the device as *given* and undertook a clarification of its *processes* without any major criticism emerging.

There were weaknesses in the concept and application of capital and in the concept of the surplus involved, but these did not affect the *principle of operation* of the device which Marx was now endeavouring to grasp.

Marx's interpretation of the *Tableau économique* in the 'Theories' manuscripts centred upon the presentation shown in Figure 10.1 (*TSV*, I, 308). The special feature of this table which gave it added clarity was the inclusion of the *sequential interdependencies* in the format. Marx inserted the letter designations (a)–(b)–(c)–(d)–, (a′)–(b′) and (a″)–(b″) in order to illustrate the links in the reproduction process implied by the *Tableau.*[11] Marx worked through an analysis of the links in great detail, but only a summary of his approach is presented here.

In each case, the letter (a) represented a 'starting point of a circulation' (*TSV*, I, 308) followed by one or more consequent links. (a)–(b) designated the outlay of rent on agricultural consumption commodities by landlords, while (a)–(c) designated their outlay on manufactured consumption commodities. The link (c)–(d) then represented the purchase by the 'sterile class' of agricultural consumption commodities. The 2,000 million that the farmers had paid in rent returned to them after facilitating the transfer of commodities to consumption. Money was involved here as both a means of payment, in the case of the rent payment by farmers to landlords, and as a means of purchase in the sequences which ensued, viz. (a)–(b), (a)–(c) and (c)–(d).

The link (a′)–(b′) comprised the transfer of manufactured means of production to the farmers to replace those used up in production. Finally, the link (a″)–(b″) represented the completion of the reproduction cycle as the raw material replacement needs of the manufacturing sector were transferred.

The above events proceeded in a strict temporal sequence for the whole circulation process was facilitated by a money supply of only 2,000 million. The sequence of exchanges followed from the movement of this money:

1 2,000 million paid by farmers to landlords as rent revenue.
2 (a)–(b) : 1,000 million paid by landlords to farmers
(a)–(c) : 1,000 million paid by landlords to 'sterile class'
3 (c)–(d) : 1,000 million paid by 'sterile class' to farmers

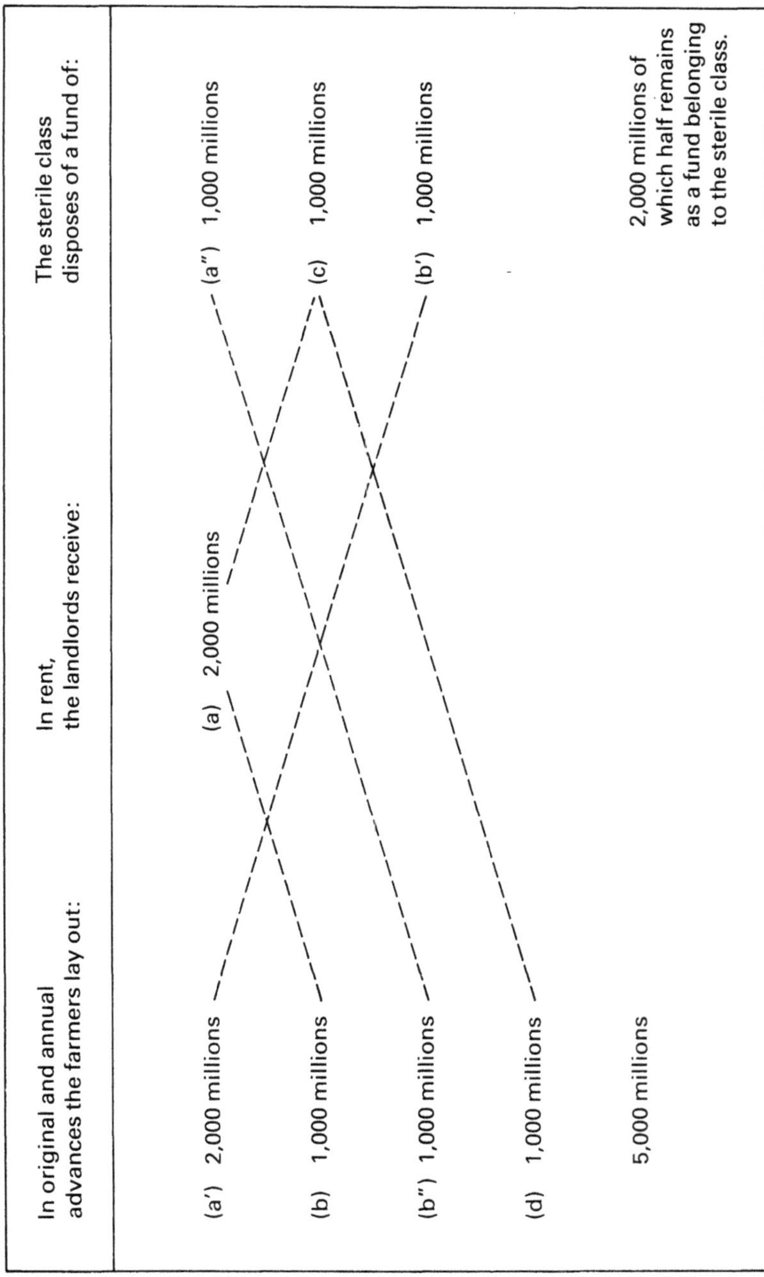
In original and annual advances the farmers lay out:
In rent, the landlords receive:
The sterile class disposes of a fund of:
(a') 2,000 millions
(b) 1,000 millions
(b") 1,000 millions
(d) 1,000 millions
5,000 millions
(a) 2,000 millions
(a") 1,000 millions
(c) 1,000 millions
(b') 1,000 millions
2,000 millions of which half remains as a fund belonging to the sterile class.

Figure 10.1

(a′)–(b′)	:	1,000 million paid by farmers to 'sterile class'
4 (a″)–(b″)	:	1,000 million paid by 'sterile class' to farmers

Ultimately the money supply returned to the farmers and was the *form* in which the surplus accrued at the end of the reproduction period. It was then paid to the landlords as rent in order to initiate the next cycle.

As is evident from the above analysis, the *Tableau économique* focused upon circulation *between* sectors. It did not consider the necessary *intra*-sector exchanges which Marx had recognised and this was a major limitation of the device as a reproduction model. For Marx, then, in formulating his own reproduction schema on the basis of the *Tableau*, this limitation would have to be overcome. Moreover, the *Tableau* would need to be modified in its division of the economy into production sectors and the role of capital and the generation of surplus Value would have to be generalised to encompass all sectors.

It was in the letter to Engels of 6 July 1863 (*MEW*, 30, 361ff.) that Marx gave the first formal outline of his own reproduction model. He stated explicitly that the table that he had prepared was a substitute for Quesnay's and that it presented the *whole* process of reproduction.

Marx noted in the letter that neither Adam Smith nor Ricardo had considered the aggregate reproduction process. They had focused only upon the distribution of net revenue as incomes. They had done this even though it was evident to them that in production, material inputs were used up and had to be replaced. In Marx's reproduction table, the revenue distribution and replacement processes were integrated.

The table involved a two-sector economy. One sector produced 'means of subsistence' upon which the wages of labour and non-wage revenues were spent. The other sector produced means of production – explicitly, 'machinery and raw materials'. These were for replacement only, for the model was of simple reproduction. Variable capital was advanced to pay wages and constant capital was advanced to purchase means of production. Some means of production were employed but not used up in the period of production. They were not part of the table itself.

In contrast to the *Tableau économique*, the sectors of production devised by Marx comprised both agriculture and manufacturing. It was the *functional use of the output* of a sector by which it was now classified. This represented a profound change in the approach to aggregate reproduction analysis. Especially did it enable Marx to make the physical role of capital more explicit in all aspects of production and to emphasise the importance of physical replacement of means of production in perpetuating capitalist production (and, ultimately, the needs for *additional* physical capital in expanded reproduction). The table then made it clear that circulation was an integral means to the achievement of these ends.

The table that Marx devised is shown in Figure 10.2. There was a uniform rate of surplus Value of 200 per cent applied in production and exchanges took place at Values expressed in money terms. The latter was made possible by each sector involving capital with a Value composition ratio (constant capital to variable capital) of 4, although Marx did not make this point explicitly. This presumption made no allowance for the constant capital advanced but not used up in the production period, and, as noted above, it was not accounted for in the table. In order that the Value basis of exchange in the table be appropriate, it must additionally be assumed that the *gross* Value compositions of capital in each sector were the same.

The analysis was carried out in arithmetical terms, but as Marx pointed out, the quantities had no significance *per se*. The total production of the 'subsistence' sector was 700. Of this, 300 was exchanged internally, 100 for wages and 200 for non-wage revenues. These internal flows were represented by the broken lines 'upwards' which were the money payouts of wages and non-wage revenues, and the solid lines 'downwards' which were the consequent expenditures. Non-wage revenues were based on surplus Value. Its immediate form of payout was as the money category 'profit' in the hands of the producing capitalists. This was then allocated by them to the three phenomenal categories 'industrial profit', 'interest' and 'rent'.

In order that the sector's used-up constant capital could be replaced, the remaining 400 of its output had to be realised. This came from expenditures by those involved in production in the 'machinery and raw materials' sector. The variable capital advanced and the surplus Value generated in this sector were chosen by Marx to total 400, for these were the sources of the

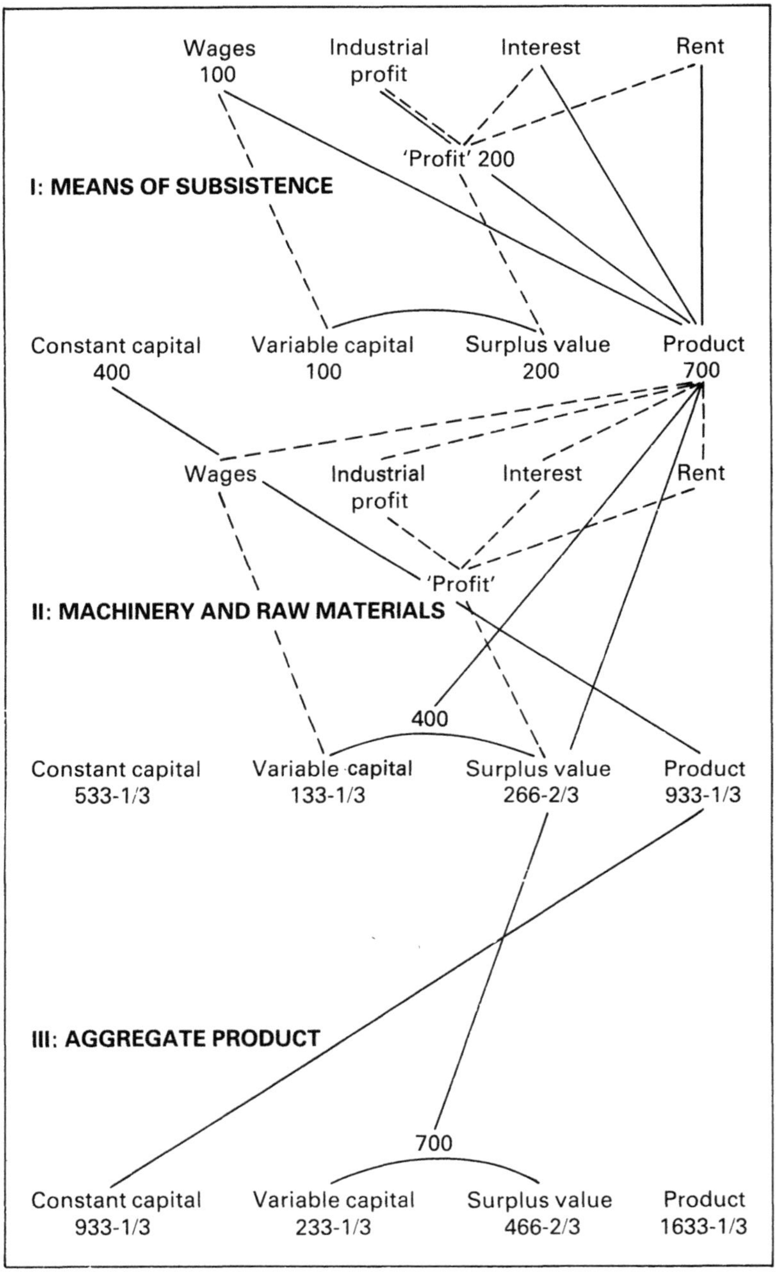

Wages
100
Industrial
profit
Interest
Rent
'Profit' 200
I: MEANS OF SUBSISTENCE
Constant capital
400
Variable capital
100
Surplus value
200
Product
700
Wages
Industrial
profit
Interest
Rent
'Profit'
II: MACHINERY AND RAW MATERIALS
400
Constant capital
533-1/3
Variable capital
133-1/3
Surplus value
266-2/3
Product
933-1/3
III: AGGREGATE PRODUCT
700
Constant capital
933-1/3
Variable capital
233-1/3
Surplus value
466-2/3
Product
1633-1/3

Figure 10.2

revenues spent in the inter-sector exchanges concerned. The payout of these revenues were represented by the 'upwards' broken lines between the sectors and the consequent expenditures by the solid line 'downwards'.

The reproduction process was then 'closed' by the receipts of 400 in money by the 'subsistence' producers being spent on means of production to replace the 400 of constant capital used up. The balance of the means of production produced was exchanged internally to replace used up constant capital in the 'machinery and raw materials' sector itself.

The table also included an aggregate level of analysis in which the total constant capital used up in production equalled the total output of the 'machinery and raw materials' sector and the total of incomes paid out equalled the total output of the 'subsistence' sector.

Marx also presented the essentials of the simple reproduction model in algebraic terms in the 'Theories' manuscripts. This analysis appeared in notebook XV and was thus written before the letter to Engels discussed above. What the algebraic form did was to express in general terms what the table version achieved in arithmetical terms. Marx's analysis (*TSV*, III, 248–9) may be summarised as follows:

Let: 0 = output
c = constant capital used up
v = variable capital
s = surplus Value

where all of these variables are measured in Value terms. For sector A ('means of subsistence'):

$$0_a = c_a + v_a + s_a$$

For sector B ('machinery and raw materials'):

$$0_b = c_b + v_b + s_b$$

The essential reproduction requirement is that:

$$0_a = (v_a + s_a) + (v_b + s_b)$$

And with $0_a - (v_a + s_a) = c_a$, this requirement becomes:

$$c_a = (v_b + s_b)$$

This last requirement reflects the necessary quantitative interdependence between the sectors that the constant capital used up in the 'subsistence' sector' is able to be replaced through purchases of 'subsistence' commodities by the workers and capitalists in the means of production sector.

The analysis so far has established the abstract potential for the capitalist economy to reproduce itself under particular, analytically imposed conditions. The next concern for Marx was to investigate the relationship of these conditions to the realities of the capitalist production and circulation processes so far abstracted from. His critico-historical investigations of these further dimensions of 'motion' are considered in the next two chapters of my study.

CHAPTER 11

The consequences of capital accumulation

THE LOGICAL DIMENSIONS OF THE CAPITAL ACCUMULATION PROCESS

The conditional analytical vision of the capitalist economic sysem, presented by Marx as the schema of expanded reproduction necessarily embraced the capital accumulation process. This process reflected what he saw as the most essential rationale of capitalist behaviour directed towards the continuing maximisation of the valorisation of capital. Capital accumulation had ramifications for the operations of the production process and its participants as well as for the circulation process. In the former, the quantitative and qualitative dimensions were directly affected by capitalists' decisions about expansion and the choice of technology to be embodied in such expansion. Here Marx was highly sensitive to the social and economic implications of any technological change for workers. The requirements for an unimpeded circulation process in expanded reproduction were stringent. Capital accumulation required quantitative and qualitative changes to the inputs available to production as well as the appropriate pattern of growth of demand in concert with decisions to produce more and/or different commodities.

Marx isolated for analytical purposes the effects of capital accumulation on production and its participants. Some crucial implications could be argued independently of the immanent difficulties of circulation which would inevitably accompany the process of production growth. The expansion of the capitalist forces of production *per se* had its own set of logical contradictions which would only be compounded by those of the analytically subsequent, but operationally integrated circulation process.

Marx did not find this analytical separation of the logical dimensions of expanded reproduction clearly developed in political economy. Capital accumulation was most frequently related immediately to its implications for the circulation of the greater output of commodities. In Marx's interpretation, it was again Ricardo who stood out in the history of political economy as the writer whose thought on capital accumulation and its effects warranted most attention. Before and after Ricardo's *Principles*, it seemed to Marx that, with a few exceptions, nothing very definitive was written about accumulation as an analytically identifiable dimension of capitalist 'motion'. The particular exceptions that he chose to emphasise were the works of John Barton, Thomas Hodgskin, George Ramsay and Antoine-Elisée Cherbuliez.

In the 'Theories of Surplus Value' manuscripts, several dimensions of capital accumulation and its consequences were analysed by Marx. Accumulation and technological change were simultaneous phenomena for Marx.[1] This led him to consider the dynamics of the composition of capital in production, including the logical problems raised in the analysis of the forms that such compositional changes could take. These dynamics were understood by Marx to be integrally and causally related to the temporal pattern of changes in the rate of surplus Value generated in production and to the appearance of changes in the rate of profits received by capitalists. Here he pursued the dialectical-logical origins of the phenomenon so often referred to in political economy as the falling rate of profits.[2]

A further dimension of capital accumulation, and the technological change that it brought with it, which concerned Marx, was the potential effect of the expanding use of machinery on the social and economic conditions of the working class. His reasoning on this aspect of 'motion' especially served to reinforce his view of the contradiction-ridden nature of capitalism as a *human* system.

In considering Marx's critical analyses of the capital accumulation origins of capitalism's 'motion', it is worth noting that he argued in terms of macro-economic aggregates. References to the micro-economic 'foundations' of such aggregates involving individual capitalist decision making processes were made in abstraction from any variations between sectors of production. This enabled Marx to carry out his analysis in *Value* terms with realised prices directly proportional to embodied abstract labour inputs. Clearly this led him to understate profoundly the complexity of the analyses in terms of linking them to the *phenomena* observed in reality. The behaviour of the *Value* composition of capital and rate of profits consequent upon capital accumulation can only be considered, at best, as a first logical step towards comprehending the *phenomenal appearances* of capitalist 'motion'. Marx did not give due emphasis to this qualification in the 'Theories' analyses.

THE DYNAMICS OF THE COMPOSITION OF CAPITAL

It was quite evident to Marx as an empirical matter, that capital accumulation under conditions of competition between individual capitalists brought with it the constant struggle to achieve leadership in the use of cost-reducing technology. Each capitalist sought to increase his access to relative surplus Value by using the maximum amount of labour-saving machinery of the most productive type available.

In analysing such processes of technological change, Marx's first task was to devise a logical framework through which the concrete forms of change could be represented in a way that was amenable to formal analysis. That is, he had to be able to 'measure', in quantitative and qualitative terms, the technologically based changes to the forces of production by means of some *analytically* consistent and coherent categories. The key category here was to be the *organic composition of capital*. However, some care is needed in ascertaining the meaning and significance of this category for Marx's critique in the 'Theories' manuscripts.

The concrete manifestation of the technological change in which Marx was interested involved a rising physical 'ratio' of machinery to the living labour required to activate it. This he referred to initially as 'the *method of production*' (*TSV*, II, 279,

380–1). Later in the manuscript he defined the 'technological composition of capital' explicitly as the '*ratio* between living labour or number of workers . . . and the *quantity of the instruments of labour*' (*TSV*, II, 455).

Now while this physical-technical 'ratio' was that required to analyse the operational and use-value aspects of production, including the implications of technological change for labour employment, there were *Value* dimensions of the processes to be considered as well. By expressing the components of the physical 'ratio' in Value terms, Marx devised his *Value composition of capital* category. It could be used immediately in the analysis of capital accumulation as a Value-orientated activity in which the requirements and consequences could be assessed in Value terms. For capitalists, the concrete forms involved were but a means to an end. What was produced and how had little or no relevance outside of the results in the books of account!

The introduction of a Value composition of capital meant that the effects of capital accumulation on the production process now had to be considered in two, potentially separate dimensions. Additional capital applied to production, and thus additional demand for machinery, raw materials and, probably, labour power, may involve a change in the 'method of production' in a physical-technical sense *and/or* a change in the composition of capital as a Value ratio (*TSV*, II, 276, 279, 380–2). By itself, the former was a sufficient but not a necessary condition for the latter to occur. The Value composition of capital could alter quite independently of any change in the concrete forms of the forces of production by virtue of a change in the relative Values of commodities comprising constant capital and variable capital.

The Value composition ratio most frequently used by Marx was that between constant capital (c) and variable capital (v) in the expression c/v. This was an ambiguous ratio in the sense that both stock and flow dimensions were involved. As would be expected, given the contemporary standards of analytical sophistication, Marx did not give any explicit attention to the precise meaning of c and v in this sense. It is clear that variable capital was intended to express the flow of outlays on labour power and will turn over at least once per analytical period. The constant capital was not so definite as two measures were possible: first, the flow of the means of production 'used up', the Value of which was 'transferred' to the commodities produced in any period; and secondly, the stock of the means of production, perhaps only *part* of which provided the flow of Value to the commodities produced, depending upon the assumptions made about durability. The capitalist expected to recoup the *flows* of capital Value through the process of realisation of the Value of the commodities produced. However, in order to analyse the effects of technological change on the Value rate of profits, which was one of the important dimensions of the 'motion' of capitalism for Marx, it would have made no sense to consider anything other than the *total* constant capital required to undertake the given 'method of production' when using the variable c, whatever the rate at which its Value was 'used up'. The Value composition of capital that was required to formulate the periodic Value rate of profits in Marx's terms necessarily required that c represent total constant capital. This can be seen in the expression for this rate: $r = s/(c + v) = e/(1 + g)$; where s = surplus Value, c = total constant capital, v = variable capital, e = rate of surplus Value (s/v), and g = Value composition of capital (c/v).

In the Value composition of capital ratio, any alteration in the Value of means of production, raw materials or necessary wage commodities, with the same 'method of production' would enter the Values of c and/or v and potentially change the composition as measured in these terms. More strictly, the requirement for a change in the ratio was that total proportional change in c should be different from that in v (*TSV*, II, 380–2). It was in the context of his endeavour to express the links between the composition of capital in technical and Value terms that Marx introduced the category he called the *organic composition of capital*.

At this stage of the evolution of his critique of political economy, Marx used the category to convey a 'combination' of the technical and Value dimensions of the composition of capital. He referred to the former as the 'first aspect' and to the latter as the 'second aspect' of the category (*TSV*, II, 276). That a change in *either* 'aspect' could bring a change in the organic composition was reiterated a few pages later. Here Marx was quite explicit that the organic composition would change with 'a change which is only due to the fact that the *Value* (*the proportional Value*) of the amounts [of capital] employed has changed' (*TSV*, II, 279; cf. 283–4, 288). The emphasis, so far, then, was on Value composition as the *manifestation* of organic composition and changes in the latter could arise from either technical *or* Value changes. Thus, in a situation where the Value effects of a technical change in composition were exactly offset by appropriate changes in the relative Values of the commodities comprising constant and variable capital, Marx noted that 'there would be no change at all in the organic composition [of capital]' (*TSV*, II, 381; cf. 387–8).

From the evidence in the 'Theories' manuscripts, it is reasonable to argue that at this time, the organic composition of capital category was used by Marx to express the composition of capital in *Value* terms as a net result of a particular technological composition, i.e. a particular 'method of production', in which the commodities involved as the means of production and as wage commodities had a given vector of Values. Any change in either the technical ratio or in the relative Values of constant and variable capital items was treated by Marx as a change in the organic composition, unless, by coincidence, the two sources of change negated each other.[3]

Capital accumulation could bring with it changes in either or both of the technical-physical and Value compositions of capital in production. The particular trend that Marx assumed existed and wanted to emphasise was that the physical 'ratio' of machinery to labour employed was 'increasing', whatever that meant *per se*, given the heterogeneous nature of the constituent elements to be added up and/or compared. This 'ratio' emphasised the choice of technique that the individual capitalist had to make in his endeavour to maximise the productivity of the labour power that he purchased at its given Value. Independently of this choice, though, the capitalist had to purchase items of constant capital and labour power at given Values, too. The all important organic composition of capital that affected the Value rate of profits was thus influenced by two aspects of the consequences of capital accumulation, viz. changes in technical composition and in the relative Values of commodities on which constant and variable capitals were spent.

The choice of more machinery-intensive 'methods of production' by capitalists affected the organic composition of capital and the Value rate of profits that could potentially be realised in circulation. At the same time, this choice had direct implications for trends in the relative and absolute employment of labour. This latter effect will be taken up again below (see pp. 244ff.). In the next section, the effect of the changing choice of technique, in combination with any changes in the Values of constant and variable capital commodities, on the organic composition of capital, and consequently on the Value rate of profits, will be analysed.

THE FALLING RATE OF PROFITS

A crucial distinction reiterated by Marx in his discussion of the effects of capital accumulation and the rising organic composition of capital was that between the Value rate of profits and its essence, the rate of surplus Value. This distinction, along with the central role of the organic composition category itself, were emphasised by Marx as the bases for his critique of the analyses of the falling rate of profits that had appeared in political economy.

For Marx, the *logic* of the 'dynamics' of the rate of profits was quite straightforward. In Value terms, using the symbols of the previous section, it could be expressed alternatively as follows:

$$r = s/(c + v) = e.v/(c+v) = e/(1 + g)$$

The effect of capital accumulation on the Value rate of profits could then be analysed in terms of the relative changes that it brought to the numerator and denominator of one of these expressions. In particular, Marx's argument was that any formal analysis of the 'dynamics' of the rate of profits rquired a co-ordinated understanding of the trends in the organic composition of capital and the rate of surplus Value induced by capital accumulation.

In the 'Theories' manuscripts, the analysis of this aspect of the 'motion' of capitalism was worked out mostly through lengthy arithmetical manipulations which belied the simplicity of the *logic* involved. At one stage, the analysis was a side product of the tortuous arithmetic of the 'tables of differential rent' (*TSV*, II, 270ff.). Here Marx's summary of his arithmetical results revealed certain generalised principles that related to a situation in which the 'method of production' remained constant but the organic composition of capital and the rate of surplus Value changed in response to changes in the relative Values of raw materials and wages commodities. The rate of profits was argued to *fall* when a proportional *decrease* in the organic composition was dominated by a proportional *decrease* in the rate of surplus Value; when an *increase* in the organic composition was accompanied by a *constant* rate of surplus Value; or when a *constant* organic composition was accompanied by a *decrease* in the rate of surplus Value (*TSV*, II, 286–8).

Some pages later in the manuscripts, Marx returned to the arithmetical analysis of the relationship between changes in the organic composition of capital and the Value rate of profits. This time, he included changes in the technical composition, i.e. in the 'method of production', as a source of change in the organic composition (*TSV*, II, 379ff.). The change in technology was first considered independently of any changes in the Value of the commodities that comprise variable and constant capital. The effect of the change was then quite readily calculated if the rate of surplus Value remained constant. Under these conditions, for example, an increase in the use of machinery and a reduction in the number of workers employed *must* raise the proportion of constant capital to variable capital in any total capital advanced. With fewer workers employed at the same rate of surplus Value, less surplus Value would be generated and this must result in a lower Value rate of profits. Marx also considered again the effects of various combinations of changes in the relative Values of variable and constant capital advanced with the 'method of production' constant. Various alternative patterns of change, with a given rate of surplus Value, could result in a rise in the organic composition of capital and a consequent fall in the rate of profits. Finally, Marx turned his attention to the more complex case of a changed 'method of production' together with changes in the relative Values of variable and constant capital commodities and changes in the rate of surplus Value. The results revealed a range of possible net effects on the organic composition of capital and hence on the rate of profits (*TSV*, II, 381–4).

Having worked through these examples and established some general principles of the logic of capital accumulation and the 'dynamics' of the Value rate of profits, Marx found Ricardo's efforts to come to grips with these aspects of the 'motion' of capitalism to have much understated the degree of complexity involved and to have failed to emphasise the appropriate causal relations. The approach to the analysis of capital accumulation in the *Principles* was quite different from Marx's, largely because of Ricardo's concern with different aspects of capitalist 'motion'. For Ricardo, the important dimensions of growth were those associated with the rising price of agricultural foodstuffs that would emerge as demand rose in the face of diminishing returns to farming coupled with import restrictions in the form of the 'Corn Laws'. Especially was he concerned with the implications of this situation for class income distribution patterns, a part of which would manifest itself as a falling rate of profits as money-wage costs rose.

In his formal analyses of these aspects of growth, Ricardo gave no explicit attention to changes in or the influence of the composition of capital as such. This was one aspect of the *Principles* analysis of the 'dynamics' of the rate of profits that troubled Marx. The other was Ricardo's emphasis, in his formal examples at least, on capital accumulation as involving wage capital only. In Marx's view, Ricardo was pursuing the 'dynamics' of the rate of surplus Value and omitting the broader and more complex arguments that arose when the rate of profits was analysed (*TSV*, II, 373–6, 426–7). Although Marx did not make the point, this appearance in Ricardo's work masked the assumption of a given and constant technologically-determined ratio between non-wage and wage capital which was only belatedly lifted in Chapter XXXI, 'On Machinery', added to the third edition of the *Principles*.[4] The fact remained, though, that Ricardo's examples employed a rate of profits expression which *explicitly* included in the denominator only wage capital and this was, in effect, for analytical purposes, nothing but a rate of surplus Value in Marx's view.

Marx was in no doubts about Ricardo's concern with the prospect of a falling rate of profits as growth proceeded: 'This is one of the most important points in the Ricardian system' (*TSV*, II, 438). And, in Marx's view, Ricardo had correctly rejected Adam Smith's idea that any tendency for the rate of profits to fall was induced by competition for the limited investment opportunities that became available as capital accumulated. Competition could only ensure the *uniformity* of the rates of profit between sectors of production and not the *level* of the general rate itself.

However, Ricardo's alternative theory of the phenomenon did not satisfy Marx either (*TSV*, II, 438–9, 467–8).

According to Marx's reading, Ricardo's argument was that the determination of the general rate of profits was immediately and predominantly dependent upon the 'dynamics' of agricultural food prices. And Ricardo's belief that there would be an inevitable secular rise in these prices was made very evident by a series of passages from the *Principles* quoted by Marx (*TSV*, II, 461–2). For example, Ricardo wrote that: 'With the progress of society, the *natural price of labour* has always a *tendency to rise, because one of the principal commodities by which its natural price is regulated, has a tendency to become dearer, from the greater difficulty of producing it*' (*Principles*, 93; quoted *TSV*, II, 461).[5] Ricardo was aware that such a tendency could be countered 'for a time' by 'improvements in agriculture, [and] the discovery of new markets, whence provisions may be imported', although the latter avenue would be hampered by the continuation of the 'Corn Laws' (*Principles*, 93; quoted *TSV*, II, 461). The key words here are 'for a time', because Ricardo went on to analyse the effects of agricultural food prices in terms that expressed their dominant tendency to rise: e.g. 'The natural price of all commodities, excepting raw produce and labour, has a tendency to fall, in the progress of wealth and population', and 'As population increases, these necessaries will be constantly rising in price, because more labour will be necessary to produce them' (*Principles*, 93–4, 101; quoted *TSV*, II, 461). In Marx's terms, then, Ricardo was arguing that growth brought with it a rise in the Value of labour power. The effect of this was to increase the variable capital required to mobilise a given quantity of living labour.

For Ricardo, this was the unequivocal origin of any fall in the rate of profits: 'in all countries, and all times, *profits depend* on the quantity of labour requisite to provide necessaries for the labourers on that land or with that capital which yields no rent' (*Principles*, 126; quoted *TSV*, II, 466). In disagreeing with Adam Smith, Ricardo reiterated this point quite explicitly when he asserted that

> *no accumulation of capital will permanently lower profits, unless there be some permanent cause for the rise of wages* . . . If the necessaries of the workman could be constantly

> increased with the same facility, there could be no *permanent alteration of the rate of profit or wages* . . . (*Principles*, 289; quoted *TSV*, II, 467.)

Thus it was that as far as Marx was concerned, the tendency of the rate of profits to fall was part of Ricardo's interpretation of the 'motion' of capitalism. The following piece from the *Principles* made this very clear: 'The natural tendency of profits then is to fall; for, in the progress of society and wealth, the additional quantity of food required is obtained by the sacrifice of more and more labour' (*Principles*, 120; quoted *TSV*, II, 462–3). And, while Ricardo recognised that this tendency may be counteracted from time to time by productivity improvements in agriculture, of one sort or another, the overall conclusion of his analysis in Chapter VI, 'On Profits', and elsewhere in the *Principles*, was that both the rate of profits and total profits would decline in a growing capitalist economic system (*Principles*, 110ff.).

For Marx, Ricardo's conclusions were correct in this matter, but his reasoning was wrongheaded on two main counts (*TSV*, II, 439). First, as Marx had already argued, Ricardo's association of rising food prices and differential rents with growth in the agricultural sector represented an error of empirical judgment about trends in productivity. The appearance of differential rent was based on an incomplete theory that omitted the category absolute rent and tied the general rate of profits exclusively to agricultural production costs in a causal sense.[6] Secondly, the arguments presented by Ricardo concerning the rate of *profits* did not adequately reflect the role of non-wage capital in the determination of the rate. In his *formal analyses*, Marx found that Ricardo was effectively dealing with a rate of surplus Value concept and this could provide only limited insights into the rate of profits issue. Ricardo frequently expressed *informal* recognition that the capital to which profit was related in formulating a rate of profits included the exchange value of the means of production in use. This recognition, though, did not form an explicit part of his *analysis* of the rate of profits in the *Principles* and, in *this* analysis, Ricardo did not concern himself with the capital composition issues that Marx thought so essential (*TSV*, II, 379–80, 438–9).

Marx's critique of Ricardo's reasoning about the falling rate of profit phenomenon, then, focused on these two limitations. With respect to the first issue concerning Ricardo's empirical judgments about the 'dynamics' of food prices and the rate of profits, supported by his theory of differential rent, Marx made some counter-observations which, at least, cast some doubt upon the veracity of the way in which Ricardo had reached his conclusions. For example, Marx expressed his belief that during the phase of history to which Ricardo referred, there was a period, specifically 1797 to 1813, in which the available statistical data indicated that the rate of profits had *risen*, despite a *rise* in agricultural prices (*TSV*, II, 459–60). A crucial factor in this rise in the rate of profits had been a *reduction* in the *real* wage calculated in terms of corn, even though the *nominal* wage had been increasing. Later in the manuscript, Marx related some additional evidence on this matter provided by John Barton in his *Observations on the Circumstances which Influence the Condition of the Labouring Classes of Society* (1817). Barton provided a table in which he showed the *real* 'wages of husbandry', measured in 'pints of wheat', as falling in several stages from 1742 to 1808, with the money wage rising significantly over the same period (*TSV*, II, 585). Marx did not relate these observations back to those made previously, but they do serve to emphasise the great difficulties that were presented in making empirical judgments that had some meaning in relation to theory. Barton's evidence was based on *market* prices for wheat; not 'natural' prices in any sense, and certainly not *Values*. Moreover, the *effect* of the real and nominal wage changes referred to by Marx just could not be ascertained by 'armchair' analyses. It may be that the *market-realised* rate of profit *in agriculture* actually rose as Marx suggested. But this cannot give any empirical indication of what happened to the 'normal' general rate or profits or the market rate realised in manufacturing industry. There was a '*void*' between the *logic* that Marx pursued in his endeavour to comprehend the effects of capital accumulation on the *Value* rate of profits and real-world phenomena to which this logic was purportedly related. Any analytical 'bridge' over this 'void' was to be very difficult to construct, although Marx did not seem to be aware of this fact.

When Marx first considered Ricardo's rent theory and its origins in the 'Theories' manuscripts, he had already argued in empirical terms that while agricultural production may not have experienced the same massive growth of labour productivity as had occurred in manufacturing industry, it had had its level of productivity raised (*TSV*, II, 18–21). This suggested an absolute reduction in the *Value* of the real, or commodity 'subsistence', wage. Both Ricardo and Marx had assumed the latter constant for analytical purposes, although both were well aware that it may change over time.[7]

Fortunately, Marx's point here was a simpler one than that which he was to tackle with empirical judgments later on. Specifically, he argued that the fact that less fertile land was to be cultivated, as Ricardo's theory of growth required, did not necessarily mean that labour productivity in agriculture would decline. Indeed, Marx suggested that it may mean that the land was now able to be made *more* productive due to technological change in spite of its innate infertility. This could explain the fact that it was now possible to cultivate such land and return the general rate of profits, plus the required rent, given current market prices (*TSV*, II, 20; cf. 244).

However, whatever Marx may have thought about the empirical significance of this observation, the simple matter of fact that he had to face was that during the period to which Ricardo referred, wheat prices had risen very rapidly. Marx reported on this in detail (*TSV*, II, 133–6) and he then admitted that the only reasonable explanation for such events was that the rapid population growth, combined with import restrictions, had forced the use of decreasingly fertile land on which labour productivity levels had fallen (*TSV*, II, 141–4, 236). Thus it could be suggested that, initially at least, improvements in cultivation techniques had not been adequate to compensate for the infertility of the required land and that the *differential* component of total rent may have risen. Marx hastened to point out, though, that the fall of wheat prices after 1819 indicated that such fertility problems must have been progressively corrected, perhaps as a *consequence* of the price 'security' afforded by the 'Corn Laws' (*TSV*, II, 236). Here again, Marx faced the 'void' between the empirical evidence and the theory that he thought supported it. The trend in observed wheat prices reflected first and foremost *market* forces. More information than Marx had available would have been required to disentangle the production-cost trends from these prices.

In Marx's reading, Ricardo had not given due emphasis even to the possibility of technical improvements in agriculture that would have qualified his views on the effects of growth on wage costs (*TSV*, II, 321–4). Ricardo was quite evidently aware of this technological potential (*Principles*, 79ff.) and Marx quoted passages from the *Principles* to this effect (*Principles*, 79; quoted *TSV*, II, 321). Ricardo argued the origins of improvements in agricultural productivity in two senses (*Principles*, 80–3; *TSV*, II, 322–4): first, changes in production methods that directly affected the productivity of the land itself; and secondly, changes in production methods that altered the way in which the land was worked, especially through improved machinery, and thereby indirectly affected the productivity of the land. The first sense meant that less land could be employed to produce a given level of use values, while the second required the same land to be worked with less labour to achieve this same output. Marx's difficulty with this analysis, as it was presented in the *Principles*, was that Ricardo had not been precise enough about the range of possible influences on the Value composition of capital that could follow from the productivity potentials explored. This represented a significant limitation on the scope of Ricardo's analysis of the effects of growth on rent and profits (*TSV*, II, 324–7).

Overall, Marx felt that Ricardo had not given enough attention to the issue of capital composition as it affected the formal analysis of the falling rate of profits. Ricardo's perception of capital accumulation appeared to be too narrow in that the *Value* implications of the rising use of machinery relative to labour were not adequately analysed. Ricardo must have observed this trend in 'methods of production' as he had occasion to comment on it several times – most importantly in Chapter XXXI added to the third edition of the *Principles*.[8] The sort of proposition upon which Ricardo based his analysis of growth and which concerned Marx was the following: 'When we say that *revenue* is *saved*, and *added to capital*, what we mean is, that the *portion of revenue*, so *said to be added to capital*, is *consumed by productive instead of unproductive labourers*' (*Principles*, 151n.; quoted *TSV*, II, 470, 535). Marx was prompted to question whether or not Ricardo was sufficiently aware of the broader analytical significance of 'productive' consumption in the context of additions to the capital stock.[9] Any notion that it was sufficient to explicate the accumulation process in terms of variable capital only was tantamount to a 'wrong approach to the whole question of accumulation' (*TSV*, II, 470). What needed to be highlighted in the *formal analysis* of accumulation was that the capitalists had the option of choosing to devote the savings to 'the *industrial consumption* of the commodities which form constant capital, and are consumed as instruments of labour or materials of labour' (*TSV*, II, 470). Ricardo had not done this adequately, in Marx's view.

Another key quotation from the *Principles* was used repeatedly by Marx to draw attention to Ricardo's analytical shortcomings in this respect, viz. 'The labour of a million of men in manufactures, will always produce the same value, but will not always produce the same riches' (*Principles*, 273; quoted *TSV*, II, 414, 473, 538). This simple little piece required careful interpretation in order to set out the possible meanings that Ricardo may have intended. It is clear that by 'value' here he meant embodied-labour exchange value and by 'riches' he referred to physical use-value production. The obvious, perhaps literal, interpretation of the piece is then that Ricardo failed to take account of the possibility that the 'million of men', employed as *living* labour, may work with different means of production that could transfer quite different amounts of *past* embodied-labour exchange value to the commodities produced. In this situation, the exchange value generated could not legitimately be said to be always the same.

This interpretation was the one to which Marx adhered when he considered the piece in the context of analysing the capital composition aspect of capital accumulation. A rising organic composition of capital meant that 'the Value of the annual product of a million men will tend to rise continuously, in proportion to the growth of the past labour which plays a part in their annual production'. To this he added the comment that 'This alone shows that Ricardo was unable to understand either the essence of accumulation or the nature of profit' (*TSV*, II, 415). The same strong critical inference was made twice more in the 'Theories' manuscript (*TSV*, II, 473, 538).

To a degree, Ricardo's own subsequent argument supported the simple interpretation taken up by Marx. Ricardo argued explicitly that, *inter alia*, superior machinery may add to the production of 'riches' by the 'million of men', but 'they will not on that account add anything to value' (*Principles*, 273; quoted *TSV*, II, 538). Moreover, he compounded the ambiguity by arguing at the same time that 'improvements in skill, by a better division of labour', that is, 'disembodied' technical change, had the *same exchange-value implications* as the introduction of improved machinery.

He went on to use an example of stocking manufacturing to affirm the point (*Principles*, 273–4). In this example, the introduction of machinery enabled physical production to be doubled with the same *living* labour input. Ricardo claimed that the total exchange value of this production remained unchanged because no additional living labour had been used in production. Marx quoted the example (*TSV*, II, 538–9) and added the simple, but pointed, comment: 'N.B. provided the newly introduced machinery costs *nothing*.'

Marx's critique of Ricardo in this particular case was not adequately *qualified* in several respects. First, as Marx was well aware, Ricardo had made it very clear in Section III of Chapter I of the *Principles* that embodied-labour exchange value included the past labour transferred from means of production (*Principles*, 22ff.). Secondly, in analysing the 'machinery' issue, Ricardo had recognised that capital accumulation brought with it increased use of machinery relative to living labour employed. Marx quoted an explicit passage to this effect (*Principles*, 395) and granted that at this point Ricardo had grasped the trends in capital composition correctly, even if only 'one-sidedly' in excluding full discussion of the Value aspects involved (*TSV*, II, 576). Thirdly, it was possible that in the arguments to which Marx referred, Ricardo was adhering to the device that he had used previously to avoid the difficulty of making explicit allowance for fixed capital in his analyses. That is, he may have continued to include in current living labour inputs an allowance for the maintenance required to restore machinery and raw materials used up to their original exchange value.[10] This approach was made evident at several points in the *Principles* (see, e.g. 39, 91, 388) and Marx even quoted two of the relevant passages (*TSV*, II, 212, 566) without noticing how Ricardo used this approach. In the present context, the labour of the 'million of men' would have indeed generated the same exchange value, independently of the method or means of production in use, if Ricardo intended such an assumption about the use of the living labour to be made.

However, with or without these qualifications, the point of Marx's critique remained that Ricardo had endeavoured to analyse and understand the effects of capital accumulation on the rate of profits in isolation from the crucial accompaniment of the rising organic composition of capital. Ricardo's recognition of this dimension of capital accumulation did not extend beyond the physical-technical composition effects which, in this particular form, were not appropriately expressed for inclusion in the formal analysis of the falling rate of profits.

Whatever the appropriateness of the *source* of the falling rate of profits argued by Ricardo, he did consider it to have a potentially significant role in the future of the growing capitalist economic system. He was quite explicit in his view that an economy such as Britain's, with a growing stock of capital and population, but with a finite access to agriculturally suitable land on which to produce food, would inevitably experience a falling rate of profits and total profits (e.g. *Principles*, 110ff.). In the short run, some respite could be obtained by improved agricultural productivity (*Principles*, 120; *TSV*, II, 544). The only viable protection for British profits in the long run, though, was the repeal of the 'Corn Laws' that restricted access to the abundant and cheap corn available elsewhere in Europe and the world (*Principles*, 126; *TSV*, II, 545).[11]

The importance of this prognosis for Ricardo was that the lowering of the rate of profits, and eventually the total amount of profits, would cause national economic stagnation. The dynamic nature of the capitalist system depended upon continued capital accumulation. This process was *motivated* by an 'adequate' rate of profits and *facilitated* by an adequate volume of profits out of which saving could take place (*Principles*, 122; *TSV*, II, 544). As Marx saw the situation that Ricardo thought capitalism to be facing, 'accumulation has the tendency to check accumulation, and the *law of the falling rate of profit* . . . hangs ominously over bourgeois production' (*TSV*, II, 541). And, even more graphically, the situation represented 'the bourgeois "Twilight of the Gods" – the Day of Judgment' (*TSV*, II, 544). Marx's view of the fate of the capitalist system was much more complex and inevitable than that envisaged as a possibility by Ricardo. The capacity of free trade in corn to overcome the effects of capitalism's contradictions as manifested in the falling rate of profits would be very limited in Marx's prognoses. In chapter 12 below, I will return to the place of the 'dynamics' of profit in the immanently generated crises experienced by capitalism.

CAPITAL ACCUMULATION AND EMPLOYMENT: RICARDO AND BARTON

Marx had found that Ricardo's *formal* analysis of capital accumulation included little explicit role for changes in the composition of capital. Indeed, most of his argument in the *Principles* proceeded in terms of a *constant*, uniform composition of capital in exchange value terms. This ensured that prices were always directly proportional to embodied-labour exchange values in a 'comparative static' context, but the *constancy* was inappropriately retained in his 'dynamics' as well and resulted in severe analytical limitations being 'built in' from the start.[12] To Marx, it had been clear that accumulation brought with it less labour-intensive 'methods of production' and that this phenomenon was an integral part of the aspects of 'motion' induced by an increasing capital stock. Ricardo gave some belated recognition to this in Chapter XXXI, 'On Machinery' added to the third edition of the *Principles* in 1821. There he dealt explicitly with the influence that capital accumulation, and the accompanying relative increase in the reliance on machinery in production, might have on the employment of labour.

Marx was also concerned with this aspect of the consequences of capital accumulation. Just prior to his critique of Ricardo's 'On Machinery', Marx reiterated his view that, in the capitalist economic system, decision-making about employment did not relate to any *human* considerations. Rather, employment was but a means to the end of maximising the generation of surplus Value (*TSV*, II, 547–8). In the context of reading Chapter XXVI, 'On Gross and Net Revenue', of the *Principles*, this meant that the capitalists were concerned about *net* revenue generation and had no interest in the gross revenue from which it came. Yet it was the latter which determined the volume of employment. Marx felt that in effect, if not in the same spirit, Ricardo argued this point, too (*Principles*, 347–8; *TSV*, II, 548–9). Here Ricardo earned Marx's somewhat exaggerated praise for drawing attention to this ahuman aspect of capitalism: 'Ricardo expressed these tendencies consistently and ruthlessly. Hence much howling against him on the part of the philanthropic philistines' (*TSV*, II, 548). The evidence for this assertion was not very well documented, to say the least.

For Ricardo, the employment implications of growth in the age of machinery were not as self-evident as they were for Marx. For much of his life as a political economist, Ricardo had held that there would be no detrimental effects on workers due to the expanding use of machinery in production (*Principles*, 386–7). In Chapter XXXI of the third edition of the *Principles*, this perception changed *to a limited and qualified extent.* Ricardo made his revised stance on this issue plain enough, in principle at least: 'I am convinced, that *the substitution of machinery for human labour, is often very injurious to . . . the class of labourers*' (*Principles*, 388; quoted *TSV*, II, 556). Later he concluded, to similar effect, that 'the opinion entertained by the labouring class, that the employment of machinery is frequently detrimental to their interests, is not founded on prejudice and error, but is conformable to the correct principles of political economy' (*Principles*, 392; quoted *TSV*, II, 570).

Once again, Ricardo drew praise from Marx for what was a quite unusual perceptiveness for an orthodox political economist of the period: 'This section . . . bears witness to his *honesty* which so essentially distinguishes him from the vulgar economists' (*TSV*, II, 555). However, had Marx considered Ricardo's arguments more carefully, and paid due regard to the subtle analytical twist involved, he may not have appeared so convinced that Ricardo held views as strong as his own on this issue. The arguments posited by Ricardo were simply not orientated towards the problem of secular capital accumulation and its effects on labour employment and it is doubtful if he intended to demonstrate any *permanent* adverse effects of technological change at all.[13] This was evident from the efforts he made to reveal channels through which displaced workers could be re-employed (*Principles*, 390) and his ultimate view that machinery paid for out of accrued savings, i.e. that associated with secular accumulation, would not have the effect of reducing employment, at least not absolutely (*Principles*, 395, 396). Moreover, Ricardo made it quite clear that he did not want any of his ideas to discourage the use of labour-saving machinery (*Principles*, 395). What he feared at this point was the export of capital if the profit opportunities opened up by the use of more efficient machinery were not taken up in Britain. The result of this would be an *absolute* decrease in the employment of labour rather than just a relative decrease (*Principles*, 396–7). Ricardo's concern here, at least, for the well-being of the workers, as far as it went, must have pleased Marx.

Marx began his consideration of Chapter XXXI of the *Principles* by critically reviewing the ideas from which Ricardo claimed to have recanted (*TSV*, II, 555ff.). He quoted Ricardo's statements on this at length (*Principles*, 386–9) and took the opportunity to discredit such ideas in his own way.

It had been Ricardo's view that with the employment of additional machinery in production, appropriate adjustments would ensue as a consequence of market forces to ensure that all current labour would remain in employment. This labour would also enjoy the added benefit of a greater purchasing power of money-wages due to the reduced prices of consumer commodities now produced more efficiently (*Principles*, 387–8; *TSV*, II, 555–6). It was Marx's opinion that in believing this, Ricardo had been overly sanguine about the capacity of self-adjustment to correct the contradictions of capitalism exposed by the increasing use of machinery. Especially did he take exception to Ricardo's assertion that all displaced workers would be directly re-employed because '*the capital which employed them was still in being, and as it was the interest of those who had it to employ it productively*', other lines of production would emerge to absorb the 'free' capital and labour (*Principles*, 387; quoted *TSV*, II, 556).

In Marx's view, there appeared to be two stages of difficulty associated with this argument (*TSV*, II, 557ff.). First, he considered the situation of the capitalists who had employed the new machine. Marx reasoned that it was probable that the *initial* move by the capitalists would be to absorb the variable capital released by the change in technology into an equivalent Value of constant capital (*TSV*, II, 558). He also reiterated a position that Ricardo had taken in Chapter I of the *Principles*. This was that the very incentive to replace labour by machinery consequent upon a rise in money-wages was based upon the condition that less labour would be required to produce the machine than the labour that it replaced in production, given that the price of the machine would be unaffected by the wage rise (*Principles*, 40–2; *TSV*, II, 550–2).

Ricardo was quite explicit about this: 'Thus *then is the public benefited by machinery: these mute agents are always the produce of much less labour than that which they displace, even when they are of the same money value*' (*Principles*, 42; quoted *TSV*, II, 551). The effect of this argument, as Marx interpreted it, was to rule out any assurance that the displaced workers would all be absorbed by machinery production.

This left any re-employment potential to the developments after the machinery was installed. Here Marx analysed the second stage of difficulty that he found in Ricardo's original position on machinery (*TSV*, II, 558–60). Ricardo's idea had been that cheaper commodities produced by more efficient machinery meant more rapid capital accumulation as net-revenue available for saving increased. The result would be a more rapidly rising demand for labour which would take up any unemployed workers. For Marx, this was an optimistic argument, at best. The additional 'free' revenue might be spent on imported commodities. And what happened to the displaced workers depended upon the growth rate of the demand for labour as well as on the growth of the supply of labour. Marx's simple conclusion was that '*by no means* does a *necessary connection exist between the revenue that has been set free and the workers that have been set free of revenue*' (*TSV*, II, 558). If anything, it was more likely perhaps that, in the longer term, growth in new undertakings and industries would absorb the volume of labour set 'free' by current technological change, 'but this is of more benefit to *those who succeed the displaced men* than to the displaced men themselves (*TSV*, II, 560).

What, then, did Marx make of Ricardo's revised position on the effects of machinery on workers? He quoted in full and discussed the key arithmetical example by means of which Ricardo demonstrated his new conclusion that machinery *may* reduce the absolute level of employment (*Principles*, 388–90; *TSV*, II, 564ff.). Ricardo's point was that where the new machine led to a reduction in the *gross* revenue of the industry concerned, the outcome was that at a given money-wage, the capacity to employ labour would be reduced.[14]

The example used by Ricardo involved a capitalist producing 'necessaries' by farming and manufacturing. The capitalist initially worked with a capital stock of 20,000*l* which, using Marx's symbols of c for constant capital (referred to by Ricardo as fixed capital only) and v for variable capital (Ricardo clearly intended to limit his definition of circulating capital here to that advanced 'in support of labour', *Principles*, 388), had a c + v composition of 7,000*l* + 13,000*l*. The profit rate assumed was 10 per cent such that on total capital employed, the *net* revenue generated was 2,000*l*. To begin with, the capitalist was assumed each year to produce a gross produce valued at 15,000*l*; comprising the net revenue of 2,000*l* and replacement for the 'variable' capital of 13,000*l*. The labour employed by the capitalist did two things: one part was, albeit implicitly, but necessarily, required to provide maintenance for the fixed capital in use which must 'every year [be] put into its original state of efficiency' (*Principles*, 388; quoted *TSV*, II, 566); and the other part of the labour was to produce commodities for sale, either to the workers themselves or to others. The division between the two tasks did not matter for Ricardo's purposes.[15]

Then in one year, the capitalist was argued to have decided to employ half of his resources in the production of 'necessaries' and the other half to produce a machine which would assist in production in subsequent years. The value of each half of the resulting product, 'necessaries' and the machine, would be 7,500*l*, thus leaving the gross product at 15,000*l*, including 2,000*l* profit as before. As the capitalist intended the machine for his own use, the 2,000*l* net revenue must be realised through the 'necessaries' produced. This would leave only 5,500*l* as 'variable' capital to employ labour in subsequent years. The obvious result was that in the *immediate short term*, the labour previously employed by the 7,500*l* now embodied in the machine must be redundant. Subsequent production involved c = 14,500*l* and v = 5,500*l*, and with the 10 per cent profit-rate still applied, *gross* product fell to 7,500*l* while the *net* product remained at 2,000*l*. The *physical* volume of the gross product now produced was not made clear by Ricardo. But it would seem that with the aid of the new machine, fewer workers probably could have had a productivity rate that ensured that the physical product did not fall in proportion to the value of the gross product. Consequently, the units of 'necessaries' produced could have become cheaper.

Now Ricardo's conclusions from this example should not have been too definitive or sweeping given its contrived nature. He had argued only the *impact* effects on employment in the short term, but even so, initially, at least, he was prepared to state quite categorically that 'there will *necessarily be a diminution in the demand for labour, population will become redundant*, and the situation of the labouring classes will be that of distress and poverty' (*Principles*, 390; quoted *TSV*, II, 568).[16] However, from this point on, the qualifications to this exaggerated conclusion began to appear.

First, he noted that the increased purchasing power of a constant net revenue may permit an increased rate of saving and capital accumulation that may employ some of the redundant labour. The modified conclusion on the basis of this point alone was that 'there would not *necessarily* [but possibly and probably! – Marx's addition] *be any redundancy of people*'. To this, Ricardo added immediately: 'All I wish to prove, is, that the discovery and use of machinery may be attended with a diminution of gross produce; and whenever that is the case, it will be injurious to the labouring class, as some of their number will be thrown out of employment' (*Principles*, 390; quoted *TSV*, II, 569–70).[17]

Secondly, Ricardo went on to argue that machinery may facilitate a substantial increase in *net* revenue such that gross revenue is not decreased. Then, 'the situation of the labouring classes will . . . be considerably improved.' Ricardo ascribed this 'improvement' to three factors: '1st, *from the increased demand for menial servants*; 2dly, from the stimulus to savings from revenue, which such an abundant net produce will afford; and 3dly, from the low price of all articles of consumption on which . . . wages will be expended' (*Principles*, 392; quoted *TSV*, II, 570–1). Marx responded to these arguments with some indignation on behalf of the workers, now implying that Ricardo had posited the 'entire apologetic bourgeois presentation of machinery' (*TSV*, II, 571; cf. 571–4).

Marx found the idea that the economic fate of so many workers should depend on their becoming 'menial servants' abhorrent, labelling this suggestion, with due irony, 'a fine result of machinery' and 'a fine prospect' (*TSV*, II, 570, 571). He objected to the added uncertainty of employment which the increasing use of machinery would bring and to the inference that any burden of adjustment to technological change should fall on the workers (*TSV*, II, 571–2). And even when workers found employment under these new 'methods of production' it would involve them increasingly in submitting to 'subjugation' by the machine with which they worked (*TSV*, II, 571). Marx found the idea of the form of man's working life being dictated by a machine an unattractive one. He also found it objectionable that increasing numbers of workers would need to be employed in providing the luxuries for the owners of the means of production and in producing the material needs of 'fleets and armies'. Again with irony: 'Fine prospects, these, for the labourer, and very desirable results of the development of the productive powers of his labour' (*TSV*, II, 572; cf. 573).

Towards the end of his chapter 'On Machinery', Ricardo softened his stance on the impact of technological change on employment even further when he considered explicitly the secular growth of the capital stock. Although Marx did not make much of it, the following passage can be argued to have represented a significant shift of emphasis on the issue by Ricardo:[18]

> To elucidate the principle, I have been supposing, that improved machinery is *suddenly* [emphasis original] discovered, and extensively used; but the truth is, that these discoveries are gradual, and rather operate in *determining the employment of the capital which is saved and accumulated, than in diverting capital from its actual employment.* (*Principles*, 395; quoted *TSV*, II, 574.)

The motivation for the increased use of machine-intensive 'methods of production' was now specified as the secular increase of the relative cost of labour due to what Ricardo saw as the declining productivity of agriculture combined with the restrictions imposed by the 'Corn Laws'. This gradualist perception of technological change brought Ricardo to a much less profound prognosis for the future of employment: '*The demand for labour will continue to increase with an increase of capital, but not in proportion to its increase; the ratio will necessarily be a diminishing ratio*' (*Principles*, 395; quoted *TSV*, II, 576). Marx's response to this was that in the end Ricardo had expressed 'the correct law of [the] growth of capital, although his reasoning is very one-sided' (*TSV*, II, 576). Thus, Ricardo had reasoned too narrowly with respect to the changing technological composition of capital as a ratio both in the context of its implications for employment and with respect to the role of its Value dimension in understanding the 'dynamics' of the rate of profits.

Prompted by Ricardo's favourable reference in a footnote to Chapter XXXI (*Principles*, 395n.), Marx briefly reviewed John Barton's *Observations on the Circumstances which Influence the Condition of the Labouring Classes of Society* (1817) in which the machinery and employment issue was discussed (*TSV*, II, 576ff.).[19] It was Marx's view that 'Indisputably, Barton has very great merit' (*TSV*, II, 577) on this issue, at least. His key contribution was a recognition of the immanent predisposition of a growing capitalist economy to adopt 'methods of production' that involved increasing the ratio of fixed capital to circulating capital, apparently in exchange value terms. While Marx rejected the dichotomy of capital used here as being relevant to the analysis of circulation but not to production *per se* that was in focus in the present argument (*TSV*, II, 578–9), the important thing was that Barton aligned the capacity to employ with the relative diminution of circulating capital advanced (*TSV*, II, 576–7).

CAPITAL ACCUMULATION ANALYSIS AFTER RICARDO

In his critique of political economy after Ricardo, Marx found only three writers whose thoughts on capital accumulation warranted attention. In their various ways and to varying degrees, Hodgskin, Ramsay and Cherbuliez related the capital accumulation process to the changing composition of capital, the tendency of the rate of profits to fall and the employment effects on workers.[20]

Thomas Hodgskin's book *Labour Defended against the Claims of Capital etc.* of 1825 contained a theory of the falling rate of profits which Marx found accorded well with his own (*TSV*, III, 298ff.). Hodgskin's argument was that because interest or profit was the source of saving by means of which capital was accumulated, the increase in the capital stock through time would be at a compounding rate. In each successive period, the profit from the previous would be included as capital and the rate of profits applied meant ever growing absolute additions to the pre-existing capital stock. This compounding accumulation process, though, was distorted by the falling rate of profits.

The fall of the rate of profits was explained by Hodgskin to be the consequence of a shortage of labour as capital accumulated at its compound rate. A rising ratio of capital per unit of labour resulted in a reduced rate of returning profit from production which in the long run would dominate any improvement in labour productivity which accompanied the capital accumulation (*TSV*, III, 298).

Hodgskin's impressionistic thesis depended essentially upon the rate of population increase falling well behind the rate of capital accumulation, as Marx noted (*TSV*, III, 299, 306). Given that this occurred, Marx felt that the principle behind the falling rate of profits in Hogskin's work was similar to his own in the sense that it appeared to involve a rise in the use of 'capital' relative to labour employed (*TSV*, III, 303–4, 306, 307). Marx considered that this trend accompanying capital accumulation was similar enough, *in effect*, to a rising organic composition of capital to credit Hodgskin with the correct insight into the source of the falling rate of profits (*TSV*, III, 302, 311, 312). At least, it could be said that he was more conscious of the appropriate forces underlying the fall than Adam Smith or Ricardo had been in Marx's judgment (*TSV*, III, 313).

In this conclusion, Marx was overgenerous to Hodgskin. Beyond a superficial appearance, there was no evidence provided by Marx that Hodgskin had grasped the essential origin of the falling rate of profits in the nature of the capital accumulation process and the changing composition of capital. In Marx's own analysis, the rising organic composition of capital was a *conscious* result of the behaviour of competitive capitalists. By contrast, for Hodgskin this outcome was an *accident* of the relative rates of expansion of capital and population. Marx integrated this rising organic composition of capital into a logical framework of analysis which, granted its limitations, produced the falling *Value* rate of profits as its result. According to Marx's own critique, Hodgskin did nothing like this.

The work of George Ramsay to which Marx referred was *An Essay on the Distribution of Wealth* published in 1836. Ramsay's merit, in Marx's view, centred upon his *effective* formulation of the constant capital and variable capital dichotomy, although he retained the fixed and circulating names for his categories (*TSV*, III, 326–7). Moreover, in the process of his analyses using this dichotomy, Ramsay had come close to formulating a concept of surplus Value akin to Marx's own (*TSV*, III, 328–9). Marx now found that Ramsay had interpreted correctly the effects of capital accumulation on the composition of capital and on the welfare of workers. Because of the former, which involved a relative reduction in the demand for labour, the latter did not increase in line with the growing wealth of the nation (*TSV*, III, 334–6).

Ramsay had come 'closer to a correct understanding of the rate of profit than the others' (*TSV*, III, 351), but the analysis of its dynamics in the context of capital accumulation which he provided was incomplete. The 'correctness' of Ramsay's conception of the determination of the rate of profits was demonstrated in the following passage quoted by Marx (*TSV*, III, 351):[21]

> the causes which regulate the rate of profit in individual cases [. . .] we have found to be, (1) The Productiveness of the Industry engaged in raising those articles of primary necessity which are required by the Labourer for Food, Clothing, etc. (2) The Productiveness of the Industry employed in raising those objects which enter into the composition of Fixed Capital. (3) *The rate of Real Wages*.

Thus Ramsay was able to go some way towards understanding the effects of capital accumulation on the rate of profits. In particular, to the extent that capital accumulation involved increased productivity in the production of 'variable' and 'constant' capital commodities, the reduced exchange values of these commodities would effect a *rise* in the rate of profits. The *exchange value* composition of capital could be affected by the relativities of these changes, but what was missing from Ramsay's treatment was the dominant effect of capital accumulation in raising the *technical* composition of capital which in Marx's analysis was the key to the tendency of the rate of profits to fall. This omission of Ramsay's was not emphasised by Marx, even though it represented a major difference from his own analysis. He simply noted in passing that Ramsay had not provided any coherent analysis of the tendency (*TSV*, III, 354).

In several ways, the ideas that Marx found in Antoine-Elisée

Cherbuliez's *Richesse ou pauvreté* of 1841 on the capital accumulation issue were similar to those of Ramsay, both in their merits and in their limitations. Cherbuliez went further in formalising the analysis of the rate of profits, but he also failed to provide any effective explanation of the dynamics of the rate of profits. Without the category surplus Value to *explain* profit, he was left without the essential foundation for an analysis of the effects of capital accumulation.

Marx's interpretation was that Cherbuliez had, in principle, grasped the constant and variable capital dichotomy, but that he had not applied it in linking capital accumulation to its effects on the rate of profits. The inkling that he had that the composition of capital was decisive in determining the rate of profits was left undeveloped (*TSV*, III, 370). As Marx saw it:

> It is an incontrovertible fact that, as capitalist production develops, the portion of capital invested in machinery and raw materials grows, and the portion laid out in wages declines. This is the only question with which both Ramsay and Cherbuliez are concerned. For us, however, the main thing is: does this fact explain the decline in the rate of profit? (*TSV*, III, 364–5.)

Evidently, for Ramsay and Cherbuliez, this particular form of this crucial question of Marx's was not an issue.

Ironically, it can be argued that at this point, Marx's own analysis was not very clear about the involvement of the changing composition of capital in the tendency of the rate of profits to fall (*TSV*, III, 364–7). In referring to the composition of capital, Marx implied the ratios $c/(c + v + s)$ and $c/(v + s)$ (*TSV*, III, 364), both of which were argued to rise as capital accumulated. The same effect was also expressed as $(v + s)/c$ falling (*TSV*, III, 367). Now these arguments were different from that which had c/v rising (*TSV*, III, 366). At the same time, Marx continued to use the rising *physical* ratio of machinery to workers (*TSV*, III, 365), and at one point he brought them together in the following confusing piece: 'It is therefore self-evident or a tautological proposition that the increasing productivity of labour caused by machinery corresponds to increased Value of the machinery relative to the amount of labour employed (consequently to the Value of labour, the variable capital)' (*TSV*, III, 366–7). Marx seemed to regard all of these expressions as moving together as capital accumulated, but a considerable degree of imprecision remained in his thought on this matter.[22]

In spite of this imprecision, Marx pressed on with his critique of Cherbuliez's endeavours. He made his attitude clear in the following passage:

> The distorted conception and bungling application of the approximately correct distinction between the elements of capital, and the vague idea that profit and rate of profit are directly connected with the ratio of these elements to one another, only lead to a repetition of the generally known phrases in a rather doctrinaire fashion, in fact merely to a statement that profit and rate of profit exist without, however, anything being said about their nature. (*TSV*, III, 374.)

According to Cherbuliez, the rate of profits *could* decline as capital accumulated, but Marx found his argument less than definitive (*TSV*, III, 374–6). Profit was defined by Cherbuliez as: $\pi = P - c$, where: P = 'the aggregate product of a given period of time', and c = 'the capital used up'. The rate of profits was then: $r = \pi/C$, where: C = 'the capital invested' (quoted *TSV*, III, 374). What happened to the rate of profits as C grew depended upon the relative rates of growth of P and c and of C itself. In this argument, there was little more than tautology, for Cherbuliez gave no *operational* reasons for the changing relativities that would actually cause the rate of profits to fall (*TSV*, III, 376).

CHAPTER 12

Reproduction and the immanent crises of capitalism

INTRODUCTION

Marx's critical analyses of two further dimensions of the 'motion' of the capitalist economic system, as they were worked out in the 'Theories of Surplus Value' manuscripts, are considered in this chapter. The first is the circulation component of expanded reproduction. As noted in the previous chapter, capital accumulation was considered by Marx to be the most essential driving force determining the nature and pace of capitalist 'motion'. So far, this process has only been considered in its production context. Such analysis enabled Marx to reveal certain effects of the logical contradictions inherent in expanding the production process under the 'rules' of capitalism. Two particular effects were argued by Marx, both of which had their origin in the rising organic composition of capital that he believed would necessarily accompany accumulation: first, the tendency of the Value rate of profits to fall; and secondly, the relative decrease in the rate at which labour power was purchased by capitalists, with its implications for growing unemployment. As Marx well knew, the logic of capital accumulation as it involved production in isolation could provide only a partial analysis of 'motion'. He had long recognised that the mode of production comprised production and circulation in an essential unity.[1] An extension of the analysis to include circulation would do two things. It would emphasise that the falling Value rate of profits exposed by the production analysis could only be considered a *notional* consequence until the realisation process of the commodities whose Values embodied the profits was made explicit in the analysis. If anything, it had been implicitly assumed by Marx in this first stage of 'motion' that the circulation process worked without impediment. Thus, the other thing that now had to be made clear was that the circulation process of capitalism was unlikely to conform to the stringent input–output conditions evident from the reproduction schema and required for unimpeded circulation. The circulation process, then, involved a set of its own contradictions that would affect the behaviour of the capitalist system as well as compounding those contradictions already exposed in the expanding production operations.

The second dimension of 'motion' considered in this chapter, and an immediate extension of the first alluded to above, is the immanently generated and recurring capitalist crisis. This represented for Marx the culmination of his analyses of 'motion' and involved the analytical integration of the 'separate' dimensions that he had considered. In the present context, at this stage of the evolution of Marx's critique, however, he largely aligned the crisis analysis with the contradictions that arose in the circulation process. The required articulation between the results of the contradictions in production consequent upon capital accumulation and those in circulation was just not pursued. Informally, of course, it is self-evident that the former were implicitly part of the 'crisis' discussion. The point is that as a formal matter, what explicit discussion Marx undertook of the crisis, and it was very limited at this stage, was directed at matters of circulation. In this sense, his perception of the crisis in 'Theories' remained narrow and impressionistic and his argument rose little above the descriptive. Some serious analytical puzzles were not given any attention and Marx had a long way to go before he could provide a coherent and consistent theoretical explanation of the capitalist crisis.

CIRCULATION, REPRODUCTION AND 'SAY'S LAW'

Capital accumulation necessarily involved demand for inputs and production of commodities on an increasing scale. By formulating his expanded reproduction schema, Marx had shown that the qualitative and quantitative input–output requirements for unimpeded growth were very stringent indeed.[2] The schema thus served to emphasise that with the unco-ordinated 'anarchy' of economic decision making under capitalism, such conditions were unlikely ever to be met. It was evident to Marx that as a result, capitalism could be expected, except by chance, to progress from one extent and degree of commodity realisation difficulties to the next. These difficulties could affect particular sectors of production or, in times of more extreme circulation failure, a *general* overproduction of commodities could emerge.

This view of the contradiction-prone nature of capitalist expanded reproduction was not widely held in nineteenth-century political economy. The orthodox and dominant belief was that while temporary circulation problems of limited extent could occur, the nature of capitalist reproduction was such as to prevent any general and sustained overproduction. This view of the capitalist economy acquired the ambiguous name of 'Say's Law', most baldly stated as 'supply creates its own demand'.[3] The ideas involved were present in the work of the Physiocrats and Adam Smith,[4] although their explication as a basic axiom of much political economy originates with Jean-Baptiste Say and James Mill around 1803–4.[5] One way or another, its influence pervaded most 'mainstream' nineteenth-century political economy after these dates. The 'Law' was embraced as a truth to be firmly defended or as a fallacy to be rejected. By expressing the 'Law' as an 'equilibrium condition', the acceptance–rejection decision depended upon exploring the actual conditions that are relevant in the capitalist economy in order to see if they comply with the demands of equilibrium. This was what Marx was doing in moving away from his reproduction schema into the analysis of circulation barriers.[6]

In principle, for the process of reproduction to proceed, the qualitative and quantitative pattern of periodic production of commodities had to match precisely the periodic, *effective* and *exercised* demand pattern. Now from the analysis of the Physiocrats, the predominant concern was with the demand for *consumption commodities*. This limitation was common to nearly all political economy prior to Marx in the nineteenth century in that the analysis of the demand for means of production for replacement and expansion was not formalised. Indeed, beyond the Physiocrats, *reproduction itself* was not really an analytical issue. What was at issue was whether adequate effective demand would always be available to purchase the growing output of consumption commodities. Any overproduction, then, would appear as an excess of these commodities only, so the issue was one of the possibility of *general underconsumption*. The proponents of 'Say's Law' rejected this possibility because, except for some short-term disproportionality, the act of production generated income sufficient to purchase what was produced. The opponents of the 'Law' prior to Marx, most notably Malthus and Sismondi, argued that underconsumption was a threat to the continuity of capitalist growth and foresaw bouts of stagnation because of the problem.[7]

This section, then, considers several aspects of Marx's critical assessment of the formulation and use of 'Say's Law' in political economy: first, the development of the idea, as Marx understood it, by Say and James Mill; secondly, the application of the 'Law' by its most significant advocate, Ricardo; and thirdly, the nature of antecedent opposition to the 'Law' and Marx's critique of this opposition.

Marx's treatment of Say in the 'Theories' manuscripts was brief and derisive.[8] He did not consider Say's political economy to be worthy of much more than disdain and thus devoted little critical effort to it, although he did at one stage envisage pursuing it more fully (*TSV*, II, 493–4).

A crucial limitation that Marx thought Say had taken over from Adam Smith was the notion that aggregate produced exchange value was all distributed as revenue. That is, no distinction was made between gross and net production in his analysis. As Marx saw it: 'It is not true that *the annual product of labour*, of which *the product of the annual labour* forms only one part, consists of revenue' (*TSV*, I, 150; cf. 103, 221). Say had failed to allow for constant capital replacement in determining aggregate exchange value (*TSV*, I, 221–1). Marx ascribed this, in part, to his emphasis upon the role of supply and demand in formulating the determination of exchange value and distribution (*TSV*, II, 133, 215, 399–400).

In conceiving of revenue as equal to aggregate produced exchange value, Say was led to the conclusion that there could not be a general demand-based failure in commodity circulation. His most serious omission in this conclusion was an appropriate understanding of the role of money in the process. It was Marx's view that Say had effectively resorted to a barter-economy model. He thus failed to perceive that money split exchange into two separate acts which comprised circulation and made it more complex to sustain (*TSV*, II, 493 and III, 119). As Marx put it, also, 'because demand is *limited* by production, it by no means follows that *production is, or was, limited by demand*, and can never exceed the demand' (*TSV*, III, 119). This reflected the 'anarchy' of production under capitalism in which the capitalist 'produces as if he were fulfilling orders placed by society' (*TSV*, III, 121). Thus, combining this lack of demand constraint upon production with the separation of sale and purchase due to money's role as a store of exchange value, predisposed capitalist circulation towards a *general* failure that Say had not envisaged.

Marx's treatment of James Mill on this issue was a little more extensive than was the case with Say. Mill was credited with the same bald belief that no general glut of commodities was possible because circulation involved what were effectively barter exchanges (*TSV*, II, 493). This amounted to a belief in the 'metaphysical equilibrium of purchases and sales' in which the commodity–money–commodity metamorphosis (C–M–C) was viewed as a necessary unity with no concern for the separable components that it involved (*TSV*, II, 503–4). Moreover, Mill had failed to perceive the commodity as the unity of use value and exchange value. This unity involved capitalism in the contradiction that while demand was based primarily upon use value, production was geared to the maximum generation of exchange value. In addition to the *will* to purchase, the *effective* demand decision involved the *means* to purchase. Mill had effectively identified these two aspects and then proceeded to assume that supply would match the resultant demand and provide the means to make it effective (*TSV*, III, 100–4).

Much more significant for Marx than the formulation of 'Say's Law' by Say and James Mill was the use made of it by Ricardo. Marx found the 'Law' to be an important component of the analysis in the *Principles* and he devoted some attention to it in his critique of that work.

Ricardo accepted the essence of the 'Say's Law' thesis that supply created its own demand and that sale was necessarily followed by purchase. It followed from this that the profitable accumulation of capital could not be impeded by *demand* problems in any general or long-term sense. Marx quoted the following passage from the *Principles* in support of this interpretation:[9]

> M. Say has . . . most satisfactorily shewn, that there is no amount of capital which may not be employed in a country, because *demand is only limited by production.* No man *produces, but with a view to consume or sell, and he never sells, but with an intention to purchase some other commodity*, which may be immediately useful to him, or which may contribute to future production. By producing, then, he necessarily becomes either the consumer of his own goods, or the purchaser and consumer of the goods of some other person. It is not to be supposed that he should, for any length of time, be ill-informed of the commodities which he can most advantageously produce, to attain the object which he has in view, namely, the *possession of other goods*; and, therefore, it is not probable that he will *continually* produce a commodity for which there is no demand. (quoted *TSV*, II, 493–4, 502.)

From this argument, Marx felt that Ricardo did not adequately understand the nature of capitalist production and circulation. Capitalists only produced commodities to be sold. Once production had taken place, a sale *had* to ensue, even if forced on the capitalist at below the commodity's immediate exchange value. The capitalist did not have the discretion whereby he would sell only if a purchase was envisaged as following immediately. His primary and necessary objective was to sell in order to convert his commodity into money as a store of exchange value and purchasing power (*TSV*, II, 502–3). Ricardo had overlooked this role of money in the present context and thus did not see that it made possible a break in the nexus of supply and demand. Marx's point was that

> At a given moment, the supply of all commodities can be greater than the demand for all commodities, since the demand for the *general commodity*, money, exchange value, is greater than the demand for all particular commodities, in other words,

> the motive to turn the commodity into money, to realise its exchange value, prevails over the motive to transform the commodity again into use value. (*TSV*, II, 505.)

The possibility of *partial* overproduction was conceded by Ricardo, Marx noted, but it was argued to be a temporary disequilibrium that would be corrected by capital mobility changing the pattern of production. Such adjustments would be in response to changes in the realised rates of profit in any sectors of production involved in which the market prices differed from those required to return the general rate (*TSV*, II, 504–5, 529). Ricardo rejected the notion that this could turn into a general glut of commodities. Marx quoted from the *Principles* to the effect that general overproduction was ruled out by the collective insatiability of needs (*TSV*, II, 505–6).[10]

This, Marx thought, represented a gross misrepresentation of the relationship between human needs and their satisfaction through effective demand under a capitalist regime. He summarised his views on this idea quite graphically in the following piece:

> If overproduction could only occur when all the members of a nation had satisfied even their most urgent needs, there could never, in the history of bourgeois society up to now, have been a state of general overproduction or even of partial overproduction . . . What after all has overproduction to do with absolute needs? It is only concerned with demand that is backed by ability to pay. It is not a question of absolute overproduction – overproduction as such in relation to the absolute need or the desire to possess commodities. (*TSV*, II, 506.)

As Marx saw it, even the 'word *overproduction* in itself leads to error' in the sense that the nature of the capitalist mode of organising production and distribution left so many genuine needs unsatisfied and therefore potential profit opportunities unrealised. For Marx, this amounted to 'constant *underproduction*' (*TSV*, II, 527). Thus capitalism fostered the absurdity that even the *producers* of a commodity (the workers) may be in dire need of it and yet it will remain unsold due to their incapacity to make their demand *effective*. As a mode of *social* production designed fully to meet *human* needs, Marx considered capitalism a failure.

'Say's Law', as espoused by Ricardo, reflected a misunderstanding of the 'anarchistic' forces at work in the production and circulation processes. It was a mistake to regard 'bourgeois production . . . as *social* production, implying that society, as if according to a plan, distributes its means of production and productive forces in the degree and measure which is required for the fulfilment of the various social needs' (*TSV*, II, 528–9). The irony noted by Marx was that 'Say's Law' was being applied to the analysis of an economic system for which it *logically* could not hold except by chance.

Marx considered the work of two main opponents of 'Say's Law', viz. Sismondi and Malthus.[11] Sismondi was another political economist of significance that Marx left relatively neglected in his critique, again in spite of his expressed intentions to correct the situation (*TSV*, III, 53).[12] He had briefly summarised Sismondi's views on the potential instability of capitalism in the *Grundrisse* manuscripts. There Marx argued that while Sismondi had effectively grasped that capital generated *immanent* contradictions in its circulation process, he had not given sufficient attention to the production process with which circulation was necessarily integrated (*G*, 410–11).

In the 'Theories' manuscripts, Marx reiterated this theme of the immanent contradictions of a production regime based on capital (*TSV*, III, 55). Sismondi understood that it was in the nature of capital to strive to expand itself. This involved an ever-growing periodic mass of commodities, the exchange value of which was to be realised through sales to those with *effective* demand. At the same time, accompanying improvements in labour productivity meant that relatively less labour would be employed with a consequent potential decrease in effective demand originating from labour incomes. For Sismondi, the realisation problems faced by capitalism were structural and systemic rather than accidental as had been the argument in much political economy (*TSV*, III, 56, 84, 259).

A difficulty with Sismondi's contribution, in Marx's view, was the suggestion that state action could correct the contradictions of capitalist production. Marx interpreted this to be a resort to past feudal-like techniques and rejected the idea outright as reflecting a deep-seated misunderstanding of the nature of capitalism and what could or should be done with it. In Marx's words, Sismondi 'wavers constantly: should the State curb the productive forces to make them adequate to the production relations, or should the production relations be made adequate to the productive forces?' (*TSV*, III, 56). For Marx, it was a fundamental premise that no amount of *reformism* could transcend the contradictions of capitalism. Sismondi's endeavours 'to exorcise the contradictions by a different adjustment of revenue in relation to capital, or of distribution in relation to production' failed to recognise that the operational dimensions of capitalism were an integrated unity in which the form of the *relations of production* dominated. Only a destruction of these relations could remove the contradictions they involved. Thus Sismondi 'forcefully *criticises* the contradictions of bourgeois production but does not *understand* them, and consequently does not understand the process whereby they can be resolved' (*TSV*, III, 56).[13] As with political economy in general, then, the limitation of Sismondi's work was its failure to penetrate the *appearances* in order to grasp the *essential* nature of capitalism. He had recognised that the system necessarily embraced contradictions, but he did not realise that even though these were exhibited at the level of appearances, they could not be *resolved* at that level.

It was Marx's interpretation that Sismondi's work had had a profound influence on Malthus. Marx railed against Malthus for what he found to be the latter's plagiarism of the work of other political economists, although he provided no specific evidence to substantiate such allegations.[14] In opposing the 'Say's Law' thesis, Malthus continued in this vein, Marx asserted, by copying Sismondi's approach, albeit with some subtlety. Thus 'he does not abandon his innate plagiarism even here. Who at first glance would believe that Malthus's *Principles of Political Economy* is simply the Malthusianised translation of Sismondi's *Nouveaux Principes d'économie politique*? But this is the case' (*TSV*, III, 53). This was a very strong accusation. Perhaps had the 'Theories' manuscripts ever reached publication, Marx may have been moved to provide the necessary evidence for it, or to drop the charge.[15]

Marx interpreted Malthus's analysis of exchange value and distribution as a regression to the circularity involved in Adam Smith's arguments. Exchange value was formulated in 'labour commanded' terms with its composition comprising the aggregate of revenues paid to those involved in production. Marx's critique of Malthus's treatment of capitalist reproduction and its problems centred upon this fallacious approach to exchange value determination. According to Marx, the key point in Malthus's rejection of 'Say's Law' was the need for a growing capitalist economy to be supported by an expanding 'unproductive-consumption' demand. This reasoning, which Marx rejected, he ascribed directly to Malthus's thought about exchange value (*TSV*, III, 40–1).[16]

The difficulty stemmed from the very nature of the 'adding-up' formulation of exchange value which Marx interpreted as involving two separate categories. There was a '*price for the producer*' reflecting the costs of actually producing a commodity and a '*price for the purchaser*' which included costs plus 'added-on' profit. The latter represented the relevant concept of exchange value for Malthus and its realisation was a condition of the continued supply of the commodity. Thus, as Marx saw things: 'The question now arises – how is this price to be realised? Who is to pay it? And from what funds is it to be paid? (*TSV*, III, 41). The logic of the situation was such that with profit 'added-on' to costs, the incomes paid as a reflection of these costs could not be sufficient to purchase commodities at their '*purchaser*' price.

In particular, the wage bill of the workers would not provide adequate aggregate demand for the reproduction of commodities and Marx quoted several passages from Malthus's *Principles of Political Economy* (2nd ed., 1836) to this effect (*TSV*, III, 57). For Marx, the issue clearly emphasised the *surplus* origin of profit, although Malthus did not make the point. In the sector producing wage commodities, 'we have a case where as a result of the nominal surcharge – the normal profit increment added to the price of the advances – a surplus fund is in fact created for the capitalist, since, in this roundabout way, he gives back to the worker only part of his product while appropriating a part for himself' (*TSV*, III, 42; cf. 47). Under these conditions of exchange value determination

> it is clear that demand by the workers can never suffice for the realisation of the surplus of the purchase price over and above the cost price . . . On the contrary, a profit fund only exists because the worker is unable to buy back his whole product with his wages, and his demand, therefore, does not correspond

to the supply. (*TSV*, III, 42.)

From this point, Marx's critique of Malthus on the probability of underconsumption went on to include the development of a multi-sector analysis of the reproduction problem (*TSV*, III, 41ff.). This rendered his critique potentially misleading because Malthus did not use such an approach, as Marx himself recognised (*TSV*, III, 41). Malthus's concern was limited to a one-sector model in which accumulation was taking place in the form of expanding advances to employ labour. The demand with which Malthus was concerned was for a *consumer* commodity only. The problem then was that once saving was allowed for, there was no guarantee that supply would not exceed demand. There was a limit to the saving ratio out of revenues beyond which a general glut of the commodity would be generated, although Malthus was not very precise about this argument. There was no explicit role for a means of production commodities sector in this analysis and by forcing Malthus's arguments into a reproduction model Marx obscured their particular limitations.[17] It was the case, though, that Malthus's one-sector approach was, in itself, a limitation which deserved to be revealed, especially as it enabled him to by-pass many of the complexities of capitalist reproduction, not the least of which was the general role of the surplus. In this sense, Marx's review of these issues was useful, but not as a critique of Malthus.

Be this as it may, Marx's finding about the invalidity of Malthus's approach to resolving the underconsumption problem was correct. The resolution using 'unproductive consumption' was erroneous irrespective of the analytical underpinnings that the problem was given. It was Malthus's argument, according to Marx, that the underconsumption issue would be resolved if

> in addition to exchange by one class of capitalists with its workers and the mutual exchange between the capitalists of the different classes, there also existed a *third class of purchasers* – a *deus ex machina* – a class which paid the nominal value of commodities [price including profit] without itself selling any commodities, . . . that is a class which transacted one phase only: M–C, but not M–C–M; [a class] which bought not in order to get its capital back plus a profit, but in order to

> consume the commodities; a class which bought without selling. (*TSV*, III, 49–50.)

From this sort of reasoning, Malthus was able to assert that even though the *raison d'être* of the capitalist was continually to increase production, the problem of overproduction would be eliminated because, as Marx put it, 'the *unproductive consumers* not only constitute a gigantic outlet for the products thrown onto the market, but do not themselves throw any commodities onto the market' (*TSV*, III, 50). Thus they do not constitute any competition for the capitalist in his endeavours to realise an increasing volume of commodities.

But, Marx was aware that such 'consumers' had to exercise an *effective demand* which in aggregate covered the 'production value' plus the 'normal profit surcharge' (*TSV*, III, 50). This caused him to ask again 'where do the annual financial resources of this class come from?' (*TSV*, III, 51). This was a crucial question. Malthus effectively answered it by referring to landowners and their rent share of the annual production which they took no direct part in producing. Any remaining shortfall of demand would be absorbed by state intervention through taxation and support of 'a mass of sinecurists in state and church, of large armies, pensions, tithes for the priests, an impressive national debt, and from time to time, expensive wars. These are the "remedies" ' (*TSV*, III, 51). Capitalism could survive, Marx concluded from Malthus's argument, only by the grace of 'parasites and gluttonous drones' (*TSV*, III, 52).

Marx did not attack the *logic* of this erroneous approach to the resolution of the overproduction problem.[18] He chose rather to turn it against Malthus in an emotional way as indicating that Malthus's work was

> an apologia for the existing state of affairs in England, for landlordism, 'State and Church', pensioners, tax gatherers, tenths, national debt, stock jobbers, beadles, parsons and menial servants ('national expenditure') assailed by the Ricardians as so many useless and superannuated drawbacks of bourgeois production and as nuisances. (*TSV*, III, 51–2.)

In this, Marx agreed with the 'Ricardians'. It was to Malthus's credit, though, that he did expose immanent contradictions of capitalism as far as he perceived them. But again, Marx hastened to ascribe ulterior motives to him:

> Malthus is interested not in concealing the contradictions of bourgeois production, but on the contrary, in emphasising them, on the one hand, in order to prove that the poverty of the working classes is necessary (as it is, indeed, for this mode of production) and, on the other hand, to demonstrate to the capitalists the necessity for a well-fed Church and State hierarchy in order to create an adequate demand for the commodities they produce. (*TSV*, III, 57.)

Thus Malthus was accused of polemicising 'in the interests of the capitalists against the workers and in the interests of the aristocracy, church, tax-eaters, toadies, etc., against the capitalists' (*TSV*, III, 61–2). Unfortunately, these assertions were not supported by any detailed evidence that Malthus's analyses implied such bias. Marx's accusations remained impressionistic at best.[19]

CRITICAL HISTORY AND MARX'S THOUGHTS ON THE CRISES OF CAPITALISM

The ultimate objective of Marx's critique of political economy was to provide a coherent explication of the crisis-prone nature of the capitalist economic system. Throughout his critique, he sought the contradictions of the system as the basis for grasping, in terms of theoretical logic, the reasons for its unstable 'motion'. In short, he sought a dialectical 'law of motion' of capitalism that would explain its inevitable trend towards the economic and social conditions required for its self-destruction at the hands of the revolutionary proletariat.[20]

In the 'Theories of Surplus Value' manuscripts, the full complexity of an analysis that could account for the recurrent crisis phenomena that capitalism was observed to experience was not evident in Marx's discussion.[21] It is worth summarising some of the crucial theoretical questions that such an analysis poses as a background against which to assess Marx's progress in the present context. First, it is necessary to settle on the observed symptoms that a state of crisis exists and, possibly, to align these indicators with separate 'types' of or, at least, components of, the crisis. Clarity in this first requirement demands, secondly, that *cause* and *effect* in the crisis analysis be carefully distinguished. In Marx's legacy on the crisis, this distinction was not clearly expressed and symptoms and causes were conflated to a significant extent.[22]

Thirdly, the crisis, as part of the continuing 'motion' of capitalism, implies some mechanism of correction, autonomous or externally applied. This view suggests a short-run, cyclical interpretation of the situation of the crisis in the process of 'motion'. The analytical puzzles posed by any 'trade cycle' argument about the nature of capitalism are well known. They include, *inter alia*, the difficulties of formulating coherent explanations for the 'turning points' that bring periodic booms and recessions (crises) to an end.[23] It is possible, as well, to suggest a longer-run form of crisis that progressively carries capitalism into experiencing more extreme symptoms. If both cyclical and secular forms of the crisis are argued to exist, their articulation needs to be explained formally. Marx's thought on this aspect of the crisis was not very precise, either.[24]

Finally, and a point which Marx himself stressed, is that revelations about the *potential* for crises in a capitalist economy based upon sound dialectical logic do not constitute the *phenomenon* of the crisis itself. The contradictions and their effects in causing the crisis must be shown to be *operational* (*TSV*, II, 502, 509).

For Marx, the impetus for the 'motion' of capitalism was capital accumulation. This was a more or less autonomous premise of capitalist behaviour. Capital accumulation exposed contradictions in both the production and circulation processes. In working themselves out, these contradictions brought negative consequences for both the capitalist and working classes. Marx was, then, faced with the task of 'combining' these consequences in order to grasp the forms and logic of the capitalist crisis, keeping in mind that he should have ideally addressed, at least, each of the issues outlined above. The particular consequences that he had to situate in his crisis analysis were the falling rate of profits and relative reduction in the demand for labour as *individual* capitalists strove to advance their profit positions by adopting increasingly capital-intensive methods of production, and the continuous partial and frequent general breakdown of the circulation process which involved the sale of commodities at prices that failed to realise the rates of profit expected by capitalists or left commodities unsold altogether.

In the 'Theories' manuscripts Marx's explicit treatment of the crisis, was brief, impressionistic and of very limited scope (*TSV*, II, 492ff.). His attention was confined largely to the crisis potential of the circulation process and virtually all of the central issues noted above were neglected. Implicitly, of course, with the benefit of hindsight, all of Marx's analyses of the dimensions of 'motion' in the present context can be read as directed towards the *goal* of formalising the crisis logic. The point that is being made is simply that the analyses were not brought together and given any interdependent coherence under the aegis of the crisis category, despite Marx's recognition of the need to do so.

Marx was concerned to repudiate the implications of 'Say's Law' for the capital accumulation process because it reflected a distortion of the nature of capitalism. For Ricardo, capital accumulation would proceed without sustained market impediments through the automatic generation of an aggregate demand equivalent to supply in all periods. Any short-run, inter-sector disporportionality problems, manifested as *partial* overproduction, would be corrected by marginal reallocations of resources through competitive, profit-maximising behaviour by capitalists. What had escaped Ricardo, in Marx's view, was the 'anarchy' of unco-ordinated production and demand and the mediation in this 'anarchy' of money acting as a store of Value.

The initiating force that drove the capitalist system into crisis was the accumulation of capital by individual capitalists. As Marx put it, 'the whole process of accumulation . . . resolves itself into *production on an expanding scale*, which on the one hand corresponds to the natural growth of the population, and on the other hand, forms an inherent basis for the phenomena which appear during *crises*' (*TSV*, II, 492). He went on to attend to some crisis-related points about accumulation and its consequences, the first of which concerned realisation problems in circulation, with the emphasis on *consumption*. Accumulation was argued to be geared to 'the unlimited desire of the capitalists to enrich themselves and to enlarge their capital' rather than to effective consumption demand, a major part of which was constrained by the relative decline in the demand for labour (*TSV*, II, 492). Secondly, and more generally with respect to realisation difficulties, the capitalist reproduction process was envisaged as involving a continuous struggle to move towards the requirements of undisturbed, balanced growth. The adjustment processes, presumably involving inter sector capital movements, were referred to by Marx as 'equalisations' and he regarded them as '*accidental*'. Thus, 'although the proportion of capital employed in individual spheres is equalised by a continuous process, the continuity of this process itself equally presupposes the constant disproportion which it has continuously, often violently, to even out' (*TSV*, II, 492). The probability was, then, according to Marx, that capitalism would experience continuous disruptions due to underconsumption and disproportionality realisation problems. The symptoms of such a crisis form would, presumably, be excessive inventory accumulation and realised rates of profit below 'normal'.

In focusing on the expanded reproduction process as the situation in which the crisis would emerge, Marx was able to emphasise the unco-ordinated interdependence of production and circulation as the source of overproduction. While the overproduction *appeared* in the failure of commodity circulation, its explanation could not be found in this sphere alone. It was the case that the

> *possibility* of crisis, which became apparent in the *simple metamorphosis* of the commodity, is once more demonstrated, and further developed, by the disjunction between the (direct) process of production and the process of circulation. As soon as these processes do not merge smoothly into one another but become independent of one another, the crisis is there. (*TSV*, II, 507.)

The interdependence of production and circulation went deeper than this, though, and Marx was soon able further to clarify the roles that each had in the crisis. The production process *by itself* also had only a partial role in explaining the crisis. The crisis was a phenomenon *realised* through circulation, even though some of its roots were in the production process. Here Marx took some first steps towards recognising the need to integrate the 'dynamics' of capital accumulation as they affected production with the realisation of their consequences in circulation.

> The mere (direct) *production process* of capital in itself, cannot add anything new in this context. In order to exist at all, its conditions are presupposed. The first section dealing with capital – the *direct* process of production – does not contribute any new element of crisis. Although it *does* contain such an element, because the production process implies appropriation and hence production of surplus Value. But this cannot be shown when dealing with the production process itself, for the latter is not concerned with the *realisation* either of the reproduced Value or of the surplus Value.
>
> This can only emerge in the *circulation process* which is in itself also a *process of reproduction*. (*TSV*, II, 513.)

There was a sense in which the production process preceded circulation for a pre-existing capital stock, but accumulation, and so 'motion', could only be accounted for by the realisation of surplus Value in circulation. The accumulation of capital then impinged upon the '*Capital and Profit*' dimension of the crisis analysis. Marx determined that he should return to this aspect in a future 'chapter' of his critique. He had, of course, already pursued the 'motion' of production in the 'Theories' manuscripts, but he evidently did not think it appropriate to try to integrate it formally with the realisation process at this stage (*TSV*, II, 513).

Marx concluded these brief notes on the unity of production and circulation by referring to the implications of their *operational* separation under capitalism. The unco-ordinated status of the two processes meant that a logically necessary unity had been sundered and the operations of capitalism must be disrupted by the perpetual endeavour to transcend the crisis effects of such a contradiction. In Marx's words: 'Crisis is the forcible establishment of unity between elements that have become independent and the enforced separation from one another of elements which are essentially one' (*TSV*, II, 513; cf. 509). The problems that could arise from such an 'enforced separation' did not seem to Marx to have been noticed by most political economists.

As Marx saw it, the expanded reproduction of the capitalist economy was founded upon the immanent contradiction that while a unity of sale and purchase was required they were in fact separate acts. The assertion of this independence was one root of the crisis and it was facilitated by money as a store of Value. Thus:

> No crisis can exist unless sale and purchase are separated from one another and come into conflict, or the contradictions contained in money as a means of payment actually come into play; crisis, therefore, cannot exist without manifesting itself at the same time in its simple form, as the contradiction between sale and purchase and the contradiction of money as a means of payment. But these are merely *forms*, general possibilities of crisis, and hence also forms, abstract forms, of actual crisis. (*TSV*, II, 512; cf. 502, 507–9.)

Moreover, this *potential* for crisis was exacerbated by Marx's understanding that the capitalist was *forced* to sell at the first stage in the circulation phase of the reproduction cycle. This raised the possibility that the sale may not realise the full Value of the commodity, especially where the capitalist was in debt and forced to 'sell in order to *pay*' (*TSV*, II, 503). In Marx's interpretation, then: 'A man who has produced, does not have the choice of selling or not selling. He must *sell*. In the crisis there arises the very situation in which he cannot sell or can only sell below the cost price or must even sell at a positive loss' (*TSV*, II, 503). What concerned Marx further was that Ricardo treated money merely as a medium of exchange (*TSV*, II, 501). This overlooked the role of money as an independent, generalised exchange value which could disrupt the barter paradigm upon which Ricardo had focused (*TSV*, II, 504, 505).

In providing an analysis of the crisis, it was essential, Marx argued, to keep the inherent *nature* of the capitalist system to the fore. It was his basic criticism of antecedent political economists that they had failed to do this and thus missed the *predisposition* of capitalism to fall into crisis. This was due, in part, he thought, to their lack of recognition of the significance of the fact that production was for exchange rather than directly for use and that exchange was not simply barter (*TSV*, II, 495). The analytical expression of this failure was the adoption of 'Say's Law' which served to obscure the distinct properties of the capitalist system which involved contradictions. These contradictions manifested themselves as crises. As Marx put it: 'In order to prove that capitalist production cannot lead to general crises, all its conditions and distinct forms, all its principles and specific features – in short *capitalist production* itself – are denied' (*TSV*, II, 501). As far as he was concerned, the political economists just did not want to face up to the *reality* of the crises experienced by capitalism. They did not want to search their theories for the very contradictions that caused such crises. In effect, they were content to believe 'that if production were carried on according to the textbooks, crises would never occur'. Thus it followed that 'the apologetics consist in the falsification of the simplest economic relations, and particularly in clinging to the concept of unity in the face of contradiction' (*TSV*, II, 500). For Marx, 'in reality crises exist because . . . contradictions exist' (*TSV*, II, 519). Some, unspecified writers were accused of a different form of evasion when it came to facing up to the observable economic problems of capitalism. Marx referred to the 'insipid . . . economists' who,

> when they are no longer able to explain away the phenomenon of overproduction and crises, are content to say that these forms contain the possibility of *crises*, that it is therefore *accidental* whether or not crises occur and consequently their occurrence is itself merely a *matter of chance*. (*TSV*, II, 512.)

For Marx, the potential for a crisis consequent upon the contradictions of capitalism was *logically* entailed. No chance conditions needed to be evoked.

Marx regarded Ricardo's denial of the crisis based upon general overproduction as an outcome of the era in which he wrote. The observed crises of the early nineteenth century Marx felt could be rationalised by various accidental events, e.g. poor harvests raising the price of corn and the effect of political events on market access (*TSV*, II, 497). Later writers were, though, faced with a more systematic periodicity of crises and were forced to provide some explanation.

> Later historical phenomena, especially the almost regular periodicity of crises on the world market, no longer permitted Ricardo's successors to deny the facts or to interpret them as

> accidental. Instead – apart from those who explain everything by credit, but then have to admit that they themselves are forced to presuppose the over-abundance of capital – they invented the nice distinction between *over-abundance of capital* and *over-production.* (*TSV*, II, 498.)

The denial of the overproduction of commodities left a critical inconsistency in these writers' attitude to the capitalist crisis, even though Marx recognised as an advance any analysis which gave emphasis to the role of capital in crises (*TSV*, II, 499).

On the theme of products as commodities produced for sale, Marx recalled that for Adam Smith, there was an internal limit to the market's ability to absorb production. This potentially constrained the growth of 'wealth'. In order to avoid this, there was a need for 'an external, colonial and world market' in which the excess domestic production which emerged as the economy grew could be realised. Ricardo had reacted against this on the basis of 'Say's Law', arguing that the use of external markets was a matter of choice (*TSV*, II, 525). For Ricardo, it was aggregate capital which limited both production *and* demand simultaneously. In the sense that only what was produced could be demanded and that effective demand could only come from incomes generated in the supply process, this was true as Marx realised. But the issue had to be posed differently in order to be meaningful, viz. 'whether – on the basis of capitalist production – as much can be consumed as is produced' (*TSV*, II, 520). In Marx's view, a significant causal element in the crisis explanation was the failure of aggregate demand to expand in concert with capacity to produce. These facets of 'motion' were based on the different motivations of different decision makers (*TSV*, II, 524–5).

Marx was also concerned with the problem of *partial* as against *general* overproduction of commodities. He noted that Ricardo had allowed for the former as a *temporary* disequilibrium phenomenon but had ruled out the latter (*TSV*, II, 529). Marx interpreted the rejection of general overproduction as implying that only the disproportionality between sectors in partial overproduction raised a problem for capitalist reproduction. Those who espoused 'Say's Law' would argue that provided the scale of production, whatever it may be, involved appropriate inter-sector balances, there could be no general glut. The only problem, then, was *relative* overproduction, that is, overproduction that was not *universal* (*TSV*, II, 530). Marx thought this argument to be 'miserable sophistry' which had the essential weakness of presuming that the sale of *final* commodities was effectively barter and thus could not be impeded (*TSV*, II, 532–3).

For Ricardo, also, a general overproduction of commodities would have implied an excess of capital. He explicitly rejected the possibility of such an excess and Marx quoted passages from the *Principles* to this effect. Included was a footnote in which Ricardo challenged an inconsistency in Say's argument in which he allowed that an excess supply of capital could lead to a reduction in the rate of interest on loans (*TSV*, II, 494, 497).[25] As far as Marx was concerned, Ricardo was correct, for an excess of commodities and an excess of capital were two ways of looking at the same thing (*TSV*, II, 533–5). Marx emphasised this when he criticised writers after Ricardo who attempted to preserve 'Say's Law' while arguing that an excess supply of capital could emerge. As Marx put it:

> Not a single responsible economist of the post-Ricardian period denies the plethora of capital. On the contrary, all of them regard it as the cause of crises (in so far as they do not explain the latter by factors relating to credit). Therefore, they all admit overproduction in one form but deny its existence in another. The only remaining question thus is: what is the relation between these two forms of overproduction, i.e., between the form in which it is denied and the form in which it is asserted? (*TSV*, II, 497.)

The question posed was not relevant for Ricardo, but very relevant for the writers referred to in the passage. They provided no answer.

The sort of crisis that Marx was concerned with in the 'Theories' manuscripts was one that recurred periodically for a short time. That is, the crisis was reflected in a cyclical recession whose precise characteristics were not discussed beyond the obvious implication that an overproduction of commodities would be evident forcing sales at prices below those that would return the 'normal' rate of profit. It was also necessarily implicit that some immanently generated corrective forces would emerge to bring the economy out of its slump. In the present context, Marx was not very informative about the analytical ramifications of formalising this cycle of events. One thing that he did emphasise explicitly was that the crisis was not to be treated as a long-run, secular phenomenon. That is: 'Permanent crises do not exist' (*TSV*, II, 497n.).

Marx was aware that in his formal analysis and explanation of the capitalist crisis he would have to confront a significant methodological problem. It was clear to him that the *potential* for crises existed in the quantitative and qualitative *structural* requirements of capitalist expanded reproduction. Such logical potential, however, did not in itself provide a *sufficient* basis for the occurrence of crises which resulted from the *operations* of capitalism. Only at the most abstract level could such potential be utilised to infer the probable crisis outcome. In reality, the potential for crisis could not be used to *explain* the existence of an *actual* crisis. Marx made this explicit when he argued:

> These factors which explain the possibility of crises, by no means explain their actual occurrence. They do not explain *why* the phases of the process come into such conflict that their inner unity can only assert itself through a crisis, through a violent process. This *separation* appears in the crisis; it is the elementary form of the crisis. To *explain* the crisis on the basis of this, its elementary form, is to explain the existence of the crisis by describing its most abstract form, that is to say, to explain the crisis by the crisis. (*TSV*, II, 502; cf. 509, 512, 514, 515.)

Just what the ultimate significance of this methodological concern would be for the *form* of Marx's crisis analysis he did not make clear. Here, as in all aspects of his endeavour to formulate a 'law of motion' of capitalism that included a fully coherent explication of the crisis phenomenon, Marx had much more thinking and development work to do. Most of the *minimal* analytical requirements outlined at the beginning of this section just had not been met.

Part V
Epilogue

CHAPTER 13

Marx's critique of political economy prior to *Capital*: a summary statement

This concluding chapter comprises two sections. In the first, I provide a chronological outline of the key developments in Marx's critique of political economy from its origins in 1844 until 1863 when he began work on the particular project designated as *Capital*. In this section, there is not much substantive detail. The intention is largely to provide some background to the summary restatement of Marx's critique of political economy as it had evolved by 1863. This summary is provided in the second section of the chapter and includes more methodological and critico-theoretical material, especially from the *Grundrisse* manuscripts, *A Contribution to the Critique of Political Economy*, and the 'Theories of Surplus Value' manuscripts.

CHRONOLOGICAL EVOLUTION

In volume I of this study, I traced the evolution and intellectual sources of Marx's critique of political economy in the period from 1844 to 1860. During these formative years, several key theoretical developments and shifts of emphasis took place as the critique progressed towards its first substantial statement in the *Grundrisse* manuscripts of 1857–8. The initial publication of some of these critical ideas came in the brief *A Contribution to the Critique of Political Economy* of 1859.

It was probably Engels's passionate critical exposé of capitalism in his article 'Outlines of a Critique of Political Economy', written in 1843 for publication in the *Deutsch-französische Jahrbücher* the following year, that drew Marx's attention to the crucial status that political economy had in any comprehension of contemporary society. Marx began reading the works of the political economists and recording his studies in notebooks in early 1844.

Prior to this, Marx spent several years in university and had a brief period as a journalist. The important legacies of these times in the present context were first, the critical skills that he had developed in his intellectual confrontations with law, philosophy and religion; and secondly, his contact with the role that 'material' conditions and interests played in determining man's form of existence and the nature and operation of the social and political institutions under which man lived. Marx's investigations as a journalist into the parliamentary debates on the wood-theft laws and the government's treatment of the poverty-stricken Moselle Valley wine-growers provided two 'real world' cases in which 'material' concerns and biases dominated the issues in one way or another.

Marx's first critical investigations into the thought of the political economists involved him in a wide range of reading. The immediate substantive results of these activities are to be found in two pieces written during 1844. The first was the short, and now inappropriately titled, 'Comments on James Mill' that appeared in one of his reading notebooks. In it, Marx exercised his burgeoning knowledge of political economy in a sweeping and emotional condemnation of capitalism as a human system. The style of the piece was similar to that adopted in the 'Outlines' written by Engels.

The second work of 1844, now referred to as the *Economic and Philosophic Manuscripts* or *Paris Manuscripts*, was more substantial. Although, like so much of Marx's writing, these *Manuscripts* remained unpublished in his lifetime, they represented a vital stage in the evolution of his critical thought in several respects.

The work began with Marx's first systematic critique of the capitalist mode of income distribution as it was posited in political economy, especially in Adam Smith's *Wealth of Nations*. At this stage, Marx accepted that political economy represented an accurate abstract presentation of the nature of the capitalist economic system. He had not yet begun his internal critique of political economy itself and, in the present context, was prepared to discuss distribution in terms of its appearances using the 'holy trinity' of categories wages of labour, profit of capital and rent of land that he would later condemn as 'false consciousness'. Be this as it may, the theme of distribution was to remain central to Marx's critique and some of his most significant conceptual developments related directly to a deeper, critical understanding of it, most especially the categories labour power and surplus Value.

The *Manuscripts* also contained a stinging critique of the human and social effects of the labour process under capitalism. Here the powerful concept of alienation was applied to an assessment of what Marx considered was man's most essential ontological activity in any stage of history. Under capitalism, the consequence of the form of man's labour was a multi-faceted and deep-seated alienation from his product, from his labour, from his fellow men, and from his human-species identity. Human potential just could not be realised under the conditions of labour dictated by the capitalists. Any post-capitalist, proletarian-dominated society that purported to be human would, first and foremost, have to bring with it a form of labour that avoided such anti-human consequences. In his later work, framed around the socio-economic class structure of capitalism, the issue of *individual* alienation was de-emphasised by Marx. However, it remained an implicit thesis of his critique and was ever-present as one aspect of the rationale for the proletariat's revolutionary transcendence to a communist society. What was soon to appear as the materialist method in Marx's analyses had a solid humanist foundation.

A third component of the *Manuscripts* comprised Marx's return to his critical study of the idealist philosophy of Hegel. His earlier extant written work on Hegel had emphasised the political dimensions found in the *Philosophy of Right.* Marx now gave some attention to the status of the dialectical method that pervaded Hegel's philosophy and his critical notes foreshadowed an emerging concern with the problem of formulating a more definitive methodological framework for his critique of capitalism.

Marx's immediately subsequent work during 1845–6, much of it in collaboration with Engels, was orientated towards a critique of philosophy. The objective was to find an appropriate way of thinking about human societies in historical motion, although this was often buried under a layer of polemic with the 'Young Hegelians'. In *The Holy Family*, the eleven 'Theses on Feuerbach' and *The German Ideology*, Marx set out, *inter alia*, the materialist interpretation of history that became a centrepiece of his critical theory thereafter. He found the essence of social motion and evolution in the working out of contradictions that had their roots in the material dimension of man's activities. Hegel's dialectical method, in an inverted form giving a *determining* role to human activity, was now enshrined in Marx's vision of history as driven by the conflicts between the material 'base' of a particular society and its ideological-institutional 'superstructure'.

Marx was soon able to apply his newly developed method in three critical contexts. First, he reacted in a highly negative way to the fallacious critical pretensions that he found in Proudhon's latest book, *System of Economic Contradictions, or the Philosophy of Poverty* (1846). On the basis of his as yet largely embryonic critique of political economy, in *The Poverty of Philosophy* (1847) Marx set out to refute the methodology and substance of Proudhon's arguments.

Secondly, late in 1847, Marx took the opportunity to prepare a series of lectures on the topic 'Wage-Labour and Capital' for the German Workers' Association in Brussels. In these lectures, published in 1849 in the *Neue Rheinische Zeitung*, Marx critically analysed the tenuous economic situation of wage-labourers as determined in their relations with the capitalists. His objective was to explain to the workers the logic of their position, given the particular requirements of a society ruled by capital. The important corollary was that it was within the collective power of the workers to transcend their predicament by ridding society of such a regime.

These themes were given a more historical and socio-political expression in the third of the contexts to be referred to in this period. The *Manifesto of the Communist Party*, written with some contributions from Engels and published in 1848, was intended to be a popular piece of propaganda. It was to provide some critico-theoretical themes for rallying the pursuit of the communist cause by proletarian groups throughout Europe. Together with the 'Wage-Labour and Capital' material, the *Manifesto* gives a complete statement of Marx's critique of capitalism as it had developed by 1847–8. The two pieces also serve to emphasise his continued adherence to the notion of a unity of theory and practice enunciated back in 1843. Thus, the *raison d'être* of the evolving critique of political economy was to establish the theoretical core of revolution. It would provide the substance of a unified proletarian consciousness to replace the 'false consciousness' that had been built and perpetuated on behalf of the capitalists.

After his move to permanent exile in London late in 1849, Marx continued his journalism and, taking advantage of the huge range of resources in the British Museum Library, began again his study of political economy. During the years until 1857, there is no evidence that he wrote anything substantial as a result of his wide-ranging studies. His mass of reading notebooks from the period are thought to be extant, but are almost entirely unpublished. It is, therefore, not possible to trace the evolution of his critical thought in the lead up to the remarkable burst of writing in 1857–8 that produced the *Grundrisse* manuscripts.

The *Grundrisse* manuscripts occupy a central place in any understanding of the evolution of Marx's critique of political economy. It was a long and involved piece of critical investigation that Marx left in its rough-drafted form and which remained unpublished as a whole in his own lifetime. The work was remarkable not only for the relative rapidity with which it was written, but also, and more significantly, for the wealth of quite sophisticated, albeit often incomplete, critical analysis that can be gleaned from it. The contents included a revealing methodological 'Introduction', left unfinished and never redrafted, a 'Chapter on Money' and a much longer 'Chapter on Capital'. Much of what appeared in these manuscripts was to provide the critico-theoretical core of Marx's 'final' but unfinished drafting of *Capital*.

Marx had hoped to prepare these manuscripts for publication quite quickly. Such ease of preparation and presentation eluded him and by early 1859 he had only two brief chapters of what was to be his book on 'Capital' prepared for the press. The *Contribution* appeared in mid-1859 and its chapters dealt with the commodity and its Value and the 'simple circulation' of commodities with the mediation of money. The main limitation of the work was that it failed to include anything on capital and production. A complementary second volume containing a 'third chapter' on capital was planned in order to redress this situation and Marx set about drafting it during the remainder of 1859. He had little apparent success before he became embroiled in the squabble with Karl Vogt which consumed him for some time. It was not until August 1861 that he made an effective start on this long-awaited 'third chapter'.

In volume II of this study, I presented an exposition and analysis of Marx's critical work from 1861 to 1863. The centrepiece of this volume has been the massive 'Critique of Political Economy' manuscripts written during this period. I focused on the most accessible parts of these manuscripts, comprising about half of the materials and having the common theme designated by Marx as 'Theories of Surplus Value'. These parts are arguably the most significant for the purposes of my study in that Marx was situating the critical theory developed in the *Grundrisse* and *Contribution*, and, implicitly, all that led up to it, in its contemporary intellectual context.

The 'Theories' manuscripts dealt ostensibly with Marx's critical reading of the works of many antecedent political economists. The work has the appearance of a draft history of the subject, and it might be argued from Marx's reference to his intentions that this was how he saw it. However, while a significant number of political economists were considered, the reading was highly selective. Marx intended the work only to be an historical study of the 'static' and 'dynamic' theoretical issues centring on the category surplus Value. His purpose was not to teach his readers intellectual history. Rather, he wanted to differentiate and distance his critical vision of the conflict- and contradiction-ridden nature of capitalism from the harmonious vision contrived and portrayed by the political economists. In the process, his draft investigations provided him with the opportunity to develop analytically more sophisticated versions of several of the critical themes adumbrated in the writings of the late 1850s.

A SUMMARY STATEMENT OF MARX'S CRITIQUE

The summary exposition of Marx's critique of political economy prior to *Capital* that follows deals only with the main categories and themes required to give it a coherent, if skeletal, form. My objective is to provide an outline of the main substantive tenets of the comprehensive critique that Marx developed through his investigations, albeit much of it *in statu nascendi*. The analytical limitations that remained will, of course, be all too obvious to modern readers. What will also be evident, though, is the great extent to which, by this stage, he had formulated a critique that anticipated many of the core theses of *Capital*.

At the beginning of the *Grundrisse* manuscripts, Marx drafted an 'Introduction' in which he explored his methodological premises. As things turned out, this part of his investigations was for self-clarification only, as he decided not to prepare it for publication. The significance of this piece in the present context is that it introduced several central features of Marx's approach to his evolving critique of political economy.

First of all, at the epistemological level, Marx posited a two-stage method of abstraction as the appropriate way to grasp intellectually the complex concrete reality of the capitalist economic system. The required abstract categories were to be 'distilled' by analysis from observed reality, with some assistance from those formulated in existing political economy. It was Marx's view, though, that these categories need not have any *immediate* empirical identification to be useful. Indeed, he asserted that political economists had been unable fully to explain the nature and operation of capitalism because their categories were limited to those which confirmed its observed appearances. Marx intended to provide categories that would enable his critique to probe beneath the appearances of capitalist processes and relations in order to grasp their *essence*.

Having established the categories to be used, Marx intended to begin with the most essential and elementary ones and build up his critique by progressively reducing the degree of abstraction from the concrete reality. Further and more complex categories would be added to the critique in a process of logical synthesis until he concluded that the appearance of the concrete was fully explained.

In the 'Introduction', Marx also made it clear that the centrepiece of the political economy of capitalism as he intended to pursue it in his critique was *social* production. In a society characterised by the division of labour, production was necessarily a social act. For the purposes of comprehending the nature and operation of production as the foundation of an economic system, the individual's situation and role had to be de-emphasised in favour of economically determined social classes.

Marx went on to reconsider the relationship between the operational categories that he intended to utilise as a frame of reference for organising his critique. He stressed that capital determined the form of and social relations involved in the production process. At the same time, the production process dominated the determination of the mode of distribution of income, the form of exchange and circulation and the structure of the consumption process. These operational categories were, however, to be treated in an essential unity. They were, therefore, only to be considered in isolation for the purposes of an analysis directed towards progressively formalising this unity. Such was Marx's intention when he began his critique with the production process of capital.

The critique opened with a formal analysis of the most elementary material manifestation of the capitalist mode of production, viz. the commodity produced for exchange. Marx explained that this commodity form represented a unity of use value and exchange value. Its exchange value was a consequence of it having the inherent property of Value by virtue of being produced by abstract labour under the auspices of capital. Value, then, originated in production as the total embodied past and immediate labour time 'socially necessary' (given the dominant method of production) to produce the particular use value form in which the commodity appeared. And, Value could be observed when realised as exchange value in the process of circulation. This process proceeded with the aid of the mediation of money and exchange values were thus expressed in money units.

For Marx, production involved the capitalist owners of the means of production purchasing labour power at some particular exchange value called the wage of labour. This wage reflected the Value of some socially- and historically-determined 'subsistence' basket of commodities assumed to be the minimum requirements for worker survival and procreation. The outlay on labour power comprised the variable capital of the capitalist and it gave him command over all of the immediate labour time which his workers could deliver in the 'accepted' or legal working day (at an 'intensity' largely regulated by the machinery with which they worked).

The capitalist also advanced constant capital in order to purchase the means of production required by the particular 'method' of producing the commodity concerned. These means included both the instruments of labour (broadly defined) and raw materials with and on which the workers were *forced* to work in order to gain access to their 'subsistence' needs. In this, they had no option beyond starvation or the 'poor house'. The capitalist, though, always had the choice of employing more or less labour as his judgment dictated. In all important respects, labour power was perceived by Marx as just another commodity input to production. As far as the capitalist was concerned its *human* dimensions were irrelevant beyond the facts of biological survival and a physiological minimum capacity to deliver labour services.

But labour power was also a very special commodity input. Given Marx's adherence to the embodied-labour theory of Value, it was only labour time that could *create* Value. The *raison d'être* of capitalism was that the capitalist could increase the Value of his capital, advanced as variable and constant capital, by engaging in production. Marx located the *source* of this increase in the Value of capital in the exploitation of labour that was facilitated by the capitalists' monopoly over the means of production. Exploitation involved the extension of the living labour time appropriated by the capitalist beyond that embodied in the Value of labour power. Surplus, and unpaid, labour was thus added to the necessary, and paid, labour and surplus Value was added to the Value of capital advanced. This surplus Value was, for Marx, the explanation of the existence of non-labour, property incomes such as profits, interest and rent.

The capitalist was assumed to strive to maximise his flow of surplus Value for any particular outlay of capital. The most immediate reflection of this in Marx's analysis was in the achievement of a maximum rate of surplus Value or rate of exploitation. This may be expressed as the ratio of surplus to necessary labour, as the ratio of unpaid to paid labour, or, in symbols (see chapter 11, pp. 229ff. above), as $e = s/v$. The value of this essential ratio could be increased by increasing the duration of unpaid labour time relative to the paid labour time by extending the length of the working day. This would increase what Marx called absolute surplus Value. The ratio could also be increased by increasing what he called relative surplus Value. In this case, the requirement was a reduction in the variable capital needed to employ a given number of workers by means of some decrease in the Value of labour power. Such a decrease could be achieved temporarily by depressing the wage below its 'subsistence' equivalent or permanently by improving the productivity of labour in the wage-commodity sectors of production.

The immediate Value of a commodity produced by labour and appropriated by the capitalist owner of the means of production comprised three components, each measured in Value terms: constant capital 'used up', variable capital and surplus Value. This was most simply expressed as $w = c + v + s$. This Value implied a particular rate of profit measured in Value terms as the ratio of surplus Value to the total capital advanced by the capitalist to facilitate production. With respect to the inclusion of constant capital, this required Marx to distinguish between the flow amount 'used up' and 'transferred' to the Value of the commodity produced, the c in the Value expression above, and the total stock advanced in order to generate this flow. For the purposes of measuring the Value rate of profit, the latter is required in the denominator of the expression. Marx usually made the simplifying assumption that the flow and the stock were equal, and thus he could express the rate as $r = s/(c + v)$ for any particular production period.

Now, for analysing the process of production and Value generation at the macro-level, or at the level of 'capital-in-general' as Marx put it, the above implied 'representative firm' approach was valid. And, he adhered to this level of analysis for most of the *Grundrisse* investigations. When it came to considering a model which included 'many capitals' employed in more than one sector of production, the analysis required careful modification to maintain its validity, except under a very special assumption.

The particular assumption required concerned the composition of the capitals used in the various sectors of production specified. In its most straightforward expression, this composition involved the ratio of the *total stock* Value of constant capital advanced to the Value of variable capital required. Provided this Value composition was uniform across the sectors of production, then the realisation of exchange values that were directly proportional to immediate Values would meet the requirement that, under conditions of competitive capital mobility, each sector capital should yield the same rate of profit. An additional requirement was that all labour was equally exploited by capital such that the rate of surplus Value was everywhere the same.

Marx considered it unlikely that such a uniform capital composition would exist, given the obviously different technically-determined methods of production required to produce different sorts of commodities. As a consequence, he realised that he would have to devise an analysis of exchange value determination that could account for a uniform rate of profit between sectors with different technical compositions of capital, expressed in Value terms as organic compositions, but with the same rate of surplus Value. This required that he formally articulate the essence of capitalist Value determination by embodied-labour time to an exchange-value vector that, when realised, would yield the same rate of profit on each capital independently of its composition. The solution that Marx developed included a vector of modified Values that he referred to variously as 'average prices', 'cost prices' and, ultimately, 'prices of production'. When exchange values were determined by these modified Values, the *realised* distribution of aggregate surplus Value would be such as to ensure that the Value rate of profit in each sector was the same.

Adam Smith and Ricardo, at least, had been aware of this puzzle of establishing consistency between embodied-labour exchange values and the distribution requirement of a uniform rate of profit under conditions where fixed capital was used to different extents in producing various commodities. Smith had abandoned the embodied-labour theory as inappropriate under such conditions. Ricardo faced up to the difficulty, but he could 'resolve' it only in an informal way by asserting that the quantitative difference between immediate embodied-labour exchange values and the modified forms required was insignificant. This enabled him to proceed 'as if' the two exchange-value vectors were effectively identical. Marx had not pursued the issue in the *Grundrisse* where his focus was largely on 'capital-in-general'. It was in the 'Theories' investigations that he took it up and formulated what he considered to be a formal, and logically consistent, solution along the lines set out above.

Marx was aware that actual market exchange values, expressed in money units, could diverge from 'average prices'. Under these circumstances, the realised rates of profits in the various sectors of production would be different. With perfect capital mobility, though, the result would be a redistribution of production resources until the pressures of supply relative to demand restored the 'average price' vector and the uniform rate of profit.

Having provided an explanation for wages as the money form of the Value of labour power, and for profit as the money form of the surplus Value generated in production by the exploitation of labour and realised in exchange, Marx gave some consideration to the ultimate distribution of surplus Value between profit and the rent that was paid to the owners of natural resources, most especially land. For Marx, rent was an income appropriated by landowners by virtue of their property rights alone. However, this did not explain the capacity to pay rent out of realised exchange values, keeping in mind that all capitals should yield a uniform rate of profit under competitive conditions irrespective of whether their methods of production involved land or not. Marx reasoned that sectors using land, agriculture in particular, must realise commodity Values such that they have available an amount of surplus Value that exceeds that required to yield the general rate of profits on capital. The 'excess' surplus Value realised can then be appropriated as absolute rent by the landowner. In order to ensure that such an 'excess' would be available, Marx argued that the Value composition of capital in agriculture had remained below the average composition in industrial production because of the historical legacy of more labour-intensive methods of production in the former sector. This meant that the immediate Value rate of profit realised in agriculture by selling commodities at their Values would exceed the average rate in industry. Thus, agricultural capital could achieve the latter rate after paying rent and preserve the uniform rate requirement of inter-sector competitive capital mobility.

It was argued by Marx that his analysis, with its focus on absolute rent, more fully and correctly explained rent than Ricardo had been able to do with the theory of differential rent. Ricardo had taken this theory over from earlier writers and developed it into a central theme of his political economy. Marx undertook a lengthy critique of Ricardo's exposition and drew three main conclusions. First, he noted that Ricardo's quantitative analysis did not give any emphasis to the socio-political nature of rent as a property income. Secondly, while he argued that differential rent was a valid category, he revealed that Ricardo's analysis of it had been unnecessarily restricted in its assumptions and scope. Thirdly, he found that Ricardo had not formulated the absolute rent category at all and, therefore, had not been able to explain the origin of *total* rent.

In the outline of the tenets of Marx's critique of political economy so far, no explicit consideration has been given to the 'motion' of the capitalist economic system through historical time. That is, the critical analysis of Value and distribution theory was conducted by Marx in 'static' terms in the sense that he abstracted from historical time. This represented but an interim stage in the formulation of the critique, for his ultimate intention was to situate this analysis in its 'dynamic' context and develop an 'economic law of motion' of the system. Such a law would account for the immanently crisis-prone nature of capitalism as it progressed under the impetus of capital accumulation.

Marx broached this 'law of motion' analysis in the *Grundrisse* and raised some of the relevant issues again in the 'Theories' manuscripts. He was able to make considerable progress in defininning the scope and component dimensions of the required analysis, but his treatment was largely impressionistic and informal at this stage. Moreover, the pieces of formal analysis of 'motion' that Marx did develop in his investigations at this stage were constrained by the fact that the relevant variables were expressed in immediate Value terms. He was aware that such analyses could only provide limited insights into the *phenomenal* form that 'motion' might take. This was especially the case where any disaggregated analysis of 'many capitals' was involved. At this level of analysis, the exchange values used had to be derived from 'prices of production'. Nowhere in the present context did Marx attempt this important modification. There remained, then, much analytical development to be undertaken before a presentation of the 'law' in published form could be contemplated. Unfortunately, the unfinished manuscripts for *Capital* would later become a lasting testament to these lacunae in Marx's critique.

Fundamental to the concept of the 'motion' of capitalism was the notion that the system must be able constantly to reproduce itself as it expanded and changed through time. In an endeavour to formalise this reproduction process, Marx developed his reproduction schema on the basis of the *Tableau économique* formulated by the Physiocrats in the mid-eighteenth century and ignored by political economists until he resurrected it. The schema enabled Marx to express formally the quantitative and qualitative requirements for reproduction to proceed without impediments and disruptions under both 'stationary' and growth conditions. The former condition, with no capital accumulation, was referred to as 'simple reproduction' by Marx and the latter, which included the effects of accumulation, as 'expanded reproduction'.

What the schema of 'expanded reproduction' especially served to emphasise was that stringent conditions had to be met for capital accumulation to proceed without disruption and crisis. It was Marx's view that the 'anarchy' of economic decision-making under the capitalist regime made it highly improbable that this complex of conditions could ever be met. The consequence of this would be that the system would experience recurrent inter-sector 'disproportionalities' of varying extents and degrees. These would manifest themselves as partial or general overproduction crises.

As far as Marx was concerned, the potential disjunctions exposed by the 'expanded reproduction' schema could not be negated by the simple proposition of 'Say's Law' as most political economists believed. Marx undertook to refute this alleged 'Law' as contradicting the essential logic of the capitalist economy and he noted that some political economists, especially Sismondi and Malthus, had detected the fallaciousness of the 'Law' before him. It was Marx's view, though, that neither of these writers had fully grasped the origin and significance of the difficulties raised by 'Say's Law'.

For most of Marx's investigations of the 'motion' of capitalism, he concentrated upon analysis at the aggregate level of 'capital-in-general'. Capital accumulation, and the technological change that he thought would necessarily accompany it, led individual 'representative' capitalists unwittingly into collective contradictions which had profound and disruptive consequences for the working class, for the structure and operations of capital and for the destiny of the system itself. In this prognosis, Marx's vision of 'motion' contrasted with the more sanguine views of most political economists. The orthodox vision gave some recognition to the remote possibility of the 'stationary state'. But, beyond this, the analyses implied a virtually infinite capacity of the system to absorb capital accumulation and technological change with the only temporary disturbances arising from 'external' events.

Capital accumulation was a process that Marx treated as immediately affecting the forces and relations of production. In investigating its contradictions and its ramifications, he therefore initially abstracted from any circulation considerations. Capital accumulation as it affected capitalist production had its own set of logical difficulties, and these would only be compounded by their integration with circulation. Again, this was intended to be only an interim abstraction, for Marx had always stressed that production and circulation (along with distribution and consumption) comprised an essential unity. As it turned out, though, in the present context, he made little progress in redressing this artificial division between the production and circulation related dimensions of the 'motion' analysis.

The technological change that Marx thought of as necessarily accompanying capital accumulation had its immediate effect on the composition of capital. However, actually identifying the nature and measuring the dynamics of this composition presented Marx with some difficulties. Both quantitative and qualitative dimensions were integrally involved in the analysis. For Marx, as an empirical matter, capital accumulation brought with it an increase in the (notional) 'ratio' of physical means of production to labour required in production processes. This rising technological composition was an immediate reflection of increasingly mechanised 'methods of production'. Marx's fundamental problem was to express this qualitative 'ratio' in unambiguous quantitative terms. His resolution was generally to assume that changes in the Value ratio of constant to variable capital would track with the rising technological composition as capital accumulated. The category that Marx used to express this relationship was the organic composition of capital. He was also aware that the Value composition could be influenced by changes in the relative Values of means of production and labour power. Such changes were, at this stage often subsumed under changes in the organic composition, too.

Capital accumulation and the rising organic composition had two significant types of effects that Marx set out to investigate: first, effects on the dynamics of the general Value rate of profits, and secondly, effects on the conditions of employment of the working class. The former effects underwent more detailed and laborious investigation than the latter in the present context. This was in spite of the fact that the *logic* of profit dynamics involved much less complex analytical puzzles than those he met in formalising the effects on the workers of the relative increase in the use of machinery in production.

The notion that the general rate of profits would fall as capital accumulated was one that pervaded political economy. Marx endeavoured to provide an analysis of this phenomenon that was firmly rooted in the essential logical contradictions of the 'motion' of the capitalist economy. Especially did he want to refute Ricardo's argument that the falling rate was a consequence of economic growth bringing with it rising agricultural food prices, and hence wage costs, due to decreasing land fertility and the protection afforded to the landowners by the 'Corn Laws' that impeded the import of cheaper foodstuffs. Marx objected to this analysis on two grounds. One was that its assumptions about the necessary trends in land fertility and food prices were empirically false. The other was that it was based upon Ricardo's theory of differential rent which Marx had gone to great lengths to expose as overly restricted in its assumptions and scope.

For Marx, the roots of the tendency for the rate of profits to fall were to be found in the dynamic factors affecting the inverse relationship between this rate and the organic composition of capital. The essential logic was able to be expressed using the formula for the Value rate of profits, $r = s/(c + v)$. Defining the organic composition of capital as $g = c/v$, and recalling that the rate of surplus Value was $e = s/v$, this became $r = e/(1 + g)$. On the basis of this expression, a rising tendency for g, *ceteris paribus*, meant necessarily that the value of r had to fall. As Marx realised, though, one effect of a rising organic composition of capital could be a rising rate of surplus Value as labour productivity in wage-commodity sectors improved. Moreover, the influence of the technical composition of capital on the organic composition could be complicated by a relative decrease in costs in the means-of-production-producing sectors. The trend of the organic composition would thus not be able to be so definitively expressed. In principle, then, the tendency of the Value rate of profits indicated by Marx's logic was not necessarily downwards. But, the textual evidence in the present context suggests that he thought of the *dominant* effect on the rate as the rising organic composition originating in technological changes. The other influences appeared only as counters to this dominance and did not negate it.

On the second matter of the effects of capital accumulation and technological change on employment, Marx undertook a critical assessment of Ricardo's thought on the issue. Ricardo had added a chapter entitled 'On Machinery' to the third edition of his *Principles*. The most obvious purpose of this chapter was to recant on his previously expressed view that the relative increase in the use of machinery would not be detrimental to the interests of the working class. Marx was in sympathy with this interpretation of the negative effects of machinery now espoused by Ricardo because he thought that they reflected an honest assessment of the situation that workers faced. A more careful reading of the chapter in question, though, would have suggested to Marx that Ricardo's resolve in arguing the view that labour must be displaced by machinery was not as strong as his. For Marx, the rising technological composition of capital was an empirically confirmed tendency as capital accumulated and this necessarily meant, at least, that *relatively* fewer jobs would be available and, probably, that there would be fewer *absolutely*. The workers should, therefore, find no joy in the wonders of the 'machine age', as increasing numbers of them were destined to end up in the 'reserve army' of unemployed labour.

The ultimate purpose of Marx's analysis of the various dimensions of the 'law of motion' of capitalism was to explain the empirically evident crisis-prone nature of the system. He considered that these fluctuating fortunes were an immanently generated consequence of the contradictions upon which this historical stage of society was founded. He rejected those pseudo-explanations which related the crises of capitalism to 'external shocks'. Such explanations were the currency of political economy, when the existence of crises was recognised at all, that is. Rather, the reasons for the observed disjunctions in economic activity were to be sought in the inner logic of the motivations and behaviours that characterised the system.

The steps that Marx was able to take towards working out a comprehensive explanation for crises in the *Grundrisse* and 'Theories' manuscripts were faltering ones indeed. Several fundamental theoretical issues were overlooked or given only superficial treatment: first, the definition of what events constitute a crisis; secondly, the distinction between cause and effect; thirdly, the place of the crisis phenomenon in the continuing short-term fluctuations of economic activity; fourthly, the situation of short-term fluctuations and crises in the secular trends of capitalism; and fifthly, the distinction between logically-adequate accounts of the potential for crises to occur and the operational events that lead to the actual realisation of this potential.

The source of the historical 'motion' of capitalism was the unlimited desire of individual capitalists to accumulate. Marx argued that under the 'anarchy' of decision making that characterised the economy, the complex of conditions required for unimpeded expanded reproduction would rarely be met. And, up until the early 1860s at least, he emphasised this as the main explanation of the crisis. The most immediate symptom of such a 'realisation crisis' was the overproduction of commodities, although its effects would soon include reduced prices, reduced profits and profit rates, reduced production and employment, and probable bankruptcy for some capitalists. In effect, these consequences reflected the fact that the capitalist market mechanism, given competitive resource mobility, reacted in a self-correcting way to overcome the recurring but temporary 'barrier' of overproduction.

In addition to this emphasis on circulation puzzles, Marx was sensitive to the potential difficulties for capitalism raised by the effects of capital accumulation in production. The dominance of a rising organic composition of capital meant that there would exist a tendency for the general rate of profits to fall, but Marx did not clarify the temporal status of this phenomenon or its relationship to the crisis concept. Evidently, though, any secular negative trend in the potential rates of profit on individual capitals would compound the difficulties experienced by capitalists during short-term crises induced by overproduction.

What was clear in Marx's tentative observations about crises in this context, was that he did not envisage economic breakdown *per se* to be the mode of transcendence to a post-capitalist society. Capitalism was perceived by Marx as having an overriding capacity of self-preservation. Just how the economic tendencies of the system would be related to its ultimate demise at the hands of the revolutionary proletariat was not considered. It can only be surmised that he foresaw the cumulative effects of periodically worsening economic conditions as consolidating the revolutionary 'consciousness' of the proletariat to the point where ultimately they would act. That is, the critical theory provided by Marx would be turned into critical practice by the pervasive effects of economic desperation.

Notes

CHAPTER 1 INTRODUCTION

1 From around mid-1859 to mid-1861, Marx was consumed with his journalism and the vituperative squabble with the German politician Karl Vogt, in between bouts of ill-health. On the Vogt affair see M. Rubel and M. Manale, *Marx Without Myth*, pp. 159ff.
2 A full discussion of the bibliographical situation of this work in the development of Marx's critical theory is provided in my *The Making of Marx's Critical Theory: A Bibliographical Analysis*, chapters 4 and 5.
3 See the discussion in Part II of volume I of the present study.
4 Throughout this study, Marx's concept of Value will be referred to with the first letter of the term in upper case. The point of this is to emphasise that he conceived of Value as an immediate and essential characteristic of commodities produced under capitalism. For Marx, the category Value could be defined independently of its apparent, phenomenal form as exchange value, even though the latter was usually simply referred to as 'value' by political economists. Cf. Anwar Shaikh's view in 'Marx's theory of Value and the "transformation problem" ', in Schwartz (ed.), *The Subtle Anatomy of Capitalism*, p. 113.
5 See note 1 above.
6 The significance of the unfinished state of *Capital* and other issues concerning its status in Marx's critical theory are discussed in my *The Making of Marx's Critical Theory*, chapters 5 and 6.
7 Marx's use of the terms such as 'section', 'part', 'chapter' and 'book' in the dividing up of his work during this period can be quite confusing. Some endeavour to clarify the situation is made in ibid., chapter 5.
8 This issue is raised again in the particular context of Marx's critique of Ricardo in notes 3 and 4 to chapter 4 below.
9 Cf. the views expressed by Salo Ryazanskaya in the editorial Preface to *TSV*, I. Ryazanskaya criticises Karl Kautsky for distorting the original arrangement of Marx's manuscript materials when he first published the 'Theories' (*TSV*, I, 20ff.).
10 In the investigations recorded in the 'Theories' manuscripts, Marx was frequently imprecise in the terminology that he used to refer to some important categories. Some clarification of the particular use of terms adopted

in the present study is therefore appropriate at this point. For most of his analysis, Marx measured economic quantities in *Value* terms (see note 4 above). As he was well aware, such quantities, even when *expressed* in commodity money units of a constant Value, were not immediately empirical magnitudes. Consequently the Value status of these quantities must be emphasised in order to distinguish them from their observed phenomenal forms to which similar names may be applied. Commodity Value embodies surplus Value, the essential source of profit (and other property incomes). Two important ratios involve surplus Value. The rate of surplus Value is the ratio of surplus Value to the Value of variable capital required to purchase the labour power commanded in the process of production. This ratio must involve Values by definition. The other ratio, the rate of profit, is not so straightforward in the sense that while it is ultimately a phenomenal category, it can be expressed in essential Value terms. That is, the ratio of surplus Value to total capital advanced may be measured in Value terms or it may be measured in terms of some phenomenal vector of exchange values linked to prices of production. It was the Value rate of profit that dominated most of Marx's analyses in 'Theories' and this term is generally used in the present study. It will be noticed also that I distinguish between the general rate of *profits*, which is a macro-category relating to capital-in-general, and the rate of *profit* that applies to individual sector capitals.

The measurement of capital also requires some clarification. In the ratio expressing a Value rate of profit, the denominator should measure the total Value of capital advanced. In order to simplify his analyses, Marx often assumed that all constant capital was used up in one production period such that capital advanced and capital embodied in commodity Value were the same. With respect to the composition of capital, the simplest expression is the ratio of constant capital advanced (and used up under the usual assumption just cited) to variable capital measured in Value terms. It should be kept in mind, though, that this Value composition has two dimensions. It is founded on a certain physical-technical 'ratio' of means of production to labour. This 'ratio' may be expressed in terms of some vector of exchange values. Where these exchange values are proportional to immediate Values, the result is the Value composition of capital. A further category used by Marx was the organic composition of capital. This became especially important in distinguishing *changes* in capital composition *vis-à-vis* the two dimensions just referred to. The organic composition is an exchange value ratio that expresses technical composition independently of the exchange-value vector used. The significance of this distinction will emerge later in the study (see chapter 4, pp. 81ff. and chapter 11, pp. 229ff.). For the present, the category Value composition of capital will be used.

11 The idea of a 'snapshot' or 'photograph' is used to convey a given *state* of the economic system observed at a point (or particular production period) in its progress through historical time. In such a 'vision' of the system, the observed level and composition of output, relative price vector, pattern of distribution and production technology are given. This approach is usually associated with the work of Piero Sraffa, *Production of Commodities by Means of Commodities*. See Geoffrey Harcourt, 'The Sraffian contribution: an evaluation', in Bradley, and Howard (eds), *Classical and Marxian Political Economy: Essays in Honour of Ronald L. Meek*, pp. 259, 264. Harcourt attributes the use of the term to Alessandro Roncaglia. I have added the notion of an 'X-ray' to express Marx's intention that his analysis should penetrate the surface appearances of the capitalist economy and expose the

essential structures and relations that underpin what is observed.

A similar methodological position is taken by Maurice Godelier in *Rationality and Irrationality in Economics*, pp. 259–60, 278–9. He distinguishes between 'synchronic' and 'diachronic' analyses. The former sets out 'what the elements of . . . [a] system are and what their relations are, at a given time (t) in the evolution of . . . [the] system', and the latter adds 'how these elements and their relations have been formed and have evolved during (*dia*) the time that this system has lasted (. . . which is theory [*sic*] both of the origin and of the evolution of a system)' (pp. 259–60). Thus:

> Synchronic analysis will seek to reconstitute, at a certain moment in the evolution of a system, the functioning of the structures of production, distribution and consumption. Diachronic analysis will seek to reconstruct the genesis of the elements of the system and of their relations, and then to follow the evolution of their functioning through a series of synchronical pictures of the system (pp. 278–9).

As a unity, these two dimensions of method emphasise the crucial analytical interdependence between a structure and its 'motion' through time.

CHAPTER 2 EXCHANGE VALUE AND DISTRIBUTION ANALYSIS BEFORE ADAM SMITH

1 Notice that Marx used the term 'modern political economy' here. Peter Grœnewegen has suggested that this term was used in order to emphasise that the Physiocrats' analyses related to the emerging *capitalist* mode of production that was subsequently to dominate as the object of political economy. See 'Thoughts on the Emergence of Economics as a Science', mimeograph, 1973, p. 12n.
2 Cf. Ronald L. Meek, *Studies in the Labour Theory of Value*, 2nd ed., p. 17.
3 Two modern interpretations of the work on interest in this period are G.S.L. Tucker, *Progress and Profits in British Economic Thought 1650–1850*, pp. 7ff., and Marian Bowley, *Studies in the History of Economic Theory before 1870*, pp. 34ff. It is interesting to notice the similarity between the interpretations of these scholars and of Marx, including the particular quotations selected to illustrate the views expressed.
4 Tucker, *Progress and Profits*, p. 8, and Bowley, *Studies in the History of Economic Theory*, pp. 53ff.
5 Tucker, *Progress and Profits*, pp. 16ff., and Bowley, *Studies in the History of Economic Theory*, pp. 37ff.
6 Tucker, *Progress and Profits*, p. 9.
7 Meek, *Studies in the Labour Theory of Value*, pp. 18ff.
8 ibid., pp. 21–3.
9 *The Economic Writings of Sir William Petty*, vol. I, p. 244. On the date of composition of the *Political Arithmetick*, see ibid., p. 235.
10 Meek, *Studies in the Labour Theory of Value*, p. 39.
11 Marx attributed the first conscious explication of exchange value as measured by labour time, 'the basic law of modern political economy', to Benjamin Franklin in his 1731 work *A Modest Inquiry into the Nature and Necessity of a Paper Currency* (*CCPE*, 55–6).
12 Petty, *Economic Writings*, vol. I, pp. 1ff.
13 Except for *An Essay Concerning the Multiplication of Mankind*, these works

have been reprinted in Petty, *Economic Writings*, vols I and II.
14 Petty, *Economic Writings*, vol. I, pp. 50–1. Cf. Meek, *Studies in the Labour Theory of Value*, p. 35, and Bowley, *Studies in the History of Economic Theory*, pp. 84–6, 91–3.
15 Petty, *Economic Writings*, vol. I, p. 43, Marx's emphasis.
16 ibid., pp. 89–90, Marx's emphasis in quoted piece.
17 ibid., p. 87, Marx's emphasis.
18 Hobbes, *Leviathan*, pp. 43, 44; Marx's emphasis after 'WORTH'.
19 ibid., p. 130, Marx's emphasis.
20 Petty, *Economic Writings*, vol. I, p. 268.
21 ibid., p. 43, Marx's emphasis. Cf. Meek, *Studies in the Labour Theory of Value*, pp. 35–6.
22 Petty, *Economic Writings*, vol. I, p. 44.
23 ibid., p. 43.
24 ibid., pp. 44ff., 181–2.
25 ibid., p. 47.
26 ibid., p. 48, Marx's emphasis.
27 ibid., Marx's emphasis. Cf. Tucker, *Progress and Profits*, p. 24.
28 Reprinted in *The Works of John Locke*, vol. 5, pp. 1ff. and 338ff. respectively. Note that *Some Considerations* was probably written around 1670–2; see Bowley, *Studies in the History of Economic Theory*, p. 22.
29 Petty, *Economic Writings*, vol. I, p. 304; quoted by Tucker, *Progress and Profits*, p. 24.
30 ibid., p. 26.
31 ibid., and Bowley, *Studies in the History of Economic Theory*, p. 54n.
32 ibid., p. 50.
33 ibid., pp. 22, 48.
34 Tucker, *Progress and Profits*, p. 26.
35 Cf. Bowley, *Studies in the History of Economic Theory*, p. 50.
36 ibid., pp. 44, 49, and Tucker, *Progress and Profits*, pp. 26–8, 34–5.
37 Locke, *Works*, vol. 5, pp. 9, 10. Cf. Tucker, *Progress and Profits*, p. 28.
38 ibid., pp. 26ff., and Bowley, *Studies in the History of Economic Theory*, p. 51.
39 Locke, *Works*, vol. 5, pp. 353–4.
40 ibid., p. 358, Marx's emphasis; cf. p. 356.
41 ibid., pp. 355–6, 358.
42 ibid., p. 365.
43 ibid., Marx's emphasis.
44 ibid., pp. 366–7.
45 ibid., p. 36.
46 ibid.
47 ibid.
48 ibid., Marx's emphasis.
49 Meek, *Studies in the Labour Theory of Value*, pp. 17, 22.
50 Locke, *Works*, vol. 5, pp. 361, 363, Marx's emphasis.
51 Cf. Meek, *Studies in the Labour Theory of Value*, pp. 21–2, and Bowley, *Studies in the History of Economic Theory*, pp. 76–9, 79n.
52 Dudley North, *Discourses upon Trade*, p. 16, Marx's emphasis.
53 ibid., p. 21 (the original has p. 20, but this is obviously a misprint).
54 ibid., p. 11, Marx's emphasis.
55 ibid., p. 4, Marx's emphasis.
56 ibid., Marx's emphasis.
57 Cf. Tucker, *Progress and Profits*, pp. 25, 32, and Bowley, *Studies in the*

History of Economic Theory, p. 55.
58 North, *Discourses*, p. 4, Marx's emphasis.
59 Cf. Tucker, *Progress and Profits*, p. 25, and Bowley, *Studies in the History of Economic Theory*, pp. 44, 48, 53, 59.
60 Cf. Tucker, *Progress and Profits*, pp. 25–6, 33–4.
61 David Hume, *Essays Moral, Political and Literary*, p. 311; Marx's emphasis except where noted as original.
62 ibid., pp. 311–12, Marx's emphasis. Cf. Tucker, *Progress and Profits*, p. 43. Tucker notes that while Hume endeavoured to refute the argument that the fall in English interest rates was due to a growth in the supply of money (ibid., p. 33), he did allow for some *indirect* influence of this factor via its independent stimulation of trade (ibid., pp. 36, 44–5).
63 Joseph Massie, *An Essay on the Governing Causes of the Natural Rate of Interest*, p. 51, Marx's emphasis. Tucker notes that Massie's view of interest as paid from profits suggests Locke's influence in spite of Massie setting out to criticise Locke: *Progress and Profits*, pp. 38–9.
64 Massie, *An Essay*, p. 51.
65 ibid.
66 ibid., p. 55, Marx's emphasis. Cf. Tucker, *Progress and Profits*, pp. 35–6, 40–1.
67 Massie, *An Essay*, p. 49, Marx's emphasis. Tucker, *Progress and Profits*, p. 39, argues that linking rent to profits gained in trade provided a justification for rent because the legitimacy of such profits at reasonable rates had never been seriously questioned.
68 Massie, *An Essay*, p. 50, Marx's emphasis. Cf. Tucker, *Progress and Profits*, p. 39 and n., where he suggests that Massie initially had in mind an equal division of immediate profit to provide for rent, but in a later work he changed this to a one-third proportion for rent.
69 James Steuart, *An Inquiry into the Principles of Political Œconomy*, in *The Works Political, Metaphisical [sic] and Chronological of Sir James Steuart*, vol. 1, p. 275; Marx's emphasis.
70 ibid., Marx's emphasis.
71 ibid., p. 244, Marx's emphasis.
72 ibid., pp. 244–5.
73 ibid., p. 245, Marx's emphasis.
74 ibid., Marx's emphasis.
75 ibid., p. 275
76 ibid., pp. 382–3; cf. ibid., vol. 3, p. 11, referred to by Marx in passing, *TSV*, I, 43.
77 See Part IV below.
78 Marx would soon use the *Tableau économique* as the basis for the more formal development of the idea of reproduction adumbrated in the *Grundrisse* (*G*, 327–8, 439ff.; and volume I, chapter 7, pp. 210ff. of the present study). This was made explicit in his letter to Engels on 6 July 1863 (*MEW*, 30, 361ff.).
79 Cf. Robert V. Eagly, *The Structure of Classical Economic Theory*, where it is argued that Classical political economy was founded on the key concept *capital*.
80 According to the work of Gianni Vaggi, the Physiocrats' concern with exchange value analysis has been much understated. See his 'Prices, Markets and Reproduction: a Study of the Role of a Theory of Value in Physiocracy', unpublished PhD thesis, University of Cambridge, 1980, and 'The Physiocratic Theory of Prices', mimeograph, 1983.

81 See note 80 above.
82 The interpretation here expressed applied especially to Quesnay. Later Physiocrats and Turgot did rescue the analysis from this limitation to some extent at least. On this theme, see Ronald Meek's essay 'The Physiocratic concept of profit' in his *The Economics of Physiocracy*, pp. 297ff.
83 Reprinted in Ronald Meek's *Turgot on Progress, Sociology and Economics*, pp. 119ff.
84 ibid., p. 133.
85 ibid., pp. 145ff.
86 ibid., p. 155.
87 On this see Ronald Meek's Introduction to ibid., pp. 19ff.; and Peter Grœnewegen's papers: 'Turgot and Adam Smith', *Scottish Journal of Political Economy*, XVI:3, November 1969, 'A reappraisal of Turgot's theory of value, exchange and price determination', *History of Political Economy*, 2:1, spring 1970, and 'A re-interpretation of Turgot's theory of capital and interest', *Economic Journal*, 81:322, June 1971; and his book *The Economics of A.R.J. Turgot.*
88 Peter Grœnewegen has pointed out to me how surprising it is that Marx did not refer to more of Turgot's works in the light of the fact that his source was the collection *Œuvres de Turgot*, nouvelle édition par M. Eugène Daire, vol. 1, Paris, 1844. This adds to the puzzles surrounding Marx's relative neglect of some of Turgot's vital contributions to the development of political economy. My discussion of Turgot here is largely limited to the aspects of his work to which Marx drew attention.
89 *Turgot on Progress, Sociology and Economics*, p. 123; Marx's emphasis.
90 ibid., p. 122.
91 ibid., p. 128, Marx's emphasis. Turgot persisted with the 'gift of nature' idea, though: see p. 146.
92 ibid., p. 128, my emphasis added.
93 ibid., p. 133 and pp. 129ff., where Turgot discussed other organisations of agricultural production that would achieve this end.
94 ibid., pp. 145ff.
95 ibid., p. 150, emphasis original; and pp. 150ff.
96 ibid., p. 151; cf. p. 147.
97 ibid., p. 155; cf. p. 153.
98 ibid., p. 152; cf. p. 171.
99 ibid., p. 154, emphasis original.
100 ibid., pp. 180 and 181 (latter piece quoted by Marx); cf. p. 147.

CHAPTER 3 ADAM SMITH'S *WEALTH OF NATIONS*

1 See chapters 4 and 5 below.
2 Quotations from Adam Smith's *An Inquiry into the Nature and Causes of the Wealth of Nations* included in this chapter are from vol. I of the edition prepared by Edwin Cannan, 1961, and are cited as *WN*. Any emphases in the quotations were added by Marx.
3 The existence of these two lines of development in the theory of value and distribution has been well established by Maurice Dobb, *Theories of Value and Distribution Since Adam Smith*, and Krishna Bharadwaj, *Classical Political Economy and the Rise to Dominance of Supply and Demand Theories.* For a different view of Adam Smith's place in this development see Samuel Hollander, *The Economics of Adam Smith.*

4 Adam Smith's concepts of productive and unproductive labour and their relationship to Marx's thought on exploitation are discussed in John Henry's paper 'Productive labour, exploitation and oppression – a perspective', *Australian Economic Papers*, 14:2, June 1975. Henry's contribution helped to clarify some of my ideas in the following discussion.
5 The complexities of Smith's discussion of rent have been set out in detail by J.M.A. Gee, 'The origin of rent in Adam Smith's *Wealth of Nations*: an anti-neoclassical view', *History of Political Economy*, 13:1, spring 1981.
6 There is a sense in which Adam Smith's view of the value aggregate was appropriate. For the purpose of national accounting, the aggregate product of an industry or the economy comprises *value added*, all of which is paid out as incomes in one form or another. The fact remains, though, that in *gross* terms the revenue from selling a commodity had to cover the cost of constant capital. It was this that Marx felt Adam Smith had not realised.

CHAPTER 4 RICARDO'S *PRINCIPLES*: EXCHANGE VALUE AND PROFIT

1 In *The Works and Correspondence of David Ricardo*, ed. Piero Sraffa, vol. I. This edition will be cited in the text below as *Principles*. All emphases in quotations are Marx's.
2 For example, G.S.L. Tucker, 'Ricardo and Marx', *Economica*, 28, August 1961, attempts to establish that Ricardo cannot be held responsible for Marx's critique of capitalism. Tucker's point is essentially that Marx's views were developed from quite different premises, with a different *raison d'être* in mind. Ricardo is presented by Tucker as taking a harmonious view of the capitalist production and distribution process that is in total contrast to Marx's dialectical vision of immanent conflict. It is unfortunate that Tucker chose to base his interpretation *only* on Marx's side remarks in *Capital*, Volume I, where the critical filiation between the two writers in both methodology and substance is not as evident as it is in 'Theories of Surplus Value'. Compare here the views of T.W. Hutchison in 'The Cambridge Version of the History of Economics', Economics Department, University of Birmingham, 1974. Hutchison allows that Marx's main intellectual source was Ricardo (p. 6), but he endeavours to downgrade the broader significance of this link by repudiating Marx's impression that Ricardo had a predominantly disharmonious vision of capitalist social relations (pp. 8–11). Unfortunately, Hutchison, too, does not consider the available evidence fully, a surprising thing given his recognition of Marx's pioneering efforts in and extensive knowledge of the history of political economy (p. 6). Had he gone beyond references to *Capital*, Volume I, and based his interpretation on the 'Theories of Surplus Value' manuscript, he would have found it much more obvious that Marx's filiation with Ricardo was *predominantly* critico-*analytical* and was only reinforced by the implied political aspects of the *Principles*. Marx knew very well that Ricardo was pro-capitalist and had a predominant belief in the system's long-run viability and economic welfare capacities. What he found so meritorious in the *Principles* in this respect was Ricardo's honesty in facing squarely the contradictions and conflicts made evident in the system by his logical analyses. On all this, see also John King's 'Marx as an historian of economic thought', *History of Political Economy*, 11:3, Fall 1979, especially pp. 383, 389ff.
3 This interpretation is largely the work of Susan de Brunhoff, 'Marx as an a-

Ricardian: Value, money and price at the beginning of *Capital*', *Economy and Society*, 2:3, August 1973, and 'Controversies in the theory of surplus Value: a reply to John Eatwell', *Science and Society*, 38:4, winter 1974–5. For de Brunhoff, there exists an 'irreducible difference between Ricardo and Marx' and she concludes that 'Marx's reasoning does not . . . consist in superseding the "bourgeois limits" of Ricardian ideas, but in *displacing the problems* of Ricardian economic theory' (emphasis original). This thesis is supported by Geoffrey Pilling, 'The law of Value in Ricardo and Marx', *Economy and Society*, 1:3, August 1972. What these two writers in particular fail to make clear is that while Marx's work was *always* critical of bourgeois society and its reflection in political economy, the *sense* of critique was that it included allowance for the *preservation* of those dimensions which incorporated contributions to general human well-being and human comprehension. Capitalism would leave a legacy of massive and sophisticated *forces* of production after the 'deluge'. Political economy provided Marx, *inter alia*, with the embodied-labour theory of exchange value and the principle of the surplus which he was able to *adapt* with such (relative) erudition to form the basis of the critical theory that he envisaged to be crucial for revolutionary praxis.

4 Joseph Schumpeter gave great weight to Marx's intellectual dependence on Ricardo's developments in political economy. The following pieces are the 'classics' of this position:

> Marx had a master then? Yes. Real understanding of his economics begins with recognising that, as a theorist, he was a pupil of Ricardo. He was his pupil not only in the sense that his own argument evidently starts from Ricardo's propositions but also in the much more significant sense that he had learned the art of theorising from Ricardo. He always used Ricardo's tools, and every theoretical problem presented itself to him in the form of difficulties which occurred to him in his profound study of Ricardo and of suggestions for further work which he gleaned from it. (*Ten Great Economists*, p. 26.)
>
> Marx used the Ricardian apparatus: he adopted Ricardo's conceptual layout and his problems presented themselves to him in the forms that Ricardo had given to them. No doubt, he transformed these forms and he arrived in the end at widely different conclusions. But he always did so by way of starting from, and criticising, Ricardo – *criticism of Ricardo was his method in his purely theoretical work*. (*History of Economic Analysis*, p. 390, emphasis original; cf. pp. 391, 596, 649, 681, 682n., 685.)

In more recent years, this has been the premise upon which many writers have based their work; most notably, Ronald Meek, *Studies in the Labour Theory of Value*, 2nd ed., pp. 166ff., and Maurice Dobb, *Theories of Value and Distribution since Adam Smith*, chapter 6, *passim*.

5 This theme is the basis of Dobbs's book cited in note 4 above and is more explicitly developed by Krishna Bharadwaj, *Classical Political Economy and the Rise to Dominance of Supply and Demand Theories*. See also the contributons to I. Bradley and M. Howard (eds), *Classical and Marxian Political Economy: Essays in Honour of Ronald L. Meek*.

6 I am referring here, of course, to Samuel Hollander whose massive and controversial study, *The Economics of David Ricardo*, along with his

numerous journal contributions, has done so much to rekindle interest in Ricardo's work at the 'front line' of scholarship. The reference to Marshall is to his Appendix I in *Principles of Economics*, 9th (variorum) ed. Hollander's article on Marx in this context, a contribution that has received much less critical scrutiny than it deserves is 'Marxian economics as "general equilibrium" theory', *History of Political Economy*, 13:1, spring 1981.

7 See, for example, the interchange between Samuel Hollander and John Eatwell in Hollander, 'Ricardo's analysis of the profit rate, 1813–15', *Economica*, 40, August 1973, Eatwell, 'The interpretation of Ricardo's *Essay on Profits*', *Economica*, 42, May 1975, and Hollander, 'Ricardo and the corn profit model: reply to Eatwell', *Economica*, 42, May 1975; that between Hollander and Alessandro Roncaglia in Roncaglia, 'Hollander's Ricardo'; Hollander, 'A reply', and Roncaglia, 'Rejoinder', in *Journal of Post Keynesian Economics*, IV:3, spring 1982; and that between Hollander and D.P. O'Brien in O'Brien, 'Ricardian economics and the economics of David Ricardo', *Oxford Economic Papers*, 33:3, November 1981, Hollander, 'The economics of David Ricardo: a response to Professor O'Brien', and O'Brien, 'Ricardian economics: a rejoinder', *Oxford Economic Papers*, 34:1, March 1982. It is worth noting that O'Brien considers the key ideas of the former two of Hollander's antagonists as 'mistaken' and Hollander's arguments to be 'equally unpersuasive'!

8 L. von Bortkiewicz, 'Value and price in the Marxian system', [1907], *International Economic Papers*, 2, 1952; and Ian Steedman, 'Marx on Ricardo', in Bradley and Howard (eds), *Classical and Marxian Political Economy*, pp. 115ff. That I consider both of these critical pieces to be misleadingly hard on Marx will be mentioned in further notes below.

9 I use the term *articulation* here advisedly to emphasise that the analytical problem is one of *difference* rather than change. Values are 'transformed' into prices that are consistent with the requirement of competitive capitalism of a uniform general rate of profits *not* in the sense that any *operational* process is involved. The process is a 'static', *abstract-analytical* one only through which modified, less abstract Values are articulated to their embodied-labour essence.

10 This is an unsettled area of controversy. See, for example, Anwar Shaikh, 'Marx's theory of Value and the "transformation problem" ' in Schwartz (ed.), *The Subtle Anatomy of Capitalism*, and the diametrically opposed views of Ian Steedman, *Marx After Sraffa*. It is interesting, but disturbing, to note that neither of these writers refer to the other's work even though their opposing views were extant well before the above pieces were published: but see H.D. Kurz, 'Sraffa after Marx', *Australian Economic Papers*, 18, June 1979.

11 Both of these works are reprinted in *The Works and Correspondence of David Ricardo*, vol. IV – hereafter cited as *Works*, IV.

12 Marx had studied the *second* edition of the *Principles* in a French translation in the very early stages of his contacts with political economy in 1844 and notes from this study are extant: *MEGA*, I/3, 415 and 493ff. For his 1850–1 study of Ricardo he used the third edition in English: *G*(EV), 765ff., contains the notes from this period. However, a few scattered references to the second edition are to be found in the 'Theories of Surplus Value' manuscript: *TSV*, I, 61; II, 400; III, 95, 105. The first of these is a quotation from the English second edition while the rest are references to Say's Notes to the French translation. Marx's grasp of the second edition was not, though, sufficiently independent of his studies of the third to enable him to notice the point made

by Steedman, 'Marx on Ricardo', p. 121.

13 *Works*, IV, 41; Marx's emphasis.

14 *Works*, IV, 248–9; Marx's emphasis.

15 Marx had previously classified as 'Classical' those political economists from Petty to Ricardo in Britain and from Boisguillebert to Sismondi in France: *CCPE*, 52. See chapter 2, pp. 15ff. above.

16 Cf. Hollander, *The Economics of David Ricardo*, p. 202.

17 Cf. *CCPE*, Chapter 1, where Marx argued the essential relationship between the commodity and its Value.

18 J.K. Rodbertus-Jagetzow, *Soziale Briefe an von Kirchmann. Dritter Brief: Widerlegung der Ricardo'schen Lehre von der Grundrente und Begründung einer neuen Rententheorie*, Berlin, 1851. For a detailed analysis of Marx's relationship with Rodbertus see Engels's Preface to *Capital*, Volume II.

19 See also Ryazanskaya's editorial note 1, *TSV*, II, 633.

20 See chapter 6 of volume I of the present study where I have considered Marx's *Grundrisse* analysis of the Value-distribution issue in detail.

21 This way of expressing Marx's abstract notions is suggested by Ian Steedman, 'Marx on Ricardo', pp. 147, 150.

22 This methodological analogy was outlined in note 11 to chapter 1 above. It has been suggested, though, that the analysis also has a logico-historical basis: see M. Morishima and G. Catephores, 'Is there an "historical transformation problem"?', *Economic Journal*, 85, June 1975; R.L. Meek, 'Is there an "historical transformation problem?": a comment', *Economic Journal*, 86, June 1976; and M. Morishima and G. Catephores, 'The "historical transformation problem": a reply', *Economic Journal*, 86, June 1976.

23 There seem to be four schools of thought on this issue. First, there are those so-called fundamentalists who argue that the articulation analysis presented by Marx was 'right' and requires no 'correction' at all: see for example David Yaffe, 'Value and price in Marx's *Capital*', *Revolutionary Communist*, 1, January 1975. Secondly, two scholars in particular have sought to give some rationale for Marx's own presentation of the analysis. They emphasise that while it was never intended to be the *end* of the story, it can be seen to be an appropriate *beginning* when its methodology and categories are understood correctly in the context of Marx's critique. Anwar Shaikh argues that Marx's analysis is the first stage in what turns out to be an iterative procedure in order to achieve the 'correction' of input Values to prices of production while maintaining the *explicit* links between the essential domain of Values and their modified form: see 'Marx's theory of Value and the "Transformation Problem" '. Ben Fine stresses the need to be clear that the difference in organic compositions of capital between sectors of production was intended by Marx to express different *technical* compositions *independently of the valuation of inputs*. Thus, for the purposes of demonstrating the articulation analysis required, the valuation of inputs at immediate Values was quite legitimate. This would have remained the case when Marx applied a price of production vector to inputs. However, as Fine notes, there is no reason why the input valuation vector should be the same as the output vector except in the case of 'equilibrium' analysis using simultaneous equation solutions to which all modern interpreters are devoted. This point is especially important in recognition of the 'dynamics' of continuously changing production methods and organic compositions of capital in the various sectors. Under these conditions, the inputs would be antecedent outputs valued at different prices of production from the current output. See Fine's 'A dissenting note on the transformation problem', *Economy and Society*, 12:4, November 1983.

Thirdly, it has been argued that Marx's procedure is wrong as it stands and must be 'corrected' directly by solving simultaneously the relevant equations with *inputs* expressed in price-of-production terms. This position has a long history and has become established as the 'text-book' version of the 'solution' to Marx's problem: for summaries see Paul Sweezy, *The Theory of Capitalist Development*, chapter VII; and M. Howard and J. King, *The Political Economy of Marx*, chapter 5. Fourthly, the view has been presented that the problem that Marx thought he had solved is, indeed insoluble: Steedman, *Marx After Sraffa*, *passim*. This adds the ultimate weight to Paul Samuelson's view that the problem is chimerical, anyway, and does not need solving: 'Understanding the Marxian notion of exploitation: a summary of the so-called transformation problem between Marxian values and competitive prices', *Journal of Economic Literature*, 9, June 1971. That there is still much momentum in this analytical puzzle is indicated in the contributions to Steedman *et al.*, *The Value Controversy*.

24 For an insightful survey of the analytical difficulties entailed by the invariance conditions, see John King, 'Value and exploitation: some recent debates', in Bradley and Howard (eds), *Classical and Marxian Political Economy*, pp. 157ff.

25 See note 23 above.

26 See note 23 above, especially the references to the work of Shaikh and Fine.

27 Cf. Piero Sraffa, Introduction to *Principles*, *ed. cit.*, pp. xlviii–ix; and Hollander, *The Economics of David Ricardo*, pp. 6–7.

28 Steedman, 'Marx on Ricardo', pp. 116–17, argues that Ricardo never *used* the term 'value' to mean embodied-labour. Rather, he used the term to mean 'cost of production' and 'natural price'. While I agree that this is the way that Ricardo's use should be read, care is needed in interpreting the *Principles* in this matter. *The important thing for Marx* was that whatever *names* Ricardo used, *the origin of exchange value remained firmly rooted in embodied-labour content.* Chapter I of the *Principles* is replete with statements to this effect, even though Ricardo was ultimately endeavouring to get at the *operational* meaning of 'relative value' in the market situation – this is the point of the phrase quoted from *Principles*, 11, by Steedman, although he chose to omit the next words, 'depends on the relative quantity of labour which is necessary for its production'. It is pertinent to note, though, that for most of the *Principles* value, cost of production and natural price *did* end up meaning embodied-labour exchange value *in effect*, at first because of Ricardo's decision that the capital induced 'modifications' were quantitatively insignificant, and then because he decided to use a uniform composition model and dispense with the problem of 'modifications' anyway (see note 31 below). Ricardo's conceptual grasp exceeded his formal analytical reach and Steedman's comment on p. 133 about Ricardo's poor standard of perspicuity and self-expression applies here too. It was not Marx who left the 'verbal muddle' (p. 120 and p. 153) to be sorted out, but rather it was Ricardo. *In another context*, Steedman follows Alfred Marshall (*Principles of Economics*, *ed. cit.*, p. 813) and suggests that the reader should make allowance for 'Ricardo's shifting and rather confusing use of terms' (p. 137). *Amen*!

29 In this passage, the word 'appears' is used in two senses. On the first occasion, 'appears' implies that market prices are *actually* based on cost prices. On the second occasion, 'appears' implies the *phenomenal* as distinct from the *essential*. At the level of observed phenomena, the cost price appears to be a summation of distribution-based costs.

30 Cf. Hollander, *The Economics of David Ricardo*, pp. 11, 202, 221, 258, 303.

31 Steedman's resort to absolutist criticism of Marx on this point ('Marx on Ricardo', p. 124) is of doubtful assistance in what I understand to be the point of doing history of political economy (and Steedman himself seems to sense this view, too, when he makes the conciliatory remarks on p. 125). What Marx emphasised in his critique was that Ricardo was bound by the entailed logic of the premises upon which the *Principles* analyses were developed, viz. the embodied-labour theory of exchange value *and* the imposed, given general rate of profits expressed as a ratio of embodied-labour exchange values. Whatever the analytical problems involved in Marx's own Value-distribution articulation analysis, they were just as much inherent in Ricardo's implicit seminal endeavours to formulate such an analysis. Steedman's criticisms of Marx on this matter (see also *Marx After Sraffa*, *passim*) therefore apply to Ricardo as well, however, less obviously so. It is beside the point that by dropping the embodied-labour principle and solving the system of production-sector equations, by Sraffa's physical commodities approach, it can be shown that Ricardo's analysis *potentially* included a logically sound theory of the rate of profits. The same potential is there, and much more readily apparent, in *Marx's* analysis, as Ronald Meek so brilliantly recognised long ago: see 'Mr Sraffa's rehabilitation of Classical economics', *Scottish Journal of Political Economy*, 8, 1961, and *Science and Society*, 25, 1961; reprinted with minor amendments in *Economics and Ideology and Other Essays*, pp. 161ff. See also Meek's later thoughts on this subject in which he repeats his emphasis on the, at least, *technical* similarity between Marx's analyses and the Sraffa derivative: Introduction to *Studies in the Labour Theory of Value*, 2nd ed., pp. xxvi ff.; and *Smith, Marx and After*, pp. 130ff. Meek's arguments have been updated by Geoffrey Harcourt in 'The Sraffian contribution: an evaluation', in Bradley and Howard (eds), *Classical and Marxian Political Economy*, pp. 255ff.

32 See note 28 above.

33 Thus, even though Marx's assertions about Ricardo's identification of exchange value and cost price represented a misunderstanding, it is not true to say, as Steedman does in 'Marx on Ricardo', pp. 121–2, that Marx failed to recognise Ricardo's appreciation that *conceptually* there existed a *difference* between the two categories even at the 'static' level of analysis. A similar overstatement is found in von Bortkiewicz, 'Value and price in the Marxian system', p. 28. The thrust of Marx's critique was that while Ricardo *sensed* the 'static' distinction correctly, he did not *formalise* it and explain precisely how a uniform rate of profit could apply without contradicting the embodied-labour Value premise.

34 Recall that Marx did not have access to Ricardo's last paper on the 'invariable standard' problem, now published in *Works*, IV, 357ff.

CHAPTER 5 RICARDO'S *PRINCIPLES*: RENT AND SURPLUS VALUE

1 At this stage, Marx planned to devote all of the second 'Book' of his six-Book critique of political economy to landed property and associated issues. The six-Book project is discussed in my *The Making of Marx's Critical Theory: a Bibliographical Analysis*, chapter 5.

2 More correctly, land not of sufficient quality to return at least the existing general rate of profits at current market prices.

3 An analytical basis for this condition was later developed by Marx and appeared in his discussions of rent in the manuscripts for *Capital*, Book III.

The reason for agricultural technology falling behind that of industry was there explained to be the relative disincentive to capital accumulation in the former because of the need to pay rent out of immediate profit revenue. On this and related issues see Ben Fine, 'On Marx's theory of agricultural rent', *Economy and Society*, 8:3, August 1979; Michael Ball, 'On Marx's theory of agricultural rent: a reply to Ben Fine' and Ben Fine, 'On Marx's theory of agricultural rent: a rejoinder', *Economy and Society*, 9:3, August 1980.

4 A more formal analysis of absolute and differential rent is provided in the Appendix to this chapter.

5 Aspects of Marx's 'tables of differential rent' are considered more fully in the Appendix to this chapter.

6 See Ian Steedman, *Marx Sraffa*, Ian Steedman *et al.*, *The Value Controversy*, and J.E. King, 'Value and exploitation: some recent debates', in Bradley and Howard (eds), *Classical and Marxian Political Economy: Essays in Honour of Ronald L. Meek*, pp. 157ff.

7 See note 7 to chapter 4 above.

8 Marx wrote as follows to Engels on 24 August 1867 on the occasion of the publication of *Capital*, Volume I:

> The best two things in my book are 1. (on which *all* understanding of the facts is based) the *twofold character of labour*, emphasised in the very first chapter, expressed, as it is, in use value or exchange value; 2. the treatment of *surplus Value independent of its particular forms*, like profit, interest, ground rent etc. (*MEW*, 31, 326.)

9 Ian Steedman, 'Marx on Ricardo', in Bradley and Howard (eds), *Classical and Marxian Political Economy*, p. 147, implies that Ricardo may have been aware of the idea that the existence of a surplus involved compulsion to perform surplus labour. That surplus labour *is* performed Ricardo obviously recognised. What he did *not* make clear was *how*, under the capitalist 'rules of the game', dictated by the nature of capital itself, the workers were *compelled* to provide surplus labour in *production*. This was distinct from the appropriation of surplus *product* by feudal landowners, where the compulsion took a different form. In drawing attention to this fact, Marx made one of his most profound contributions to the *critical* comprehension of capitalism as a human-social system. Especially, then, is Steedman's argument on p. 152 quite wrong. There he ascribes to Marx the position of simply *asserting* and *describing* the existence of the difference between the Value of labour power and the Value generated by living labour. Rather, Marx had a very clear theory of exploitation based upon monopolised private property rights over the means of production *and* what is produced with them.

10 Overall, Steedman insists that Marx's critique of Ricardo's handling of the valuation of 'labour' was misdirected in that the similarities between the two writers on this matter outweighed their differences ('Marx on Ricardo', pp. 141ff.). As I have already suggested in the previous note, this underestimates the *additional* insight which Marx contributed. At the purely *physical* level, Marx followed Ricardo's ideas about the 'real' commodity wage Value as the basis of the Value of labour power and those about the modifications to the actual market Value because of supply and demand effects. Now while it is not appropriate to overemphasise the significance of the category labour power *in isolation*, it was important for the clarity of Marx's socio-political thesis on the origin of surplus Value. Just how important is emphasised by Steedman's use of the observer X and Z example (p. 151). There he misses the

crucial point by not noting that observer X's statement simply cannot be correct under capitalism, for the very existence of the surplus depends on the worker *not* being 'paid' the Value of each of the N hours he works. The idea of labour power, as observer Z is aware (although Steedman's scripting understates what Z might have said), is to emphasise that there is a commodity form of labour purchased by the capitalist at a Value below its capacity to deliver living labour as the source of new Value. How effectively the capitalist supervises the exercise of this capacity is irrelevant to the essential point here.

11 Some modern interpreters are also of this opinion: see, e.g., Luigi Pasinetti's formal 'Ricardian' model in his *Growth and Income Distribution: Essays in Economic Theory*, chapter I, especially pp. 7, 20.

12 The lack of clarity that Marx faced in formulating his critique of Ricardo's handling of the category fixed capital is still evident in modern readings of the *Principles*. For example, even Samuel Hollander's detailed study reflects an ambivalence on this point: see *The Economics of David Ricardo*, pp. 162, 206, 213, 259, 340. Cf. Steedman's reservations about Ricardo in this respect, too: 'Marx on Ricardo', pp. 133, 137.

13 Again, in 'Marx on Ricardo', pp. 140–1, Steedman understates the crucial significance *for Marx* of isolating the category variable capital and does not give enough emphasis to Ricardo's *de facto* use of the same category. Ricardo used wage capital advances so explicitly for the very same reason that Marx did: viz. in order to highlight that labour is the *only* source of exchange value, even though such values may be 'modified' quantitatively by other considerations.

CHAPTER 6 REACTIONS TO RICARDO'S THEORY: THE 'MAINSTREAM' CRITICS

1 The status of James Mill, McCulloch and de Quincey as 'disciples' of Ricardo was confirmed some thirty years ago by Schumpeter in his *History of Economic Analysis*, pp. 476–8. Since then, this status has been questioned by various interpreters with respect to the second two. The 'revisionist' interpretation of McCulloch is to be found in D.P. O'Brien's *J.R. McCulloch: a Study in Classic Economics*, *passim*, and in his *The Classical Economists*, pp. 4–5, 43, 93. The status of de Quincey in this respect has been questioned by Mark Blaug, *Ricardian Economics: a Historical Study*, p. 169. O'Brien, *The Classical Economists*, p. 9, puts de Quincey down as a disciple of Ricardo, but later in the book expresses some reservations about this (pp. 43, 96–7, 136, 229). Most recently, though, Peter Grœnewegen has shown de Quincey to have shifted ground with respect to his adherence to Ricardo's ideas in the second of his major economic works, *The Logic of Political Economy* (1844): see 'Thomas de Quincey: faithful disciple of Ricardo?', *Contributions to Political Economy*, 1, March 1982. The 'Ricardian' status of all three writers, though, has been re-affirmed by Samuel Hollander, 'The reception of Ricardian economics', *Oxford Economic Papers*, 29:2, July 1977, thus denying the significance of the evidence elicited by the above writers. The source of this controversy is very easily found: it is simply that the characteristic features of a '*Ricardian*' analysis have been defined differently by giving different weights to the various dimensions of Ricardo's doctrinal heritage.

2 See Thomas Sowell, *Say's Law: an Historical Analysis*, chapter 2; and Sowell,

'Sismondi: a neglected pioneer', *History of Political Economy*, 4:1, spring 1972.

3 The history of political economy in the post-Ricardian period is extremely complex. Just what happened to the intellectual legacy left by Ricardo has been the subject of much controversy between historians, often arguing at cross-purposes because of differing views of what the legacy comprised (cf. note 1 above). It is not appropriate to try to develop this issue here, but the reader is directed to the following literature in which the substance of the debate is evident: Blaug, *Ricardian Economics*, pp. 58ff., R.L. Meek, *Economics and Ideology and Other Essays*, pp. 51ff., M.H. Dobb, *Theories of Value and Distribution since Adam Smith*, pp. 96ff., and Hollander, 'The reception of Ricardian economics'.

4 T.W. Hutchison, 'The Cambridge Version of the History of Economics', Economics Department, University of Birmingham, 1974, pp. 13–14, makes far too much of Marx's passing reference to the year 1830 as critical in this respect (*K*(PE), I, 97). Clearly Marx's assertion was an exaggeration, but this should not be allowed to obscure the point that he wanted to make about the *trend* in political economy after Ricardo's death. Compare the more reasoned assessment in John King, 'Marx as an historian of economic thought', *History of Political Economy*, 11:3, Fall 1979.

5 Again Hutchison's judgment is astray when he exaggerates the significance of accusations of social and political bias as an element in Marx's critique of the political economists: see 'The Cambridge Version of the History of Economics', pp. 14–16. As I hope my study shows in some detail, Marx's critique had much more substance than Hutchison would have us believe. Cf. King, 'Marx as an historian of economic thought'.

6 See, for example, Salim Rashid, 'Malthus's *Principles* and British economic thought, 1820–1835', *History of Political Economy*, 13:1, spring 1981, pp. 77–8.

7 On the Physiocratic origins of Malthus's ideas see B. Semmel, 'Malthus: "Physiocracy" and the commercial system', *Economic History Review*, XVII:3, 1964–5. I owe this reference to Peter Grœnewegen.

8 For Marx, only a classless society could avoid the ideology of minority material interests. And, it was the proletariat that could act as a social 'bottom line', so to say, and absorb all economic class minorities under a banner of common interest.

9 See *The Works and Correspondence of David Ricardo*, ed. Piero Sraffa, vol. II for the 'Notes on Malthus's *Principles of Political Economy*', and vols VI to IX for the correspondence with Malthus.

10 Rashid, 'Malthus's *Principles* and British economic thought, 1820–1835', pp. 56–7.

11 See note 7 above.

12 T.R. Malthus, *Principles of Political Economy Considered with a View to their Practical Application*, 2nd ed., pp. 69ff.

13 The idea of a labour based surplus as the source of profit was expressed in passing by Malthus, ibid., p. 292.

14 ibid., pp. 267–8.

15 ibid., pp. 70, 78.

16 ibid., pp. 260–1, 291ff.; and Malthus, *Definitions in Political Economy etc.*, pp. 31–2. Cf. Hollander, 'The reception of Ricardian economics', pp. 226–7.

17 Malthus, *Principles of Political Economy*, p. 267 and n.

18 Malthus, *Definitions in Political Economy, ed. cit.*, pp. 29–30; quoted by Marx, *TSV*, III, 33.

19 R. Torrens, *An Essay on the Production of Wealth*, pp. vi, vii.

20 ibid., p. v.

21 ibid., pp. v–vi.
22 ibid., pp. vii, 27ff.
23 James Mill, *Elements of Political Economy*, 2nd ed., p. 94.
24 Torrens, *An Essay on the Production of Wealth*, p. vii.
25 ibid., pp. 38–40.
26 ibid., pp. 51–5.
27 ibid., pp. 41–2, 50ff.
28 ibid., pp. iii, x.
29 ibid., pp. 28ff., 51ff.
30 ibid., pp. 28–9.
31 Cf. Piero Sraffa's reference to Torrens on this idea and his use of it in *Production of Commodities by Means of Commodities: Prelude to a Critique of Economic Theory*, pp. 94–5 and chapter X.
32 Torrens, *An Essay on the Production of Wealth*, pp. 51–3.
33 ibid., pp. 10ff.
34 It seems unlikely that it was written by Bailey, in spite of its having the same publisher and expressing similar ideas. See R.M. Rauner, *Samuel Bailey and the Classical Theory of Value*, p. 89n., and S. Hollander, *The Economics of David Ricardo*, p. 644n. It is a curious fact that the pamphlet has been reprinted without comment, *as if* it were Bailey's, along with *A Critical Dissertation on the Nature, Measure and Causes of Value.*
35 This pamphlet has also been reprinted in the Kelley edition of *A Critical Dissertation* . . . cited above. Regarding the author of the *Westminster Review* article itself, see Rauner, *Samuel Bailey and the Classical Theory of Value*, pp. 149ff. Rauner's conclusion is that the author was James Mill.
36 See Blaug, *Ricardian Economics*, pp. 52ff. For a dissenting view that Bailey's disagreement with Ricardo has been much exaggerated see Hollander, 'The reception of Ricardian economics', pp. 227ff.
37 Bailey, *A Critical Dissertation* . . . , pp. x, xii ff., 9–10, 14ff.
38 See volume I, chapter 8 of the present study.
39 Bailey, *A Critical Dissertation* . . . , pp. 1, 4ff., 26, 33–4.
40 ibid., pp. 1–2.
41 ibid., p. 7.
42 Cf. Diane Elson, 'The Value theory of labour', in Diane Elson (ed.), *Value: the Representation of Labour in Capitalism*, pp. 136–7.
43 Bailey, *A Critical Dissertation* . . . , pp. 4–5, Marx's emphasis.
44 ibid., pp. 5, 95ff.
45 ibid., pp. 182–3, Marx's emphasis.
46 ibid., pp. 181–2, 198ff.
47 See ibid., pp. 185ff., for a discussion of monopoly markets.
48 ibid., p. 182, my emphasis added.
49 Cf. Rauner, *Samuel Bailey and the Classical Theory of Value*, pp. 67, 80, where the point is made that Bailey's discussion of cost price was not the best part of his work.
50 This version is discussed in pp. 148ff. above.
51 Bailey, *A Critical Dissertation* . . . . , pp. 201ff.
52 See the discussion of the Value-distribution articulation issue in chapter 4, pp. 81ff. above.
53 Bailey, *A Critical Dissertation* . . . , pp. 97, 112.

CHAPTER 7 REACTIONS TO RICARDO'S THEORY: THE 'PSEUDO-DISCIPLES'

1 Regarding the present 'Ricardian' status of these writers in the literature, see note 1 to chapter 6 above.

2 Peter Grœnewegen has argued that de Quincey's *Dialogues of Three Templars on Political Economy* (1824) represented 'a masterly exposition of Ricardo's theory of value'; see 'Thomas de Quincey: faithful disciple of Ricardo?', *Contributions to Political Economy*, 1, March 1982, p. 52. Cf. pp. 172ff. below.
3 See note 3 to chapter 6 above.
4 The Prefaces to the 2nd and 3rd eds of the *Elements* are reprinted in James Mill, *Selected Economic Writings*, ed. Donald Winch, pp. 205–6.
5 These early notes on Mill's *Elements* are reprinted in *MEGA*, I/3, 411, 414, 520ff. Marx's so-called 'Comments on James Mill', which had little to do with Mill *per se*, are in CW, 3, 211ff., and this piece is discussed in volume I, chapter 1, pp. 36ff., of the present study.
6 Mill, *Selected Economic Writings*, p. 204; cf. Donald Winch's comments, pp. 188–9.
7 James Mill, *Elements of Political Economy*, 2nd ed., p. 94.
8 ibid., p. 99.
9 ibid., pp. 97–8.
10 ibid., pp. 86ff.
11 ibid., p. 94.
12 ibid., p. 41, Marx's emphasis.
13 Anwar Shaikh provided me with some clarification of this example.
14 Mill, *Elements of Political Economy*, pp. 41–2, Marx's emphasis.
15 ibid., pp. 42–3.
16 ibid., p. 78; see also pp. 70ff.
17 Refer to chapter 5, pp. 102ff. above.
18 D.P. O'Brien has prepared a substantial bibliography of McCulloch's works in *J.R. McCulloch: a Study in Classic Economics*, pp. 406ff.
19 McCulloch's ideas on these issues were not very well defined or argued and changed as his work progressed: see Blaug, *Ricardian Economics: a Historical Study*, pp. 46ff., and O'Brien, *J.R. McCulloch: a Study in Classic Economics*, pp. 121–2, 126ff.
20 While Marx used the 1828 version of the 'Notes and Dissertations', the references here are to the textually very similar version which dates from 1849 and appeared in Adam Smith, *An Inquiry into the Nature and Causes of the Wealth of Nations*, with . . . Notes and Supplemental Dissertations by J.R. McCulloch, Esq., pp. 435ff. The piece quoted here is from p. 443n., with Marx's emphasis.
21 Somehow, Mark Blaug finds in McCulloch's piece quoted here the idea that profit is the reward of 'waiting', *Ricardian Economics*, p. 48.
22 McCulloch, 'Notes and Dissertations', p. 439. It should be noted that this 1849 version replaces '*exchangeable value*' and '*real* or *cost value*' from the 1828 version with '*value*' and '*cost*' respectively. Beyond this, the two versions are virtually identical.
23 McCulloch, 'Notes and Dissertations', p. 435, Marx's emphasis.
24 Cf. the discussion in Blaug, *Ricardian Economics*, pp. 49–50; and in O'Brien, *J.R. McCulloch: a Study in Classic Economics*, pp. 139ff.
25 Ricardo, *On the Principles of Political Economy and Taxation*, vol. I of *The Works and Correspondence of David Ricardo*, p. 286n., Marx's emphasis.
26 McCulloch, 'Notes and Dissertations', p. 435.
27 Ricardo, *Principles*, p. 287.

28 With good reason, at least as far as the *Dialogues of Three Templars* was concerned: see note 1 to chapter 6 and note 2 to this chapter.
29 Reprinted in Thomas de Quincey, *Political Economy and Politics*, pp. 37ff.
30 Reprinted in ibid., pp. 118ff.
31 See note 28 above.
32 de Quincey, *Dialogues of Three Templars*, p. 54, de Quincey's emphasis.
33 ibid., pp. 82, 83, 86.
34 ibid., p. 78.
35 ibid., pp. 55–6, 86, 91.
36 See the editorial notes by J.M. Robson in *The Collected Works of John Stuart Mill*, vol. IV, 'Essays on Economics and Society', p. 230 and p. 290.
37 Marx's treatment of Mill has been considered more generally by Bela Balassa, 'Karl Marx and John Stuart Mill', *Weltwirtschaftliches Archiv*, 83, 1959, and Bernice Shoul, 'Similarities in the work of John Stuart Mill and Karl Marx', *Science and Society*, 29, 1965. Balassa gives some attention to the exchange value–distribution issue, while Shoul's paper is devoted entirely to aspects of the 'law of motion' of capitalism.
38 J.S. Mill, *Essays on Some Unsettled Questions of Political Economy*, 2nd ed., p. 90, Marx's emphasis.
39 ibid., p. 91, my emphasis added.
40 ibid., pp. 91ff.
41 ibid., p. 90.
42 ibid., p. 92, emphasis in original.
43 Quoted in Balassa, 'Karl Marx and John Stuart Mill', p. 149.
44 For an excellent discussion of the comparative *social* positions adopted by Marx and Mill in their writings see: Graeme Duncan, *Marx and Mill: Two Views of Social Conflict and Social Harmony*. Mill's views on capitalism are summarised at pp. 238ff.
45 Mill, *Essays on Some Unsettled Questions*, pp. 94ff.
46 ibid., pp. 99ff. The summary of Mill's example below is taken from M.H. Dobb, *Theories of Value and Distribution since Adam Smith*, pp. 126ff.
47 Mill, *Essays on Some Unsettled Questions*, p. 101.
48 ibid., p. 103.

CHAPTER 8 REACTIONS TO RICARDO'S THEORY: THE 'RADICAL CRITICS' OF CAPITALISM

1 Cf. Mark Blaug, *Ricardian Economics: a Historical Study*, p. 140.
2 The well-known work on these 'radicals' is Esther Lowenthal, *The Ricardian Socialists*. As the title of this work suggests, the traditional name for this group has been the 'Ricardian Socialists'. Their 'socialist' status stemmed from nineteenth-century ideas of capitalist reformism and they varied in their attitudes to how 'radical' such reform should be. They certainly were not 'scientific' revolutionary socialists in Marx's sense: but cf. ibid., pp. 13–14, and Blaug, *Ricardian Economics*, p. 140. In recent times, the 'Ricardian' *bona fides* of the group has been questioned and the evidence elicited suggests that they cannot be usefully classified in this way: see E.K. Hunt, 'Value theory in the writings of the Classical economists, Thomas Hodgskin, and Karl Marx', *History of Political Economy*, 9:3, Fall 1977, and Samuel Hollander, 'The post-Ricardian dissension: a case-study in economics and ideology', *Oxford*

Economic Papers, 32:3, November 1980.

3 Marx had intended to deal with the 'critique and history of political economy and socialism' together in the one, separate work as late as 1858 (see letter to Lassalle, 22 February, *MEW*, 29, 549ff.). Beyond this, the critical history of political economy became of more immediate concern and it acquired an independent status in the 1859 *A Contribution to the Critique of Political Economy*. It remains unclear what Marx's intentions were for the critical history of socialism. On these matters see my *The Making of Marx's Critical Theory: a Bibliographical Analysis*, chapter 4, Section 4.3, and chapter 5.

4 Cf. Lowenthal's coverage in *The Ricardian Socialists*. She includes in her book William Thompson and John Gray, who were omitted by Marx from the present critique, but did not include the anonymous work of Ravenstone.

5 Ravenstone was probably a pseudonym and his true identity is not known with any certainty. It has been suggested that he might have been an Anglican minister, Edward Edwards: see Joseph Dorfman, ' "Piercy Ravenstone" and his radical Tory treatise', in P. Ravenstone, *A Few Doubts as to the Correctness of Some Opinions Generally Entertained on the Subjects of Population and Political Economy*, pp. 16ff.

6 For some reason, Marx did not refer to Ravenstone's *A Few Doubts* cited in the note above. This was a broader work which treated explicitly several topics that would have been of interest to Marx, including property, capital, exchange value, distribution and the surplus.

7 Ravenstone, *Thoughts on the Funding System and its Effects*, p. 7, Marx's emphasis.

8 ibid., pp. 12, 13, 20, 71.

9 ibid., pp. 11, 14.

10 ibid., p. 11; cf. pp. 14–15.

11 ibid., p. 13.

12 For a discussion of Hodgskin's life and work see Élie Halévy, *Thomas Hodgskin*.

13 The place of Hodgskin in the evolution of political economy and his intellectual affiliations are important, though, and have been carefully assessed by Hunt, 'Value theory in the writings of the Classical economists, Thomas Hodgskin, and Karl Marx', and Samuel Hollander, 'The post-Ricardian dissension'. See also T.W. Hutchison, 'The Cambridge Version of the History of Economics', Economics Department, University of Birmingham, 1974, p. 28n.

14 Thomas Hodgskin, *Labour Defended Against the Claims of Capital, etc.*, pp. 19–28, 80.

15 ibid., p. 108.

16 ibid., pp. 91, 64–5.

17 ibid., pp. 31ff.

18 Thomas Hodgskin, *Popular Political Economy, etc.*, p. 247, Marx's emphasis.

19 Hodgskin, *Labour Defended*, pp. 31, 75, 80–2.

20 ibid., p. 60, Marx's emphasis; cf. pp. 26–7.

21 See volume I, chapter 4, pp. 114ff. of the present study.

22 J.F. Bray, *Labour's Wrongs and Labour's Remedy; or, the Age of Might and the Age of Right*, p. 48.

23 ibid., pp. 49–50, Bray's emphasis.

24 ibid., p. 49, Bray's emphasis.

25 ibid., p. 57.

26 ibid., p. 61.

27 ibid., p. 59.
28 ibid., p. 83.

CHAPTER 9 SOME PARTICULAR POST-RICARDIANS

1 Ramsay, *An Essay on the Distribution of Wealth*, pp. 21ff.
2 ibid., pp. 23–4.
3 ibid., p. 24, the first emphasis is Ramsay's, the latter emphases are Marx's.
4 ibid., p. 49; cf. p. 52 where this assertion was reiterated.
5 ibid., pp. 137ff., 193.
6 ibid., pp. 182ff.
7 ibid., pp. 25–6, 41ff., 47, 56–7, 59, 79ff., 137ff.
8 ibid., pp. 42ff., 163.
9 ibid., p. 46.
10 ibid., p. 172; see also the discussion of wages, pp. 84ff.
11 Richard Jones, *An Essay on the Distribution of Wealth, and on the Sources of Taxation*. The other two main pieces used by Marx, the *Introductory Lecture* and the *Textbook of Lectures*, were included in William Whewell's 1859 collection of Jones's works entitled *Literary Remains Consisting of Lectures and Tracts on Political Economy*. It is evident, though, that these pieces must have been published prior to 1859, even though Whewell gave no indication of this in his 'Prefatory Notice'. Marx's quotations from these pieces carry page numbers which bear no relation to the pagination of the Whewell edition and they were cited as being published in London and Hertford respectively (*TSV*, III, 413 and 419). The 'Syllabus of a Course of Lectures on the Wages of Labour', evidently published with the *Introductory Lecture* in 1833, was not included in the Whewell collection for some reason.
12 Jones, *An Essay on the Distribution of Wealth*, p. vii.
13 On Jones's method of analysis, see the two papers by William L. Miller: 'Richard Jones: a case study in methodology', *History of Political Economy*, 3:1, spring 1971, and 'Richard Jones's contribution to the theory of rent', *History of Political Economy*, 9:3, Fall 1977.
14 Miller, 'Richard Jones: a case study in methodology', pp. 201, 204, 206–7; and 'Richard Jones's contribution to the theory of rent', p. 352n.
15 Ronald Meek referred to Marx's method as a 'logical–historical' one in 'Karl Marx's economic method', reprinted in *Economics and Ideology and Other Essays*.
16 Marx's own thoughts on the method to be adopted in the critique of political economy were rough drafted in the 'Introduction' to the *Grundrisse* manuscripts (*G*, 100ff.). See the discussion in volume I of the present study, chapter 5, pp. 146ff.
17 Jones, *An Essay on the Distribution of Wealth*, pp. xii-xv, xviii–xx, xxii–xxiv, xl–xli.
18 ibid., pp. xxiv ff., 2–3.
19 ibid., pp. xxxviii–xxxix; cf. Blaug, *Ricardian Economics: a Historical Study*, pp. 149, 169, 223.
20 Jones, *An Essay on the Distribution of Wealth*, p. xxxix.
21 ibid., pp. ii–iii.
22 ibid., p. 2.
23 ibid.
24 ibid., p. 4.
25 ibid., p. 11, Marx's emphasis; cf. p. 188.
26 Jones discussed the types of 'peasant' rents in ibid., pp. 3–16, and *passim*. See

also Miller, 'Richard Jones's contribution to the theory of rent', pp. 348ff.
27 Jones, *An Essay on the Distribution of Wealth*, pp. 11–14, 185ff.
28 ibid., pp. 12, 187–8.
29 ibid., pp. 188–9.
30 ibid., p. 188, emphasis original; cf. pp. 13, 191.
31 ibid., pp. 189ff.
32 See chapter 5, pp. 102ff. above.
33 Jones, *An Essay on the Distribution of Wealth*, p. 191.
34 ibid., pp. 190ff.
35 ibid.
36 ibid., pp. 199–200; cf. Blaug, *Ricardian Economics*, pp. 150–1, and Miller, 'Richard Jones's contribution to the theory of rent', *passim*.
37 In Marx's subsequent development of the critique of rent theory in *Capital*, Book III, he argued the relationship between rent, capital accumulation and agricultural technology more fully. See n.3 to chapter 5 above.
38 Jones, *An Essay on the Distribution of Wealth*, pp. 231–2.
39 Marx's critique of the political economists on this issue will be considered in Part IV of this study.
40 Jones, *An Essay on the Distribution of Wealth*, pp. 257ff., 273.
41 See Jones, *Literary Remains*, pp. 539ff. and pp. 337ff. respectively, although as pointed out in note 11 above, the 'Syllabus' referred to by Marx was not included in this collection.
42 Jones, *Textbook of Lectures*, in *Literary Remains*, pp. 414ff.
43 On Ramsay, see pp. 193ff. above.
44 Jones, *Textbook of Lectures*, in *Literary Remains*, p. 454, Marx's emphasis.

CHAPTER 10 THE DIMENSIONS OF 'MOTION'

1 'Valorisation' is the translation of *Verwertung*, a term which Marx used to convey the idea of capital preserving and expanding its Value dimension.
2 It is unnecessary and potentially confusing to attribute the assumption of 'Say's Law' to Marx here as Bernice Shoul does in her 'Karl Marx and Say's Law', *Quarterly Journal of Economics*, 71:4, November 1957, pp. 611–14. There is no evidence that I am aware of to suggest that Marx took this view of any of his analyses in which the problems of circulation were abstracted from. Such abstraction was undertaken for purely analytical reasons and had nothing to do with the issues raised by 'Say's Law'. Moreover, the concept of 'Say's Law' itself is open to several different interpretations, as Shoul realises, and this renders Marx's analytical assumptions more complex and ambiguous than they need to be.
3 These matters are discussed fully by Paul Sweezy, 'Karl Marx and the Industrial Revolution', and by Ronald Meek in his 'Discussion' of Sweezy's paper, in R.V. Eagly (ed.), *Events, Ideology and Economic Theory*, Wayne State University Press, Detroit, 1968, pp. 107ff. and 120ff. respectively.
4 This point is made by Michael Bleaney, *Underconsumption Theories: a History and Critical Analysis*, p. 95.
5 See volume I, chapter 7, pp. 210ff. of the present study.
6 Salo Ryazanskaya, the editor of *Theories of Surplus Value*, points out that this table format was taken from the work of Theodor Schmalz rather than directly from the work of Quesnay or any other Physiocrat. Ryazanskaya goes on to note that this 'Digression' on the *Tableau économique* which opens notebook X of the manuscripts was probably written in Manchester during

Marx's visit there in April 1862. The lack of quotations from Physiocratic works could then be explained by the absence of any access to these works. See *TSV*, I, 484 n.88.

7 The *Analyse* article is reprinted in its English translation in R.L. Meek, *The Economics of Physiocracy: Essays and Translations*, pp. 150ff. The relevant table is on p. 158.

8 *Physiocrates. Quesnay, Dupont de Nemours, Mercier de la Rivière, l'abbé Baudeau, Le Trosne.* Avec une introduction sur la doctrine des Physiocrates, des Commentaires et des notices historiques, par M. Eugène Daire, Parts I and II, Paris, 1846. Marx referred explicitly to this collection on two occasions in 'Theories' (*TSV*, I, 53, 380).

9 I owe this point to Peter Grœnewegen.

10 My exposition of Marx's treatment of the *Tableau économique* was improved through reading B.N. Ganguli's erudite paper 'Karl Marx on Quesnay', *Indian Economic Review*, 7:2, October 1972.

11 Ryazanskaya summarises the meanings of these links which, he notes, were provided by Marx and did not originate from Schmalz or Quesnay: *TSV*, I, 484–5 n.89.

CHAPTER 11 THE CONSEQUENCES OF CAPITAL ACCUMULATION

1 It has been argued that Marx was writing in a better age to make such a judgment than some of his antecedents. Paul Sweezy sees this interpretation by Marx as flowing immediately from his observations of the emerging age of 'modern industry' in which the rate of mechanisation was high compared to that in the preceding age of 'manufacture'. The analytical consequences of this were that the classical political economists had displayed less awareness of the significance of technological change than Marx and encompassed less of its effects in their work. In the age of 'manufacture', it was less obvious that far reaching dynamic changes were proceeding to transform capitalism 'from a relatively conservative and change-resistant society into a super-dynamic society headed, in Marx's view, for inevitable revolutionary overthrow': 'Karl Marx and the Industrial Revolution', in R.V. Eagly (ed.), *Events, Ideology and Economic Theory*, Wayne State University Press, Detroit, 1968, p. 112, and *passim*. In his 'Discussion' of Sweezy's paper, Ronald Meek concluded that the most important point in this background to Marx's theory of capital accumulation was:

> The primary stress which Marx laid on changes in the methods of production – which was undoubtedly derived from the characteristics of the particular historical stage in which he was living – introduced a vital change into the theory of economic development. Before Marx, theories of development had been framed in terms of the more or less smooth, more or less uninterrupted accumulation of capital, and its continued and unintermittent interaction with population growth, the progress of diminishing returns in agriculture etc. With Marx, the dynamic development of industry and the technological change associated with it becomes for the first time a major determining factor. Since technological change is highly unstable, the concept of a smooth and uninterrupted development goes by the board, and the material foundation for a theory of the trade cycle is laid. (Eagly (ed.), *Events, Ideology and Economic Theory*, p. 121.)

Meek did not, however, agree with the degree of 'conservatism' ascribed by Sweezy to the age of 'manufacture': 'Discussion', p. 120.

A similar judgment by Michael Howard and John King led them to posit technological change as the most essential dimension of Marx's analysis of capital accumulation and its implications for the fate of capitalism: *The Political Economy of Marx*, p. 182.

2 Indeed, Angus Walker goes as far as to argue that Marx found all of the 'economic problems' that concerned him 'not in the real world, but in the teachings of the British Classical economists': 'Karl Marx, the declining rate of profit and British political economy', *Economica*, 38, November 1971, p. 373. Given the appalling conditions for workers that Marx *observed*, such a sweeping generalisation cannot be taken seriously. It should be granted, though, that in the case of the falling rate of profits, its predominance in political economy probably predisposed him towards pursuing the issue analytically.

3 Controversy surrounds Marx's analytical expression and 'measurement' of observed changes in technology, although too often the issues raised concern the demands of algebra rather than criteria of understanding. It is now generally accepted that in its 'final' form, in contrast to the argument traced above, a change in the organic composition of capital was confined to a change in the Value composition that was due to a change in the technical composition. In Marx's *definition* of the organic composition category, it was not possible for changes in the Value composition to do anything but track with changes in the technical composition in the absence of compensating changes in capital Values. Many writers have expressed their acceptance of this interpretation. However, the literature in which this is evident manifests widely differing views on other important issues of interpretation. See, for example: Mario Cogoy, 'The fall of the rate of profit and the theory of accumulation: a reply to Paul Sweezy', *Bulletin of the Conference of Socialist Economists*, winter 1973, p. 57, Ben Fine and Laurence Harris, 'Controversial issues in Marxist economic theory', *Socialist Register*, 1976, pp. 160–1, Michael Howard and John King, *The Political Economy of Marx*, p. 197, Michael Lebowitz, 'Marx's falling rate of profit: a dialectical view', *Canadian Journal of Economics*, 9:2, May 1976, pp. 243–4, Anwar Shaikh, 'Political economy and capitalism: notes on Dobb's theory of crisis', *Cambridge Journal of Economics*, 2 June 1978, p. 250, Trent Schroyer, 'Marx's theory of the crisis', *Telos*, winter 1972, pp. 113–14, and David Yaffe, 'The Marxian theory of crisis, capital and the state', *Economy and Society*, 2:2, May 1973, p. 194.

But, acceptance that Marx *defined* the organic composition of capital in this way on sound methodological grounds, given his interpretation of the nature of capitalism, does not remove all ambiguity from the way in which he *applied* the category. Marx observed the increasing mechanisation of production and drew from it that as capital accumulated, the organic composition of capital would be rising. In Ian Steedman's view, this requires an act of faith for not only was there no way of meaningfully assessing the changing technical composition of capital in *quantitative* terms, but also there was no way of observing the composition of capital in *Value* terms. Value was an *essential* category and not a *phenomenal* one and it did not manifest itself as an appearance. It was measurable only in principle, important as it was in Marx's thought. The only empirical indication of the change in technology would have been a rising ratio of market-price weighted value of machinery to labour employed. The linking of this to the organic composition of capital was a complex process not considered by Marx at all. See *Marx After Sraffa*, pp. 124–5, 133–4.

In a rare patch of agreement, neither Paul Sweezy nor David Yaffe is troubled by Steedman's misgivings about the empirics of the organic composition of capital. Sweezy, 'Some problems in the theory of capital accumulation', *Monthly Review*, 26:1, May 1974, p. 46, *explicitly* asserts that there exists *empirical* evidence of a rising organic composition of capital in the nineteenth century. How this could have been *observed* in accordance with Marx's definition he does not say. Yaffe's 'fundamentalism' allows him to resort to the *logic* of capital in order to justify a rising organic composition. For him it simply follows that this *must* have been the case because in striving to maximise the generation of surplus value in a competitive environment, each capitalist would be required to employ a higher ratio of machinery to labour in order to improve productivity and lower costs. Measuring this seems to be beside the point for Yaffe: 'The Marxian theory of crisis, capital and the state', pp. 195–6. Sweezy objects to Yaffe's *approach*, but the outcome for Marxological interpretation is the same: 'Some problems in the theory of capital accumulation', p. 45.

Both Howard and King, and Steedman establish *analytically* that the Value composition of capital is not strictly proportional to the technical composition of capital and that changes in these ratios may be of opposite sign. On this basis, there is no reason beyond an act of faith to assume that the special conditions for a rising organic composition of capital were present beneath the phenomena of the nineteenth century. See: *The Political Economy of Marx*, pp. 198–9, and *Marx After Sraffa*, pp. 133–5 respectively.

4 Cf. Mark Blaug, *Ricardian Economics: a Historical Study*, p. 70, Luigi Pasinetti, *Growth and Income Distribution: Essays in Economic Theory*, pp. 20–1, and Samuel Hollander, *The Economics of David Ricardo*, p. 340.

5 References are to Ricardo's *On the Principles of Political Economy and Taxation* in *The Works and Correspondence of David Ricardo*, ed. Piero Sraffa, vol. I. All emphases in quotations are Marx's unless otherwise noted.

6 See chapter 5, pp. 102ff. above.

7 Regarding Ricardo's assumption, see Hollander, *The Economics of David Ricardo*, pp. 309–10.

8 See pp. 244ff. below.

9 Cf. Hollander, *The Economics of David Ricardo*, pp. 314, 316.

10 This point was discussed in chapter 5, pp. 113ff. above.

11 For an interpretation of Ricardo's views on this issue that is less pessimistic, even with retention of the 'Corn Laws', see Hollander, *The Economics of David Ricardo*, pp. 600ff.

12 Cf. Pasinetti, *Growth and Income Distribution*, pp. 20–1.

13 A point made by Blaug, *Ricardian Economics*, p. 67, and Hollander, *The Economics of David Ricardo*, p. 343.

14 As Hollander puts it: 'The concept of exogenous (non-induced [by wage changes]) technical change, which has the effect of actually *reducing* employment capacity, constitutes the striking novelty of the chapter "On Machinery" added in 1821', *The Economics of David Ricardo*, p. 341, emphasis original; cf. p. 342.

15 Cf. Oswald St Clair, *A Key to Ricardo*, p. 238.

16 The strength of this conclusion based on purely short-run results has been questioned by Blaug, *Ricardian Economics*, p. 67.

17 Cf. Hollander, *The Economics of David Ricardo*, p. 343 and n. 104.

18 On this argument, see St Clair, *A Key to Ricardo*, p. 241, Blaug, *Ricardian Economics*, pp. 68–9, and Hollander, *The Economics of David Ricardo*, p. 355.
19 As Hollander notes, any view that Barton *influenced* Ricardo on the machinery issue requires careful interpretation: *The Economics of David Ricardo*, pp. 346ff.
20 See also the earlier discussions of Marx's views on these three writers in chapter 8, pp. 187ff. and chapter 9, pp. 193ff. and pp. 196ff. respectively.
21 George Ramsay, *An Essay on the Distribution of Wealth*, p. 172, Marx's emphasis.
22 See the discussion on pp. 229ff. above. Marx's handling of the organic composition in the context of discussing Cherbuliez is considered by Steedman, *Marx After Sraffa*, pp. 135–6.

CHAPTER 12 REPRODUCTION AND THE IMMANENT CRISES OF CAPITALISM

1 This was argued in the methodological 'Introduction' to the *Grundrisse* manuscripts (*G*, 88ff.). See chapter 5, pp. 140ff. in volume I of the present study.
2 Probably more so than Marx was aware of at this stage as is demonstrated by Donald Harris, in 'On Marx's schema of reproduction and accumulation', *Journal of Political Economy*, 80, May/June 1972.
3 Regarding the multiple interpretations of 'Say's Law', see William Baumol's 'Say's (at least) eight laws, or what Say and James Mill may really have meant', *Economica*, 44, May 1977.
4 These origins have been discussed by Joseph Spengler, 'The Physiocrats and Say's Law of markets', *Journal of Political Economy*, 53, September and December, 1945, Ronald Meek, *The Economics of Physiocracy*, pp. 313ff., Thomas Sowell, *Say's Law: an Historical Analysis*, chapter 1, and Michael Bleaney, *Underconsumption Theories: a History and Critical Analysis*, chapter 5. Peter Grœnewegen has argued that Turgot's saving and investment analysis also foreshadowed what was to become 'Say's Law': see 'A re-interpretation of Turgot's theory of capital and interest', *Economic Journal*, 81, June 1971, p. 335.
5 The emergence of 'Say's Law' and the relevant dates are discussed in Baumol, 'Say's (at least) eight laws, or what Say and James Mill may really have meant'.
6 Cf. Sowell, *Say's Law*, pp. 35–8.
7 The history of the analysis of underconsumption is fully dealt with by Sowell, *Say's Law* and Bleaney, *Underconsumption Theories*.
8 See chapter 6, pp. 129ff. above.
9 *On the Principles of Political Economy and Taxation* in *The Works and Correspondence of David Ricardo*, ed. Piero Sraffa, vol. I, p. 290, Marx's emphasis.
10 ibid., p. 292.
11 Marx had also considered the work of Rodbertus at length in the context of the critique of rent theory (*TSV*, II, 15ff.) and his main source for this was the third of Rodbertus's published 'letters' to von Kirchmann. The second of these 'letters' published in *Soziale Briefe an von Kirchmann* dealt with overproduction and crises. For some reason, it was not discussed or cited at all by Marx. Bleaney discusses Rodbertus's work on underconsumption in *Underconsump-*

tion Theories, chapter 4.

12 See chapter 6, pp. 129ff. above. The significance of Sismondi's contributions is discussed in Sowell, *Say's Law*, chapter 2, and Bleaney, *Underconsumption Theories*, chapter 3.

13 Shades of the eleventh of the 'Theses on Feuerbach': 'The philosophers have only *interpreted* the world in various ways; the point is to *change* it' (*CW*, 5, 5).

14 See chapter 6, pp. 141ff. above.

15 Recent research has, however, rejected these plagiarism allegations. Thomas Sowell's reading is that there were strong overlaps in the writings of Malthus and Sismondi, but that there were also significant differences in their analyses as well. Sowell also makes the point that plagiarism by Malthus is less probable than Marx alleged because many of Malthus's ideas appeared in correspondence with Ricardo prior to the publication of Sismondi's work: *Say's Law*, pp. 89–90. Michael Bleaney also reveals some significant differences between the approaches of Malthus and Sismondi to the underconsumption issue: *Underconsumption Theories*, chapters 2, 3, and 5. These, too, cast doubt upon the bald plagiarism allegations made by Marx against Malthus. It is evident, then, that even though Marx would not have known about the correspondence between Malthus and Ricardo, a more careful reading of Malthus's published work should have caused Marx to temper his assertions.

16 Later writers find a much richer content in Malthus's work on the overproduction problems of capitalism. See J.M. Keynes, 'Thomas Robert Malthus', in *Essays in Biography*, *The Collected Writings of John Maynard Keynes*, vol. X, Sowell, *Say's Law*, chapters 3 and 4, and Bleaney, *Underconsumption Theories*, chapters 2 and 5.

17 These limitations are brought out clearly by Michael Bleaney, *Underconsumption Theories*, pp. 42ff. and 98ff.

18 Cf. ibid., pp. 54–5.

19 It is important to keep in mind, though, that Marx's attack on Malthus's motives was only a complement to his substantive critique: see chapter 6, pp. 148ff. and note 5 above.

20 Maurice Dobb's words emphasise for us the systematic scope of the crisis phenomenon in Marx's thought:

> Marx clearly regarded crises, not as incidental departures from a predetermined equilibrium, not as fickle wanderings from an established path of development to which there would be a submissive return, but rather as themselves a dominant form of movement which forged and shaped the development of capitalist society. To study crises was *ipso facto* to study the dynamics of the system; and this study could only be properly undertaken as part of an examination of the forms of movement of class relations (the class struggle) and of the class revenues which were their market expression.

This passage appeared in Dobb's *Political Economy and Capitalism*, 2nd ed., pp. 80–1. Some decades later, this interpretation was reiterated by Trent Schroyer, 'Marx's theory of the crisis', *Telos*, winter 1972, p. 109:

> Marx's crisis theory was an attempt to reconstruct the constitutive dynamic

of capitalist accumulation *and* the social consequences of this dynamic.

> . . .
>
> Marx's theory of capitalist crisis attempted to grasp the totality of the dynamic of the capitalist epoch. Its intention was to show how this dynamic recurrently generates intensified constraints upon societal and human development. (emphasis original.)

Such, then, was the grand design of Marx's analysis of the crisis. A useful survey of aspects of Marx's theory of crisis is Erik Olin Wright's 'Alternative perspectives in Marxist theory of accumulation and crisis', in J. Schwartz (ed.), *The Subtle Anatomy of Capitalism.*

21 Referring to the *totality* of Marx's efforts to formulate a satisfactory crisis theory, Joseph Schumpeter summarised the results in his essay on Marx in *Ten Great Economists*, p. 47:

> Marx's performance in the field of business cycles is exceedingly difficult to appraise. The really valuable part of it consists of dozens of observations and comments, most of them of a casual nature, which are scattered over almost all of his writings, many of his letters included. Attempts at reconstruction from such *membra disjecta* of a body that nowhere appears in the flesh and perhaps did not even exist in Marx's own mind except in an embryonic form, may easily yield different results in different hands . . .

The roots of this assessment are clearly evident in the 'Theories' manuscripts.

22 The symptom–cause–effect puzzle has caused considerable controversy in the literature on Marx's crisis analysis, especially with respect to the situation and role of the falling rate of profits and the status to be ascribed to realisation problems in the analysis. Readers interested in pursuing these issues will find the following works useful: Paul Sweezy, *The Theory of Capitalist Development*, chapters VIII–X, Bernice Shoul, 'Karl Marx and Say's Law', *Quarterly Journal of Economics*, 71:4, November 1957, David Yaffe, 'The Marxian theory of crisis, capital and state', *Economy and Society*, 2:2, May 1973, Mario Cogoy, 'The fall of the rate of profit and the theory of accumulation: a reply to Paul Sweezy', *Bulletin of the Conference of Socialist Economists*, winter 1973, Paul Sweezy, 'Some problems in the theory of capital accumulation', *Monthly Review*, 26:1, May 1974, Makoto Itoh, 'The formation of Marx's theory of crisis', *Bulletin of the Conference of Socialist Economists*, 4:1, February 1975, Michael Howard and John King, *The Political Economy of Marx*, chapter 6, Ben Fine and Laurence Harris, 'Controversial issues in Marxist economic theory', *Socialist Register*, 1976, Michael Lebowitz, 'Marx's falling rate of profit: a dialectical view', *Canadian Journal of Economics*, 9:2, May 1976, and Anwar Shaikh, 'Political economy and capitalism: notes on Dobb's theory of crisis', *Cambridge Journal of Economics*, 2, 1978.

23 See Howard and King, *The Political Economy of Marx*, pp. 210ff.

24 Cf. ibid. and the early work of Maurice Dobb, *Political Economy of Capitalism*, pp. 121–2, Joseph Schumpeter, *Ten Great Economists*, pp. 50–2, and Paul Sweezy, *The Theory of Capitalist Development*, pp. 190–2.

25 Ricardo, *Principles*, ed. cit., pp. 290, 290n., 297.

Bibliography

A PRIMARY SOURCES

1 *Karl Marx*

Grundrisse der Kritik der politischen Ökonomie, Europäische Verlagsanstalt, Frankfurt, n.d..

Grundrisse: Foundations of the Critique of Political Economy (Rough Draft), ed. and trans. with a Foreword by M. Nicolaus, Allen Lane, London, 1973.

A Contribution to the Critique of Political Economy, ed. M. Dobb, trans. S. Ryazanskaya, Lawrence & Wishart, London, 1971.

Theories of Surplus Value, three Parts, ed. S. Ryazanskaya, trans. E. Burns, Progress Publishers, Moscow, 1963–71.

Capital: a Critique of Political Economy, three vols, Progress Publishers, Moscow, 1971.

Capital: a Critique of Political Economy, Volume I: introduced by E. Mandel, trans. B. Fowkes; Volumes II and III: introduced by E. Mandel, trans. D. Fernbach, Penguin, Harmondsworth, 1976–81.

2 *Karl Marx and Friedrich Engels*

Historische-kritische Gesamtausgabe, Sections I and II, Verlag Detlev Auvermann and Dietz Verlag, Berlin, 1970–80.

Werke, 42 volumes, Dietz Verlag, Berlin, 1961–71.

Collected Works, 50 volumes forthcoming, Lawrence & Wishart, London, 1975–

3 *Other writers*

Bailey, S., *A Critical Dissertation on the Nature, Measure and Causes of Value; Chiefly in Reference to the Writings of Mr. Ricardo and His Followers etc.* [1825], Augustus M. Kelley, New York, 1967.

Bray, J.F., *Labour's Wrongs and Labour's Remedy; or, the Age of Might and the Age of Right* [1839], London School of Economics and Political Science, Reprints of Scarce Tracts in Economics and Political Science, no. 6, London, 1931.

de Quincey, T., *Political Economy and Politics*, Augustus M. Kelley, New York, 1970.

Hobbes T., *Leviathan* [1651], with an Introduction by K.R. Minogue, Everyman's Library, Dent, London, 1976.

Hodgskin, T., *Labour Defended Against the Claims of Capital; or, the Unproductiveness of Capital Proved, etc.* [1825], Augustus M. Kelley, New York, 1963.

Hodgskin, T., *Popular Political Economy: Four Lectures Delivered at the London Mechanics' Institution* [1827], Augustus M. Kelley, New York, 1966.

Hume, D., *Essays Moral, Political and Literary*, Oxford University Press, 1963.

Jones, R., *An Essay on the Distribution of Wealth, and on the Sources of Taxation* [1831], Kelley & Millman, New York, 1956.

Jones, R., *Literary Remains Consisting of Lectures and Tracts on Political Economy*, ed. with a Prefatory Notice by W. Whewell [1859], Augustus M. Kelley, New York, 1964.

Locke, J., *The Works of John Locke* [1823], vol. 5, Scienta Verlag, Aalen, 1963.

Malthus, T.R., *Definitions in Political Economy etc.*, John Murray, London, 1827.

Malthus, T.R., *Principles of Political Economy Considered with a View to their Practical Application*, 2nd ed., William Pickering, London, 1836.

Marshall, A., *Principles of Economics*, 9th (variorum) ed., ed. C.W. Guillebaud, Macmillan, London, 1961.

Massie, J., *An Essay on the Governing Causes of the Natural Rate of Interest; wherein the Sentiments of Sir William Petty and Mr. Locke, on that Head, are Considered* [1750], Johnson Reprint Corporation, New York, 1970.

Mill, James, *Elements of Political Economy*, 2nd ed., Baldwin, Cradock, & Joy, London, 1824.

Mill, James, *Selected Economic Writings*, introduced and ed. Donald Winch, Oliver & Boyd, Edinburgh, 1966.

Mill, J.S., *Essays on Some Unsettled Questions of Political Economy*, 2nd ed. [1874], Augustus M. Kelley, New York, 1968.

Mill, J.S., *The Collected Works of John Stuart Mill*, vol. IV, 'Essays on Economics and Society', ed. J.M. Robson, Routledge & Kegan Paul, London, 1967.

North, D., *Discourses upon Trade; principally directed at the Cases of the Interest, Coynage, Clipping, Increase of Money*, Tho. Basset, London, 1691.

Petty, W., *The Economic Writings of Sir William Petty*, two vols, ed. C.H. Hull [1899], Augustus M. Kelley, New York, 1963.

Ramsay, G., *An Essay on the Distribution of Wealth* [1836], Augustus M. Kelley, Clifton, N. J., 1974.

Ravenstone, P., *A Few Doubts as to the Correctness of Some Opinions Generally Entertained on the Subjects of Population and Political Economy* [1821], Augustus M. Kelley, New York, 1966.

Ravenstone, P., *Thoughts of the funding System and its Effects* [1824], Augustus M. Kelley, New York, 1966.

Ricardo, D., *The Works and Correspondence of David Ricardo*, ed. P. Sraffa with the collaboration of M.H. Dobb, eleven vols, Cambridge University Press, 1951–73.

Smith, Adam, *An Inquiry into the Nature and Causes of the Wealth of Nations* [1776], with a Life of the Author, an Introductory Discourse, Notes and Supplemental Dissertations by J.R. McCulloch, Esq., Adam and Charles Black, Edinburgh, 1855.

Smith, Adam, *An Inquiry into the Nature and Causes of the Wealth of Nations* [1776], two vols, ed. Edwin Cannan, Methuen, London, 1961.

Steuart, J., *The Works Political, Mètaphisical [sic] and Chronological of Sir James Steuart* [1805], six vols, Augustus M. Kelley, New York, 1967.

Torrens, R., *An Essay on the Production of Wealth* [1821], Augustus M. Kelley, New York, 1965.

Turgot, A.-R.-J., *Turgot on Progress, Sociology and Economics*, trans., ed. with an Introduction by R.L. Meek, Cambridge University Press, 1973.

B SECONDARY SOURCES

Balassa, B., 'Karl Marx and John Stuart Mill', *Weltwirtschaftliches Archiv*, 83, 1959.

Ball, M., 'On Marx's theory of agricultural rent: a reply to Ben Fine', *Economy and Society*, 9:3, August 1980.

Baumol, W.J., 'Say's (at least) eight laws, or what Say and James Mill may really have meant', *Economica*, 44, May 1977.

Bharadwaj, K., *Classical Political Economy and the Rise to Dominance of Supply and Demand Theories* [R.C. Dutt Lectures on Political Economy, 1976], Centre for Studies in Social Science, Calcutta, 1978.

Blaug, M., *Ricardian Economics: a Historical Study* [1958], Greenwood Press, Westport, Conn., 1976.

Bleaney, M., *Underconsumption Theories: a History and Critical Analysis*, Lawrence & Wishart, London, 1976.

Bortkiewicz, L. von, 'Value and price in the Marxian system' [1907], *International Economic Papers*, 2, 1952.

Bowley, M., *Studies in the History of Economic Theory before 1870*, Macmillan, London, 1973.

Bradley, I. and Howard, M.C. (eds), *Classical and Marxian Political Economy: Essays in Honour of Ronald L. Meek*, Macmillan, London, 1982.

Cogoy, M., 'The fall of the rate of profit and the theory of accumulation: a reply to Paul Sweezy', *Bulletin of the Conference of Socialist Economists*, winter 1973.

de Brunhoff, S., 'Marx as an a-Ricardian: Value, money and price at the beginning of *Capital*', *Economy and Society*, 2:3, August 1973.

de Brunhoff, S., 'Controversies in the theory of surplus Value: a reply to John Eatwell', *Science and Society*, 38:4, winter 1974–5.

de Vivo, G., 'Notes on Marx's Critique of Ricardo', *Contributions to Political Economy*, 1, March 1982.

Dobb, M.H., *Political Economy and Capitalism*, 2nd ed. [1940], Routledge & Kegan Paul, London, 1968.

Dobb, M.H., *Theories of Value and Distribution since Adam Smith: Ideology and Economic Theory*, Cambridge University Press, 1973.

Duncan, G., *Marx and Mill: Two Views of Social Conflict and Social Harmony*, Cambridge University Press, 1973.

Eagly, R.V., *The Structure of Classical Economic Theory*, Oxford University Press, New York, 1974.

Eatwell, J., 'Controversies in the theory of surplus value: old and new', *Science and Society*, 38:3, Fall 1974.

Eatwell, J., 'The interpretation of Ricardo's *Essay on Profits*', *Economica*, 42, May 1975.

Elson, D., 'The value theory of labour', in D. Elson (ed.), *Value: the Representation of Labour in Capitalism*, CSE Books, London, 1979.

Fine, B., 'On Marx's theory of agricultural rent', *Economy and Society*, 8:3, August 1979.

Fine, B., 'On Marx's theory of agricultural rent: a rejoinder', *Economy and Society*, 9:3, August 1980.

Fine, B., 'A dissenting note on the transformation problem', *Economy and Society*, 12:4, November 1983.

Fine, B. and Harris, L., 'Controversial issues in Marxist economic theory', *Socialist Register*, 1976.

Ganguli, B.N., 'Karl Marx on Quesnay', *Indian Economic Review*, 7:2, October 1972.

Gee, J.M.A., 'The origin of rent in Adam Smith's *Wealth of Nations*: an anti-neoclassical view', *History of Political Economy*, 13:1, spring 1981.

Godelier, M., *Rationality and Irrationality in Economics* [1966], trans. B. Pearce, New Left Books, London, 1972.

Grœnewegen, P.D., 'Turgot and Adam Smith', *Scottish Journal of Political Economy*, 16:3, November 1969.

Grœnewegen, P.D., 'A re-appraisal of Turgot's theory of value, exchange and price determination', *History of Political Economy*, 2:1, spring 1970.

Grœnewegen, P.D., 'A re-interpretation of Turgot's theory of capital and interest', *Economic Journal*, 81, June 1971.

Grœnewegen, P.D., 'Three notes on Ricardo's theory of value and distribution', *Australian Economic Papers*, 11, June 1972.

Grœnewegen, P.D., 'Thoughts on the Emergence of Economics as a Science', mimeograph, 1973.

Grœnewegen, P.D., *The Economics of A.R.J. Turgot*, Martinus Nijhoff, The Hague, 1977.

Grœnewegen, P.D., 'Thomas de Quincey: "faithful disciple of Ricardo?" ', *Contributions to Political Economy*, 1, March 1982.

Halévy, E., *Thomas Hodgskin*, ed., trans. and with an Introduction by A.J. Taylor, Benn, London, 1956.

Harcourt, G.C., 'The Sraffian contribution: an evaluation', in Bradley and Howard (eds), *Classical and Marxian Political Economy*.

Harris, D.J., 'On Marx's scheme of reproduction and accumulation', *Journal of Political Economy*, 80, May/June 1972.

Henry, J., 'Productive labour, exploitation and oppression – a perspective', *Australian Economic Papers*, 14, June 1975.

Himmelweit, S., 'The continuing saga of the falling rate of profit: a reply to Mario Cogoy', *Bulletin of the Conference of Socialist Economists*, autumn 1974.

Himmelweit, S. and Mohun, S., 'The anomalies of capital', *Capital and Class*, 6, autumn 1978.

Hodgson, G., 'The theory of the falling rate of profit', *New Left Review*, 84, March-April 1974.

Hollander, S., *The Economics of Adam Smith*, Heinemann, London, 1973.

Hollander, S., 'Ricardo's analysis of the profit rate, 1813–15', *Economica*, 40, August 1973.

Hollander, S., 'Ricardo and the corn profit model: reply to Eatwell', *Economica*, 42, May 1975.

Hollander, S., 'The reception of Ricardian economics', *Oxford Economic Papers*, 29:2, July 1977.

Hollander, S., *The Economics of David Ricardo*, Heinemann, London, 1979.

Hollander, S., 'The post-Ricardian dissension: a case study in economics and ideology', *Oxford Economic Papers*, 32:3, November 1980.

Hollander, S., 'Marxian economics as "general equilibrium" theory', *History of Political Economy*, 13:1, spring 1981.

Hollander, S., 'The economics of David Ricardo: a response to Professor O'Brien', *Oxford Economic Papers*, 34:1, March 1982.

Hollander, S., 'A reply', *Journal of Post Keynesian Economics*, 4:3, spring 1982.

Howard, M.C. and King, J.E., *The Political Economy of Marx*, Longman, Harlow, 1975.

Hunt, E.K., 'Value theory in the writings of the Classical economists, Thomas Hodgskin, and Karl Marx', *History of Political Economy*, 9:3, Fall 1977.

Hutchison, T.W., 'The Cambridge Version of the History of Economics', Occasional Paper no. 19, Economics Department, University of Birmingham, January 1974.

Itoh, M., 'The formation of Marx's theory of crisis', *Bulletin of the Conference of Socialist Economists*, February 1975.

Keynes, J.M., 'Thomas Robert Malthus', in *Essays in Biography* [1933], *The Collected Writings of John Maynard Keynes*, vol. X, Macmillan, London, 1972.

King, J.E., 'Marx as an historian of economic thought', *History of Political Economy*, 11:3, Fall 1979.

King, J.E., 'Value and exploitation: some recent debates', in Bradley and Howard (eds), *Classical and Marxian Political Economy*.

Kurz, H.D., 'Sraffa after Marx', *Australian Economic Papers*, 18, June 1979.

Lebowitz, M., 'Marx's falling rate of profit: a dialectical view', *Canadian Journal of Economics*, 9:2, May 1976.

Lowenthal, E., *The Ricardian Socialists* [1911], Augustus M. Kelley, Clifton, N. J., 1972.

Medio, A., 'Profits and surplus value: appearance and reality in capitalist production', in E.K. Hunt and J.M. Schwartz (eds), *A Critique of Economic Theory*, Penguin, Harmondsworth, 1972.

Meek, R.L., *The Economics of Physiocracy: Essays and Translations*, Allen & Unwin, London, 1962.

Meek, R.L., *Economics and Ideology and Other Essays*, Chapman & Hall, London, 1967.

Meek, R.L., 'Discussion', in R.V. Eagly (ed.), *Events, Ideology and Economic Theory*, Wayne State University Press, Detroit, 1968.

Meek, R.L., *Studies in the Labour Theory of Value* [1956], 2nd ed., Lawrence & Wishart, London, 1973.

Meek, R.L., *Turgot on Progress, Sociology and Economics*, trans. and ed. with an Introduction by R.L. Meek, Cambridge University Press, 1973.

Meek, R.L., 'Is there an "historical transformation problem?": a comment', *Economic Journal*, 86, June 1976.

Meek, R.L., *Smith, Marx, and After: Ten Essays in the Development of Economic Thought*, Chapman & Hall, London, 1977.

Miller, W.L., 'Richard Jones: a case study in methodology', *History of Political Economy*, 3:1, spring 1971.

Miller, W.L., 'Richard Jones's contribution to the theory of rent', *History of Political Economy*, 9:3, Fall 1977.

Morishima, M. and Catephores, G., 'Is there an "historical transformation problem"?', *Economic Journal*, 85, June 1975.

Morishima, M. and Catephores, G., 'The "historical transformation problem": a reply', *Economic Journal*, 86, June 1976.

Oakley, A., 'Two notes on Marx and the transformation problem', *Economica*, 43, November 1976.

Oakley, A., *The Making of Marx's Critical Theory: a Bibliographical Analysis*, Routledge & Kegan Paul, London, 1983.

Oakley, A., *Marx's Critique of Political Economy: Intellectual Sources and Evolution*, vol. I: *1844 to 1860*, Routledge & Kegan Paul, London, 1984.

O'Brien, D.P., *J.R. McCulloch: a Study in Classic Economics*, Allen & Unwin, London, 1970.

O'Brien, D.P., *The Classical Economists*, Oxford University Press, 1975.

O'Brien, D.P., 'Ricardian economics and the economics of David Ricardo', *Oxford Economic Papers*, 33:3, November 1981.

O'Brien, D.P., 'Ricardian economics: a rejoinder', *Oxford Economic Papers*, 34:1, March 1982.

Pasinetti, L., *Growth and Income Distribution: Essays in Economic Theory*, Cambridge University Press, 1974.

Pilling, G., 'The law of Value in Ricardo and Marx', *Economy and Society*, 1:3, August 1972.

Rashid, S., 'Malthus' *Principles* and British economic thought 1820–1835', *History of Political Economy*, 13:1, spring 1981.

Rauner, R.M., *Samuel Bailey and the Classical Theory of Value*, Bell, London, 1961.

Roncaglia, A., *Sraffa and the Theory of Prices*, Wiley, Chichester, 1978.

Roncaglia, A., 'Hollander's Ricardo', *Journal of Post Keynesian Economics*, 4:3, spring 1982.

Roncaglia, A., 'Rejoinder', *Journal of Post Keynesian Economics*, 4:3, spring 1982.

Rosdolsky, R., *The Making of Marx's 'Capital'*, trans. P. Burgess, Pluto Press, London, 1977.

Rubel, M. and Manale, M., *Marx Without Myth: a Chronological Study of His Life and Work*, Blackwell, Oxford, 1975.

St Clair, O., *A Key to Ricardo* [1957], Augustus M. Kelley, New York, 1965.

Samuelson, P.A., 'Understanding the Marxian notion of exploitation: a summary of the so-called transformation problem between Marxian values and competitive prices', *Journal of Economic Literature*, 9, June 1971.

Schumpeter, J.A., *Ten Great Economists* [1952], Allen & Unwin, London, 1966.

Schumpeter, J.A., *History of Economic Analysis*, Allen & Unwin, London, 1954.

Schwartz, J. (ed.), *The Subtle Anatomy of Capitalism*, Goodyear, Santa Monica, 1977.

Semmel, B., 'Malthus: "Physiocracy" and the commercial system', *Economic History Review*, 17:3, 1964–5.

Shaikh, A., 'Marx's theory of Value and the "transformation problem" ', in Schwartz (ed.), *The Subtle Anatomy of Capitalism*.

Shaikh, A., 'Political economy and capitalism: notes on Dobb's theory of crisis', *Cambridge Journal of Economics*, 2, June 1978.

Shoul, B., 'Karl Marx and Say's Law', *Quarterly Journal of Economics*, 71:4, November 1957.

Shoul, B., 'Similarities in the work of John Stuart Mill and Karl Marx', *Science and Society*, 29, 1965.

Shoul, B., 'Karl Marx's solutions to some theoretical problems of Classical economics', *Science and Society*, 31, 1967.

Shroyer, T., 'Marx's theory of the crisis', *Telos*, winter 1972.

Sowell, T., 'Sismondi: a neglected pioneer', *History of Political Economy*, 4:1, spring 1972.

Sowell, T., *Say's Law: an Historical Analysis*, Princeton University Press, 1972.

Spengler, J., 'The Physiocrats and Say's Law of markets', *Journal of Political Economy*, 53, September and December 1945.

Sraffa, P., *Production of Commodities by Means of Commodities: Prelude to a Critique of Economic Theory*, Cambridge University Press, 1960.

Steedman, I., *Marx After Sraffa*, New Left Books, London, 1977.

Steedman, I., 'Marx on Ricardo', in Bradley and Howard (eds), *Classical and Marxian Political Economy.*

Steedman, I., *et al.*, *The Value Controversy*, Verso, London, 1981.

Sweezy, P., *The Theory of Capitalist Development* [1942], Monthly Review Press, New York, 1968.

Sweezy, P., 'Karl Marx and the Industrial Revolution', in R.V. Eagly (ed.), *Events, Ideology and Economic Theory*, Wayne State University Press, Detroit, 1968.

Sweezy, P., 'Some problems in the theory of capital accumulation', *Monthly Review*, 26:1, May 1974.

Tucker, G.S.L., *Progress and Profits in British Economic Thought 1650–1850*, Cambridge University Press, 1960.

Tucker, G.S.L., 'Ricardo and Marx', *Economica*, 28, August 1961.

Vaggi, G., 'Prices, Markets and Reproduction: a Study of the Role of a Theory of Value in Physiocracy', unpublished PhD thesis, University of Cambridge, 1980.

Vaggi, G., 'The Physiocratic Theory of Prices', mimeograph, 1983.

Vygodski, V., *The Story of a Great Discovery: How Karl Marx Wrote 'Capital'*, Abacus Press, Tunbridge Wells, 1974.

Walker, A., 'Karl Marx, the declining rate of profit and British political economy', *Economica*, 38, November 1971.

Wright, E.O., 'Alternative perspectives in Marxist theory of accumulation and crisis', in Schwarz (ed.), *The Subtle Anatomy of Capitalism.*

Yaffe, D., 'The Marxian theory of crisis, capital and the state', *Economy and Society*, 2:2, May 1973.

Yaffe, D., 'Value and price in Marx's *Capital*', *Revolutionary Communist*, 1, 1975.

Index

For Product Safety Concerns and Information please contact our EU
representative GPSR@taylorandfrancis.com
Taylor & Francis Verlag GmbH, Kaufingerstraße 24, 80331 München, Germany

www.ingramcontent.com/pod-product-compliance
Ingram Content Group UK Ltd.
Pitfield, Milton Keynes, MK11 3LW, UK
UKHW022111190926
475702UK00013B/1382
* 9 7 8 1 1 3 8 8 7 8 6 1 7 *